THE PICARESQUE HERO
IN EUROPEAN FICTION

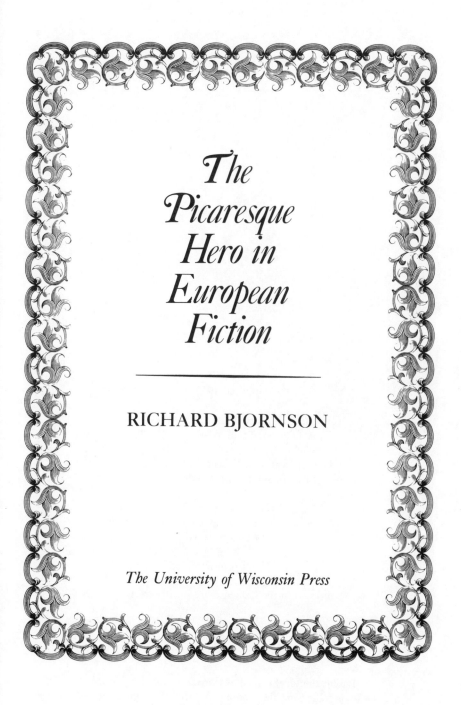

The Picaresque Hero in European Fiction

RICHARD BJORNSON

The University of Wisconsin Press

Published 1977

The University of Wisconsin Press
Box 1379, Madison, Wisconsin 53701

The University of Wisconsin Press, Ltd.
50 Great Russell Street, London, England

First printing

Printed in the United States of America

For LC CIP information see the colophon

ISBN 0-299-07100-6

Publication of this book was made possible in part
by a grant from the Andrew W. Mellon Foundation

CONTENTS

ILLUSTRATIONS

PREFACE

Many aspects of picaresque fiction have already received intense scrutiny, but there have been relatively few attempts to synthesize a comprehensive overview of its origins and early development. From the beginning of my interest in the picaresque, I have been convinced that such an overview could contribute significantly to an understanding of its role in the evolution of the modern novel. By offering detailed interpretations of individual texts and placing them in appropriate historical, ideological, and moral contexts, I have tried to provide the perspective from which this overview can be obtained. Without the work of previous scholars, such a task would have been impossible, and my indebtedness to their ideas is amply indicated in the notes; more specifically, I feel deeply appreciative toward all those who freely and generously shared their views with me. Benito Brancaforte, Don Larson, Hugo Bekker, Jim Battersby, George M. Kahrl, Ron Rosbottom, David Miles, Don Wayne, Art Kunst, Fannie Le Moine, David Hayman, and Prospero Saíz all read portions of the manuscript at various stages; their insightful comments prevented me from committing a number of errors, and their suggestions often prompted me to rethink my own conclusions. In a more general way, I would like to thank Merton M. Sealts, Walter Rideout, Germaine Brée, Niels Ingwersen, Bill Berg, Peter Boerner, Gerhild Bjornson, Roger Asselineau, and Mme Jacques-André Lubin for their help and encouragement. A summer research stipend from the Wisconsin Alumni Research Foundation permitted me to begin my work in this area, and a generous grant from the Humanities College of the Ohio State University helped me to complete it. Sections of the present study have appeared, in somewhat different form, in *Romanische Forschungen*, *Revista de estudios hispánicos*, *Romanic Review*, *Ibero-romania*, *Comparative Literature*, and *Studies in Scottish Literature;* I would like to thank the editors of these journals for permission to use materials contained in these earlier essays. The final version of the manuscript was considerably improved by the careful, critical readings of Sue Lanser, who typed it, and Elizabeth Uhr, who edited it; Janet Needs was extremely helpful in typing corrected copy, and Allen Bjornson provided valuable assistance with the illustrations. Throughout the writing and revising of the manuscript, I have been aided by the sound critical suggestions and loving support of Aija Kuplis Bjornson, and I would like to express my gratitude by dedicating this book to her.

R. B.

Columbus, Ohio
July 1976

THE PICARESQUE HERO
IN EUROPEAN FICTION

INTRODUCTION

In 1554 an anonymous short novel was published almost simultaneously in Alcalá, Burgos, and Antwerp. Nowhere in this novel do the words "pícaro" or "picaresque" appear; nevertheless, *Lazarillo de Tormes* was later commonly linked with works like Alemán's *Guzmán de Alfarache* (1599, 1604) and Quevedo's *El Buscón* (1626). Together with a great number of minor works which appeared between 1600 and 1646, these three novels form the core of a Spanish "picaresque" tradition. Following the translation of these works into other European languages, picaresquelike fiction began to emerge in England, France, and Germany—Grimmelshausen's *Simplicius Simplicissimus* (1668), Lesage's *Gil Blas* (1715, 1724, 1735), Defoe's *Moll Flanders* (1722), Smollett's *Roderick Random* (1748). Each of these novels is a unique fusion of existing conventions and an imaginative response to specific historical circumstances, but within the novel-writing traditions of their respective countries, they all performed similar functions. By breaking down the traditional separation of styles and expanding the range of acceptable subject matter to include the morally serious treatment of nonaristocratic characters,[1] they constituted one of the most important stages in the transition between earlier literary prose and the modern novel, which itself became the dominant mode of fictional expression in eighteenth- and nineteenth-century Europe.

Among these novels, however, important distinctions must be made. Some of them portray character as a process during which the picaresque hero's personality emerges; others depict character as a function of the protagonist's inherent nature. Some create fictional worlds in which the picaresque hero can plausibly attain wealth and psychological well-being; others situate "pícaros" in worlds where they cannot possibly escape a "double-bind" situation in which they are compelled to choose between survival and integrity.[2] In order to obtain a conceptually valid, historically accurate idea of picaresque fiction and its crucial contribution to the emergence of the European novel, one must first determine its essential components and then examine the circumstances under which they recur.

At the same time, a theory or explanation of picaresque fiction should account for differences between individual novels in the tradition.

Because the form-giving principles which organize literary conventions and influences into fictional entities inevitably reflect an ascertainable world view—a series of implicit assumptions about what is possible, desirable, or imaginable in human life—it seems possible to interpret the evolution of picaresque fiction as a sequence of different world views operating within the limitations of a relatively constant formal or thematic structure. During the two-hundred-year period in which picaresque fiction flourished, European society was undergoing significant changes in social organization; as the feudal order declined in most countries, the increasingly important middle classes began to provide a dynamic but often frustrated impetus toward a redefinition of established aristocratic values and modes of perception. Picaresque novels written against the background of these conflicting ideologies manifest numerous different attitudes toward the rise of bourgeois individualism, but because the essential picaresque situation involves the paradigmatic confrontation between an isolated individual and a hostile society, these novels almost invariably reflect a world view defined in terms of the author's position on precisely this question.

Like modern writers of science fiction and detective novels, authors of the early picaresque novels did not consciously adhere to formal or compositional rules which together might serve to define a genre; in fact, the term "picaresque novel" is a synthetic, somewhat arbitrary label for a collection of works which critics and scholars have retrospectively grouped together on the basis of rather vaguely delineated similarities. In broad general terms, it is usually employed to describe episodic, open-ended narratives in which lower-class protagonists sustain themselves by means of their cleverness and adaptability during an extended journey through space, time, and various predominantly corrupt social milieux.[3] For seventeenth-century Spaniards who wrote and read this type of fiction, the crucial factor was the presence of a "pícaro" at the center of the narrative, and although a common subject matter may have implied the use of certain conventions, motifs, and narrative structures, it hardly constituted a literary genre in the true sense of the word.

Scholarly discussions of the picaresque are generally based upon one of two assumptions: either it is regarded as an historical phenomenon, or it is viewed in terms of an ideal form or type. Both approaches have their disadvantages, and both must somehow resolve the difficult problems of defining a category which has no *a priori* existence and of determining which works legitimately belong in that category.[4] If a narrow historical definition is adopted, the critic is prevented from drawing fruitful analogies among works which have much in common, despite the fact that none of them were directly influenced by the others. However, when critics derive abstract generalizations from an inductive examination of one or more novels, their definitions tend to be circular, because works drawn upon to establish the model necessarily manifest the principal characteristics of the model itself; furthermore, by focusing upon incidental resemblances between novels, this approach often blurs fundamental distinctions between them, while overlooking the relationships of impact and influence by means of which ideas, techniques, and conventions are transmitted from one work to another.[5] The word "picaresque" can be applied to works written before 1550 and after 1750, but if it is to retain its usefulness, it must be defined in such a way that it implicitly subsumes novels from the historical period in which picaresque fiction first achieved a recognizable identity.

Without general agreement upon definitions and critical methodologies, differences of opinion are inevitable, and it is not surprising that the picaresque hero has been characterized in so many different and contradictory fashions. Variously described as a social conformist in avid pursuit of material possessions and a rebel who rejects society and its rewards, an optimist and a pessimist, a good-for-nothing without scruples and a wanderer with potentialities of sainthood, he has been called immoral, amoral, and highly moral.[6] In actuality, picaresque heroes have at one time or another exhibited all these and many other characteristics; their fictional lives have served as vehicles for the expression of diametrically opposed ideologies and moral systems, but if the pícaro and the context of values in which he is portrayed are subject to infinite variation, they cannot serve as defining characteristics of picaresque fiction. What is needed is not an inductively established list of picaresque elements, but a dynamic model sufficiently flexible to encompass the unique individual works and their historical contexts while clearly identifying the shared elements which justify their inclusion in the same category.

It might be impossible to reconstruct faithfully every dimension of a complex literary phenomenon like the European picaresque novel, but perspective can be gained by focusing upon three of its most significant aspects: the primitive prenovelistic "mode" or "myth" of the lower-class, wandering hero,[7] the thematic and structural conventions which become associated with it, and the specific works which integrate these conventions into individualized forms with their own ideological, aesthetic, and moral assumptions. Within this frame of reference, problems created by attributing specific moods, attitudes, or character traits to all pícaros are eliminated, and the argument between those who reserve the label "picaresque" for a limited number of Spanish Golden Age novels and those who employ it to signify a type of narrative becomes superfluous. Because every specific example of picaresque fiction is a mixed form, there is no such thing as an ideal picaresque hero or a pure picaresque novel; the picaresque myth or mode is an essential component of novels associated with the Spanish picaresque tradition, but nothing prevents it from reappearing in the lives of characters who possess a wide variety of personality traits and meet with diverse experiences. This fictional possibility is clearly not bound to any specific era or geographical location, although it might occur in some times or places and not in others.

After capturing the imagination of an entire generation of Spanish writers, it reemerged in the works of early French, English, and German novelists, but its primary elements are already present in *Lazarillo*. The book's anonymous author probably did not intend to invent a new form; in fact, there is nothing particularly new about *Lazarillo*. Nearly all of its incidents and themes can be traced to literary sources or traditional folklore anecdotes and motifs.[8] However, by incorporating disparate, fragmentary materials into the life of a clever and adaptable lower-class character in a corrupt environment, the anonymous author traces the outlines of a story with mythic proportions. Essentially this story involves a rootless, unattached individual who must secure his own survival and psychological well-being in a society which openly espouses traditional ideals, while actually sanctioning the most dehumanizing modes of behavior. Characterized by an ambiguous or nonexistent link with his father, this outsider (or "half-outsider")[9] inherits no place which can be considered a home, no trade by means of which he can sustain himself, and no social position to provide him with well-defined relationships to other people. Prematurely made responsible for his own welfare, he usually undergoes a rude awakening (or initiation) which shocks him into an awareness of what he must do in order to survive. Because he lacks the strength and absolute integrity to impose his will upon a hostile world, he adapts himself to diverse situations by serving different masters, inventing clever ruses, or wearing a variety of masks during a peripatetic life of alternating good and evil fortune. During the two centuries following the original publication of *Lazarillo*, variations upon this myth proliferated, and many different attitudes toward the picaresque hero were expressed; however, a characteristic pattern of experience—ambiguous links with the past, departure from home, initiation, repeated contacts with a dehumanizing society and its pressures to conform—recurred with striking regularity.

But only a limited number of the myth's possible permutations appeared, and many similarities among specific picaresque novels occurred because writers tend to portray similar subject matter in similar conventional terms. In every historical period, certain stereotyped ways of perceiving, evaluating, and communicating gain ascendancy. Governing what is commonly considered real, pleasant, or just, these conventions enable an author to conceive works which will be intelligible to anticipated audiences. He may adopt conventions in their usual form or distort them in some recognizable fashion, but he cannot escape them, and once his works have been published and read, they too swell the body of material which exemplifies conventional thinking and helps to determine the expectations of subsequent readers; thus, the parody or modification of a convention might itself become a convention.

In *Lazarillo*, the picaresque myth is intimately linked with two literary conventions: the pseudoautobiographical perspective and the panorama of representative types. Neither is necessarily associated with the picaresque myth, but both almost invariably reappear in subsequent picaresque fiction. Sixteenth-century readers would have been familiar with the techniques of first-person narration in genuine autobiographies and in late classical works like Apuleius' *Golden Ass*, [10] but most previous examples of postmedieval European prose fiction (novella collections, jest books) had been loosely organized within a frame story. By creating the persona of an adult narrator telling his own story in the past tense, the author of *Lazarillo* was able to shape traditional or folklore elements into a cohesive, aesthetically satisfying unity based upon the illusion that they constituted parts of the same life. Insofar as most later writers of picaresque fiction also adopted this technique, their plots can be defined as functions of their central characters' lives—a relationship generally emphasized by the inclusion of the picaresque hero's name or epithet in the titles of their novels. The best picaresque novels are not, as has often been claimed, patchwork collections of randomly selected episodes. Although they characteristically employ materials from diverse sources, these materials are subordinated to a narrator's unifying perspective which focuses upon a recurrent human situation and often reconciles the traditional opposition between the comic and the serious.

In the case of *Lazarillo*, the pseudoautobiographical format permits the author to obtain a comic effect without relinquishing claims to moral seriousness and verisimilitude. No matter how exaggerated or obviously conventional his materials might be, his fictive narrator remains a psychologically plausible point of reference, because in the context of first-person narration, the primary level of reality is that of the storyteller, not of the story told. The same holds true with regard to the sermonizing digressions and fantastic episodes of later picaresque novels. In each of them, the narrator is a complex, highly individuated character whose motives and preoccupations color his story and organize it into a meaningful plot. The obtrusiveness of the narrator varies, and some few picaresque narratives abandon the first-person technique altogether, but in general the picaresque hero's life is filtered through his own consciousness as he reflects upon the meaning of what he has seen and experienced.

The author of a simulated autobiography may provide clues to indicate that a narrator is unreliable or uncongenial, but the very choice of this conventional means of ordering experience implies the use of mental constructs traditionally associated with genuine autobiography. Thus, the narrating Lázaro and most of his successors in the picaresque tradition present the events of their lives in logical sequences which plausibly culminate in their present state of consciousness. They might be selecting and shaping these events to project a favorable image of themselves, to justify their manner of having coped with societal pressures, to instruct readers or simply to make them laugh, but a limited illusion of reality nearly always derives from the inclusion of information which permits an implied reader to trace their picaresque journeys through authentic-seeming sequences of temporal, spatial, and social relationships. As in genuine autobiography, the reader tends to believe and sympathize with such narrators, and the author of *Lazarillo* relies upon this tendency to convey the moral and social ramifications of his "vulgar" protagonist's experiences in a harsh and hypocritical world. Furthermore, by cultivating the impression that *Lazarillo* can be read as the plausible account of actual experience, the anonymous author is breaking with traditional practices of portraying vulgar characters as inherently comic and of maintaining a strict separation between "high" and "low" styles.

Another dominant convention of the European picaresque novel—its panoramic overview of the types and conditions of human life—is suggested by the very nature of the myth. Because picaresque heroes wander from place to place and traverse various social milieux, they encounter many different people, and by momentarily focusing upon these secondary characters, the author can depict a cross section of contemporary manners, morals, and idiosyncrasies.[11] By satirizing or parodying these characters, an author may be distorting reality, but because distortions are produced according to recognizable principles, it is usually possible to identify the ideological and moral assumptions which mediate between perceived reality and the literary representation of it. Taken together, these assumptions govern the way an author construes the picaresque myth and employs the various conventions associated with it.

A novel's reception can also be strongly influenced by the world view which, rightly or wrongly, readers perceive in it. For nearly fifty years *Lazarillo* had remained an isolated example of fictional possibilities, but when Alemán adopted the conventions of first-person narration and panoramic vision to present his version of the picaresque myth in *Guzmán*, he achieved an enormous popular success which helped establish the picaresque novel as a respectable literary form and the lower-class individual as a legitimate protagonist in morally serious works of fiction. To a large degree, this success is attributable to the eloquent overlay of seemingly orthodox religious opinions in the novel.

On the surface, the long, digressive, overtly didactic *Guzmán* seems to have little in common with *Lazarillo*, a short, humorous narrative which focuses upon the major character's experience; evidence for Alemán's indebtedness to his anonymous predecessor remains inconclusive.[12] And yet, attracted to the entertainment provided by the adventures of apparently insouciant rogues in both works, seventeenth-century Spaniards persisted in linking them together.[13] During the next forty years, literary conventions established by *Lazarillo* and *Guzmán* were frequently revived and recombined; in fact, the linking of these two novels produced a commonly accepted idea of picaresque fiction—an idea which shaped the expectations of readers and itself coalesced into a convention which later Spanish writers adopted for a variety of purposes. Like Quevedo, they reduced picaresque heroes to one-dimensional caricatures; like Espinel, they elevated them to the level of respectable individuals who defend traditional conceptions of honor and status. Modified by these variations upon the myth, the idea of picaresque fiction nevertheless tended to remain within boundaries established by the *Lazarillo-Guzmán* model.

Translated into all the major European languages, these Spanish novels helped shape traditions of prose fiction in Germany, France, and England, but as they were assimilated into social and literary contexts quite different from those of Golden Age Spain, they themselves underwent curious modifications. The most dramatic changes occurred in France, where translations of picaresque novels became closely linked with the "romans comiques" (comic novels) of writers like Charles Sorel and Paul Scarron. Although openly reacting against the pretension and artificiality of popular romances, the authors of these comic novels often simply transferred romance conventions to the depiction of less exotic events, characters, and settings; thus, when La Geneste, who was working in this tradition, translated *El Buscón*, he transformed Quevedo's disreputable pícaro into a generous-hearted and ultimately successful picaresque adventurer like Sorel's Francion or Scarron's Destin.[14]

To comprehend such metamorphoses, one must recognize how conventions of thought and narrative structure change and sometimes disappear in the ongoing dialectic between abstract idea and particular historical case. For example, if the adventures of a lower-class, wandering protagonist are to be understood by a contemporary audience, they must relate in some meaningful way to conventional preconceptions about such characters, the worlds in which they live, and the technical devices by means of which they can be rendered plausible, entertaining, or morally instructive; however, what is considered true, entertaining or right varies from one period to another, from one culture to another, and even from one writer to another. As a consequence, picaresque novels drawing upon one set of conventions can be reinterpreted in terms of other conventions, and when this occurs, their original meaning is often modified or lost. It is quite possible that Lesage and Grimmelshausen conceived of their works as belonging to a tradition which included previous works of picaresque fiction. *Gil Blas* and *Simplicius Simplicissimus* do share basic elements of the picaresque myth and its allied conventions with *Lazarillo* and *Guzmán*, but because the frames of reference are different, the significance of these elements changes drastically; thus, literary conventions can be transmitted from one country to another, retaining similar outward shapes while undergoing radical shifts in meaning.

The conventions of picaresque fiction are common property. At any particular moment, they are potentially the same for everyone in a given culture. Influences operate upon individual writers. Quevedo, Úbeda, Lesage, Grimmelshausen, and Smollett had read previous picaresque fiction, and their reactions to it affected the way in which they wrote their own novels, but each of their works reflects a personal synthesis of conventions and influences. All writers arrange stereotyped materials according to implicit compositional laws which are in turn governed by their own attitudes toward the world. One of Unamuno's characters is only partially correct when he asserts, "invento el género, . . . y le doy las leyes que me place" ("I invent the genre, . . . and give it the laws which please me"),[15] but his comment is instructive. Each work has its own form, and if conventions are shared, form is the fusion of organizing principles that distinguishes one picaresque novel from all others which employ the same materials and techniques. When an artist tailors a convention to bring it into harmony with the informing purpose of a literary work, changes in the convention may be far more interesting or significant than what is retained; for this reason, the bulk of the present study will be devoted to individual picaresque novels and the ways in which their authors adapted conventions and influences to express their conceptions of the world.

In its broadest sense, the picaresque myth functions as one possible paradigm for the individual's unavoidable encounter with external reality and the act of cognition which precedes and shapes his attempts to cope with a dehumanizing society.[16] During their respective journeys, picaresque heroes continually come in contact with a constantly changing reality outside the self. In situations exacerbated by rootlessness and poverty, they may or may not become delinquents,[17] but they are invariably confronted by a choice between social conformity (which is necessary for survival) and adherence to what they have learned to consider true or virtuous. Their responses to this double-bind situation reflect an author's implicit assumptions about the self and the fictional universe in which people become aware of themselves. In the European picaresque, the self is frequently depicted in the traditional manner as an inherent "nature" which is tested and revealed for what it is during the course of the hero's fictional adventures.

What the anonymous author of *Lazarillo* portrayed was something quite different. Faced with the common human problem of providing himself with both physical sustenance and a psychologically satisfying self-image, his picaresque hero internalizes the dehumanizing behavior patterns of the dominant society and thus acquires a character which he did not have by nature. In novels where character is a function of nature, the spectrum of possible picaresque heroes ranges from inherently corrupt figures like Quevedo's Pablos and Úbeda's Justina to noble, generous-hearted individuals like Marcos de Obregón, Francion, Gil Blas, and Roderick Random. In novels like *Lazarillo*, *Guzmán*, and *Moll Flanders*, however, the protagonist's character is susceptible to a socializing process. Although most of Alemán's contemporaries failed to recognize the social criticism implicit in his portrayal of character as "process," he (like Defoe and the author of *Lazarillo*) demonstrates how necessity and social pressure constrain lower-class, wandering heroes to adopt the characteristic attitudes and behavior patterns of the society in which they must live. If these attitudes and behavior patterns are dehumanizing or morally reprehensible, the implication is that the society itself is responsible for implanting them in the individual.

But whether character is portrayed as nature or as process, there is one striking similarity which unites the picaresque novels written outside Spain and distances them from their Spanish predecessors. Whereas the fictional careers of nearly all the Spanish pícaros terminate unhappily or ambiguously, *Simplicissimus*, *Moll Flanders*, *Gil Blas*, and *Roderick Random* are all, in one way or another, success stories. They all culminate in a peace and harmony which permits the hero to reconcile his needs for physical and psychological security in a corrupt society after having traversed the same basic sequence of experiences as Lazarillo and Guzmán. The type of happy ending and the context of values in which it becomes meaningful differ in each case. Simplicissimus' ascetic withdrawal to an island in the Indian Ocean implies a state of heightened vision and serves as the device by means of which Grimmelshausen retains the plausibility of his narrative while endowing it with a symmetrical plot structure and a complex astrological symbolism. Drawing upon conventions of criminal biography, journalism, and religious literature, Defoe portrays Moll as capable of reaching the elevated social station to which she aspires, because in her fictional world, consummate role-playing and the shrewd investment of available resources justify upward social mobility. Lesage's and Smollett's picaresque heroes possess an inherited or acquired nobility which prevents them from totally succumbing to the socializing process, and after a series of adventures which test their virtue, they both retire to the countryside, where they enjoy material comfort, a good reputation, and a happy marriage. A chain of direct and verifiable influences leads from the Spanish picaresque through *Gil Blas* to *Roderick Random*, but despite a continuity suggested by the recurrence of the picaresque myth, the first-person narration, and the panoramic perspective, differences in social and literary conventions bring about a change in the picaresque hero and reflect points of view which are diametrically opposed to those commonly associated with the earlier Spanish novels.

The picaresque hero's fate is largely determined in the interaction between character and a fictional world governed by a series of implicit but ascertainable laws. When the picaresque hero is portrayed in terms of innate qualities, the fictional world almost always operates within the framework of a limited "poetic justice"; that is, fate corresponds in some recognizable way with what the hero deserves by virtue of a good or bad nature. Quevedo's Pablos suffers repeated humiliations for his pretensions to a higher social position than the one to which he is entitled by birth; and though the actions of Gil Blas and Roderick Random might not always reflect their virtuous natures, they both ultimately enjoy a wealth and marital bliss which recompenses them primarily for what they are, and only incidentally for what they have done. The situation is quite different when the picaresque hero's character is perceived as resulting from interaction with the external world. In this case, the character's fate depends upon the way in which assimilated social practices are judged. For Moll Flanders, role-playing and the subordination of emotional concerns to the enlightened pursuit of gentility actually enable her to reconcile her physical and psychological needs. Although Lazarillo and Guzmán do the same thing and pursue the same goals, there is never the slightest possibility that their lives would culminate in the sort of happy ending experienced by Moll. In their fictional worlds, lying and petty materialism are incompatible with psychological well-being, and even if they attain the "height of all good fortune," they can only do so by compromising their integrity. Because the many different permutations of the myth and the variety of moral values and ideologies connected with it are manifested in divergent attitudes toward character (which can be portrayed as nature or as process) and the fictional world (which may or may not allow the picaresque hero to experience a happy ending), they provide clues to the interpretation of individual novels and to the entire European picaresque tradition.

There is no simple correspondence between the actual existence of rogues or vagabonds and their emergence as popular fictional heroes between 1550 and 1750; however, in choosing to portray lower-class wandering characters, individual authors do tend to adopt conventional ideas about such people and their usual patterns of behavior. Even in the same society, the range of attitudes toward real pícaros may be extremely wide, but if literary pícaros are to be comprehensible, they and their situations must be somehow related to that which contemporary readers consider to be "real." In most European picaresque novels, authors attempted to create at least a limited impression of verisimilitude, and in doing so, they were obliged to obey certain laws of credibility. As early as *Lazarillo*, an emphasis upon commonplace objects, plausible chronologies, recognizable place-names, and money as a *sine qua non* of survival establishes space-time coordinates which foster the illusion that the fictional autobiography is a genuine account of what could have happened to a person like Lázaro.

Picaresque fiction seldom involves the direct mirroring of actual social conditions in Spain, France, England, or Germany, because literary representation was frequently based upon caricatural distortion, polemic effect, or imaginative projection into fantastic realms; and even when authors sought to convey an authentic picture of reality, it was bound to be colored by their personal views. In fact, the way in which the European picaresque novel emerged and evolved becomes increasingly intelligible when placed against the background of conflicting world views which dominated the period 1550–1750. In most European countries at this time, feudal society was gradually being supplanted by a bourgeois-dominated social order, but the transition was halting, never fully consummated; and just as the roots of bourgeois ideology can be traced back to the Middle Ages, aristocratic assumptions about character and society persisted until long after the French Revolution, even among the most successful bourgeois. As a self-made man apparently proud of his rise in society, Lázaro is a representative of the new social order, but so is Moll Flanders and so is Gil Blas. If the recurrent sequence of events in the picaresque myth can be linked to the ambitious commoner's struggle for physical and psychological survival in a hostile, highly competitive world, different attitudes toward the picaresque hero might actually reflect different attitudes toward a much more important socio-cultural phenomenon—the rise of bourgeois individualism.[18]

The medieval world view hardly constituted a unitary system, but there was widespread acceptance of the idea that society was (or was supposed to be) a harmonious "chain of being" descending from God through the king and the nobility to the lowest commoner.[19] Strengthened during the Renaissance, this essentially neoplatonic conception was generally based upon the assumption of an ordered universe and discussed in terms of morality and the Thomist hierarchy of laws—eternal law, natural law, revealed law (i.e., the Bible), and codified or human law. In theory, every individual belonged to one of three estates (nobility, clergy, commoner), each of which had well-defined prerogatives and responsibilities.[20] A healthy state of society (like that of the human body or the well-regulated family—the two analogies most commonly cited to support the hierarchical model) occurred when each member of the whole was fulfilling its proper function. According to this world view, inequality of wealth and condition was natural, because it reflected the will of God and allowed each person to contribute to the harmonious working of the entire society. On the level of individual morality, this meant recognizing one's place in the universe, accepting it, and performing the duties which it entailed; within a larger framework, justice implied an attempt to obtain the closest possible correspondence between reality and God's plan. The idea that society was one part of a divinely ordained, rationally organized, harmoniously functioning universe was reassuring to many people, for it gave them the impression that they had well-defined identities in a secure and stable world order.

Based upon the assumption that all people inherit the nature of their parents and a corresponding place in the social hierarchy, such a world view provided a powerful rationalization for maintaining the *status quo*, but even during the Middle Ages there were individuals (especially merchants, professional men, and rich farmers) who did not fit into a system of three estates; social mobility did exist. During the sixteenth and seventeenth centuries, European cities were expanding rapidly. Ambitious commoners were drawn to these cities, where some of them succeeded in accumulating wealth, thus swelling the ranks of a nascent "middle" class. The urbanization and bourgeoisification of society did not develop in the same ways or with the same rapidity in all European countries, but wherever a middle class did emerge, it served a mediating function, absorbing commoners and occasionally providing new members of the aristocracy. Beneath a surface adherence to traditional ideas and under the influence of Renaissance humanism, the interests and preoccupations of this class began to surface in political theory, theology, philosophy, art, literature, and popular culture. In opposition to the idea that society was or was meant to be an unchanging, harmonious order where everyone dutifully fulfilled the obligations of an inherited place, a new ideology began to take shape. By stressing the autonomy of individuals whose powers and talents might entitle them to higher social stations than the ones into which they were born, the bourgeois world view provided a theoretical justification for upward social mobility.

Because social advancement was generally based upon the acquisition of wealth, greater emphasis was placed upon money as a determinant of social status, upon practical education, and upon the virtues which enhanced the ambitious commoner's chances of obtaining material success—virtues like economy, rational calculation, perseverance, industriousness. Although this new ideology implied that individuals were free to realize their potential and define themselves in terms of their own efforts, actual bourgeois attitudes toward individual freedom remained extremely ambiguous. On the one hand, the bourgeois felt justified in aspiring toward a higher social station; on the other, successful bourgeois tended to consider themselves inherently superior to vulgar commoners, and their own ultimate goal was inclusion in a class (the nobility) which they themselves regarded as superior to their own. Because their life-style and tastes were generally modeled upon those of the aristocracy, these bourgeois tended to de-emphasize the very virtues and assumptions upon which their own original aspirations were premised; by marriage, purchase of lands or titles, and service to the king, many bourgeois even acquired patents of nobility. For this reason, it would be misleading to speak about the unequivocal triumph and dominance of a bourgeois value system; in actuality, the rise of bourgeois individualism was a complex historical phenomenon which frequently involved the assimilation and reinterpretation of aristocratic values.[21]

The emergence of bourgeois ideology influenced the early development of the European novel in several ways. Technical advances in printing and increased literacy among the rising middle classes transformed book production into an important industry. In Germany, France, and England, a growing bourgeois reading public made it possible for writers like Grimmelshausen, Defoe, Lesage, and Smollett to support themselves at least partially with income from the sale of their works. This public tended to prefer books which contained useful knowledge or morally edifying sentiments, preferences which the almanac-compiler Grimmelshausen and the journalist Defoe obviously respected in writing their novels. Moll Flanders, Gil Blas, and Roderick Random all achieve security after demonstrating self-reliance and acquiring money. Based upon hard work, piety, and a careful husbanding of resources, even Simplicissimus' withdrawal from society constitutes a type of bourgeois independence. The happy endings of the non-Spanish picaresque novels all correspond in one way or another to fates which middle-class readers would consider plausible or desirable for characters with whom they could empathize. The ambiguity of bourgeois attitudes toward individualism and social mobility is even suggested by the fact that romance conventions and aristocratic assumptions reappear in picaresque novels which depict real-seeming heroes, situations, and geographical locations. Writers of French, English, and German picaresque novels were thus not necessarily advocates of a bourgeois world view, but in adapting the picaresque myth to the conventional hopes and expectations of prospective readers, they recorded their own attitudes toward individual freedom and social order—concepts defined in contradictory terms by competing ideologies as they were variously expressed in French, English, and German contexts.

In Spain, the situation was somewhat different. During the fourteenth and fifteenth centuries, an embryonic bourgeoisie had already come into existence, but until the eighteenth century, there was no Spanish equivalent for the word "bourgeois," suggesting that the Spanish middle class lacked the well-defined sense of identity possessed by its French, English, and German counterparts.[22] As in other European countries, the successful bourgeois aspired to the privileges and adopted the socio-cultural assumptions of the aristocracy, but a rigidly structured social hierarchy and a dearth of opportunities for social advancement frequently transformed the talented, ambitious Spaniard into a "superfluous man" with no meaningful outlet for his energies. Spain reached the apex of its economic development in the mid-sixteenth century, and during the period when picaresque literature flourished, it was becoming increasingly difficult to acquire the wealth associated with a rise in social status.

This situation was rendered more complex by the fact that the nascent bourgeoisie of fifteenth- and sixteenth-century Spain was largely composed of "conversos" (converts to Catholicism) with Jewish ancestors.[23] Even before the expulsion of the Jews in the late fifteenth century, there were over 300,000 conversos living in Spain.[24] When Jews were prohibited from practicing certain professions and finally expelled from the country, many conversos benefited from the situation. During the fifteenth and early sixteenth centuries, they occupied important positions in commerce and the civil bureaucracies; some acquired considerable wealth and successfully integrated themselves into the existing social hierarchy; a few even managed to obtain patents of nobility.[25] As the Inquisition developed into a powerful institution and the statutes of "limpieza de sangre" (purity of blood) were promulgated during the sixteenth century, the plight of conversos worsened. Most Spanish New Christians had actually become Catholics, and although a strong movement developed against the absurd practice of condemning sincere Christians for their distant origins, a renewed impetus for the persecutions arose when Portuguese New Christian merchants settled all over Spain after Philip II's 1580 annexation of Portugal.[26] Because both Spanish and Portuguese New Christians tended to practice bourgeois professions, the statutes of "limpieza de sangre"— which excluded them from marriage to Old Christians, public service, and church office—effectively prevented some of Spain's most dynamic and ambitious people from achieving higher social stations. In supporting the persecution of conversos, the petty nobility was defending the basically feudal order which guaranteed their privileged status in society, but the new wealth and respectability of bourgeois conversos irritated the Spanish lower classes, and Inquisitorial persecutions of New Christians undoubtedly also appeased their feelings of resentment.

Considered guilty on the basis of "impure" origins, conversos could be denounced at any moment and their property could be seized. Many counterfeited respectable genealogies and avoided traditional Jewish professions, but psychologically their situation was untenable. In addition to the constant fear of persecution, they were often obliged to assimilate the very values of "blood" and "honor" which would have condemned them if their heritage ever became public. Permanently alienated from the Jewish culture which they had abjured, as well as from the Christian one in which they had to live, these conversos could hardly escape an awareness of their own compromised identity, even if they succeeded in passing as Old Christians.[27]

The primary determinants of status in late sixteenth- and early seventeenth-century Spanish society were noble birth and purity of blood; those who lacked these innate qualities possessed no legitimate means of rising in society, and characteristic middle-class virtues—rational calculation, industriousness, economy—were often regarded as demeaning. Because respectability was largely unrelated to an individual's actual behavior, an unbelieving Old Christian could be less subject to persecution than a devout New Christian, and immoral noblemen retained privileges from which virtuous commoners were excluded. Under such circumstances, it is not surprising that people frequently attached greater significance to maintaining the appearances of honor and purity of blood than to cultivating genuinely noble sentiments and sincere religious belief. As exceptionally talented people who had previously prospered in Spanish society, many conversos turned to literature, where their anxiety, their frustration, and their longing for a more equitable society found expression. Both their background and their present situation predisposed them to adopt elements of an essentially bourgeois ideology, especially the ideas of individual freedom and of character as process. Overt criticism of the Inquisition was subject to rigorous ecclesiastical censorship, and even eighteen years after his death Fray Luis de León was denounced for merely having expressed sentiments of human equality in one of his poems.[28] Ironically, the very orthodoxy which the Inquisition was purportedly defending could be adduced to attack the premises upon which its persecution of conversos was based; in fact, converso writers tended not to reject Christianity, but to lament the fact that Spanish society was insufficiently Christian.

This is precisely what Alemán was doing in *Guzmán*. For a converso like him, the advantage of viewing character as process must have been obvious, because if the primary source of corruption derives from pressures which condition individuals to act as they do, no one can be condemned on the basis of impure origins. The aristocratic, anti-Semitic Quevedo undoubtedly understood the thrust of Alemán's novel, and in *El Buscón* he reversed the significance of the picaresque narrative structure, endowing his hero with an inherently corrupt converso nature and implicitly attacking the ideas of freedom and equality associated with bourgeois individualism. Although a few Spanish picaresque novels (especially those written by exile conversos) portrayed the self as subject to a socializing process, most of them were specifically written for the amusement of socially elite readers who were decidedly antagonistic to the aspirations of ambitious commoners, and it is for this reason that they almost invariably reverted to the traditional aristocratic conception of character as nature.

The anonymous author of *Lazarillo* may or may not have been a converso,[29] but by giving literary form to a myth which draws attention to the interaction between the self and society at a moment when traditional concepts of the self were being questioned, defended, and redefined, he helped to establish a literary convention which would subsequently be adopted by Spanish, French, German, and English authors whose works reflect diverse attitudes toward conditions like those confronted by conversos in Spain: the disintegration of traditional value systems, the rise of bourgeois ideology, and the increasing difficulty of reconciling aspirations for upward social mobility with psychological needs for security and self-respect in a hostile, dehumanizing society. Because Simplicissimus, Moll

Flanders, Gil Blas, and Roderick Random live in fictional worlds which permit them to cope successfully with problems posed by these conditions, each of them succeeds in his or her own way—each of them can experience a happy ending. For the Spanish pícaro, as for the Spanish converso or the Spanish bourgeois, there was generally no way out.

THE BIRTH OF THE PICARESQUE:
Lazarillo de Tormes
AND THE SOCIALIZING PROCESS

Lazarillo provides an excellent example of the no-exit situation experienced by so many Spanish pícaros. This anonymous little book contains elements borrowed from numerous popular and literary sources; yet its disparate materials are so skillfully integrated into the pseudoautobiographical perspective that they coalesce into the semicredible account of an individual whose beliefs and values are distorted during an extraordinarily harsh childhood.[1] Even if particular episodes are recognizable exaggerations or lies, they are psychologically plausible insofar as they either reveal the narrator's motives in telling his story or represent stages in his development from a relatively naive young boy into a rather cynical adult. Readers are distanced from the narrating Lázaro by their awareness that his character is subject to satiric distortion; this awareness prevents them from accepting his story as literally true, but it does not prevent them from recognizing that his fictional autobiography follows a pattern which also occurs in real life. Molded into conformity by his encounters with pain, hunger, fear of death, and universally corrupt models of behavior, Lázaro is subjected to a process through which numerous low-born individuals in a competitive, acquisitive, hypocritical society have had to suffer.

For sixteenth-century Spaniards, the very name Lázaro had connotations of suffering and death. The diminutive form "Lazarillo" is phonically linked to one of the key recurrent words in the text—"laceria" (misery, poverty)—and since Lázaro is the same as the English Lazarus, it clearly echoes two Biblical characters of that name—a man raised from the dead by Christ (John 11:1–44) and a beggar who reclines in the bosom of Abraham while the rich man who refused him alms is suffering in hell (Luke 16:19–31). In both Biblical passages, Lazarus dies physically and is reborn into a new life of the spirit; in *Lazarillo*, however, the central

La vida de Lazarillo de
Tormes, y de sus fortunas: y
aduersidades. Nueuamente impressa,
corregida, y de nueuo añadi:
da enesta següda im:

Fig. 1. Title page of the 1554 Alcalá edition of *Lazarillo*

character undergoes a symbolic death of the spirit as the price which he must pay for being reborn into a life of physical well-being.[2]

All people must suffer, and all people must die, but like most of them, Lázaro seeks to avoid suffering and knowing through suffering that he will

Fig. 2. Title page of the 1554 Burgos edition of *Lazarillo*

die—to avoid the knowledge of who and what he is. Throughout the first three "tratados" (chapters; literally "tractates"), all his thoughts and actions are engaged in attempts to escape his misery, and when an itinerant tinker provides him with a key to the chest in which the miserly priest hoards his bread, Lazarillo momentarily believes that he has discovered a way to leave his "laceria" behind him, but he is mistaken, for he can escape neither poverty nor a deeply felt awareness of his own mortality until he successfully assimilates the modes of survival and avoidance acceptable to his society.

During the first two tratados, Lazarillo repeatedly prays for his own death as an end to his suffering, but these prayers remain on an abstract, intellectual level. When confronted with the real possibility of death, however, he responds in an entirely different manner. One of his reasons for remaining with the priest is a fear that he actually will die if a third master proves "más bajo" (more poverty-stricken) than the first two. His anxiety proves justified, and the third tratado is structured around an elaborate metaphor which links the squire's "enchanted" house with the sepulchre. Observing that his master has less desire to eat than a dead man, Lazarillo describes the house as a "sad and gloomy" place devoid of furnishings or even footsteps to indicate possible human habitation; its entryway evokes fear in passersby. On one occasion, after the squire has unearthed a "real" (a silver coin) and commanded the boy to buy them a meal at the local market, Lazarillo rushes into the street, where he encounters a funeral procession and overhears the dead man's widow lamenting the fact that her husband is being taken to the "sad and gloomy" place where "no one ever eats or drinks." Immediately associating the funeral's destination with his master's house, Lazarillo rushes back to bolt the door and prevent the mourners from entering with the corpse. He is afraid. The anticipated meal gives him no pleasure, and for three days his face remains pale. In actuality, the incident is probably based upon a popular folk anecdote, but within the context of Lázaro's life it becomes the basis for a symbolically significant human experience. By trying to "lock out" the uncomfortable proximity of death, the young boy is fleeing from his own fate. In real terms of course no one can permanently lock out suffering and death, but an awareness of them can be suppressed, and that is precisely what Lazarillo's society teaches him to do.[3]

In the prologue, when Lázaro admits that he is no more saintly than his neighbors, he is also implying that they are no better than he is. Based upon a retrospective consideration of his own experiences, this conclusion

Fig. 3. Lazarillo encounters the funeral procession (Bramer, ca. 1600)

Fig. 4. Lazarillo attempting to lock out death (Leloir, 1886)

is undoubtedly justified. Selfishness and petty materialism are pervasive in his fictional world; genuine virtue is absent behind the respectable façades which people erect to preserve the appearances of honor and religious faith. Unlike the nobleman who inherits wealth and a well-defined station in life, Lazarillo is obliged to seek what everyone needs in some form—a psychologically satisfying self-image and a means of securing physical survival. Only through contact with other people can he discover ways of satisfying these needs; in fact, besides serving to caricature particular types of folly, each of the secondary characters in *Lazarillo* teaches or reinforces a lesson which subsequently becomes an integral part of the adult Lázaro's world view.

By virtue of the suffering they impose upon him and the examples of successful behavior they offer him, he learns that he must choose between integrity and survival. He cannot have both; that possibility has been removed from his range of options by a society which reserves physical well-being for people who successfully practice deception, ignore unpleasant truths about themselves, and remain constantly on guard against the selfish designs of others. From the blind beggar and the priest, Lazarillo

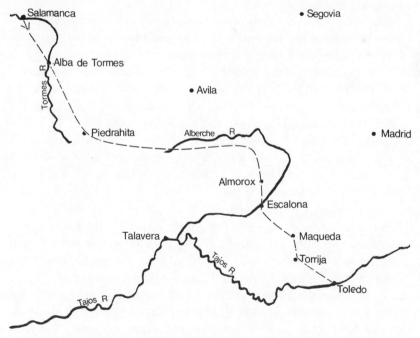

Fig. 5. Lazarillo's journey (map by Allen Bjornson)

27

learns to mask his true feelings and to regard everyone as a potential enemy to be outwitted in the continual combat which seems to characterize human relationships in his society. When he serves the squire, he sees how outwardly respectable individuals retain their self-esteem by lying to themselves and others. The pardoner and the "alguacil" (constable, justice of the peace) demonstrate to him that clever and unscrupulous people can survive in a corrupt society by manipulating appearances and disregarding the harm they inflict upon their fellow human beings. This "education" is indeed a dehumanizing process which deprives Lazarillo of any real opportunity to develop his potential for a truly human existence, but he is not the sole victim of this process: he is only one of the many who are conditioned to accept mistrust, anxiety, solitude, and selfishness as the price of survival in a society which requires adherence to Christian principles while withholding material rewards from anyone who actually practices them. Not only are these people locked in the prison house of their own deformed characters; they contribute to the socialization of others whenever they act according to the prevailing value system. The corrupt society is thus self-perpetuating, and Lázaro represents but a single link in an ongoing process.

The entire narrative of *Lazarillo* is ostensibly a memoir-letter written by Lázaro in response to a request, by a friend and superior of the archpriest of San Salvador, for a complete and detailed account of "el caso" (case, incident, situation). In the seventh tratado, it becomes clear that Lázaro had married the archpriest's mistress to assure himself a materially comfortable existence. On one occasion, after speaking to his wife and the archpriest about various rumors concerning their relationship, he promises never to discuss the matter again; in fact, he admits that "hasta el día de hoy nunca nadie nos oyó sobre el caso" (79) ("until now no one has heard about the situation from us").[4] It is probable that the incident which interests "Vuestra Merced" is the same incident which Lázaro had previously discussed with the archpriest.[5] In any case, he clearly allows Vuestra Merced to surmise the facts of the situation. Because Lázaro's complacent cuckoldry would undoubtedly appear shameful when judged according to socially sanctioned standards of behavior, he must have some motive for revealing the truth. He is obviously proud of himself, for he still doesn't regret having contracted the marriage, and he considers his materially comfortable position an adequate recompense for all his previous hardships; in fact, if the archpriest and his mistress are using Lázaro as a cover for their relationship, he is also using them, and he is apparently

Fig. 6. Lázaro discussing rumors with his wife and the archpriest (Leloir, 1886)

willing to admit his own rather ambiguous role in the affair to show Vuestra Merced how well he copes with reality by exploiting human relationships for profit.

The pragmatic, materialistic mentality behind Lázaro's attitude toward "el caso" does not suddenly appear in the seventh tratado; it is the plausible culmination of a conditioning process which began while he was still a child. As he leaves home to enter the blind beggar's service, Lazarillo listens to his mother's final words of advice—"válete por ti" (13) ("Watch out for yourself"). This expression is certainly a commonplace one, but in a world where human relationships are reduced to a continual battle in which each participant wears a series of masks and every action is a blow or counterblow, it is particularly appropriate for a boy who up to this time has been living "como niño" (like a child). The experience which renders his mother's words meaningful to him occurs on the bridge at Salamanca, where the beggar, taking advantage of his new servant's gullibility, smashes Lazarillo's head against a bull-shaped stone to impress upon him that a blind man's boy must always be one step ahead of the devil. At this point, Lazarillo concludes that he must indeed watch out for himself— "me cumple... pensar cómo me sepa valer" (13) ("I need to... think about how to take care of myself"). By obliging his servant to recognize the harshness of the world in which he is living, the blind beggar performs a crucial role in Lazarillo's development, for he translates the mother's commonplace advice into experiential terms and forcibly initiates the boy into the utilitarian mode of thinking which governs his actions in the seventh tratado.

During the first two tratados, this lesson of the stone bull is repeatedly reinforced by the continuous combat which characterizes Lazarillo's relationships with the beggar and the priest. Battles are usually fought over the food which he covets and which his masters withhold from him, and the intermediary is often the container in which the food is kept. For example, while serving the blind beggar, Lazarillo develops a taste for wine and delivers a preliminary blow by stealing his master's wine jar; the suspicious blind man counters by holding the jar in his hands. Lazarillo places a straw in the bottle; the beggar covers the mouth of the jar with his hands. Lazarillo drills a hole in the jar and allows the wine to trickle into his mouth as he lies between his master's legs; the blind man pretends not to notice the ruse so that he can smash the jar into the unsuspecting boy's face.

Later, a similar combat develops when Lazarillo attempts to gain access to the bread in the priest's chest. The entire sequence is dominated by images of battle and locked doors. In traditional terms, a clergyman opens doors to the spiritual life, but the priest of Maqueda locks up his "hacienda" (wealth), and Lazarillo is continually seeking to open doors which separate him from sustenance and physical life. The priest "arms" the chest, which itself resembles "ancient pieces of armor," and after trying to decide "cómo me podría valer" (36) ("how I could take care of myself"), Lazarillo "attacks" it, until it is "wounded," and finally "surrenders" to him. When the priest discovers that it is Lazarillo who had "made war" on him, he mercilessly beats the boy. Whether the intermediary in this incessant battle is the blind beggar's wine jar or the priest's chest, the fundamental situation remains the same: individuals are separated by a lack of generosity and trust, and the only viable approach to survival is a pragmatic one, involving selfishness, petty materialism, and deceptiveness.

Many other episodes in the first two tratados reveal a similar pattern. The entire episode of the blind beggar exists within a framework of blows. It opens with the blow Lazarillo receives on the bridge at Salamanca and closes with the blow he deals the beggar by tricking him into jumping against a stone pillar at the end of the tratado. Lazarillo's original "calabazada" (knock on the head) is paralleled by a concussion which causes the beggar's head to resound like a "calabaza" (pumpkin), and just as the blind man had derived pleasure from the pain he inflicted on someone who trusted him, Lazarillo taunts his victim for imprudently trusting the words of a blind man's servant. Actually the second incident is merely a practical application of the principles inculcated in Lazarillo during the first one, for by smashing the boy's head against the stone bull, the beggar implicitly rejects trust as a possible basis for their relationship.

When the narrating Lázaro avers that the blind man "guided and enlightened" him on the pathway of life, he means, among other things, that his first master taught him to trust no one and to always "watch out for himself." For anyone whose behavior is governed by these principles, all other people become opponents to be outwitted, rather than fellow human beings with whom joys and sufferings, thoughts and emotions may be shared. As a consequence of assimilating the blind beggar's philosophy, Lazarillo condemns himself to a life of solitude and anxiety. By the end of the second tratado, incessant hostility is the only model of human interaction to which he has been exposed, and it is hardly surprising that he begins to view all society as a jungle in which everyone is the potential enemy of everyone else.

This is the attitude which later lies behind Lázaro's willingness to accept a cuckold's role in return for the archpriest's patronage, but before succumbing completely to the dictates of a dehumanizing personal morality, Lazarillo experiences the rudimentary possibility of a human relationship based upon values other than those he had learned from the blind beggar and the priest. In the third tratado, during his stay with the squire, he has vague intimations of generosity, compassion, and authentic communication. Initially he reacts to the squire as his first two masters had conditioned him to act. When Lazarillo pulls three pieces of bread from his bosom, the squire immediately appropriates the largest piece and ravenously devours it. Just as he had grabbed the grapes of Almorox three at a time to protect his share from the blind beggar, Lazarillo gulps down the remaining pieces of bread to prevent the squire from obtaining them. He is treating the squire as a hostile opponent. But unlike the beggar and the priest, the squire is not stingy; he offers to share all that he possesses—a jug of water—with his servant. Whereas the priest's selfishness had been symbolized by the way in which he jealously guarded the keys to the attic and the chest, the squire's openness is suggested by his willingness to give Lazarillo the key to his house. Indeed, when the squire obtains a "real," he doesn't gorge himself in secret; he gives the money to Lazarillo and declares that they shall both eat "like counts."

The squire is the first person to express an interest in Lazarillo's past, and he doesn't hesitate to tell the young boy about himself. Both of them obviously embellish their stories, but Lazarillo does respond to the squire's humanity. As a gesture of politeness toward his master, who apologizes for not having any wine to offer him, Lazarillo claims that he doesn't drink wine, although in actuality he had developed a taste for it during his service with the blind beggar.[6] In the entire narrative, the squire is the only person who is less powerful than he is, and for this reason Lazarillo feels free to pity rather than distrust him. He humors the older man's need for respect and even denies himself food so that his master might have something to eat. For the first and perhaps only time in his life, Lazarillo realizes that another person is susceptible to the same gnawing hunger which he himself is experiencing. Neither master nor servant takes pleasure in the other's suffering, for they are not hostile combatants but two human beings confronted by common enemies—the deprivation and hunger which threaten to destroy them. In a corrupt and lonely world, men might find some solace in a sense of community and shared destiny, but they are imprisoned in a society which conditions them to repudiate their feelings of compassion and generosity. Ironically, their fear that others will take advantage of them if they fail to "watch out for themselves" causes them to behave in ways that endanger their own peace of mind and even, as in the case of the blind beggar, their lives. Almost totally dependent upon the charity of others, he inculcates his servant with a philosophy of absolute mistrust and suffers a broken head as a consequence of his own momentary need to trust the boy. The episode with the squire indicates that humane alternatives to the combat situation do exist; unfortunately, Lazarillo's society demands only lip service to them, while actually distributing its rewards to those who pragmatically pursue their material self-interest at other people's expense.

The disjunction between apparent and actual morality in this fictional society engenders duplicity (or masking) for purposes of satisfying both physical and psychological needs. In practical terms, it represents a necessary survival technique, allowing clever individuals to extract what they want from people who would never give it to them if they simply requested it. Traceable to the simulated amiability which permits the beggar to smash Lazarillo's head against the stone bull as a means of alerting him to the deceptiveness of appearances, Lazarillo's awareness of the necessity to dissemble underlies all his contrivances to obtain food from the blind beggar and the priest; in fact, he himself shows how well he has understood the beggar's object lesson when he camouflages his true desires (revenge, escape from a cruel master) and adopts a similar mask of friendly solicitude while carefully positioning his mentor in front of the stone pillar. But as long as he stays with the beggar and the priest, they remain capable of making Lazarillo appear guilty to onlookers, who laugh at the boy's sufferings and approve of the beatings meted out to him. These people's interpretations of the situation are obviously being manipulated, just as the pardoner and the alguacil later manipulate the opinions of credulous townspeople by staging an elaborate performance to demonstrate the efficacy and authenticity of the pardoner's worthless bulls. To assure his own physical well-being, Lázaro ultimately emulates the two frauds, because in agreeing to accept the conditions of the archpriest's patronage, he is actually devising a way to convince others of his good intentions, while maneuvering to get what he wants.

In a society which demands an outward show of respect for traditional concepts of honor and religious faith, masking also serves a psychological function. If people are obliged in practice to contravene values which they are supposed to espouse in theory, they must develop some means of coping with the dichotomy between what they are and what they say they are. In *Lazarillo* the most common method of resolving this dilemma is to pretend that it does not exist. For example, the niggardly priest actually treats Lazarillo quite uncharitably, but in keeping with his image as a clergyman, he wants others to regard him as a generous man. Although he allows his servant to eat but a single onion every four days, he makes a show of handing him the key to a room where the onions are stored, and he grandiloquently instructs the boy to relish the dainty tidbits there. The priest himself refuses to eat what he believes to be mouse-eaten bread, but he does cut off the nibbled areas and hand them to Lazarillo with the assertion that the mouse is a "clean thing." Only by blinding himself to the absence of charity in his actions can the priest continue to regard himself as a charitable person, but he keeps up the pretense because that is the only way in which he can maintain his self-respect.

This sort of hypocritical masking is even more apparent in the squire, all of whose energies are directed toward convincing others of a respectability which has no basis in fact. Although literally starving to death, the squire pretends not to be hungry and insists that he left his estates in Old Castile merely because a neighbor failed to salute him properly. He wants to be considered an "hombre de bien" (gentleman; literally "good man") whose honor remains intact despite his present misfortunes, but if he could obtain a position with a high-ranking nobleman, he would lie, flatter, and cheat to curry favor, and he would willingly remain silent about anything which might displease such a master. In the squire's eyes, the honor of an "hombre de bien" depends not upon the integrity with which he actualizes virtuous principles, but upon his ability to convince other people to accept his respectable façade, no matter what immoral actions he might commit. Like the priest, the squire can believe in himself as long as he believes that others believe in him.

The same principle underlies the narrating Lázaro's claim to be a successful man whose autobiography illustrates the virtue of rising from poverty. In the prologue, he implies that all people want their "obras" (works) to be seen and praised by others. Whether his own "obras" are his literary efforts or the actions reported in them, he too presumably desires a favorable reception for them. The actual events of his life are relatively insignificant, and when judged according to traditional norms, his involvement in "el caso" is shameful or dishonorable. Nevertheless, his prologue is characterized by an elevated style usually reserved for important persons. Like the squire's sword and cape, this elevated style is a comic expression of Lázaro's unwarranted pride, but it also reflects an understandably human impulse to reassert his self-worth in the face of a reality which threatens to deprive him of it.

In fact, the adult Lázaro's self-deceptions are strikingly similar to those of the squire. In the sixth tratado, as soon as he earns enough money to buy a sword and a cape, he abandons his position as a water-seller, dresses "muy honradamente" (very honorably), and calls himself an "hombre de bien." Later he leaves his "laceria" behind him in precisely the manner prescribed by the squire, for he actually attaches himself to a wealthy patron, whose favor he retains by remaining silent about unpleasant subjects. He receives gifts of food from the archpriest, but in order to maintain his sense of honor, he must overlook the fact that they represent payments for his willingness to marry another man's mistress. In this instance, Lázaro reconciles his physical and psychological needs in the same hypocritical manner adopted by the squire, who, to assuage his hunger, must eat bread stored in Lazarillo's filthy shirt while attempting to satisfy his obsession with "limpieza" (cleanliness in a physical sense but also in terms of "limpieza de sangre") by casually expressing confidence that the bread had been prepared by "manos limpias" (clean hands).[7] Like the squire's pathetic claim to "honor," Lázaro's attempt to retain his self-respect drives him to accept an endless round of half-lies and self-deceptions, for otherwise he would be forced to recognize his own degradation.

This, however, he is unwilling to do, and when he responds to the request for a detailed account of "el caso," he develops a rhetorical strategy to justify his own apparently dishonorable relationship with the archpriest. Although Vuestra Merced is probably more interested in the archpriest's behavior than in that of an obscure town crier, Lázaro insists upon describing his own life from the beginning, because he desires to portray his complacent cuckoldry as defensible within the context of his previous experiences. Vuestra Merced presumably knows only the surface facts of the case, and by showing him the human reality behind those facts, Lázaro proposes to convince him that under similar circumstances anyone would have acted as he did; in fact, he twice comments upon the credit due to people who rise from humble origins, and he contrasts them with those who inherit wealthy estates or fall from high social positions. By emphasizing the harshness of fortune and the almost insurmountable obstacles which he himself overcame, he is inviting Vuestra Merced to apply these generalizations to the specific case of a town crier who, despite incriminating appearances, is merely following the rules of a society which demands compromise. The implication is that such a man deserves not censure for his moral flexibility, but praise for his skill and cleverness in bettering his social position.

Conditioned by his previous experiences, Lázaro realizes that he cannot openly acknowledge the shameful truth about his arrangement with the archpriest, because such an admission would endanger his physical as well as his psychological well-being; however, his situation is not without its difficulties, and Lázaro does make several oblique references to them. For example, while describing his service with the priest, he equates hunger with light, because it sharpens the mind, but he goes on to say that the opposite is also true, as he himself could testify. The only time at which Lázaro truly experiences the opposite of hunger is during his marriage to the archpriest's mistress; therefore, if he knows by personal experience that satiety dulls the mind, he is probably referring to the self-imposed blindness with which he views his role in "el caso." Similarly, before he relates the episode about the squire's "real" and the funeral procession, he asks a proverblike rhetorical question: "¿Qué me aprovecha, si está constituido en mi triste fortuna que ningún gozo me venga sin zozobra?" (57) ("What good does it do me, if it is decreed in my sad fate that no joy will come to me unaccompanied by worry?"). In context, the question concerns Lazarillo's inability to relish a long-desired feast, but on another level, he might be admitting that the pleasure he receives from his arrangement with the archpriest is accompanied by anxiety. Sprinkled throughout the text are similar hints that the narrator, fully aware of his ambiguous situation, is not altogether comfortable with the mask he is wearing.

There are two possible explanations for this uneasiness. Either Lázaro knows that discomfort is an appropriate response to his present circumstances and feigns it to gain the sympathy of Vuestra Merced, or he actually feels discomfort as a consequence of undergoing a socializing process which obliges him to renounce any possibility of establishing open, honest relationships with others, of attaining genuine self-awareness, or of developing a morality based upon more than petty materialism and pragmatic self-interest. In the first instance, his narrative would become an artfully contrived mask calculated to deceive readers into according Lázaro the approbation which he, as a "self-made man," claims to deserve; in the second, the autobiographical memoir-letter would be merely a final and somewhat pathetic expression of a mentality conditioned to accept society's dehumanized values as normal and natural. The situation resembles that posed by a figure-ground problem in Gestalt psychology. Lázaro must be seen either as a victim or as a deceiver; in the reader's eyes, the narrator cannot be both at the same time, and yet both interpretations of the text are possible.

Thus, when Lázaro employs sententious statements which apply equally well to incidents he describes in the text and to his own involvement with the archpriest's mistress, he could be signaling his awareness of how others might judge him, or he could be unwittingly condemning himself for what he sees in others but fails to perceive in himself. On three occasions, he employs the exclamation: "¡Cuantos . . . !" ("How many!") in drawing attention to the widespread practice of a vice or weakness which he has observed in a particular instance. When his mulatto stepbrother flees in fear from the blackness of his own father, Lazarillo exclaims upon the number of people who flee from others because they fail to look at themselves. After observing the proud bearing of the starving squire, he exclaims upon the number of people who would suffer for their honor what they would never suffer for God. Finally, when he recognizes how cleverly the pardoner and alguacil have tricked the credulous congregation, he exclaims upon the number of such swindlers who circulate among the people. In each case, the adult Lázaro is himself among the "cuantos" upon whose number he is speculating. Faced with rumors about his wife's relationship to the archpriest, he flees from others to avoid looking at himself. As a self-proclaimed success, he would never suffer for God the humiliations which he suffers for his own honor, and like the two frauds, he is a swindler who knows the rules of the game and exploits "el caso" for his own material benefit.

None of these exclamations is explicitly linked with Lázaro's situation in the seventh tratado, but they are all clearly applicable to it. Because there is no way of determining with absolute certainty the degree to which the narrator intended these exclamations as allusions to his present circumstances, the text itself is ambiguous, and the reader's interpretation of it oscillates between two views of what is there—the inadvertant admissions of a dehumanized victim or the contrivances of a mask-wearing trickster. This ambiguity extends to the narrator's vocabulary, for the reader never knows whether Lázaro's words reflect the assimilation of a debased language system or the conscious manipulation of that system.

Lázaro's use of terms associated with honor and religion clearly illustrates this ambiguity. Commonly assumed to denote actual virtue or faith, these terms undergo a systematic reversal of meaning in *Lazarillo;* for example, "bueno" (the good, the good individual) and "bien" (good) become ironically reversed key words which indicate the presence of evil beneath the appearance of goodness. In sixteenth-century Castile, an "hombre bueno" was a person who, lacking noble blood, had acquired a certain fortune and participated in the "concejos" (city or town councils). [8]

Both "bueno" and "bien" had connotations of virtue and social respectability; in Lázaro's vocabulary, only the respectability remains, the virtue having been replaced by physical comfort and an ability to play by society's rules. In real terms, this must be what Lazarillo's mother has in mind, when she gives her son into the blind beggar's care and cautions him to be "good." She regards her husband as a "buen hombre" (good man), because he knew how to provide his family with something to eat; similarly, she considers the blind beggar a "bueno amo" (good master) because he would presumably do the same for Lazarillo. After her husband is convicted as a thief and exiled, she determines to "arrimarse a los buenos, por ser uno dellos" (10) ("attach herself to the good people in order to be one of them"). For her, the "good people" are stable boys like Zaide, who steals to support her and her family while attempting to maintain the appearance of honesty.

Just as his mother willingly prostitutes herself to Zaide for food and firewood, Lázaro later sells himself to the archpriest for the same amenities. The similarity between the two situations is emphasized by Lázaro's admission that his own "buena vida" (good life) results from a decision to "arrimar[se] a los buenos" (79). Claiming that he has reached both a "buen puerto" (good harbor) and the summit of "toda buena fortuna" (all good fortune), he considers his wife "tan buena mujer" (as good a woman) as any living within the gates of Toledo. In each case, the word "good" implies the moral compromise necessary to live well and maintain the appearance of goodness in a corrupt society. Having lost all connotations of genuine virtue, Lázaro's idea of "good" contrasts sharply with the conventionally accepted definition of the term.

The same reversal of meaning occurs in nearly all his references to God, prayer, and the sacraments. Exposed to many commonplace usages for the word "God," Lazarillo learns to pray, not for spiritual consolation but for physical well-being.[9] On one occasion, he even prays for the death of others so that he might eat at their funeral banquets. The God who fulfills such prayers and inspires Lazarillo to trick his first two masters is the same God from whom Lázaro claims to have received his reward for marrying the archpriest's mistress—"me hace Dios con ella mil mercedes y más bien que yo merezco" (80) ("with her God grants me a thousand favors and more good than I deserve"). Actually his prosperity at this point derives from a successful application of what he had learned from the blind beggar, who "guided and enlightened" him on the path of life; however, in the seventh tratado, Lázaro claims that it was God who enlightened him and placed him on a profitable path. Because the inspiration which comes from God and the inspiration which comes from the blind beggar result in the same type of behavior, Lázaro's religion is revealed as a highly secularized belief in a God who accords material comfort to those who "watch out for themselves."

Within this context, the sacraments retain a certain symbolic value, but rather than ministering to the eternal life of the spirit, they provide sustenance for the body. Throughout the second tratado, bread is described in terms usually reserved for the communion. When Lazarillo opens the chest, the bread appears to him as the "face of God" and offers him "consolation." He speaks of "adoring" it and "receiving" it, but what he is referring to is its power to satisfy his hunger. Similarly, he learns to drink the blind beggar's wine as a means of reaching a state of physical well-being, but he depicts it in terms of religious ecstasy. Despite Lazarillo's painful encounter with the wine jar, the beggar assures him that he will be "blessed" by wine, and if wine can be considered as a synechdoche for the institutional church served by the archpriest, the town crier does indeed owe his physical blessings to wine. Associated with the fulfillment of physical needs and symbolizing the "good" life which Lázaro attains through deception and compromise, the sacraments in *Lazarillo* take on a secular meaning diametrically opposed to their traditional religious one.

If Lázaro is viewed as a victim of society, these reversals of meaning reflect his assimilation of current but debased language. If he is regarded as a deceiver, they reveal both a calculated use of words associated with traditional values and a cynical disregard for the values themselves. The possibility that the narrator's attitude can be interpreted in different ways creates a fundamental ambiguity in the reader's reaction to the text, but when it comes to judging the values espoused by the narrator, the ambiguity disappears. Whether Lázaro is a victim or a trickster, he has clearly adopted a dehumanized value system in attempting to cope with the schizophrenic demands of a society in which "good" people must act in one way while pretending that they are acting in another.

In either case, Lázaro is implicitly condemned, but because he is the product of repeated contacts with a harsh world where people must learn to play by rules which require them to suppress their impulses toward generosity, compassion, truthfulness, and genuine religious belief, the anonymous author of *Lazarillo* is actually drawing attention to (and commenting upon) the nature of that society. By revealing the debased mentality behind Lázaro's pretentious and self-serving letter to Vuestra Merced,

he is implicitly questioning the societal values internalized by his picaresque hero. No character in the book lives according to traditional concepts of honor and religion, though many pretend to do so for their own selfish purposes. The blind beggar might adopt a humble and devout pose, but
his only purpose is to "sacar el dinero" (get money); the squire parades his
meticulously arranged rags through town and attends mass daily, but he
only desires to convince others that he is a man worthy of respect. Without exception, the clergymen ignore their spiritual vocation, abuse the
trust placed in them, and devote themselves to worldly concerns. In claiming to have attained the summit of all good fortune as a consequence of his
arrangement with the archpriest, Lázaro has simply become like everyone
else.

However, Lázaro's claim is undercut by the fact that hardly anyone in
sixteenth-century Spain would have considered the town crier's situation
as a summit of good fortune; furthermore, it is unlikely that Vuestra
Merced would accept Lázaro's contention that a man's virtue can be measured in terms of his ability to rise in society by means of shrewdness,
deception, and moral compromise. It is unclear whether Lázaro desires to
be respected for his success or for his insightfulness in recognizing the
conditions of success, but it is clear that he wants to be respected for an
accomplishment which, when judged according to a truly humane set of
values, is no accomplishment at all. The emptiness of his pretension becomes apparent when compared with that of the squire. Lázaro himself
recognizes the worthlessness of "la negra que llaman honra" (50) ("the
wretched thing which men call honor") when he sees it in others, but he
apparently fails to perceive that his own storytelling is motivated by a
desire for a similar type of honor.

Similarities between Lázaro's behavior and that of other characters link
his mentality to prevalent attitudes in his society; his failure to recognize
these similarities suggests that his own moral vision is biased and incomplete. If the reversed meanings of terms associated with honor and religion
signify a debasement of language traceable to general social practices, and
if Lázaro's habits of mind represent an interiorization of the prevailing
ethos in a society where he hopes to survive and prosper, the meaning of
the picaresque myth in *Lazarillo* becomes apparent; it serves as a paradigm
for the process by means of which the dehumanizing values of a corrupt
society are imprinted upon the mind of a lower-class individual. Lazarillo's lack of respectable parentage and his departure from home expose him
to a rude initiation and a struggle for physical and psychological survival.

Modeling his behavior upon that which he observes around him, he learns to attain his own selfish, materially defined goals by deceiving and exploiting others. Because all people are presumably responsible for protecting their own interests, he feels no compulsion to deal honestly or compassionately with them. Obliged to compromise and then camouflage the nature of his compromise by hypocritically defending his honor, Lázaro is locked into a life devoid of truthfulness, compassion, and self-awareness, for this is the price he assumes everyone must pay for success.

Lázaro's self-justificatory memoirs are thus perhaps more persuasive than he himself realizes, because his own personality constitutes an implicit condemnation of the society in which he is living. If he were a self-made man, as he claims to be, Lázaro would incur responsibility for his own dehumanization. In actuality, this dehumanization results from society's arbitrary limitation of the ways in which needs can be satisfied. Behavior that is necessary for survival continues to be discussed in terms of traditional values which no longer possess any genuine moral or spiritual significance. But even in Lazarillo's fictional world, it remains possible to conceive of alternative values—like the generosity and self-awareness he experiences in the third tratado—and to recognize that people could lead more humanly satisfying lives if they dealt honestly with themselves and charitably with others. If Lázaro's personality has been warped in the socializing process, it is on the basis of these implied alternative values that judgment can be passed upon the society which conditions him to accept hypocrisy and the pragmatic pursuit of his own materialistic self-interest as normal ways of coping with reality. In the juxtaposition of pseudovalues assimilated by the fictive narrator with genuine values according to which his attitudes are condemned, an implied world view emerges, and it is within the context of this world view that the anonymous author's elaboration of the picaresque myth must be understood.

During a time when there was considerable interest in questions about inherited qualities and the legitimacy of upward social mobility, this author succeeded in redefining the problem and giving it fictional form. Without explicitly defending his hero's right to rise in society, he depicted the comic and tragic consequences of a low-born individual's encounter with the conflicting demands of a no-exit situation. It is for this reason that readers can laugh at Lázaro's pretentiousness while feeling sympathy for someone who, like him, has been subjected to a dehumanizing socialization process. The picaresque myth in *Lazarillo* thus corresponds to a complex situation outside the narrative, and when readers react ambiguously to a narrator whose life embodies the principal elements of that myth, they are indirectly responding to the difficulty of knowing the truth about a social reality in which traditional values no longer obtain.

If *Lazarillo* reflects particular historical relationships as perceived by its anonymous author, it also established a precedent which would be followed under quite different circumstances in later picaresque novels. Besides delineating the major outlines of this myth, the anonymous author contributed to the evolution of the modern European novel. Earlier works—anatomies of roguery like *Liber vagatorum* (1510) or jest books like *Till Eulenspiegel* (1515)—had depicted low-life scenes and drawn upon popular anecdotes, but by sustaining a consistent pseudoautobiographical perspective while allowing readers to glimpse the flaws and inadequacies of the narrator's personality, the author of *Lazarillo* achieved a much higher degree of artistic organization and moral seriousness than did his predecessors. Furthermore, his extended portrayal of a lower-class character's life placed a new emphasis upon the primacy of individual experience and reflected a heightened interest in creating the illusion of verisimilitude, suggesting that the anonymous author of *Lazarillo* was among the first Europeans to seize upon the novel's potential as a serious form of literary expression.

3

THE DISSEMINATION OF
THE PICARESQUE:
Guzmán de Alfarache
AND THE CONVERSO PROBLEM

Nearly fifty years after the publication of *Lazarillo*, Mateo Alemán's *Guzmán de Alfarache* (1599, 1604) appeared in Madrid and immediately achieved an extraordinary popular success.[1] In the meantine, *Lazarillo* had become a well-known literary character, although the anonymous author's text repeatedly suffered multilation at the hands of editors and censors. In a 1555 Antwerp edition, the book's unity and symmetry were destroyed by the addition of a poorly written sequel. Four years later, both *Lazarillo* and the sequel were placed on the Index, although an expurgated version was published in 1573. Bound together with the apocryphal continuation, this text was reissued at Milan in 1587 and at Bergamo in 1597. Perhaps influenced by popular romances, the sequel describes how Lázaro departed from Toledo and survived a shipwreck. Because he was drunk, the wine coursing through his veins prevented water from entering his body and permitted him to live among the fish. Despite the possibility of an allegorical interpretation,[2] the 1555 continuation has little intrinsic merit, and except for the fact that its first chapter was often printed as the final tratado in later editions of *Lazarillo*, the fantastic journey to the realm of the fish was soon forgotten and never became popularly linked with the original story.

For Spanish readers, the proscription and expurgation of *Lazarillo* had more serious consequences. Within a year after the establishment of the Index, *Lazarillo* was included among the books considered dangerous to the faith or morals of good Catholics. However, five Spanish editions had already appeared and others were being printed abroad. Because Lázaro's story could not be completely suppressed, Juan López Velasco (a secretary to the Council of Overseas Territories) received approval to publish a censored version. Frequently bound together with Lucas Gracián Dantisco's courtesy book *Galateo español*, this so-called "Lazarillo castigado"

(Lazarillo punished or corrected) was presented more as an entertaining story than as a profound social and moral commentary; the monk and the pardoner episodes were missing, and isolated observations about clergymen and court customs were excised, although satiric portraits of the priest, the canon, and the archpriest remained, presumably because they could be interpreted as recognizable *topoi* and not attacks upon the church or its hierarchy.[3]

López Velasco's censored version did not seriously impair the book's picaresque narrative structure, and since four more editions appeared in the next quarter century,[4] it seems unlikely that Alemán could have remained unaware of *Lazarillo* during the time that he was writing *Guzmán*. There are several verbal and thematic parallels which indicate that he might have been consciously echoing the anonymous novel, but if he was influenced by *Lazarillo*, he undoubtedly viewed it as a narrative form with potentialities for expansion rather than as a model to be followed scrupulously.[5] Despite the fact that *Guzmán* is many times longer than its predecessor, however, there are fundamental similarities between the two novels. In both of them, a lower-class narrator finds himself in humiliating circumstances (Guzmán is a galley slave) and writes his autobiography in an attempt to justify himself. Both Lazarillo and young Guzmán lack the well-defined social position which respectable birth might have given them; both leave home and undergo a painful initiation into the deceptive world of appearances where everyone is pursuing earthly vanities and seeking to outwit everyone else. While serving a series of corrupt masters, they both learn to participate in perverse but commonly accepted patterns of behavior, paying for their survival by a loss of genuine human values. In both *Lazarillo* and *Guzmán*, a profound, compassionate moral vision emerges from behind the constantly implied juxtaposition of conventional ideals and the actual behavior of people living in a society supposedly governed by those ideals.

Guzmán and *Lazarillo* thus share the autobiographical perspective, a panoramic view of society, and a series of narrated experiences which retrace the basic outlines of the picaresque myth, but Alemán's novel differs from *Lazarillo* in that it is filled with the fictive narrator's self-analyses and sermonizing digressions. There is even evidence to indicate that Alemán intended his novel to be read as a miscellany—a collection of borrowed and invented examples of eloquent style and effective argument. In fact, when Part I of *Guzmán* became popularly known as "El Pícaro," he objected strenuously and preferred to subtitle his entire work "atalaya de la vida humana" ("watchtower of human life").[6] As the vantage point from which everything in the novel is seen and interpreted, this "atalaya" presupposes the attitudes and assumptions of the narrating Guzmán, an ostensibly sincere Christian and repentant sinner struggling to impose a comprehensible order upon his perceptions of the world. Unlike Lázaro, however, Guzmán is not merely concerned with his own life, but with all of human life. Alemán's insistence upon the "atalaya de la vida humana" subtitle undoubtedly serves to emphasize the universality and underlying seriousness of the work, but it is his artistry in contriving this "watchtower" that makes *Guzmán* extremely significant in another way. By adapting elements of traditional rhetoric, spiritually uplifting literature, and anecdotal humor to the simulated autobiography of a vulgar "hero," he succeeds in fusing a profoundly tragic sense of life to a traditionally comic subject matter. In *Guzmán*, expository prose is transformed into a fictional medium capable of representing plausible, lower-class characters without denying the moral seriousness and psychological depth of their experiences. The subsequent European novel would develop in precisely this direction, and it is not an exaggeration to say that *Guzmán*'s extraordinary popularity in Spain and other countries contributed to the acceptance of the novel as a serious literary form.

Despite its length, diffuseness, and bewildering diversity, *Guzmán* does have a unity of focus to the degree that it revolves around a coherent presentation of the converso problem. Himself the victim of social injustice, Alemán was refused permission to emigrate to Peru in 1582, at least partly because he was unable to establish the purity of his blood; thirty-five years later, he succeeded in going to Mexico only by bribing a government official and relinquishing his rights to Part II of *Guzmán*. All verifiable historical dates in the book indicate that Guzmán's chronology parallels that of the author. Like his fictional character, Alemán apparently underwent a conversion. When he visited Cartagena in 1591, the burning plug from a ceremonial cannon salute grazed his cheek. Fearing for his life, he invoked the protection of Saint Anthony of Padua, and when he escaped unhurt, he vowed to publish a biography of the saint—a project which he completed in the Seville prison, where he had been incarcerated for debt in 1602. If McGrady is correct in linking this incident with Guzmán's unjust imprisonment in Bologna, Alemán may have been allegorically describing how he himself had been unfairly treated while attempting to obtain justice after the original manuscript of Part II had been stolen and published, because the preceding and following episodes contain veiled allusions to the affair.[7] Like Alemán, then, Guzmán is a converso who writes a theologically orthodox book while he is in prison and after he has undergone what he considers to be a religious conversion.

But within contemporary Spanish society, such a conversion would not necessarily have preserved a converso from Inquisitorial persecution, and if the fictional Guzmán's memoirs are self-exculpatory, it is quite possible that they also serve as a more universally applicable apologia, providing a practical and theoretical justification for the converso's right to existence in society and to salvation after death. As the fictive narrator, Guzmán not only relates the story of his life; he also makes numerous philosophical comments of a general nature. These digressions conform so closely to the tenets of Counter-Reformation Catholicism that the book itself was praised by the censors; even today, *Guzmán* is frequently discussed as an orthodox theological tract, although the primacy of the converso problem has become increasingly evident in recent years.[8] When properly understood, the entire novel—its narrative, its religious doctrine, its anecdotes, tales, parodies, and allegories—constitutes a converso's eloquent plea for a recognition of his humanity and the legitimacy of his claims to religious and secular equality.

In the preface to Part II of *Guzmán*, Alemán defines the book's purpose as the presentation of an "hombre perfeto" (perfect man); somewhat later, the narrator echoes the author's avowed intention by declaring that his goal too is the creation of an "hombre perfeto." If a perfect man is someone who recognizes the truth, the allusion is presumably to the narrating Guzmán; however, within the social context of late sixteenth-century Spain, it would have been impossible for Guzmán to reach perfection because he could never escape his converso heritage. And yet, whether or not he actually attains salvation, he is portrayed as a man capable of penetrating deceptive appearances, recognizing a deeper spiritual truth, and guiding the unenlightened away from the evil path of sin and toward the path of perfection. Like Luis de Granada or Saint Teresa, he combines descriptions of intensely personal experience and arguments drawn from literary and historical sources in an attempt to persuade readers that they must practice introspection, examine their consciences and improve their own behavior, if they wish to reach a new state of awareness. It is significant that Alemán portrays a converso as the credible "watchtower" of human life, for if all the religious and philosophical ideas expressed by the narrator are genuinely orthodox (and no one in the seventeenth century seems to have seriously doubted this), any man—even a converso—can be regarded as a defender of the true faith. The implication is that, if all men are essentially similar, Guzmán might be considered a representative man, and his life might serve to illuminate the condition of all men. In terms of the justification of conversos, it makes little difference whether or not Guzmán's ultimate conversion is genuine. According to orthodox theology, there is no reason why a converso cannot reach perfection and provide a universally applicable view of human existence.

Attempting to project himself as a man of wisdom and faith, the narrating Guzmán introduces the various episodes of his life under the pretext that they illustrate the validity of orthodox religious principles. Defined by the Council of Trent and defended by the Spanish throne, these principles represent an officially proclaimed version of the truth; however, as he demonstrates in the narrative sections of the novel, society does not encourage more than a superficial adherence to this doctrine, for it conditions people to cultivate the appearance of virtue while avidly following the most selfish and materialistic motives. Thus, although the proclaimed values of Guzmán's society are patently orthodox, its actual practices conform to an altogether different ethic. From Guzmán's own apparently orthodox position, that society seems more corrupt and immoral than the poor, homeless pícaro who is obliged to adopt its customs if he hopes to survive. In condemning the very people whose lives have been twisted and deformed by the inescapable pressures which it exerts upon them, society itself emerges as a hypocritical villain, and by satisfying an impulse to reassert his own self-worth in the face of such a judgment, Guzmán creates the basis for a convincing defense of an entire class of alienated and outcast Spaniards.

Ironically, his argument makes use of the same literary techniques and traditions as the popular religious guides of the period. On the surface, Guzmán's autobiography is a record of his own progress toward perfection as well as a manual of spiritual instruction. Like the religious guides, *Guzmán* is at the same time intensely personal and highly rational, because every experience, no matter how charged with anguish or anxiety, is introduced as a specific illustration of a larger truth. Assuming that all people are rational and, if not blinded by appetite or passion, would reach the same conclusions, Guzmán claims to guide his readers toward an emotional and rational acceptance of universally valid principles. For example, before relating an episode from his own life, he usually generalizes about the type of experience involved. Presented within the context of a moral or religious discussion, the episode is thus transformed into an illustrative example. A sermon on charity precedes a description of Guzmán's involvement with a truly charitable man; a lecture on the appetites of the flesh introduces an account of his service with the lascivious French ambassador; a discussion of friendship is immediately followed by an episode which reveals how false friends mistreat him. Never does Guzmán stray from orthodox Catholic doctrine, but one general conclusion seems to emerge from both his sermons and the narrative episodes which illustrate them: all people are essentially alike, and if this is true, a pícaro or a converso has every right to consider himself a good Christian.

Even the intercalated allegories and novellas serve a rhetorical function in Guzmán's apologia for his converso identity. At one point, he relates the story of Pantelón Casteleto, a miserable Florentine beggar who incongruously wills his filthy, unkempt burro to the duke of Tuscany. The duke takes his legacy seriously and discovers 3,600 escudos hidden on the animal. Similarly, Guzmán is bequeathing the story of his own life to his readers. Behind the odiousness, poverty, and apparent failure of that life, there lies something extremely valuable, and readers who take it seriously will be enriched beyond their expectations. Another anecdote with a similar moral appears near the end of the novel. In this case, a painter has been commissioned to portray a horse. When he finishes, he leaves the canvas upside-down on a chair; his patron enters the room, sees the upside-down horse and becomes furious, although he is completely satisfied as soon as the painter rights the canvas. For Guzmán, the painting is like the works of God. As soon as they are viewed from an appropriate vantage point, all things appear to be created as perfectly as anyone could desire. By a logical extension of this principle, Spaniards who condemn the converso need only perceive him properly to understand that he, like them, has been created to perfection by God. Like the duke of Tuscany or the gentleman who commissioned the painting, Guzmán's readers will obtain full satisfaction if only they regard his apparently miserable life from a suitable "atalaya."

The same basic argument is reiterated in one of Guzmán's deceptively simple allegories: truth is equated with a peg and illusion with a string attached to the peg. Although the string can cover the peg and twist it for long periods of time, the string will break long before the peg. Within the context of Guzmán's orthodoxy, the allegory illustrates the premise that truth will always emerge from behind illusory appearances. Applied to society, this general statement suggests the futility of attempting to disguise the truth beneath the masks people wear to defraud others or the false identities which social pressures oblige them to adopt. If readers follow Guzmán's line of reasoning, they should apply it to conversos as well as to Old Christians, for regardless of their social roles people will ultimately be revealed for what they are.

Within the rhetorical framework of Guzmán's apologia for conversos, the four long novellas also become illustrative examples. In the first novella, "Ozmín and Daraja," two noble young Moors are separated, subjected to a series of misfortunes, and finally reunited under the protection of Ferdinand and Isabella. Adopting the Christian names of their royal patrons, the two Moors marry and live happily ever after. The monk who narrates the story interprets it as an example of how God's grace manifests itself in apparent misfortune, but there are similarities between Guzmán's own story and that of the Moors. In both cases, young people are the victims of undeserved suffering, but their difficulties are ultimately overcome by a conversion to orthodox Catholicism. When the Spanish monarchs sponsor two attractive, young conversos for Christian baptism, they indirectly vouchsafe Guzmán's own right to be considered a Christian in good standing.

Similarly, the "Dorotea and Bonifacio" story ostensibly illustrates God's punishment of those who mistreat the innocent and the just, but it also demonstrates the fragility of worldly honor, which is always vulnerable to forces beyond one's control; in the background lies the suggestion that a true personal honor exists and resides in the purity of one's intentions. Dorotea and Bonifacio are happily married commoners, but when the nobleman Claudio abducts and seduces Dorotea, his action threatens to destroy their happiness; however, his own house burns down, revealing his sister's liaison with a butler and destroying his reputation as well as his possessions. Claudio himself is arrested, but Dorotea returns surreptitiously to her husband, and because she never tells him about the loss of her honor, they continue to live happily together. Just as Guzmán would be considered tainted if people knew about his converso origins, Dorotea would be disgraced if her shame were known. In real terms, however, both Guzmán and Dorotea (her name means "gift of God") are morally superior to the society which would condemn them.

In *Guzmán*, then, both expository generalizations and specific narrative examples tend to destroy any meaningful rationale for distinguishing between Old and New Christians. Because Guzmán's world view is essentially Augustinian and corresponds closely to that expressed in the Tridentine profession of faith, he is actually condemning accepted

Spanish social practices by juxtaposing them with the very principles which that society claims to enforce; however, Guzmán's emphasis differs from that of orthodox dogma in that he is more concerned with human equality than with doctrinal purity.[9] For him as for the Council of Trent, all existence is divided into an infinite, eternal, spiritual realm and a limited, transitory, material one. By their nature, all people participate in both realms. Echoing and elaborating upon the orthdox idea that everyone is susceptible to sin and death, Guzmán observes, "Todo ha sido, es y será una misma cosa. El primero padre fue alevoso; la primera madre, mentirosa; el primero hijo, ladrón y fratricida" (355)[10] ("Everything has been, is and will be the same thing. The first father was treacherous; the first mother, deceitful; the first son, a thief and fratricide"). By emphasizing the recurrence of this pattern, Guzmán is pointing out that everyone is imprisoned in a physical body which is subjected to appetite, passion, imperfection, and decay. Because people's perceptions are limited by the grossness of their senses, they can be deluded by appearances. If Guzmán's major premise (everyone confronts a similar destiny) is valid, then his own life can be considered a representative example of the human journey through a world of sin, suffering, and death.

At the same time, Guzmán insists that all people have a spiritual existence and a potential for salvation. Underlying the constantly changing, physically limited temporal world, Alemán's orthodox theology posits an ultimately real substratum of spiritual being. By knowing and acknowledging the superiority of this realm, one becomes aware of universal, rationally comprehensible laws, which are always operative beneath the apparent arbitrariness of the material world. Condemned to a fate of sin, suffering, and death in their physical existence, human beings are also endowed with reason, which permits them to recognize the transience of earthly things and the immutability of the spirit; furthermore, they have an inalienable soul, which potentially unites them to the mystical body of God, as Guzmán says: "Todos somos hombres y tenemos entendimiento... también eres miembro deste cuerpo místico, igual con todos en sustancia" (266, 268) ("We are all men and have understanding... you too are a member of this mystical body, equal to everyone else in substance"). If this is true, everyone has a God-given access to salvation, which may be attained by perceiving the truth and willing the good.

Because this truth is neither visible nor tangible, it can never be comprehended through the senses, but only by means of introspection and rational understanding; it follows that all people have a moral obligation to know themselves, for only through self-knowledge can they know the truth, which is the Divine. According to the Tridentine profession of faith, justification involves the sanctification and renewal of the inner self through the voluntary acceptance of grace and gifts—"et sanctificatio et renovatio interioris hominis per voluntariam susceptionem gratiale et donorum."[11] The implication is that no one is damned from the beginning; every person is free to choose between the authentic truth of the spirit and the false truths of the physical world. Guzmán illustrates the nature of this choice by comparing man to a little child learning to walk. Unless the child moves his own feet, he will fall upon the floor and not into the waiting arms of a loving father. Similarly, man must make an effort to define himself in terms of his soul; otherwise, he will fall into perdition and lose the salvation which God holds out to him. Within this context, socially sanctioned honor and purity of blood become irrelevant. Because all people have material and spiritual being, they are equally capable of attaining salvation or suffering perdition. If an individual's ultimate destiny depends solely upon the recognition and acceptance of grace, an Old Christian has no more right to claim religious legitimacy than a converso.

According to Saint Augustine, moral evil derives from a perversion of will, which impels people to neglect their spiritual being and devote themselves to the pursuit of earthly vanities that provide only momentary, insubstantial satisfactions and are lost forever at the moment of death. Corresponding to Augustine's earthly city (founded upon a pervasive love of self and contempt for God), the entire society in *Guzmán* is dominated by men who steal, lie, cheat, and neglect their obligations, while boasting about their actions. In such a world, justice is a reward for those who can afford to pay the highest bribes, and commerce is no more than the sum of people's attempts to cheat each other. In Guzmán's symbolic terms, this society is variously characterized as a battlefield, a turbulent ocean, or a card game in which each player maximizes his own gain while seeking everyone else's ruin.

One of Alemán's own favorite emblems—a spider descending its thread toward the head of a sleeping snake—is mentioned twice by Guzmán, who clearly identifies it with the way people regard each other in this corrupt, hostile society (Fig. 7).[12] On one occasion, he expands upon the idea behind the emblem, "Todo anda revuelto, todo apriesa, todo marañado. No hallarás hombre con hombre; todos vivimos en asechanza los unos de los

Fig. 7. Frontispiece to Part I of *Guzmán de Alfarache* (1599), showing the author pointing to the emblem which depicts the spider-snake allegory

otros, como el gato para el ratón o la araña para la culebra, que hallándola descuidada, se deja colgar de un hilo y, asiéndola de la cerviz, la aprieta fuertemente, no apartándose della hasta que con su ponzoña la mata" (280) ("Everything is turned around, ephemeral, and full of intrigue. You will not find one man with another; all of us are living in ambush for each other, like the cat for the rat or the spider for the snake—the spider which, finding the snake off guard, descends a thread, grasps the snake by the neck and holds fast, not letting go until it has killed it with its poison"). Both the spider lurking in ambush and its victim are portrayed as vile, disgusting creatures, and the implication is that a society characterized by egoism and rapacity is necessarily a jungle, where each person is alienated from all others. In his dedication to Francisco de Rojas, Alemán expresses a fear of vulgar readers, whom he describes as "cazadores" (hunters) lying in wait for "nuestra perdición" (our perdition). Even after they succeed in wounding their prey, these hostile readers never explain why they wanted to harm him in the first place.[13] On one level, he is referring to the self-righteous people who persecute conversos; on another, he is delineating a society in which trust has become impossible. Everyone seems to consider himself in perpetual combat with everyone else, but because overt selfishness is not a commonly admired trait, people construct ambuscades by dissimulating their true motives behind façades of honor and respectability. Fearing detection, they tacitly agree to respect the pretensions of others so that their own pretensions might also be respected. Corruption and hypocrisy are thus institutionalized by a kind of unwritten social contract.

As long as the virtues of the poor are despised as vices and the vices of the wealthy are admired as virtues, a successful man will tend to "hincharse" (puff himself up) or "entronizarse" (exalt himself). In actuality, he is merely parading his own moral blindness, for the earthly vanities which he regards as supremely important can provide no more than fleeting, empty pleasures. Basing his self-esteem upon honor, wealth, power, and sensual gratification, he must live in constant fear that his entire life will be rendered meaningless if the physical trappings of his identity are destroyed or lost, as they inevitably will be. Such a man exhibits a state of mind which corresponds to a self-image based solely upon life in the material world; he is opting for what Guzmán calls death in life.

There is, however, another possible way of achieving self-definition. If the test of a man's faith lies not in what he possesses but in what he does with what he possesses, every man is free to repudiate what Augustine calls self-love, or a contempt for the Divine within one's self. Whether a person is a converso or an Old Christian, he can act with integrity, eschew his natural inclinations toward evil, deal charitably with others, and know himself by calmly accepting his own suffering and death. Contrary to the assumptions underlying the persecution of conversos, evil in society derives from a general perversion of the will, and it cannot be attributed to the inherent qualities of those Spaniards who happen to have Jewish ancestors. According to the dominant social values of honor and purity of blood, Guzmán ought to be condemned and ostracized, but his society formally recognizes the truth of an orthodox religious doctrine which, when accepted at face value, permits him to respect himself and repudiate society's rejection of him. As a galley slave without wealth, honor, or Old Christian blood, Guzmán effectively cites society's own principles in proclaiming his right to salvation and denying the validity of its standards for determining status.

In contrast to *Lazarillo*, the moral vision in *Guzmán* is repeatedly and expressly defined, because it is an integral part of the autobiographical perspective or "atalaya" from which the adult narrator is speaking. Desiring to project himself as a wise man who has acquired a deeper understanding of himself and his world, Guzmán tries to disavow his former perverse motivations and dissociate himself from his previous sins and follies. In doing so, however, he describes a socializing process which resembles that of *Lazarillo* in many ways: a young boy without respectable origins leaves home, undergoes an initiation into the corrupt practices of a dehumanizing society, and finally adopts the accepted forms of behavior in order to survive. Like Lazarillo, Guzmán must choose between integrity and physical well-being, but unlike his predecessor, he discovers a theoretically plausible solution to the picaresque identity crisis. Viewing himself in terms of his basic human characteristics (which he shares with all other people) and accepting the major tenets of a socially sanctioned religious orthodoxy, he can minimize the importance of his physical needs and believe that he has as much right as anyone to respect himself. From this perspective, the picaresque pattern of experience as depicted in *Lazarillo* is transformed into the life of a typical sinner, a man who can transcend the moral blindness inculcated in him by a perverse society. Near the beginning of Part II, Guzmán himself declares, "A mí me parece que son todos los hombres como yo, flacos, fáciles, con pasiones naturales y aun estrañas" (481) ("To me it seems that all men are like me, weak, pliant, with natural passions and even unnatural ones"). If this is true, an account of how his environment conditioned him—an unreflective young converso—to renounce his spiritual identity and follow his inclinations toward evil traces the process to which any poor sinner is subjected in a society that has institutionalized covetousness, vulgar materialism, and an obsessive concern for honor and purity of blood.

Even in his childhood home, Guzmán is exposed to this corrupt system of values. His parents attach supreme importance to material wealth, sensual pleasure, and the superficial appearance of honor, but although young Guzmán leaves home to escape the anguish and shame of being associated with them, he redefines himself in noble terms and sets out to obtain the same sort of sham honor which characterized their disreputable lives. His father was descended from a Genoese Jewish family of usurers and money-changers. After abjuring Christianity while in Algerian captivity, he stole his Mohammedan wife's fortune and returned to Seville, where he flaunted a false piety, gambled, simulated several bankruptcies, and accumulated sufficient wealth to buy a villa in nearby San Juan de Alfarache. Although Guzmán's mother believes that she might be an illegitimate offspring of the noble and wealthy Guzmán de Medina Sidonia family, she owes what wealth she does possess to prostitution. Guzmán himself is supposedly conceived when his mother deceives an elderly lover and meets the converso in an edenic garden at his villa. Sometime after their reenactment of the Original Sin and the death of the older lover, the converso and the prostitute marry. While she pursues her profession, he seems content to wallow in conspicuous luxury; however, rumors begin to circulate, and Guzmán feels himself the victim of daily public insults.

Confronted with a heritage that fills him with undeserved guilt and shame, he determines to run away, but after reaching this decision, his first action betrays the moral blindness which renders him susceptible to corruption in a perverse society. He rejects the name of his putative father and invents a more respectable-sounding one: Guzmán de Alfarache. However, by naming himself after the most noble candidate for his mother's paternity and the villa where he was conceived, he is actually reaffirming the corrupt values and false honor of his parents. During these opening episodes, the narrating Guzmán seems to be revealing shameful details about himself, but he is really placing the blame for his own corruption upon circumstances beyond his control. How could he be held responsible for his converso blood, his parents' cupidity, or their degenerate behavior? He even emphasizes that, being so disgusted with them, he was the one who attempted to deny his relationship with them and terminate it, although in doing so, he unwittingly imitates them and the worldly society to which they belong. He has no conception of the honor which presumably accompanies a respectable-sounding name, but he adopts such a name to gain the favorable opinion of others, and this desire to be respected for qualities which he does not possess impels him to take the first step toward an immoral career. Within the context of his childhood experiences, however, the step appears to result from the perfectly justifiable decision of an inexperienced young boy who desires to escape from a dishonorable situation and succeed in the only manner in which he has ever seen anyone succeed.

However, when Guzmán departs from his native Seville and finds himself alone on the path to Madrid, he soon discovers that society is essentially hostile; it will cheat and beat and starve him unless he finds some way of defending himself. At the first inn, a filthy, bleary-eyed hag serves him unhatched chicks and calls them an omelet; at the second inn, a respectable-seeming proprietor complains bitterly about the old woman, but he serves mule meat as suckling pig and steals the young boy's cape. After leaving the second inn under the threat of imprisonment for his altercation with the dishonest proprietor, Guzmán is unjustly beaten by two "cuadrilleros" (patrolmen of the Inquisition) and charged an exorbitant price by a mule-driver who had appeared quite charitable when he originally invited the tired young boy to mount upon one of his mules. Leaving Seville, Guzmán still has money, fine clothes, and a high opinion of himself. Along the way, he is reduced to the level of a poor, hungry wretch who has even lost his cape, a traditional symbol of honor. Reflecting upon this situation, Guzmán begins to perceive that he has acted like a "bozal" (greenhorn), but although he would like to ask for advice, there is no one to help him. Because his pride will not allow him to return home, he accepts the offer of a menial job at the third inn, where he waters the wine and fodder, thus actively participating in the same type of deception which had been practiced upon him. During these early stages of his journey, Guzmán is effectively initiated into the usages of a corrupt society. If he hopes to avoid being preyed upon by others, he must beware of deceptive appearances, whether they are ugly (the first innkeeper) or pleasant (the second innkeeper, the mule-driver). In any case, he cannot expect justice from social institutions (the "cuadrilleros"). He himself finally chooses to accept a position which involves dishonest behavior, but he is virtually constrained to do so in order to survive in a society which rewards dissimulation and egoism but punishes naive honesty and virtue.

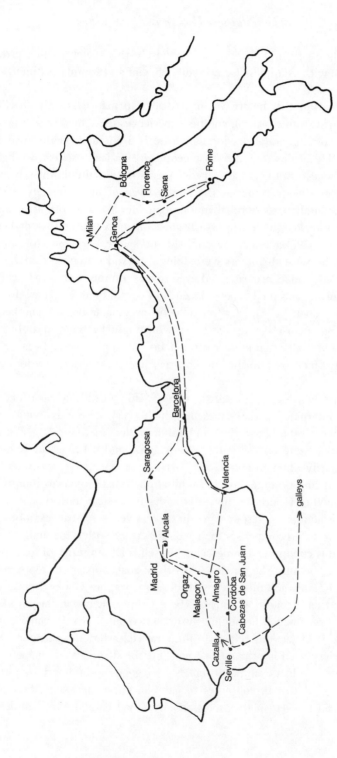

Fig. 8. Guzmán's journey (map by Allen Bjornson)

As in the story of Lazarillo, it is precisely this society which provides Guzmán with examples of successful behavior and stimulates him to adopt them.

By the time that he arrives in Madrid, Guzmán is already "hecho pícaro" (made into a pícaro), and his experiences there merely reinforce the patterns of immoral behavior which he had adopted on the road from Seville. He begins to realize that people are basically selfish, irreligious, and dishonest, but because everyone seems to be acting in the same way, he accepts their conduct as the normal way of life in society. "Todos jugaban y uraban, todos robaban y sisaban: hice lo que los otros. . . . Y no lo tenía por malo, que aun a esto llegaba mi inocencia; antes por lícito y permitido" (297). ("Everyone gambled and swore, everyone stole and pilfered: I did what the others were doing. . . . And I didn't consider it evil, because my innocence extended even to this; on the contrary, I held it to be lawful and accepted.") As in Lazarillo's world, there is no basis for trust in such a society. All men seem to be preying upon one another and protecting themselves against those who might be lying in ambush for them. They all attempt to maintain honest appearances, because they know that men are punished not for their dishonest actions but for getting caught.

If Guzmán develops a selfish, materialistic attitude toward life, he is merely internalizing the values by which everyone else is living. As an "esportillero" (basket-carrier) and scullery boy in Madrid, a dandy in Toledo, a rogue on the path to Barcelona, and a beggar in Rome, he momentarily obtains money and social acceptance, but he always loses them and suffers some form of humiliation. What he fails to comprehend is that neither wealth nor honor provides more than illusory and ephemeral satisfaction. In response to the pervasiveness of bad examples in a society which recompenses men who get away with lying and cheating, Guzmán is conditioned to perceive himself solely in terms of his physical existence, because the pursuit of worldly goals appears to represent the only commonly accepted means of self-actualization. Under these circumstances, there is nothing unusual about his persistence in the sinful, dishonest career which he adopts by necessity on the road from Seville to Madrid. If his actions reflect an immoral character, the narrator implies that society itself is primarily responsible for shaping that character.

Even when bad example is replaced by good, and poverty by physical well-being, Guzmán continues to gamble, cheat, and steal, because he cannot rid himself of the "malas mañas" (bad habits) which he learned from others. In Rome, he feigns various maladies to elicit charity from passersby, but when a sympathetic cardinal takes pity on him, pays for his "cure," and employs him as a page, Guzmán deceives his benefactor and gambles away the new clothes which had been given to him. He cannot abandon his former ways because constant repetition has etched them indelibly into his character. When his next master, a degenerate French ambassador, applauds Guzmán's clever ruses and rewards him for procuring attractive women, the young pícaro's impulses toward evil are again reinforced, and he becomes even more incapable of judging himself and realizing the futility of pursuing earthly vanities.

After a series of humiliating experiences, however, Guzmán decides to lead a new life—to leave his former self behind and rise like a Phoenix from the ashes—but an unjust society prevents him from carrying out his resolve. He departs from Rome to visit a friend in Siena, but his trunks are stolen and his friend becomes hostile. Although Sayavedra, a former acquaintance and a minor accomplice in the crime, is apprehended for the theft and exiled from Siena, Guzmán remains without his possessions, and when he publicly accuses Alejandro Bentivoglio, who had engineered the theft of the trunks and actually wore the stolen clothes in the streets of Bologna, he himself is imprisoned for defamation of character. Through no fault of his own, he has been humiliated, his wealth has been lost, and his friends have proven false. As a result, he consciously chooses to become a confidence man and thief.

In the company of a repentant Sayavedra, whom he meets on the road to Florence, Guzmán perpetrates a series of successively more profitable ruses. During these episodes, the implicit lesson promulgated by a corrupt society becomes evident: people who desire wealth and respect are justified in deceiving others as long as they maintain appearances of honesty. Furthermore, if human life is no more than sin, suffering, and death, why should anyone do otherwise than "look out for himself"? Although Guzmán manages to transport his newly acquired fortune to Madrid, it is clear that his success is of questionable value. First, the goal of his actions is the accumulation of material wealth, which is subject at every moment to deterioration and loss. During the return voyage to Barcelona, a violent storm carries away the ship's tiller and Sayavedra becomes so disoriented that he jumps overboard in a fit of madness.[14] If the ship had foundered, Guzmán would have lost his possessions and quite possibly his life. Second, no one who commits a crime can escape an awareness of what he has done. Guzmán himself later admits, "Mis obras mismas me persiguieron"

(778) ("My own works persecuted me"). Even a converso can achieve material success, Guzmán seems to be saying, but that success is as worthless to him as it would be to anyone else. Not only is it contingent upon the possession of fleeting, insubstantial things; it also fosters a state of consciousness in which peace and harmony are impossible.

But before Guzmán realizes this truth, he descends even further toward total depravity. In Madrid he marries the daughter of a wealthy merchant and, like his father, employs stolen money as capital for questionable business ventures, fakes bankruptcies, and buys a villa. By unconsciously emulating his disreputable father, Guzmán becomes a success according to the most commonly accepted worldly standards. In real terms, however, his success is transitory and unsatisfying. His wife is querulous, and her extravagant expenditures leave him deeply in debt when she dies. Motivated primarily by the knowledge that ecclesiastics are well fed and exempt from prosecution, he decides to study for the priesthood, but even at the university he is subject to social injustice: the valedictory honors which Guzmán earns are awarded to the son of a wealthy nobleman. Similarly, when he abandons his studies to marry a beautiful young innkeeper's daughter, society deprives him of the anticipated comfort of a prosperous inn by condoning the seizure of all their possessions to redeem a defaulted loan for which the innkeeper had countersigned shortly before his death.

Like his father before him, Guzmán encourages his second wife's prostitution. Submitting himself to a world of false appearances and ethical egoism, he wants only to amass wealth. "Dinero y más dinero era lo que yo entonces buscaba" (837). ("Money and more money was what I was looking for at that time.") But wealth is transitory, and this fact is once again illustrated when his wife sequesters their possessions and absconds with a Neapolitan galley captain. By this point, Guzmán is so inured to his own immorality that he reverts to cape-snatching and petty thievery before devising a clever ruse to become overseer on a wealthy estate. Feigning charity, piety, and moral righteousness, he secretly takes a mulatto mistress and gorges himself on sweets. He tells the mulatto that he loves her, although he actually intends to embezzle money from the estate, flee to America, and leave her in Spain. His moral deterioration is now complete. His entire life is no more than a lie, and when his employer's relatives discover discrepancies in the overseer's reports, Guzmán's respectable façade crumbles, and he is sentenced to six years in the galleys. Supposedly he is being punished for his dishonesty, but the pervasiveness of

successful dishonesty suggests that he is really suffering for his careless-
ness in getting caught. On a deeper level, his punishment might be appropriate to the moral blindness which underlies all his sins and crimes, but in
terms of social justice, Guzmán's actions merely reflect the assimilation of
perverse but commonly accepted values and modes of behavior.

In the galleys, he claims to have undergone a religious conversion which
awakens him to the falsity of these values, but his spiritual regeneration is
apparently rather short-lived, because in discussing a possible continuation of his book, the narrator promises to relate how he "gasté" (wasted)
the rest of his life. A momentary insight followed by a relapse into immoral behavior would not be inconsistent with his history. After leaving
the French ambassador, Guzmán had resolved to amend his behavior, and
even as a child the spirit within him had frequently sharpened his vision
until he realized that he was leading a life of self-deception, but despite
these flashes of insight, he can never avoid the subsequent necessity of
conforming to the corrupt society in which he is obliged to live.

Similarly, after the alleged conversion, his first act involves the denunciation of a mutiny planned by the other galley slaves. The betrayal of his
fellow sufferers may prevent them from usurping a power which they
would undoubtedly abuse, but Guzmán's decision hardly reflects the dis-
interestedness and charity of a genuine convert. He displays no compassion when seven of the mutineers are brutally executed and others muti-
lated for life. Furthermore, informing upon the plotters actually represents his support for the corrupt social order which licenses the galley to
pursue its highly un-Christian course as a privateer preying upon unsuspecting victims. In fact, this is the very society which had allowed him to
be unjustly beaten for a missing hatband—the society which had bombas-
tically threatened him that he would have to give up the hatband or his
life. The object itself is a trifle, but the importance attached to it illustrates
how thoroughly the system is dominated by selfish materialism and an
exaggerated respect for honor. As an informer, Guzmán not only helps to
preserve this corrupt and unjust system; he is also preserving himself,
because the captain apologizes for the unjust beating, grants him freedom
of movement on the ship, and promises to request a pardon for him. In
many ways, the galley is merely an extension of the society which had
conditioned Guzmán to adopt immoral attitudes. Even within such a
limited sphere, success depends upon one's ability to disguise self-interest
behind a socially acceptable façade, and Guzmán's newfound faith is an
integral part of his façade. Although this faith would seem to imply a

disdain for worldly concerns, it actually helps him to acquire material advantages.

Nevertheless, the final irony of the book is that Guzmán's ultimate imperfection does not impair the validity of his argument in favor of converso legitimacy. The corrupting factor is not his tainted blood but his attachment to earthly vanities. Condoned by society and firmly rooted in his own character, this attitude produces anxiety and a deep-seated self-hatred. Guzmán himself suggests as much when he admits, "las obras buenas del bueno son el premio de su virtud, así los males que obra un malo vienen a serlo de su mayor tormento" (779) ("The good works of a good man are the reward of his virtue; similarly, the evil things done by an evil man come to be his worst torment"). In itself, virtuous action is not a reward, and vicious action is not a torment; rather, man's awareness of having done good or evil results in a state of mind which corresponds to the nature of his actions. If he dedicates himself to the pursuit of wealth or pleasure, he is defining himself entirely in terms of his physical existence and cutting himself off from the peace and inner harmony of life in the spirit.

Like all other men, Guzmán remains subject to evil inclinations during his life in the temporal world. Although he travels through much of Spain and Italy, his picaresque life is less a geographical than a moral journey. As he acquires the material and moral perquisites of a worldly self-image, he becomes blind to the impermanence of worldly things and nourishes his pride in the belief that he has found security and honor, but he always falls back into poverty and humiliation. During his travels an inverse correlation between physical well-being and self-awareness gradually emerges, but as long as he lives, it is not his impure blood but his attachment to earthly vanities that subjects him to loss, humiliation, and a tendency to forget flashes of insight which momentarily illuminate his condition.

As in *Lazarillo*, the perversion of human values is suggested by the ironic reversal of terms which actually mean the opposite of what they are commonly assumed to mean. For example, when Guzmán's mother appropriates the money of her recently deceased, elderly lover, she places her hand where his "corazón" (heart) had been, and when Guzmán steals 2,500 "reals" from a Madrid spice merchant, the money becomes for him "la sangre de mi corazón" ("the blood of my heart"). The association of material wealth with traditional symbols for spiritual life (heart, soul) and honor (blood) draws attention to the corrupt state of mind which characterizes Guzmán, his mother, and the society which has conditioned them to act as they do. Even when reduced to a galley slave, Guzmán continues to accumulate small sums of money and hoard them in a "landre" (small pocket) near his heart. Ironically, a "landre" is not only a pocket but also a small tumor—a malignant growth which threatens to destroy the very core of his being.

This corrupt state of mind is also suggested by the use of religious imagery. For example, Guzmán's relationship with his second wife is a surrogate religion of secular rather than spiritual values. Her name is "Gracia" (Grace), and Guzmán first encounters her when he is invited to share a picnic with her and her family; the meeting itself takes place on a Sunday afternoon near the church Santa Maria del Val. Although he will be ordained if he completes only three more weeks of divinity school, he abandons his studies, marries Gracia, and happily anticipates fine meals in her mother's inn. Originally Guzmán had begun his theological studies not because he felt a genuine spiritual calling but because he knew that priests always had enough to eat. Having never truly desired the spiritual "food" of communion, he readily accepts the physical food which Gracia offers. By receiving Gracia as his wife, he is accepting a false or worldly "grace" subject to loss and decay. Rather than exaltation or wisdom, this sort of "grace" fosters degradation and moral blindness. As in *Lazarillo*, the confusion of material wealth and spiritual value in Guzmán's mentality (and by extension in his world) is appropriately suggested by the ironic reversal of terms and practices commonly linked with authentic religious devotion.[15]

Like everyone else, Guzmán is a sinner with a corrupt state of mind, but he is also like everyone else in that his humanity grants him access to salvation. The important point is not whether Guzmán becomes a sincere penitent at the end of the novel; it is the fact that he, a vulgar pícaro and converso, has experienced a spiritual journey which could lead to salvation. It is obvious to Guzmán that all men live through an eternally recurrent pattern of sin, suffering, and death, but he also insists that they exhibit "señales de su salvación" (signs of their salvation), and he quotes this phrase while relating the story of his father. He implies thereby that even such a disreputable, hypocritical converso has the potential to attain salvation, and if this is true of Guzmán's father, it is certainly applicable to Guzmán himself.

Superimposed upon Guzmán's fluctuating fortunes and mental states during his picaresque journey is a circular movement which reinforces the idea that he can be saved despite his humble origins and tainted blood. When he leaves home, Guzmán gradually loses his religious inclinations. The first time he enters Madrid, Barcelona, Genoa, and Rome, he is poor and dressed in rags; when he returns to Genoa, Barcelona, Madrid, and Seville, he appears respectable and materially comfortable; however, in each instance, he is more corrupt than he had been during his first visit. As long as he persists in pursuing a worldly self-image, he is denying his identity as a man who, though susceptible to the temptations of physical existence, is endowed with spiritual being. According to orthodox theology, however, he could overcome his blindness by returning to the faith he knew as a child, and this is precisely what happens in the galleys. After being unjustly punished for a crime that he did not commit, Guzmán feels himself "inocente y con carga ligítima cargado" (899) ("innocent and burdened with a legitimate burden"). Relegated to the dirtiest and most irksome position in the galleys, he actually does reach a type of perfection in his humble acceptance of unjust suffering and his conscious imitation of Christ. Guzmán undoubtedly fails to sustain the intensity of faith which he attains during his "crucifixion" and "conversion," for he is still subject to the reward-punishment system of a corrupt society, but the fact remains that a converso is clearly portrayed as having unqualified access to salvation.

In both practical and theoretical terms, Alemán created an extremely effective apologia for conversos. If honor, wealth, and purity of blood are earthly vanities, one who lacks them is not inherently inferior to his more prosperous and respectable neighbors. If all men are fundamentally similar, no one is condemned at birth to eternal damnation, and a converso is not automatically less human or less Christian than those who pride themselves on their Old Christian blood. There is an underlying artistic unity in the fine sense of irony with which Alemán demonstrates that the most despised pícaro is morally superior to the society which engendered him, and this suggests a crucial affinity between *Guzmán* and *Lazarillo*. Despite the fact that Alemán employs literary conventions associated with miscellanies and spiritual guides, *Guzmán* is a unified work, largely because an autobiographical format integrates the book's diverse materials into a plausible narrative framework, within which the picaresque myth and a panorama of contemporary vices and follies come to illustrate a coherent moral vision. In *Lazarillo* and *Guzmán*, fictive narrators develop rhetorical arguments to justify their own behavior, and both imply that a corrupt society dehumanizes the lower-class, wandering character by requiring him to adopt its selfish, materialistic values. In each case, the actual practices of society are revealed to be in direct contradiction with its own most frequently proclaimed principles of honor, justice, and religion. Like the anonymous author of *Lazarillo*, Alemán displays a profound sympathy for the tragedy and pathos of those whose lives have been distorted by the society which hypocritically disdains them.

IN THE WAKE OF
Guzmán:
VARIATIONS ON THE
PICARESQUE-LIFE THEME

While Part I of *Guzmán* was enjoying its unprecedented vogue, people had already begun to associate it with *Lazarillo*, although the loosely defined conception of picaresque fiction which emerged from this conjunction tended to obscure the moral seriousness as well as the overtones of social criticism in both novels. Upper-class readers might have been amused by a pícaro's cleverness, gaiety, and apparent freedom from responsibility, but because their own social and moral superiority was based upon the superficial, hypocritical assumptions attacked so effectively by Alemán and his anonymous predecessor, these readers had a vested interest in overlooking the tragic dilemma of a lower-class, wandering character whose personality is warped by its contact with a society which fails to abide by its own most frequently proclaimed ideals. As a consequence, they generally viewed *Lazarillo* and *Guzmán* as entertaining stories of happy-go-lucky rogues who served many masters and often succeeded in outwitting them. The favorable reception of *Guzmán* undoubtedly helped arouse a widespread contemporary fascination with pícaros and picaresque subject matter. This fascination in turn augmented the novel's success, although it did not necessarily foster a full appreciation of Alemán's world view.

It was not until shortly before 1600 that the words "pícaro" and "picaresco" achieved currency in Spain.[1] Alemán himself used the terms rather sparingly and attempted to discourage superficial readings of *Guzmán* by insisting that it be identified as an "atalaya de la vida humana" rather than simply "El Pícaro." In the imitations and apocryphal sequels of *Guzmán*, however, the word "pícaro" generally figures prominently in the titles as well as in the texts. Not only was Juan Martí's *Segunda parte de la vida del pícaro Guzmán de Alfarache* (1602) more popular than the authentic Part II;[2] it and Lopez de Úbeda's *La pícara Justina* (1605) represent precisely the sort of trivialization against which Alemán had reacted so

vehemently. By portraying the pícaro as an amusing but inherently immoral rogue without cares or duties, these novels reconcile the literary
representation of vulgar characters with a reaffirmation of commonly accepted social and moral values. In fact, the attitude toward picaresque-life
themes reflected in Martí's continuation and Úbeda's *Justina* undoubtedly
influenced the way in which both *Lazarillo* and *Guzmán* were interpreted
by early seventeenth-century readers.

Within the context of a taste for picaresque subject matter among
readers from the privileged classes, the linking of *Lazarillo* and *Guzmán*
may have fostered a superficial reading of Alemán's novel, but it also
promoted a resurgence of interest in *Lazarillo*. By 1595 only seven Spanish
editions of *Lazarillo* had appeared, but within the following eight years,
the anonymous little book was reissued ten times.[3] Nine weeks after the
first publication of *Guzmán*, the Madrid publisher Luis Sánchez brought
out an edition of *Lazarillo*, and editors in Barcelona and Saragossa simultaneously published both *Guzmán* and pirated editions of the anonymous
novel.[4] Among the first writers to associate the protagonists of the two
novels was Agustín de Rojas. In *El viaje entretenido* (1603), he asks what
Guzmán de Alfarache or Lazarillo de Tormes had served as many masters
or played as many tricks as he had, indicating that the link was based upon
the idea that both of them were clever tricksters and servants to many
masters.[5] Úbeda's *Justina*, published two years later, repeatedly echoes
Lazarillo and *Guzmán* and even includes an elaborate frontispiece in which
the book's comic heroine appears next to Guzmán and in close proximity
to Lazarillo. In the same year, Cervantes portrayed a minor character in
Don Quixote, Ginés de Pasamonte, who resembles Guzmán in that he
claims to have composed his autobiography in the galleys, but in boasting
about his memoirs the unrepentant rogue compares them with *Lazarillo*
and asserts that they are so good that their publication will bode ill for all
such works that have been or will be written.[6] In ensuing years, the
association of the two novels became a critical commonplace, and when
Gaspard Ens published a Latin translation of *Guzmán* in 1623, he actually
replaced the "Ozmín and Daraja" story with his own version of *Lazarillo*.
In every instance, however, the coupling of the two novels was based
upon their being considered entertaining stories of clever, carefree rogues.

Although Alemán was primarily concerned with describing what he
considered to be a true picture of human destiny and demonstrating how
people were conditioned to turn their backs upon this picture, *Guzmán*
does contain allusions to the picaresque life as an "almíbar" (sweet syrup)

Fig. 9. Frontispiece to *La pícara Justina* (1605)

to be savored, a "bocado sin hueso" (mouthful without a bone), a "lomo descargado" (unburdened back) and an "ocupación holgada y libre de todo genero de pesadumbre" (leisurely occupation free from all sorts of worry).[7] This vision of the picaresque life exercised an undeniable appeal in the increasingly secular atmosphere at Philip III's court, where women even adopted the custom of disguising themselves in ragged clothes and claiming to be dressed "a lo picaresco" (in picaresque fashion); the assumption that pícaros led free and happy lives reappears in Rojas' *El viaje entretenido*, Covarrubias' dictionary definition of the word, and numerous poems and plays of the period,[8] but it is perhaps *La pícara Justina* which provides the most detailed elaboration of the idea.

Grouping *Justina* with *Lazarillo, Guzmán, The Golden Ass,* and *Celestina,* Úbeda implies that these books comprise a literary tradition of works dealing with the picaresque life, which is defined pictorially in the frontispiece to the first edition of his novel (Fig. 9). Around the border of this curious engraving are squares containing images of musical instruments, food, drink, and gambling equipment; a letter appears in each square and forms a part of the emblem "El aguar de la vida picaresca" (the small chest or baggage of the picaresque life). The central image is dominated by "la nave de la vida picaresca" (the ship of picaresque life) steered by Time and occupied by Celestina, Justina, and Guzmán. The portrait of a sleeping woman and the word "ociosidad" (idleness, laziness) are inscribed on the side of the ship, and Cupid and Ceres are depicted on the sails. Bacchus, holding wine and grapes, appears at the top of the mast. Rowing with an oar labelled "siguales" ("follow them"), Lazarillo sits next to the bull of Salamanca and a post inscribed "oliste" (smell) in a small skiff attached to the ship by a mooring line. Although the border images and the mythological figures suggest a life of play and self-indulgence, there are also stark reminders that these pleasures are earthly vanities. A banner flying from the foremast proclaims "el gusto me lleba" ("pleasure carries or conveys me"), but an inscription upon Time's tiller reads "llebolos sin sentir" ("carry them without noticing"), and the ship is bearing them down the River of Forgetfulness toward a harbor guarded by a skeleton, who holds up a mirrorlike object containing crossed bones and the word "desengaño" (the elimination of illusion). The ostensible moral is obvious: while people like Justina, Guzmán, Lazarillo, and Celestina are leading picaresque lives and gratifying their worldly desires, they remain unaware that time is carrying them closer and closer to the harbor of death, where all pleasures and illusions will be revealed as meaningless.

By placing Justina, Celestina, Guzmán, and Lazarillo in a single picture and associating them with a carefree life of sensual pleasure, Úbeda was reaffirming an ideological assumption which must have been particularly congenial to socially elite readers. Such people might enjoy reading about vulgar characters and even imitating them in superficial ways, but no matter how strongly they felt attracted to a gay and carefree life of drinking and dancing, eating, playing music, devising clever ruses, and making witty speeches, they would of course never abandon the perquisites of their respectable positions to experience the actual hardships of lower-class existence, and Úbeda's implicit pejorative judgment of picaresque insouciance served to reassure them that their own "serious" concerns were more valid than the "trivial" pursuits of pícaros. As a poor but ingenious and happy-go-lucky rogue who wastes his life upon sensual pleasures, the pícaro appealed to readers who felt morally and socially superior to him, because he offered them entertainment without either engaging their sympathy for his sufferings or questioning society's responsibility for his corrupt behavior.

There was a great wave of interest in picaresque subjects between 1599 and 1606, and this interest did help to sustain the popularity of *Lazarillo* and *Guzmán*, but with the exception of Spanish works written by exiles living in France, the majority of novels conceived directly or indirectly in response to the success of *Guzmán* and *Lazarillo* were specifically written for readers from the privileged classes. Although these early seventeenth-century works repeatedly echo *Lazarillo* and *Guzmán*, they omit crucial elements of the earlier novels and completely transform the meaning and significance of the literary pícaro. In broad general terms, the immediate successors in the picaresque tradition can be divided into four categories: novels like Juan Martí's apocryphal continuation of *Guzmán*, Vicente Espinel's *Marcos de Obregón* (1618), and Jerónimo de Alcalá Yáñez y Ribera's *El donado hablador Alonso: Mozo de muchos amos* (1624, 1626), which retain the morally serious tone, encyclopedic tendency, and autobiographical perspective of *Guzmán*; novels like *Justina* and Quevedo's *El Buscón*, which parody *Guzmán* and reduce the pícaro to a one-dimensional, comic caricature; the picaresque adventure stories of Salas Barbadillo and Castillo Solórzano; and socially critical novels written by exiles like Juan de Luna and Dr. Carlos García. Works in the first two categories are obviously related to the popularity of *Guzmán*, and it is in them that one discovers the clearest indications of an emerging conception of picaresque fiction based upon the *Lazarillo-Guzmán* model. In García's *La desordenada codicia de los bienes ajenos* (1619) and Luna's *Segunda parte de Lazarillo de Tormes* (1620), Alemán's thesis about human quality and his veiled criticism of an arbitrary and dehumanizing social system are openly adopted by writers who fled Spain to escape Inquisitorial persecution, whereas the novels of Salas and Castillo exemplify a tendency to regard the pícaro as a colorful adventurer whose experiences provide vicarious excitement for leisure-class readers.

"Alonso", "Marcos", and the Apocryphal "Guzmán"

On the surface *Marcos, Alonso,* and Martí's *Guzmán* bear some resemblance to Alemán's novel; they are all simulated autobiographies of lower-class, wandering characters whose experiences furnish pretexts for expository sermons and panoramic views of society. Obviously desirous of creating the impression that his continuation was genuine, Martí imitated the format of the original *Guzmán*, included numerous disgressions (often borrowed verbatim from previous writers),[9] and alluded to events, characters, and analogous situations in the authentic Part I; he even chose a pen name (Mateo Luján) and a place of birth (Seville) which might cause unsuspecting readers to confuse him with Alemán. An ecclesiastic, poet, and musician who frequented Madrid literary circles and undoubtedly knew Alemán personally, Espinel recorded his opinion of *Guzmán* in a sixteen-line Latin epigram which appeared among the eulogies to Part I of the novel, and when he composed his own semiautobiographical *Marcos*, he created a work that corresponded rather well with his interpretation of the earlier book. Like Guzmán in the epigram, Marcos suffers from heat and cold and bears "all things that are harsh." He "touches upon" music, banquets, and putrescence, while proposing to teach moral "laws" and "serious things . . . mixed with sweet trifles"; he observes the variety and contradictions of human life, while preaching a higher morality of the spirit and offering sweet balm for the sad and the wretched—"Tristibus, et miseris dulce leuamen ades."[10] Strongly influenced by *Marcos*, Alcalá Yáñez undoubtedly considered himself to be writing in the same tradition.

Despite *Guzmán*'s obvious impact upon these writers, however, none of them was completely successful in following the path indicated by Alemán. Martí failed to sustain the highly ironic pseudoautobiographical perspective, and many of the digressions in his *Guzmán* are merely historical or descriptive excurses with no discernible relationship to the protagonist's experience. In *Marcos* the narrator is handled inconsistently, and *Alonso* degenerates into a patchwork collection of stereotyped images and situations drawn from earlier picaresque novels.[11] Such flaws suggest that these novels are artistically and intellectually inferior works written to take advantage of the enormous popularity of "El Pícaro," but in any consideration of the picaresque novel they remain historically important, because they illustrate how the narrative techniques and overt didacticism of *Guzmán* could be employed for purposes diametrically opposed to those of the converso author Alemán.

Espinel, Alcalá Yáñez, and Martí accepted the norms and values of a society which Alemán regarded as irrevocably corrupt. For that reason, their works tended to support the existing order. Because Espinel occupied a subordinate social position and depended upon noble patronage, his espousal of an essentially aristocratic world view seems perfectly natural, and as the only truly middle-class writers of Spanish picaresque fiction, the Valencian lawyer Martí and the pious Segovian doctor Alcalá Yáñez behaved in a characteristically bourgeois fashion by assimilating the attitudes of a superior social class.[12] In *Marcos, Alonso*, and the apocryphal *Guzmán*, a lower-class protagonist experiences difficulty when he attempts to improve his station in life. This difficulty reflects the implicit acceptance of a world view which presupposes a stable, harmonious order and precludes change, including social advancement. Within the framework of these assumptions, each of the three authors rejects Alemán's portrayal of character as process, reverting to the traditional idea that character is a function of one's nature. In attempting to reconcile the demands of this world view with the aspirations of their respective picaresque heroes, they all effectively reinforce the idea that people who are born into subordinate positions in the social hierarchy must learn to be submissive.

The traditionalist ideology adopted by Martí, Espinel, and Alcalá Yáñez was posited upon the assumption that individuals can fulfill their moral obligations, achieve happiness, and contribute to social harmony by resigning themselves to the limitations and realizing the potential of their God-given stations. The principle behind this assumption is aptly illustrated by one of Alonso's allegorical anecdotes in which Venus transforms a favorite cat into a lady-in-waiting. Forgetting her new form, the lady runs after a mouse, grasps it between her teeth, and deposits it triumphantly upon her mistress's lap. The goddess immediately perceives that she has made a mistake and changes the lady back into a cat. The lesson behind Alonso's story involves the belief that every creature has its own natural qualities and corresponding types of behavior; just as it is appropriate for a cat and inappropriate for a lady-in-waiting to hunt mice, each person has a well-defined nature and incurs a moral obligation to act in conformity with it. To do otherwise would be foolish or dangerous. It is for this reason that Marcos, who at one point acquires a reputation as a great magician, refuses a dwarf's request for a charm to make him grow; he justifies his decision on the basis that "las obras de naturaleza son tan consumadas, que no sufren emienda; nada hace en vano, todo va fundado en razón; ni hay superfluo en ella, ni falta en lo necessario; es naturaleza como un juez, que después que ha dado la sentencia no puede alteralla . . ." ("the works of nature are so perfect that they cannot be improved; nothing is done in vain, everything is based upon reason; there is never anything superfluous nor the lack of anything necessary; nature is like a judge, who once he has passed sentence cannot alter it").[13]

According to this world view, inequality of condition is good, and the existing distribution of wealth and privilege is justified because the prevailing order reflects the will of God. In contrast to Alemán, the authors of *Marcos, Alonso,* and the apocryphal *Guzmán* assumed that the actual organization and laws of society are just; for example, Martí accorded lengthy encomiums to the valorous soldiers and glorious history of Mother Spain. Whereas Alemán portrayed lawyers as corrupt and avaricious, Martí praised them as honorable men who separate truth from falsehood, defend justice, judiciously interpret the statutes, protect the poor, and liberate the oppressed. Himself a lawyer, he conceived of truth not in terms of Alemán's religious insight, but as that which emerges from a supposedly disinterested winnowing of all available information. Like Espinel and Alcalá Yáñez, he reduced reason to commonsense reasonableness. In *Marcos*, the appropriateness of this attitude is illustrated during a brief episode in a cemetery. Upon hearing strange noises emanating from a sepulchre, Marcos is nearly overcome by fear, but he investigates the disturbance and soon discovers that the noises are being made by a stray dog. No matter how mysterious an event may appear to be, it can always be explained in a commonsense fashion.

For those on the middle or lower rungs of the social hierarchy, this reasonableness dictates a morality of prudent circumspection, patient resignation, and dutiful perseverance. According to Marcos, it is not difficult to perceive distinctions of power, wealth, and position, and it is only sensible to respect them. "Esta humildad y cortesía es forzosa para conservar la quietud y asegurar la vida. . . . La humildad con los poderosos es el

fundamento de la paz, la soberbia, la destruición de nuestro sosiego."
("This modesty and civility is necessary to preserve one's calm and assure
one's self of life. . . . Humility in the presence of powerful men is the basis
of peace; arrogance, the destruction of our tranquility.")[14] Within this
context, patience becomes the divine virtue—the only virtue necessary in
all stations and situations of human life—because it allows even the most
humble people to bear unavoidable hardships and bring their good intentions to fruition. "Al fin con ella se alcanzan todas las cosas de que los
hombres son capaces."[15] The reward for submissiveness and patience is a
"quietud del animo" (tranquility of mind), which is praised and desired in
all three novels.

Allied with an intelligent perseverance, this attitude can even yield a
quite tangible "milagroso fruto" (miraculous fruit), as Espinel implies by
recounting a simple parable in his prologue: two students traveling toward
Salamanca pause at a well, where they decipher a barely legible inscription, "Conditur unio, conditur unio," on a small stone; one of them dismisses the words as a drunkard's incoherent scribblings, but reflecting
that "conditur unio" can mean "the pearl is hidden" as well as "the union is
hidden," the second student remains at the well, lifts the stone, and discovers a valuable pearl which had been buried with two unfortunate lovers
who found "union" in death. By carefully scrutinizing a perplexing situation, the student discovers its true significance and obtains a "miraculous
fruit" as his reward. In figurative terms, Espinel is advising readers to
exercise the same prudence and perspicacity in evaluating the life of his
fictional hero, but what is perhaps even more important, he is suggesting
that people will be rewarded for comprehending truths revealed by physical appearances and apprehended by the senses.

The rational process implied in this tale is quite different from the one
advocated in the original *Guzmán,* and the difference exemplifies the way
in which all three writers diverge from Alemán's socially critical perspective. Whereas Guzmán uses reason to penetrate false appearances and
preaches a withdrawal into one's self as the only path to genuine knowledge, Marcos applies reason to decipher puzzling appearances and coun-
sels an opening of the self to impressions from the external world. The
implication is that Guzmán's fictional universe is inherently chaotic and
deceptive, while the worlds of Marcos, Alonso, and Martí's Guzmán are
fundamentally just and harmonious. For Marcos, life is filled with direct
manifestations of God's will. Rather than distrusting that which his senses
register as beautiful, he seems to refine and sharpen his senses to become
more intensely aware of the perfection in the universe.

Malicious and hypocritical individuals can disrupt this equilibrium, but in *Marcos*, a natural tendency toward order or poetic justice serves as a countervailing force to reestablish the divinely ordained harmony. In Alemán's *Guzmán*, appropriate punishments occasionally overtake guilty individuals: innkeepers who take unfair advantage of the young pícaro are subsequently chastised, a woman who defrauds him of an expensive meal is arrested, Sayavedra and Guzmán's Genoese relatives pay dearly for their ill treatment of him, and his own condemnation to the galleys is fitting for a man who has become totally dishonest and immoral. However, none of these punishments is specifically related to the social rank or inherent qualities of the people involved. In contrast, Marcos possesses a "noble breast," and although he might suffer momentary setbacks for failing to exercise prudent circumspection, he is eventually rewarded when he recognizes and fulfills the duties of his station in life. In *Alonso* this force exists only on a theoretical level, for despite the fact that Alcalá Yáñez's hero virtuously follows his nature, there seems to be no place for him in a corrupt society.

In Martí's continuation, poetic justice obtains in the sense that the apocryphal Guzmán's impure blood represents an inescapable corrupting factor which prevents him from gaining insight and becoming an "atalaya de la vida humana." Viewed and condemned from a position of moral superiority, Martí's Guzmán does not perform the unifying function of Alemán's narrator. In this respect *Alonso* and *Marcos* are closer to the original *Guzmán*, for the autobiographical perspective in both novels integrates expository digressions with narrative episodes by fostering the illusion that they are expressions of a single individual's point of view; theoretical justifications for an attitude of prudent conformity are accompanied by episodes illustrating the validity of such an attitude. In *Marcos* and *Alonso*, temporary defeats or humiliations are inevitably followed by some form of vindication. Because the heroes of both novels are fulfilling the obligations of their respective positions in the established order, this narrative pattern reinforces the assumption that the order itself is fundamentally just. By attempting to project themselves as men who had always possessed virtuous natures, Marcos and Alonso are reaffirming their good opinions of themselves, but they are also exhorting readers to recognize the virtue of keeping to one's proper place in the divinely ordained social hierarchy.

For Espinel and Alcalá Yáñez, the autobiographical format thus serves both as a unifying fictional device and as an ideologically biased assertion about the nature of reality. In this regard their works are considerably more complex and interesting than Martí's continuation, although all three tacitly adopt an aristocratic value system. Marcos and Alonso themselves accept this value system, and because they both leave home to improve their situations, the difficulty in reconciling an ambitious, talented individual's aspirations with his assumptions about a stable, rigidly stratified social order emerges more clearly in their stories than it does in the apocryphal *Guzmán*.

In *Marcos* the author's attitude toward this situation is complicated by the fact that there are two different narrators (or one narrator at two different stages in his life). On the first level of narration, Marcos is a well-read, contemplative seventy-year-old recording his memoirs for the amusement of the archbishop of Toledo. To justify his own behavior, he composes a lecture on the necessity of patience and illustrates the futility of impatience by inserting an account of his service with Doctor Sagredo—a man incapable of controlling his anger. Having apparently forgotten his original pretext for relating the incident, he proceeds to relate how, after losing his position with Sagredo, he becomes stranded in a rude hermit's shelter during a violent rainstorm. Because the hermit recognizes him as a former soldier and expresses a desire to hear about his adventures, the middle-aged Marcos orally recounts his experiences in Spain, Algeria, and Italy. At this point, the elder narrator's written account of the spoken narrative should terminate, but the middle-aged narrator anachronistically continues to inform the hermit about events which actually took place after their meeting. It is only at the end of the novel that the seventy-year-old memorialist describes his parting from the hermit and returns to the didactic tone of the first chapter. Both narrators advocate the same philosophy of prudent conformity, and both project themselves as honorable men who experienced the rewards of acting properly. Within this context, Marcos' life is presented as an exemplary model of virtuous behavior; in fact, if Marcos' social station reflects divine order, his autobiography becomes a never-ending education which repeatedly teaches him the necessity of recognizing, accepting, and abiding by the sentence which a righteous Providence passed upon him by causing him to be born Marcos de Obregón.[16]

The situation in *Alonso* is somewhat different. The novel is divided into two parts, both of which involve a series of conversations with a sympathetic ecclesiastic. As a thirty-four to thirty-five-year-old lay brother at a monastery in Navarra, Alonso tells the first part of his story to a vicar. Years later, after undergoing an Algerian captivity and becoming a hermit, he encounters a local priest who recognizes him as the former lay brother and expresses curiosity about the events which brought him from the monastery to the hermitage. The story which he recounts to the vicar and to the priest is frequently interrupted by exchanges between himself and his respective interlocutors. Like Marcos, Alonso presents himself as a worldly-wise man calmly lecturing others on their moral flaws, and his proverblike exhortations to prudent behavior focus more upon the practical concerns of daily living than upon the fundamental social and theological issues broached by Guzmán. Rather than criticize the dynamics of a world which unjustly operates to his detriment, he accepts the basically aristocratic idea of inherent nature and advocates a morality of getting along under existing circumstances.

Like Marcos, Alonso is a self-confident individual who has assimilated the ideology of his social superiors, but unlike Marcos he does not usually receive tangible recognition for acting according to his nature. He nearly always applies himself with intelligence, industry, and skill to the tasks of any position which he happens to hold, and his perceptiveness is repeatedly vindicated by subsequent events; nevertheless, none of his positions proves permanent, and by withdrawing to the hermitage at the end of Part II he is virtually admitting that there is no place in society for a talented, honest, ambitious man like himself. His dilemma might even serve to illustrate the paradoxical demands placed upon the Spanish middle class, to which Alcalá Yáñez himself belonged. Having adopted fundamental tenets of an aristocratic world view, many members of this class confronted a reality in which justice and harmony were absent and opportunities for social advancement were severely limited. The impossibility of reconciling theory with practice in this situation is clearly reflected in the fate of Alonso, who can only circumvent his typically bourgeois dilemma by withdrawing completely from society.

Both Marcos and Alonso internalize a value system which relegates them to subordinate social positions and predisposes them to conceive of themselves as having static natures which persist essentially unchanged during their respective encounters with the external world. The tranquility of mind that supposedly rewards those who faithfully actualize the potential of their natures frequently eludes these two picaresque heroes, but unlike Alemán's Guzmán, they are never menaced by a loss of self-esteem or constrained to choose between integrity and survival. Even under the most difficult circumstances, they never relinquish a belief in their own righteousness, and they nearly always act in conformity with their own ideas of virtue. For this reason, they escape most of the anxieties to which Alemán's hero is subject.

The concept of character as inherent nature clearly demands a modification of the picaresque myth as defined in *Lazarillo* and *Guzmán*, and that is precisely what occurs in *Marcos*. Unlike the earliest Spanish pícaros, Marcos inherits a stable sense of honor and identity from a father to whom he is sincerely attached, but although birth and genealogy do not function as obstacles to his self-esteem, he leaves home because he fears that the poverty of his family will inhibit the development of "el natural talento que Dios y naturaleza me habían concedido" ("the natural talent which God and nature had bestowed upon me").[17] Before he leaves, his father hopes that God will guide Marcos and make him a good man. What he actually desires is that his son become respectable, and he even passes on a symbolic token of the familial honor by giving the boy a sword, although it is nearly as large as Marcos himself and merely impedes his progress along the way. Only when he matures physically and psychologically will he be capable of carrying the sword and sustaining the honor which it symbolizes.

The true nature of this honor and Marcos' means of defending it are clearly illustrated during his journey from Ronda to Salamanca. At this time he undergoes a series of initiation experiences, but rather than forming his character, they provide him with opportunities to gain confidence in himself by opposing his "noble breast" to hostile circumstances. Marcos' first two experiences follow a single pattern: after being duped, he perceives the true nature of the situation and cleverly turns the tables on those who tricked him. At an inn near Ronda, he listens complacently to the flatteries of a young rogue and proves sufficiently gullible to permit the entire company to eat at his expense; he is even made the butt of a practical joke, but he avenges himself by pawning his coat and pretending that one of the rogues had stolen it. At a second inn, a mule-driver with whom Marcos is traveling desires to seduce a beautiful woman. Pretending that someone has stolen his purse, he threatens to prosecute all the students who are staying there. Overcome by fear, Marcos runs into the woods, becomes lost, and spends the night in a hollow cork tree, where he sleeps poorly because "ants" are continually crawling across his face. At dawn, he discovers that the "ants" are actually worms feeding upon two corpses—the husband and the dead lover of a mourning emaciated woman who stands nearby. Guzmán would have exploited such an image to expatiate upon death and original sin, but Marcos merely refers to the incident as a good reason for avoiding solitude and staying in the company of other people.

When he returns to the path and accepts the mule-driver's invitation to mount upon a mule, he remains silent about the experience and rationalizes that not everyone is capable of understanding serious things. Because the mule-driver failed in his attempted seduction and received a reprimand from the local "alcalde" (justice of the peace), he is contrite and refrains from mocking Marcos for his earlier gullibility. In the eyes of others, Marcos' honor remains intact, and the mule-driver has been appropriately punished for his effrontery. During these early episodes, Marcos might have avoided embarrassing situations if he had followed his father's advice and "taken the pulse" of things before undertaking them; nevertheless, in both instances he salvages his honor and appears to triumph, although his conception of honor strongly resembles that of the squire in *Lazarillo*. Marcos himself later admits that "la honra o infamia de los hombres no consiste en lo que ellos saben de sí propios, sino en lo que el vulgo sabe y dice" ("the honor or infamy of men doesn't consist in what they know about themselves, but in what the common man knows and says").[18] Early in life, he recognizes that gullibility and foolish pride can blind a person to the actual facts of a situation, and that a good reputation is often more valuable than self-knowledge. Within this context, the honor which he inherits from his father becomes a highly malleable virtue, but just as he readily adjusts to the difficulty of carrying his father's sword, he soon accustoms himself to the necessity of maintaining the appearance of honor.

Nearly all his subsequent experiences illustrate the appropriateness of his noble self-image and the validity of his father's advice. In returning to Ronda after four years at the university, Marcos perpetrates a number of clever ruses, but in contrast to Lazarillo, whose tricks are necessary for survival, Marcos dupes others to restore a divinely ordained social equilibrium, when it has been momentarily disrupted by the unjust or dishonest actions of others. In effect, he becomes an agent of the prevailing value structure and strives to counteract forces of evil and disharmony. In the process he is faithfully accepting his place in society, and he soon learns that if he performs his role with integrity, he will be rewarded. For example, when he observes an innkeeper stealing money pouches from cardsharps who have just swindled several gullible merchants, Marcos places himself behind the innkeeper and softly suggests passing the money to him. Thinking that he is giving the pouches to his wife, the innkeeper hands them to Marcos, who returns them to the merchants. By deceiving the innkeeper, Marcos takes money from a thief and restores it to its rightful owners, and when the grateful merchants pay for his mule during the remainder of the journey, he receives a material reward that corresponds to the integrity with which he played the role of submissive subordinate. In a similar fashion he recovers a stolen mule and unmasks a fig thief. As an Algerian captive, he later devises a clever ruse to convince the king that a trusted minister has embezzled royal funds. The dishonest minister is removed from office and the stolen money recovered. Even though he is temporarily living in a society implacably hostile to his own Catholic Spain, Marcos can restore it to a just and harmonious order, and as a reward for doing so, he receives his freedom. On other occasions, he reestablishes mutual trust in a marriage menaced by the husband's jealous gullibility, recovers his own money after being duped by a Venetian prostitute, and manages to obtain fifty doubloons for having been unjustly incarcerated in a Barcelona prison; in fact, whenever he suffers an unjust imprisonment, his good reputation or his ingenuity facilitates his return to freedom and restores the outward signs of his inner nobility.

Throughout Marcos' autobiography, the dominant narrative pattern remains the same: someone disturbs a socially sanctioned relationship or treats the hero unfairly, and although his predicaments are partially caused by his own lack of circumspection, Marcos always exercises his patience and opposes his "noble breast" to adverse fortune. He may resort to ingenious disguises or picaresquelike ruses, but they are always justifiable devices which bring about a return to a previous norm (the merchants' ownership of their money, his own possession of a mule, a farmer's right to his figs, the removal of a dishonest minister from a position of power, trust in a marriage, respect for himself in the eyes of others). Behind this pattern lies the assumption that the world is fundamentally just and has a natural tendency toward order. This order may be disrupted by malicious or hypocritical individuals, but appropriate rewards and punishments are ultimately distributed according to people's noble or vulgar characters. The implication is that anyone who acts honorably and prudently will eventually receive tangible compensation for his efforts. Such action implies conformity to one's place in society, and because virtue in this sense is linked with profit, Marcos' version of reality actually constitutes a justification of the existing social order. Even the wearing of masks becomes acceptable if they are employed to cope with momentary aberrations from the social norm. In Marcos' case, role-playing actually serves to consolidate his position and reinforce his self-esteem. Operative on both psychological and social levels, the pattern of temporary defeat and ultimate victory reaffirms his belief in himself and in the natural justice of the world in which he is living.

From the narrator's perspective, the success of his ruses provides one reason for judging his life favorably; another is suggested by his beneficient influence upon people like the Sagredos and the children of his Algerian master. Despite the power which he exercises over Dr. Sagredo's wife, doña Mergelina, and the attraction which he feels for the Algerian girl Alima, Marcos sublimates his sexual desires in an attitude of paternal solicitude. From the beginning, his vision of the emaciated woman, the tree, the two dead men, and the bed filled with worms links sexuality with the corruptibility of the flesh. Only once does Marcos actively pursue a woman. The incident occurs in Bilbao and results in humiliation and physical illness. Subsequently he retains his inner calm by avoiding romantic entanglements and abstaining from the passions of love. For Alima and doña Mergelina, he becomes a wise, advice-giving father figure, not a lover. His example of calm wisdom so influences Alima that she desires to leave Algiers and become a Christian—to become like him—and he fosters this desire by giving her his rosary and encouraging her to adopt the name María. In the Sagredo episode, Marcos saves the intemperate doctor and his beautiful but vain wife from a potentially embarrassing situation by hiding doña Mergelina's young suitor when her husband returns unexpectedly. After Marcos reprimands her, she resolves to mend her ways and requests that he become a father and spiritual guide to her.

By precept and example, Marcos transforms the infidel Alima into the Christian María and the frivolous Mergelina into a faithful wife. During the final scenes of the novel he reencounters them, and the fact that they continue to practice the virtues which he taught them bears testimony to his lasting influence over them. Returning to Ronda, he stops in Malaga and discovers that Alima (now María) and her brother (who now calls himself Jesús) have been rescued from the sea by a ship's captain who agrees to grant them their "Christian liberty." When they receive baptism, a process begun eight years earlier in Algiers reaches a successful climax, justifying Marcos' sense of self-worth and permitting him to believe that his teachings had saved two infidels from the error and everlasting death of their former religion. They acknowledge their indebtedness when they address him as father and master, the identical terms used by Sagredo and doña Mergelina when they unexpectedly encounter him in a bandit's lair.

In a literal sense, Marcos remains childless, but he becomes a spiritual father for Alima-María, Mustafa-Jesús, and doña Mergelina, because he awakens them to an awareness of truth and honor. Having guided others toward moral perfection, he feels justified in viewing himself as a wise and prudent man. In actuality, he inculcates in others the same conformity which guarantees his own psychological and physical survival in a rigidly stratified social order.

Like Marcos, Alonso defines himself in terms of a God-given character and recognizes that one who seeks "tranquility of mind," as he does, must patiently and prudently subordinate his conceptions of truth and justice to those of his social superiors; at the same time he realizes that he can only achieve happiness when he acts according to his nature. Because the most prominent feature of his character is a compulsively frank talkativeness, he finds it impossible to remain silent even if it is clearly in his interest to do so. To suggest that he act differently would be to "pedir peras al olmo" ("seek pears on an elm tree").[19] As an inveterate talker, he should theoretically be able to achieve tranquility of mind by saying what he thinks, but in contrast to Espinel's fictional universe, where the virtuous are rewarded for being themselves, Alonso is trapped in a society which constantly subjects him to the hostility of hypocritical individuals and to the arbitrariness of fortune.

Characterized by the narrator's commonplace images of a storm-tossed sea, a battlefield, or a theater of masks, Alonso's world seems irreconcilable with his assumption of a divinely ordained harmony. Marcos escapes this contradiction by regarding the temporal order as a puzzling but ultimately comprehensible reflection of God's will. As an "escudero," he might suffer temporary setbacks, but his world always functions to restore him to his proper place in the social hierarchy. Having internalized the same stereotyped cultural assumptions as Marcos, Alonso lacks a well-defined place, and even when he is acting in perfect harmony with his own nature, his good intentions and virtuous behavior go unrewarded. As a consequence, he finally adopts an ascetic attitude which is in total disaccord with his characteristically bourgeois qualities of industry, frugality, and perseverance.

A rationalization for his withdrawal to the hermitage could be provided by his insight into the corruptibility of the flesh; in fact, the first two episodes in Part II seem to illustrate a heightened awareness of death and the vanity of earthly things. After being forced to leave the monastery, Alonso is captured by gypsies, who steal his clothes but eventually allow him to appropriate the ragged garments of a recently deceased old gypsy. While wearing them he proves extremely adept in carrying out the cleverest ruses and swindles. When he leaves the gypsies, he finds a wealthy nobleman's body on the road. Exchanging his gypsy costume for the dead man's respectable garments, he goes to Saragossa, where he parades as a nobleman and partakes of a good many banquets before he becomes known as a freeloader and has to abandon his act. On two successive occasions, Alonso covers his body with the clothes of dead men, and although the success of his role-playing is reflected in the gypsies' admiration of his cleverness and his ability to deceive the respectable people of Saragossa, both episodes suggest that Alonso is subject to the same fate which overtook the previous owners of the clothes he was wearing; however, if reputation and wealth are no more than external trappings and if everyone is subject to death and the arbitrariness of fortune, Alcalá Yáñez' basic idea of a divinely ordained hierarchy is placed in question, because all social distinctions would then be clearly based upon earthly vanities.

Furthermore, the morally blind, self-satisfied individuals who dominate society cannot tolerate a compulsively honest talker. It is for this reason that Alonso withdraws from secular society and becomes a lay brother at the end of Part I, but the monastery itself is a microcosmic social organization, and after fourteen years of faithful service, the monks dismiss him for meddling in their affairs. If he had known how to flatter and dissimulate, he might have remained at the monastery, where he believed himself secure and free to speak his mind, but his subsequent adventures reveal that a man of his nature can remain true to his character and achieve peace only by renouncing all attempts to reconcile his self-image with a viable social role. From the perspective of the narrator's situation in Part II, his service as a lay brother in Part I is an intermediate stage on a path toward the wisdom which he supposedly acquires when he finally becomes a hermit.

Alonso's latent alienation from society emerges long before his withdrawal to the hermitage; in fact, both parts of the novel are organized around a series of futile attempts to find security and tranquility of mind in the secular world. In his own eyes Alonso is a talented individual whose good intentions, industriousness, and honesty are nearly always repaid with animosity and ill treatment. On several occasions he mentions his own generous, pacific nature, and he repeatedly insists that he has never experienced inclinations toward evil. These virtuous impulses constitute for him a "señal evidente y clara de la buena sangre que me dejaron" ("a clear and evident sign of the good blood I inherited").[20] This "good blood" undoubtedly represents his claim to "limpieza de sangre," but it also finds expression in his physical features. Prospective employers are always impressed with his handsome figure and honest face, and they frequently engage him, even when he is unable to produce character references. Once employed, he applies himself skillfully and diligently to his work. However, as a compulsive talker who can't refrain from reproaching others with their faults, he is repeatedly obliged to leave masters whom he had served faithfully and well, although the narrator always emphasizes that they were the ones who refused to listen to "lo que fuera justo" (that which was just).[21] Because a disregard for his advice usually has unpleasant consequences for such masters, readers can conclude that Alonso's inability to remain in any position is actually a sign of his moral superiority over a society which rejects him.

From the beginning, Alonso lacks the traditional guarantees of self-esteem, for he inherits neither money nor social position from his parents. Shortly after the young boy's birth, his father dies, and his mother leaves him with an uncle who lives in a small and distant village. For fifteen years Alonso suffers countless beatings in a joyless house presided over by a miserly, hypocritical uncle, but when he leaves and attempts to find a more satisfactory life by emulating the corrupt manners of students and soldiers, he learns that such people offer him neither genuine friendship nor security. Nevertheless, he momentarily sees himself as a member of a group and uses the first-person plural pronoun "nosotros" during his brief association with them.

After the students are expelled from the university and the soldiers are routed by a band of irate farmers, Alonso never again employs the term "nosotros" to designate himself as part of a group. But even during these early episodes he doesn't actually communicate with the corrupt, self-satisfied people around him. His uncle is greedy and querulous; students and soldiers fight among themselves and steal from innkeepers and peasants. Although Alonso temporarily feels a rudimentary solidarity with them, the students subject him to a degrading initiation, and the soldiers mock his aborted attempt to enter a widow's house by climbing down her chimney. But each humiliation stimulates Alonso's inherently virtuous nature, impels him to perceive the perversity of his companions' lives, and prompts him to reproach them for their corrupt behavior. In both cases his admonitions prove justified when misfortune strikes his former companions. Alonso begins to see himself as a virtuous character in a corrupt society, but if this self-image strengthens his inclination toward self-righteous garrulousness, it also isolates him from all those who dislike being informed of their vices and follies.

Having failed to find security in family tradition or social groups, Alonso engages himself to six different masters. His duties are always performed faithfully, but he never remains in any one service for an extended period of time because he cannot avoid calling his masters' vices to their attention or instructing them in the exercise of their offices. Sometimes a master cannot bear to hear the truth about himself and dismisses the presumptuous young man; sometimes Alonso becomes so disgusted with a master's folly that he departs voluntarily.

In contrast to Alonso's experiences with students, soldiers, and secular masters, the final episodes in Part I are specifically designed to illustrate the arbitrariness of fortune. In the first instance, Alonso advises a poor but respectable Valencian widow to place her son with a wealthy "caballero," but she refuses and moves to the country, where a mulatto servant forces his way into her house, kills her beloved son, and unsuccessfully attempts to rape her. Unjustly imprisoned for abetting the crime, Alonso obtains his release only after he has been tortured and starved for a month. In the second case, Alonso travels to Mexico City, where he accumulates a large fortune by underwriting commercial ventures in the colonies, but he squanders his money on gambling and women, arrogantly refuses to give alms to the poor, and ultimately loses all his earthly possessions when they are jettisoned in an attempt to save a foundering ship. In poverty and in wealth, the implicit lesson is the same: individuals can never maintain an absolute control over their own destinies. Whether Alonso acts virtuously and gives good advice or acts foolishly and fails to take good advice, he cannot escape the inconstancy of earthly life.

Even the utmost diligence and good will cannot protect him. For a year and a half after returning to Spain, he tends wardrobe for a group of strolling players and observes how the weather and the whims of princes are often more important than the quality of actors' performances in determining the success or failure of a play. He himself demonstrates a good-natured perseverance by memorizing the company's repertoire, playing the tambourine in war scenes, and acting various bit parts. Recognizing the youth's talent and dedication, the manager offers him a major role, but before Alonso can debut, the manager is convicted of murder and the troupe is disbanded. Once again he received nothing for the virtuous exercise of his typically bourgeois qualities. No matter how assiduously he applies himself to learning any role, a chance occurrence can deprive him of the opportunity to play it.

It is after this experience that Alonso retires to the monastery in Navarra. Believing that he occupies a position where he can freely express his opinions without sacrificing his integrity, he serves with industry and devotion for fourteen years. But like his secular masters, the monks resent his well-intentioned criticism and eventually discharge him. Once again, his frankness causes him to lose a position, but on this occasion the loss is particularly painful, because Alonso had, he thought, found what he had been looking for since childhood—peace and security in a place which corresponded to his nature.

As in Part I, the narrative structure in Part II culminates in Alonso's acceptance of a situation which seems to represent a safe harbor in a chaotic world. Since he is older and more mature than he had been in Part I, the story which he relates from this "atalaya" reflects the disillusionment which he had suffered after leaving the monastery. For example, the first two episodes resemble his earlier involvement with students and soldiers; he readily adapts himself to the corrupt practices of gypsies and false noblemen, but in Part II he never defines himself as part of a group, and his experiences are clearly linked to death and the transience of earthly things. Subsequently he seeks security in marriage to a seventy-two-year-old widow, service to a wealthy Portuguese nobleman, apprenticeship to a painter, and employment in the weaving mills of Segovia, but the widow's two sons deprive him of the estate when she dies, and he voluntarily leaves the other situations because he knows that he can never find tranquility of mind by staying in them.

As a hermit, Alonso embraces one possible solution to the dilemma of a submissive subordinate who accepts a world view that contradicts his perceptions of reality and denies the validity of the motivations, goals, and values which give meaning to his life. Potentially, a similar dilemma exists in *Marcos* and in Martí's continuation, but Espinel circumvents it by imagining a fictional world which rewards an "escudero" for faithfully expressing his nature in his actions, and the problem is never even confronted in the apocryphal *Guzmán*, because its vulgar hero doesn't assimilate the basically aristocratic world view according to which he is judged and condemned. By declaring psychological independence from earthly vanities (subject to the arbitrariness of fortune) and social approbation (subject to the caprices of others), Alonso discovers a place where he can act according to his nature without being punished for doing so, but by acknowledging that there is no place in society for a man who possesses all the principal bourgeois virtues, he is also revealing the inadequacy of his own ideological assumptions. Essentially a conformist caught in the inherent contradiction between a stereotyped world view and his own experiences in an arbitrary, unjust society, Alonso represses the dilemma of the submissive subordinate by simply reaffirming the justice of the existing order. Like Espinel and Martí, Alcalá Yáñez was unquestionably influenced by Alemán's novel, but by portraying character as nature rather than as process and by adopting a traditionalist ideology, all three authors transformed the socially critical format of *Guzmán* into a vehicle for the defense of social conformity.

"Justina" and the Caricature of the Picaresque Hero

A second variation upon the *Lazarillo-Guzmán* model is exemplified by novels like Úbeda's *Justina* and Quevedo's *El Buscón*, in which picaresque protagonists are reduced to one-dimensional caricatures. Echoes of *Lazarillo* and *Guzmán* abound in both works. Úbeda's heroine quotes directly from Alemán's novel, humorously puns upon Lázaro's proverbial locutions, facetiously improvises upon the root word "pícaro," and even claims to have married Guzmán.[22] The narrative format and the treatment of several secondary characters in *El Buscón* are reminiscent of *Lazarillo*, and the major outlines of its plot are strikingly similar to those of *Guzmán*.[23] But whereas Alemán and the anonymous author of *Lazarillo* implicitly recognize that the lives of pícaros are distorted by the dehumanizing pressures of society, Úbeda and Quevedo portray similar characters in terms of inherently corrupt natures. Both Pablos and Justina are vulgar, lower-class conversos whose aspirations to a respectable place in society are *a priori* condemned as hypocritical and pretentious. As autobiographical narrators, they unwittingly reveal their own vulgarity and presumptuousness. Calculated to amuse the largely aristocratic audience for whom *Justina* and *El Buscón* were written, such characters are clowns to be laughed at, not human beings to be empathized with. The same ideology and reductionist techniques appear in both works, and although Úbeda's novel hardly achieves the same level of artistic integration and moral seriousness as *El Buscón*, it clearly illustrates one type of response to the enormous popularity of *Guzmán*.

Like Alemán, Úbeda was a converso, but unlike his predecessor in the picaresque tradition, he curried favor at the court of Philip III (Cervantes portrayed him as a sycophant in *El viaje del Parnaso*) and mocked the converso heritage in which he himself shared. Dedicatory eulogies to the illustrious, ancient, pure blood of Lerma's powerful secretary don Rodrigo Calderón and the presence of Calderón's recently invented coat of arms on the title page of *Justina* indicate that Úbeda was openly supporting the secretary's campaign for ennoblement, which he didn't receive until six years after the publication of *Justina*.[24]

Despite frequent allusions to *Lazarillo* and *Guzmán*, Úbeda's novel lacks many of the most important elements of the picaresque myth. Justina never undergoes a process of initiation and social conditioning. From the beginning, she is presented as an "estatua de libertad que é fabricado" ("statue of free living which I contrived").[25] The idea that the heroine is a "statue of free living" suggests Úbeda's intention to employ her as a symbolic embodiment of the picaresque-life themes illustrated in the frontispiece, but the word "statue" also expresses his willingness to accept the traditional notion that lower-class individuals like Justina are most fittingly portrayed as static comic characters.

This reductive approach is clearly evident in the attitude with which she describes her own ancestors. Claiming that people, like sponges, "soak up" the qualities of their forebears, she announces that her book will achieve its goal if it demonstrates that picaresqueness is inherited. To establish the purity of her own picaresque blood, she traces her genealogy back to all eight grandfathers, implying that her ability to invent entertaining deceptions and defraud others, her wit and her inclination toward dancing, gaiety, music, and traveling are in her blood. Named Justina because she upholds the honor of the picaresque family in the "justa de la picardía" (joust of roguery), she dismisses doctors, lawyers, and notaries as useless, humorless people, but rather than inflicting serious harm upon those whom she is mocking, her facetious statements reflect her own vulgarity. In her continuing state of moral blindness, she boasts about her sins and dishonest ruses because she considers them clever, but she stands condemned by what she reveals about herself.

As narrator, Justina prides herself upon a unique ability to create humorous sobriquets for people and things. In fact, both she and Úbeda declare that a "sauce" of curious details and clever witticisms is more important than a sustained account of the pícara's life. The claim that they are presenting numerous examples of rare and original styles of composition might well constitute a satiric parody of *Guzmán*'s miscellany qualities, but the author intentionally distances himself and the imagined reader from the narrating Justina by reproving her in satiric verses and moralizing "aprovechamientos" (useful commentaries) before and after each chapter. As a consequence, the illusion of a coherent autobiography is destroyed, and the novel itself becomes a long, fragmentary joke in which language and reality are distorted for the sole purpose of producing a humorous effect.

Justina's most important single characteristic is her wit, but unlike Lazarillo and Guzmán, she is not obliged to develop it in order to survive. Cleverness is simply an inherent part of her nature. It is the quality which allows her to steal mules from mule thieves, dupe a student who jokes at her expense, and turn the tables upon relatives who attempt to appropriate her share of her parents' estate. When applied to events which would normally arouse strong emotional responses, however, this ingenuity reveals her to be as cold as a "statue." For example, when her father dies, Justina calmly relates the fact and uses it as a pretext to exhibit her own verbal dexterity. An innkeeper, her father is killed by a "caballero" who discovers water in his horse's fodder. Seemingly unperturbed about the incident, Justina and her mother shroud the dead man and store him in the oven. While dogs are gnawing at the corpse, the two women graciously accept a banquet offered by the man's killer. The narrator concludes that her father might not be placed "honradamente" (honorably) in his new apartment, but he was at least there "hornadamente" ("ovenably"—like a batch of bread). The effectiveness of the passage depends not upon the description of an event from the narrator's past, but upon her success in surprising readers by unexpectedly juxtaposing two long, similar words. By suppressing the emotional dimension of her own experiences, however, Justina becomes a jester at whose witticisms readers might laugh but with whom they could never empathize.

A similar trivialization characterizes her attitude toward death and the corruptibility of the flesh. On one occasion, she holds a dead rabbit and reflects that, if she believed herself to have repented, she would actually be penitent—"acuerdate Iustina, que eres conejo, y en conejo te has de boluer" ("remember Justina, that thou art rabbit and unto rabbit shalt thou return").[26] By substituting rabbit for dust in a well-known Biblical passage about the impermanence of human life, she is satirically refuting the sense of the original, for rabbits are traditionally associated with promiscuity and rapid breeding. At the same time she is parodying the style of *Guzmán:* the underlying implication is of course the idea that repentance involves more than good intentions and that Guzmán's pious statements are comparable to those of Justina.

The primary level of communication in *Justina* exists between an author witty enough to "contrive" a "statue of free living" and socially elite readers capable of appreciating his wit and sanctioning his assumption that lower-class characters are best portrayed as caricatures or comic figures. In fact, the extraordinary lexicography of the novel and its numerous veiled allusions to contemporary events suggest, as the narrator herself intimates, that if her memoirs are to be properly understood, they must be read according to the "ley girolifica" (hieroglyphic law).[27] The knowledge necessary to perceive the true meaning of Justina's allusions and word constructions was largely restricted to a relatively small readership at the court of Philip III, and it is perhaps for this reason that the book received a somewhat restrained reception.

At the same time, its intended function becomes clear. It is, as Úbeda's subtitle suggests, a "libro de entretenimiento" (book of entertainment) designed to amuse upper-class readers. For their benefit, the picaresque heroine is reduced to a one-dimensional comic character—a presumptuous commoner who fails to recognize the absurd futility of her pretensions to respectability. Elegant variations upon themes of picaresque life are devised, and the serious treatment of vulgar characters in literature is parodied. Characterized by an inherently corrupt nature and viewed from a position of moral and social superiority, Justina epitomizes a dehumanized image of lower-class life—an image obviously designed to please a pseudosophisticated court audience and an especially powerful secretary well known for his willingness to accept bribes.

The Picaresque Adventure Stories of Salas and Castillo

Somewhat later than the satiric picaresque parodies of Úbeda and Quevedo, the successful dramatists Salas Barbadillo and Castillo Solórzano began to capitalize upon themes of picaresque life by incorporating the situations, descriptions of costumes, techniques of characterization, and decorative circumlocutions of the comic stage into novels with an adventure-story format. Influenced by the Italian novella, which was extremely popular in early seventeenth-century Spain, their picaresque fiction is characterized by a continuous impulse toward novelty and superficial diversity. When Salas revised *La hija de Celestina* and reissued it as *La ingeniosa Elena* (1614), he added a melange of light entertainments in response to a taste for this type of embellishment among his upperclass readers. The same is true of Castillo's many depictions of pícaros: Domingo Estrianquer in the short story "El Proteo de Madrid" (1625);

two older women and their four daughters in *Las harpias en Madrid y coche de las estafas* (1631); Teresa in *La niña de los embustes, Teresa de Manzanares* (1632); Hernando de la Trampa and Estefania in *Aventuras del bachiller Trapaza, quinta esencia de embusteros y maestro de embelecadores* (1637); and their daughter Rufina, who allies herself successively with an older rogue, Garay, and a younger one, Jaime, in *La garduña de Sevilla y anzuelo de las bolsas* (1642). Songs, satires, short plays, poems, and novellas are often arbitrarily introduced, and the narratives themselves are divided into episodes which are more like short stories than integral parts of novels. With the exception of *Teresa* and a brief section in Salas' *La hija de Celestina*, the autobiographical perspective is absent, and even when there is a first-person narrator, the picaresque protagonists are portrayed as static characters whose corruption is inherent, not the result of a socializing process as it had been in *Lazarillo* and *Guzmán*.

The pícaros of Salas and Castillo may appear to lead lives of gaiety and carefree insouciance, but they are always viewed from a distance and implicitly condemned. The two authors frequented the same literary circles and wrote for the same upper-class audiences, although Castillo was somewhat younger than Salas. The serious moral implications and trenchant satire of Salas' works reflect the influence of Quevedo, but although these qualities are largely absent from Castillo's novels, both authors were clearly catering to a public fascinated by the cleverness and apparent freedom of rogues. Because this public did not generally accord vulgar characters the potential for a fully dimensioned human existence, Salas and Castillo depicted their picaresque adventurers not as tragic victims in a corrupt society, but as corrupt excrescences upon a fundamentally sane social order.

This attitude is exemplified by the treatment of love in the picaresque adventure novels of Salas and Castillo. Portrayed as an ennobling sentiment in an honorable person and as a degrading or ridiculous indulgence in a pícaro, love becomes contingent upon the possession of a noble nature. The same assumption obtains in *Justina* and *El Buscón;* in fact, Úbeda makes the point quite clearly in one of his satiric verses:

> En fin, verás que amor, si es pobre y pícaro,
> Alas da, pero son alas de Icaro.

> (In the end, you'll see that love, if it's poor and picaresque,
> Gives wings, but they're wings of Icarus.)[28]

Although a pícara may appear to be in love, she is incapable of experiencing genuine human sentiment. Her exuberance might allow her to fly, but her wings are destined to melt when she overreaches herself. The Icarus image appears frequently in *Justina*, and it serves as a highly appropriate emblem for a widespread conception of picaresque life. Justina's own disreputable mother is named Perlicarlo, fusing "perla" (pearl) and "Icaro" (Icarus) in a name which also contains the word "pícaro." This ingenious coinage combines a traditional symbol of beauty (the pearl) with an allusion to self-destructive overconfidence (Icarus). It also suggests that Justina's inherited picaresqueness exists at least partly in a tendency to view herself unrealistically.

In the novels of Salas and Castillo a dominant place is accorded to the relationships between men and women, but neither Elena nor any of Castillo's picaresque heroes ever experiences love as an ennobling sentiment. On the contrary, amorous passions are invariably portrayed as distractions which prevent the characters from rationally conceiving and carrying out their schemes for acquiring wealth. To characterize Elena, Salas relies upon hyperbole and stereotyped images as descriptive labels: his heroine is more beautiful than Helen of Troy, her eyes execute lovers, her heart is the abode of falsehood. Her own emotions are never portrayed from her point of view, and it is only in the most ironic terms that "love" binds her to her companions, because their love is no more than "razón de estado" (reason of diplomacy, self-interest). Her deep-seated egoism removes all possible basis for trust, for if she sees a potential profit in betraying others, she doesn't hesitate to exploit the opportunity. This attitude reveals a dehumanized mentality, but because Elena's personality is a function of her nature, Salas is actually reinforcing an aristocratic assumption about the inability of vulgar commoners to experience genuine emotional attachments.

Castillo's picaresque adventurers are most successful when they induce love in others without engaging their own feelings, for only by remaining calm can they manipulate appearances in order to "lucir" (shine brilliantly) and present themselves as persons of quality. When they themselves fall in love, their schemes usually miscarry. Each of the four "harpies" successfully carries out a plan to dupe a prospective suitor, but they all agree to refrain from either falling in love with their intended victims or having sexual relationships with them. In contrast to these pícaras, Trapaza is handicapped in his marriage schemes by his infatuation with the young noblewomen whom he is courting, and Teresa regrets her love for Sarabia, a rogue who gambles her money away. For all of these characters, love is a blinding passion in themselves or a weakness to be exploited in others. As in the works of Úbeda, Quevedo, and Salas, it is assumed that lower-class characters are incapable of noble sentiments.

If Úbeda and Quevedo reduce pícaros to morally corrupt, comic carica-tures, Salas and Castillo endow them with the physical attributes of romantic heroes. Their picaresque adventurers retain the ingenuity and acquisitiveness of earlier pícaros, but their physical attractiveness, grace, and skill render them virtually indistinguishable from genuinely noble individuals. In fact, they possess the innate ability to simulate honesty and nobility so well that only chance can unmask them, despite the fact that they are fundamentally dishonest. For example, Teresa can sing, play musical instruments, and imitate the manners of her social superiors. At first her restlessness—she is like "bullente azogue con alma" ("boiling mercury with a soul")—is channeled into practical jokes, but her talent and energy enable her to become the most successful wigmaker at the court and the most popular actress in Seville. On a subsequent occasion, she acts so convincingly that an elderly merchant believes her to be his own daughter, and only the sudden appearance of the real daughter after a twenty years' absence prevents Teresa from inheriting a fortune. Later, a fortuitous encounter with an actor-acquaintance exposes her while she is parading as a noble widow. Similarly, Trapaza can dress handsomely, and three young noblewomen accept him as a worthy suitor. He doesn't suc-ceed in marrying them, but his own actions never betray him. He is only unmasked when characters who knew him in other circumstances happen to appear or when a jealous Estefania informs on him. During the entire story, however, readers know that Teresa is a child of "embustes" (artful lies, baubles) and Trapaza a man whose name means fraud, deceitful trick, or, as his grandfather often exclaimed, anything which did not have the color of truth.

Castillo's picaresque heroes are essentially social climbers, and if their adventure stories are to sustain the reader's interest, characters like Teresa, Trapaza, and Rufina must be accorded some chance of success. Despite orthodox moral commentaries, these clever, attractive, talented rogues can and do enjoy the fruits of their deceptions. Since they bear no visible signs of their vulgar origins, they feel perfectly justified in attempt-ing to obtain enough wealth to require that others treat them as persons of quality. Teresa even advances a rudimentary philosophy to defend her dishonest behavior when she asserts, "cada uno está obligado a aspirar a valer más" ("Everyone is obliged to aspire to better herself").[29] Her own actions are always motivated by this desire to "valer más," which she conceives in terms of a more tranquil, physically comfortable existence. Although her fortune is acquired by a series of confidence tricks, she herself is never punished, and she ultimately marries a merchant in Alcalá. Like Rufina's pleasant life with Jaime in Saragossa and the harpies' retirement in Granada, her marriage demonstrates that a pícara could achieve upward social mobility and escape the poetic justice meted out to Salas' Elena, who dies on the gallows after poisoning her lover.

Castillo's pícaras are sufficiently prudent to retire when they have accumulated enough money to live comfortably, but his pícaros tend to gamble away their earnings, ally themselves with deceitful associates, and frequently spend time in the galleys, although readers are assured that "bien la había favorecido la suerte a Trapaza si él supiera usar bien después de haber adquirido mal" ("fortune would have smiled upon Trapaza if he had known how to use wisely what he had acquired wickedly").[30] Even he is not condemned for his vulgar birth or his immoral activities, but for his lack of prudence in gambling away fortunes capable of sustaining him for the rest of his life. The implication is that Trapaza too could have risen in society and lived happily if he had played his role more carefully. Because the dishonest activities of these picaresque adventurers frequently remain unpunished and because their victims are always uncongenial characters, the explicit morality (contained in brief expository passages) of Castillo's novels conflicts with the implicit morality of his narratives.

Actually these narratives are generated by stringing together variations upon a single pattern: the protagonist, a physically attractive commoner, accidentally becomes aware of a potential victim and demonstrates his or her cleverness by devising a "maquina" (scheme, apparatus) or "quimera" (chimera, mirage) to deceive the victim. The ruse is generally rationalized on the grounds that anyone with money is like a fish waiting to be caught or an animal waiting to be trapped. Disguise is the lure which engenders confidence, and the ruse itself is the net in which the victim becomes entangled. For example, in *La garduña de Sevilla*, Rufina repeatedly obtains someone's trust by pretending to be a woman of quality. With her extraordinary beauty and musical talent, she ensnares her victim and steals what she desires. Although Castillo's heroes never succeed in defrauding genuinely noble individuals, they do deceive many unappealing or ignoble characters. Because the "maquinas" also serve to reveal the follies or vices of unsympathetic victims, their fishing expeditions appear to be justified in that the fish deserve to be caught.

For both Salas and Castillo, the picaresque adventurer is so absorbed in seeking selfish, materialistic goals that he or she places more confidence in physical possessions than in other people. For example, Rufina conceals most of her wealth from Garay, and after meeting Jaime, she allows her first companion to languish in the galleys. But whereas Castillo makes no attempt to portray the psychological consequences of such an attitude, Salas follows the example of Quevedo in attempting to suggest the state of mind which accompanies a life based upon acquisitiveness and deception. At the beginning of *La hija de Celestina*, Elena dupes a wealthy Toledan nobleman into giving her 2,000 ducats by claiming that she needs the money to enter a convent because the nobleman's nephew has raped her and ruined her reputation. Once this fraud has been perpetrated, however, she can never completely repress feelings of anxiety, for, as the narrator contends, if one person is cheated, all people become potential enemies. Fearing arrest, she flees from Toledo to Madrid, to Burgos, and finally to Seville. Even three years after the crime, she worries about encountering the nobleman's nephew when she returns to Madrid.

While in Seville, Elena and her two companions masquerade as humble, saintly people until one of their own servants informs on them. Although the old woman Méndez is apprehended and dies after receiving four hundred lashes, Elena and her lover Montúfar are forewarned. Without informing Méndez, they escape to Madrid, where they live upon the earnings of Elena's prostitution. But tiring of her companion's complacency, Elena poisons Montúfar just before she herself is arrested and hanged. Because Elena is concerned only with her own welfare, she feels no compunction about causing the deaths of her two closest companions; yet despite her pragmatic ruthlessness, she is never free from the fear that some chance occurrence will reveal her true identity.

Beneath the light entertainment provided by the adventure-story plot, Salas was actually condemning the moral blindness and lack of genuine nobility in a pícara who could maintain a convincingly respectable façade of honor and religion. Throughout the novel, an omniscient narrator comments ironically upon Elena's behavior and satirizes her vanity and hypocrisy, allowing readers to follow the adventure-story plot and enjoy Elena's ingenious confidence tricks without having to consider her a fully dimensioned, morally responsible individual. Salas was of course a playwright, and the atmosphere of his novel resembles the artificial world of the stage; like the audience at a play, readers of *La hija de Celestina* can momentarily accept the illusion that Elena is real, but they simultaneously recognize that her actions, invented for their amusement, are not to be taken seriously.

A similar atmosphere pervades the novels of Castillo, but rather than dramatizing the moral corruption of the picaresque adventurer, he transforms similar characters into vaguely outlined actors in stereotyped scenes on a stage manipulated by the author. These were precisely the types of characters with whom leisure-class readers could most easily identify, although if they met them in real life they would undoubtedly regard them as calculating, unsympathetic individuals; however, because Castillo's picaresque adventurers are imaginary people in a fictional world without ultimate consequences or tragic potential, upper-class readers could momentarily suspend disbelief and take pleasure in the outwitting of uncongenial victims by handsome and talented rogues. When kept on the level of harmless stage entities, these clever and audacious picaresque heroes proved highly entertaining to members of Spain's privileged classes.

The *"Desordenada codicia"* and Luna's *"Segunda parte"*

Among the rash of novels which followed in the wake of *Guzmán*, only two retained Alemán's critical perspective and his conception of character as process, and both of these novels were written in France by exile Spaniards who took advantage of their freedom from Inquisitorial pressure to indict arbitrary and irrational Spanish customs. For Carlos García and Juan de Luna, the *Lazarillo-Guzmán* model served as a precedent for the expression of viewpoints which had been largely suppressed in early seventeenth-century Spain. Both men had good reason to resent the treatment they had received in Spain. A native Toledan, Luna was persecuted by the Inquisition in Saragossa before moving to Paris (where he earned his living by teaching Spanish to wealthy Frenchmen) and London (where he eventually became a Protestant preacher for a Spanish community in Cheapside).[31] Although he may have been a New Christian, Luna's difficulties in Saragossa probably stemmed from the same Protestantism which prompted him to dedicate his *Segunda parte* to Henriette de Rohan, a member of the Protestant Huguenot branch of her family. García was a converso doctor who left Spain under Inquisitorial pressure and traveled to Paris, where he became associated with a group of Jewish professionals who lived near the Louvre and enjoyed considerable court patronage during the regency of Marie de Medici. Even in France, however, García experienced an eight-month imprisonment which he considered unjust and attributed to the machinations of a Jewish rival.[32]

Under these circumstances it is not surprising that Luna and García recognized that the picaresque novel could serve as a rhetorical device to plead for the justice and tolerance which had been denied them. In the prologue to his *Segunda parte de Lazarillo de Tormes* (1620), Luna recounts the parable of a farmer whose pears become so famous that the Inquisitor desires to sample them. Apprised of the request, the farmer is so frightened that he uproots the pear tree and sends it, hoping thereby to forestall any further visits from the Inquisitor's servants. If the pear tree stands for fruitful human endeavor, the invidious consequences of the Inquisition become evident: it inspires an irrational fear capable of destroying not only the products of human labor, but also the very capacity to produce.

A similar criticism is implied in García's *La desordenada codicia de los bienes ajenos: Antigüedad y nobleza de los ladrones* (1619). The entire narrative takes place in a prison during a conversation between a worldly-wise narrator and the French thief Andrés. Near the beginning the narrator observes that a loss of freedom reduces one to a "nothing" in a forest where wild animals devour each other—a "nothing" in a Tower of Babel where everyone talks and no one understands. Whether guilty or innocent, individuals condemned to this "hell" are indelibly marked by the experience, and that is precisely what was happening to many innocent people in a Spain dominated by the Inquisition. The expression of such antiestablishment views could hardly be expected to elicit favorable reactions from Spanish authorities, and it is not surprising that both novels were placed on the Index and that Luna's continuation remained on it even when the original *Lazarillo* was removed.[33] Despite the popularity of *Desordenada codicia* and *Segunda parte* in England, France, and Germany, they were not published in Spain until well into the nineteenth century.

Critics have often accused Luna of failing to understand the complex artistry of *Lazarillo;* in actuality, the *Segunda parte* represents a remarkably ingenious elaboration upon the principal themes and techniques of the anonymous novel.[34] As a teacher of Spanish, Luna had already compiled several texts which introduced students to pure Castilian and provided a taste of Spanish culture by including proverbs, idiomatic expressions, and bowdlerized excerpts from well-known Spanish novels. The version of *Lazarillo* bound with the *Segunda parte* was a bilingual Spanish-French edition first brought out by Pierre Bonfons in 1601.[35] This edition was specifically intended for language instruction, and it is quite possible that Luna conceived of the continuation as an attractive, amusing supplement to one of the works which he himself had taught to his students—a possibility heightened by the fact that 1623 and 1628 editions of the work were augmented by Pierre d'Audiguier's facing-page translations. In any case, it is true that many of the phrases, literary allusions, and syntactical patterns which characterize the *Segunda parte* first appeared in Luna's own language-instruction manuals.

Lazarillo undoubtedly appealed to Luna by virtue of its subtle condemnation of a society which compels people to engage in endless self-deceptions and compromises if they desire to survive and prosper; however, critical judgments merely suggested by the original are rendered explicit in the *Segunda parte*. After learning the principles of survival in a dehumanizing society, the original Lázaro acquires physical well-being at the expense of integrity, and he adopts a joking tone to describe an essentially humiliating sequence of events. At the end of the *Segunda parte*, Luna's Lázaro has been further disgraced, and he flees into a church, where he drapes a tomb-cover over his naked body and vows to adopt an ascetic attitude for the remainder of what he assumes will be a short and miserable life. He too adopts a facetious tone, but he has learned the unstated lessons of *Lazarillo*. His attitude has evolved into the reverse of the original Lázaro's cynicism, for he resigns himself to suffering and accepts poverty as the price of insight. The endings of the two books are different, but the dilemma of a lower-class, wandering character in a corrupt society remains the same.

Luna's insightfulness as an interpreter of *Lazarillo* is evident in the way he echoes scenes, characters, and structural techniques from the original novel. For example, Lazarillo's assimilation of the squire's hypocritical value system is symbolically indicated by a parallel between the squire's clothes and those which he himself buys after earning money for four years as a water-seller. In the *Segunda parte*, Luna's Lázaro reencounters the squire in Murcia and shares a bed with him. The following morning, the squire absconds with Lázaro's respectable garments, leaving only a pile of rags for his former servant to wear; however, Lázaro himself later acquires a similar set of rags, and just as the squire had done in Murcia—he accompanies women who desire an escort to support their pretensions to respectability. As in the original novel, Lázaro chooses clothes and modes of behavior similar to those of the squire, and his choice implies an acceptance of the squire's value system. In neither case is attention drawn to the parallel, but when the scenes are juxtaposed in the reader's mind, the similarity between the two men becomes obvious.

As in *Lazarillo*, Luna ironically reverses the meanings of terms associated with honor and religion to indicate the widespread hypocrisy with which they were used in contemporary Spanish society. Near the end of the *Segunda parte*, Lázaro is offered shelter by a white-bearded hermit. Venerated as a saint by the local populace, the hermit actually maintains a mistress in town and hoards a small fortune in the altar of his oratory. Just as the original Lazarillo had once been fooled by the squire's meticulously arranged rags, Luna's Lázaro is deceived by the hermit's appearance and saintly reputation, but after the older man dies, Lázaro discovers the money and agrees to marry the hermit's "widow" under the same conditions of complacent cuckoldry accepted by the original Lázaro during his marriage to the archpriest's mistress in Toledo. Like the bread and wine which provide him with physical (not spiritual) sustenance, the hermit and the altar are traditionally associated with genuine devotion. By linking them with the pursuit of earthly vanities, Luna transforms them into symbols of a secular religion. In a more fortunate moment, Lázaro himself exclaims, "¡O dinero, que no es sin razón la mayor parte de los hombres te tienen por Dios!" ("O money, it is not without reason that the majority of people consider you to be God!")[36] Behind a façade of traditional religion lies only the religion of money, the religion practiced with such devotion by the hermit at his altar.

A similar society of masks reappears in the background of the *Desordenada codicia*, but although Luna's Lázaro and García's Andrés serve as foils to a pervasive hypocrisy in their respective fictional worlds, the assumptions behind their critiques of society differ. The picaresque protagonists of both novels are perpetual victims, whose repeated humiliations result not from any inherent blemish in their characters but from the depravity of Spanish institutions, their own moral blindness, and the transitoriness of earthly things. In the *Desordenada codicia*, García's argument is basically the same as that of Alemán: Andrés is no different from the respectable people who condemn him to prison, and the distortion of his personality results from the pressures of a corrupt society. Luna's Lázaro is subject to these same pressures, but whereas García implies that corruption can be alleviated by the rational exercise of will and the practice of good works, Luna's Protestant theology decrees that the only viable solution is an absolute dependence upon God's grace, and this is presumably the attitude adopted by Lázaro when he retreats into the church at the end of the *Segunda parte*.

Like Alemán, García is adducing orthodox Catholic doctrine to reveal the disparity between the actual practices of Spanish society and its most frequently proclaimed ideals. To reveal the hypocrisy of religious intolerance, he devotes almost half of his novel to Andrés' expository defense of the thesis that all men are equal in the sense that all men are thieves. Because no one is satisfied with his station in life and everyone covets what does not belong to him, Andrés concludes that "el hurtar es naturaleza en el hombre y no artificio. . . . Nuestro pecado original será una inclinación y natural deseo de hurtar" ("stealing is inherent in man and not acquired. . . . Our original sin is a predilection and natural desire for stealing").[37] Invented in heaven by the fallen angels and practiced by Adam, Cain, Jacob, David, and a host of Greek and Roman heroes, the noble art of thievery, he contends, is emulated by the lower classes, but when practiced openly it is punished; consequently all men—office-holders, shoemakers, tailors, doctors, notaries, lawyers, innkeepers, butchers, alguacils, and clergymen—seek ways of disguising their dishonest acquisitiveness. "Todos hurtan y cada oficial tiene su particular invención y astucia para ello." ("Everyone steals and each member of a profession has his own artifice and guile for doing it.")[38] In the broadest sense, thievery becomes a synechdoche for the inescapable corruptibility of the flesh. If everyone is like Andrés—born in sin and incapable of repressing a natural "desordenada codicia de los bienes ajenos," there can be no valid justification for persecuting some men on the basis of their allegedly impure blood. Reduced to its fundamental terms, Andrés' arguments are quite similar to those of Alemán's Guzmán. The "respectable" people who disdain petty thieves are actually the greatest hypocrites, because their own actions are governed by the same principles as those of the people whom they condemn. By placing the good-natured Andrés within a context of universal thievery, García is actually advancing an argument which no orthodox Catholic could have refuted, yet if his argument is taken seriously, the entire basis for the Inquisition's persecution of conversos is reduced to absurdity.

In contrast to García's exploitation of orthodox Catholic doctrine as a vehicle of social criticism, Luna openly attacks Catholic clergy and ritual. In the *Segunda parte*, justice and privilege are sold to the highest bidder; every priest is portrayed as miserly, lazy or licentious; the lighting of candles and the worshiping of relics are mocked; but even more important from a doctrinal point of view, Luna's narrator suggests that God can extend or withhold grace from anyone, implying that works alone never insure salvation. At one point he declares, "La industria de los hombres es vana; su saber, ignorancia, y su poder, flaqueza, cuando Dios no le fortalece, enseña y guía" ("The ingenuity of man is vain; his knowledge, ignorance, and his power, weakness, if God does not strengthen, teach and guide him").[39] By asserting that all people's efforts are vain if or when God does not strengthen, teach, and guide them, he is denying a fundamental tenet of the Tridentine profession of faith: that God extends His grace to everyone, and everyone must exercise free will in accepting or rejecting it.

Couched in narrative terms and expressed by the fact that the morally corrupt Lázaro is actually superior to the society around him, the socially critical perspective of the *Segunda parte* exists against a background of rising and falling fortune.[40] Luna's narrator himself announces this theme when, in his introduction, he declares that "mudanza" (change) is an inescapable part of his fate. By adopting Bonfons' inclusion of the first chapter in the 1555 continuation as the last section of *Lazarillo*,[41] Luna eliminated the anonymous author's emphasis upon Lázaro's claim to have reached the summit of all good fortune. Already an adult with a fully formed character, Luna's Lázaro integrates the apocryphal account of drunken German soldiers into his autobiography, for it is after his experiences with them that restlessness and a desire for wealth motivate him to leave the "good life" in Toledo and follow Tomé González' footsteps by enlisting for military service in North Africa; however, to fulfill his dreams of wealth, he must cross the sea—a traditional symbol for instability. When the ship on which he is traveling founders, the captain and other respectable people save themselves and leave the commoners behind. Consoling himself with wine, Lázaro survives a plunge to the bottom of the sea, where he has visions of great treasure and finally becomes entangled in the nets of local fishermen, who dredge him up and bribe the Inquisition for permission to exhibit him throughout Spain as a curious sea monster. Perishing of hunger and imprisoned in a stinking fish tank, he calls himself a "cautivo en tierra de libertad" (captive in a land of freedom),[42] but because he is not strong enough to liberate himself, he remains silent about the fraudulence of his new masters until they reach Toledo, where his pregnant wife and the archpriest unwillingly testify that he is not a sea monster but a former town crier. The roguish fishermen are punished, and Lázaro receives twenty ducats, which allow him to eat well and buy fine clothes, but when he brings a lawsuit against his wife and the adulterous archpriest, his small fortune proves insufficient to combat their superior resources, and he finds himself reduced to poverty and exiled from the city.

Just as the original Lázaro claimed to have found a "buen puerto" (good harbor) at the end of his autobiography, Luna's picaresque hero believes that he has arrived in a "puerto de descanso" (harbor of peace or rest) while he is enjoying his twenty ducats, but every time he attains a materially comfortable situation, he is thrust back into humiliation, poverty, solitude, and scabrousness. His own decisions to seek wealth as a soldier and as a plaintiff against the archpriest might contribute to his disgrace, but the most important determining factors always lie beyond his control, for they include the unpredictability of the sea, the cowardliness of the ship's captain, the cruelty and acquisitiveness of the fishermen, and the corruption of a religious hierarchy which sells its permission for him to be exhibited as a monster as well as the "justice" executed upon him in Toledo. Just before he enters the church and entrusts himself to God's grace, Luna's Lázaro suffers his ultimate misfortune when the dead hermit's mistress and her mother mock him, appropriate the money from the altar, and leave him naked and alone on a public street. More sinned against than sinning, this Lázaro is a suffering victim in a world where petty thieves are often severely punished while the worst criminals go free. By drawing such a picture of society, Luna is not betraying *Lazarillo* but expanding upon its unstated assumptions as a means of expressing his own resentment against a Spain which had forced him into exile.

The *Desordenada codicia* also resembles *Lazarillo* in that its portrayal of Andrés demonstrates that a corrupt personality develops in the interaction between the self and a corrupt environment. While still a young boy, Andrés escapes public execution only because he agrees to testify against his parents. Whether or not they are guilty, he cannot be held responsible for their actions; but when society offers him a choice, he is confronted by two unsatisfactory alternatives: he can either repudiate his parents and save himself or maintain his loyalty to them and die. In a sense, he is responsible for his actions, but it is society which determines the conditions of his choice and rewards him for betraying his parents.

After leaving his native town, Andrés apprentices himself to a shoemaker, but because the work is difficult and his master beats him, he runs away after having stolen a single shoe from every shoemaker in town. Burdened with such a heavy load, he is quickly apprehended, punished, and exiled from the city. With the exception of a brilliantly successful ruse by means of which he tricks a love-sick captain to escape from the galleys, Andrés' schemes invariably miscarry because his booty generally proves as useless and cumbersome as the shoes. Caught red-handed, he nearly always loses more than he gains.

In early seventeenth-century Spain, writers like Úbeda, Martí, and Castillo Solórzano praised the picaresque life as happier and freer than the lives of more responsible people, but they could only do so because they and their upper-class readers did not ultimately take these eulogies seriously. Luna's Lázaro seems to be following this tradition when he equates the "vida picaresca" (picaresque life) with the "vida filósofa" (philosophical life) and claims that it represents the "camino más libre, menos peligroso y nada triste" (freest, least dangerous, and perpetually happy path).[43] However, in light of his own sufferings and humiliations, the hypocrisy of anyone who pretends to envy the carefree gaiety of pícaros becomes obvious. Lázaro's attitude toward picaresque freedom is just as ironic as the hypocritical hermit's praise of asceticism. Judged in terms of their own lives, the statements of both men are revealed as mock eulogies. In *La oposición y conjunción de los grandes luminares de la tierra* (1617), García recounts an apparently autobiographical anecdote to illustrate a similar point. Chased, insulted, and beaten each time he enters a French village, a young Spaniard soon learns that people will accept him if he is wearing French clothes. Although the injustices inflicted upon him are irrational, he can avoid them by conforming to superficial customs. Luna's parody of stereotyped notions about the gaiety of picaresque life illustrates the same idea as García's suggestion that respectable people differ from alienated pícaros primarily in terms of their clothes (or masks). In both cases, exile writers are subtly undercutting the self-righteous hypocrisy of Spain's dominant classes by employing techniques similar to those used in *Lazarillo* and *Guzmán*. In fact, for them the picaresque novel itself becomes a rhetorical device to plead for justice and tolerance in a society which had unfairly persecuted them.

After the initial success of *Guzmán* and its linkage with *Lazarillo*, a great number of picaresque novels were published in Spain, but with the exception of García's *Desordenada codicia* and Luna's *Segunda parte*, they adopted socially conformistic attitudes and a trivialized interpretation of the picaresque myth. Various elements of the *Lazarillo-Guzmán* model reappeared in these novels, but the epigons of the picaresque tradition generally failed to unify their materials, as Alemán and the anonymous author had done by subordinating them to the identifiable motivations of their narrating characters. Like *Guzmán*, the picaresque works of Martí, Espinel, and Alcalá Yáñez are constructed around narrators who relate anecdotes, allegories, fables, and the story of their own lives from an "atalaya de la vida humana" in the attempt to justify their previous behavior and project favorable images of themselves, but the autobiographical perspective in these three novels lacks the coherence and consistency it possesses in Alemán's *Guzmán*. Playing upon the stereotyped image of the pícaro as a clever and carefree but immoral rogue, Úbeda and Quevedo adopted *Lazarillo*'s practice of allowing a disreputable narrator to condemn himself by his own boasts, whereas Salas and Castillo exploited the adventure-story potential of the picaresque format.

Only the exile writers García and Luna followed *Lazarillo* and *Guzmán* in representing the process by means of which lower-class wandering individuals suffer the distortion of their personalities as a consequence of pressures imposed upon them by a corrupt society. Lazarillo and Luna's Lázaro, Guzmán and Andrés all must assimilate dehumanizing attitudes if they hope to survive and prosper. They might be corrupt, but it is society which makes them corrupt. In contrast to them, the picaresque heroes of Martí, Úbeda, Quevedo, Salas, Espinel, Alcalá Yáñez, and Castillo are portrayed as innately good or evil characters, whose natures express themselves in a series of contacts with the world. By reverting to the traditional assumption that society is and ought to be a divinely ordained hierarchy in which everyone's place is predetermined by an inherent nature, these writers were denying the role of conditioning as a factor in social corruption and reinforcing the values of the dominant classes in seventeenth-century Spain.

The tragic and pathetic overtones of picaresque existence emerge in *Marcos, Alonso, Desordenada codicia* and Luna's *Segunda parte*, but in the novels written for courtly audiences—*Justina, La hija de Celestina, El Buscón,* and the adventure stories of Castillo—the pícaro is no longer a plausible human character but a one-dimensional caricature or adventure-story hero. Ostensibly gay and carefree, his or her life is viewed and condemned from a position of moral superiority. The readers for whom these novels were written might have been amused by the apparent insouciance of a lower-class protagonist, but they hardly considered the actual thoughts and feelings of pícaros as appropriate subject matter for serious literary treatment. To them the very idea of a picaresque identity crisis was absurd, because the pícaro was by definition dishonorable, corrupt, and incapable of genuine human feelings.

The reification of the picaresque hero is but one consequence of the rapprochement between the *Lazarillo-Guzmán* model and the traditionalist ideology; in addition, the fictional worlds in most of the later novels are constructed upon the very premises which Alemán and the anonymous author had so eloquently called into question. Justina, Elena, and Martí's Guzmán all have impure blood, but within the context of an essentially aristocratic world view, the converso problem recedes into the background, because tainted blood is assumed to be a primary determinant of the pícaro's vulgar character. Unlike Alemán's original, Martí's Guzmán is enough of an adventurer to engineer his own escape from the galleys, but his corrupt nature prevents him from ever achieving tranquility of mind by means of an authentic religious conversion. Espinel obviates the possibility of meaningful social criticism by assuming that the physical world operates according to a principle of poetic justice, which reflects divine order and ultimately rewards all people of good will. Alcalá Yáñez espouses similar ideas of character as nature, but Alonso's failure to find an appropriate place in society illustrates the difference between a noble-hearted retainer like Marcos and a declassed bourgeois like himself. From the beginning Salas' Elena is unambiguously identified as corrupt, and her personality remains unchanged by its contact with society. The same is true of Castillo's picaresque adventurers, but whereas Elena is appropriately punished, they neither experience the latent sterility of their own lives nor suffer punishment for their dishonest actions.

By reconciling the literary portrayal of pícaros with an acceptance of traditionalist social values, Spanish writers with socially elite audiences in mind drastically altered the meaning of the picaresque myth as delineated by Alemán and his anonymous predecessor. Free from the constraints of Spanish censorship, García and Luna did portray the dehumanizing impact of a corrupt society upon the lower-class consciousness, but even they failed to fully exploit the unifying potential of the pseudoautobiographical perspective. The artistic unity of *Lazarillo* and *Guzmán* derives from a skillful handling of this perspective, just as the force of their moral commentary is posited upon the assumption that character is process, not nature. Because this assumption did not correspond to the dominant ideology in early seventeenth-century Spain, it was seldom adopted by writers obviously aware of the *Lazarillo-Guzmán* model, and even when it was, it did not necessarily enable them to create unified literary works.

5

El Buscón:

QUEVEDO'S ANNIHILATION
OF THE PICARESQUE

There was one man who understood the implications of Alemán's critique
and possessed the genius to successfully adapt the *Lazarillo-Guzmán* model
to his own world view, and that man was the brilliant wit, scholar, and
courtier don Francisco de Quevedo y Villegas. Himself the member of an
aristocratic family, Quevedo shared the traditionalist sentiments expressed
in most seventeenth-century picaresque novels, and he could hardly be
expected to regard a lower-class, wandering character as the fully dimensioned, tragic victim of a dehumanizing socialization process. In his *La
vida del Buscón llamado don Pablos* (1626),[1] he borrows themes and techniques from *Lazarillo* and expresses many of the same philosophical
assumptions which appear in *Guzmán*, but he is using the picaresque-novel
format as a means of demonstrating the absurdity of considering the life of
a pícaro as suitable subject matter for serious literary treatment. Like
Alemán, Quevedo does create an "atalaya de la vida humana," but his
ideological assumptions and his caricatural technique cause him to locate
his fictive narrator among those who are observed from the perspective of
truth, not among those who have the insight and knowledge to judge
others. At the time that *El Buscón* was written, the novel had not yet
achieved full recognition as an accepted form of literary expression, and
Quevedo probably viewed his only venture into the genre as a somewhat
immature *tour de force*, but within the context of his own world view, it still
represents a trenchant commentary upon the picaresque hero as he existed
in contemporary Spanish literature and society.

Although *El Buscón* is filled with jokes, puns, and caricatures, it is also a
morally serious work of art.[2] Throughout his life Quevedo was concerned
with the transience of earthly things, the corruption of contemporary
society, and the inevitability of death. Although he later regretted the
frivolity of his early works, he was never indifferent to ideas of morality
and death. He might have been a youthful court wit when he wrote *El*

Buscón, but he was already one of the most profound thinkers of his age. As early as 1604, he wrote to the well-known Dutch scholar Justus Lipsius, expressing an avid interest in Seneca and describing his own country in the same sad tones as Lipsius had used in talking about his war-ravaged homeland. "Quid de mea Hispania non querula voce referam? Vos belli praeda estis. Nos otii, & ignorantiae. Ibi miles noster, opesque consumuntur. Hic nos consumimur: & desunt qui verba faciant, non qui dent." ("What can I relate about my own beloved Spain without speaking in a querulous tone of voice? You are the spoils of war. We of laziness and ignorance. There our soldiery and wealth are devoured. Here we are devoured: honest men are lacking, not those who deceive.")[3] In broad philosophical terms, there is no contradiction between this letter, written during Quevedo's student days at Alcalá, and his later religious or political tracts; a nascent fascination with Senecan stoicism and an awareness that he was living in an Iron Age of ignorance, hypocrisy, and costly, useless wars were already present in his mind. A short time later Quevedo began working on the earliest *Sueños*. In them as well as in his letter to Lipsius, he was clearly attributing the widespread moral blindness in his own country to selfishness and materialism.

Although Quevedo developed many of his ideas further in the later *Sueños*, several assumptions are consistently made throughout his writings. The two most important ones in terms of any interpretation of *El Buscón* involve his attitude toward earthly vanities and his adherence to the traditional, rigidly stratified social hierarchy. For him, death was inherent in all human life—"lo que llamáis morir es acabar de morir, y lo que llamáis nacer es empezar a morir, y lo que llamáis vivir es morir viviendo" ("that which you call death is only the end of dying, and that which you call birth the beginning of death, and that which you call life is living death").[4] For this reason, he characterized the wise man as one who is constantly aware of his own inevitable death—"Cuerdo es sólo el que vive cada día como quien cada día y cada hora puede morir" ("Only he who lives every day as if he might die on any day and at any moment is wise").[5] Judged from this vantage point, most people are engaged in trivial matters, although they tend to repress a recognition of this fact, because their self-esteem is contingent upon a belief in the importance of their own activities.

In "Las zahurdas de Plutón," Quevedo portrayed life in terms of two alternate paths which men may choose: a broad highway congested with horses, carriages, and well-dressed, apparently happy people, or a narrow trail filled with thistles and potholes. The few people who venture down the second path are dressed in rags, and pieces of flesh have been torn from their bodies by bushes and rocks along the way, but these people never look behind them, for they are following the path of truth and virtue. In contrast to them, the people on the broad highway are pursuing the "way of the world." Their behavior is accepted as perfectly normal by their companions, but according to Quevedo's world view, everyone on the broad highway fails to see that wealth, amusement, and false honor will be rendered worthless by the death which none of them can avoid. Commoners and noblemen are equally susceptible to the seductions of the broad highway, and they are equally capable of virtue, but they must act within the traditional social hierarchy. In Quevedo's eyes, corruption in contemporary Spain was largely attributable to people's disregard for tradition and their refusal to perform the duties and responsibilities of their social stations. According to him, the truly religious man would be profoundly aware of his own mortality and the transience of earthly things, and the truly honorable man would voluntarily accept his place in society and act in an appropriate fashion.

In many of his writings and particularly in the *Sueños* and *El Buscón*, Quevedo incorporated his critique of society into panoramic satires of the ways in which people blinded themselves to the irreligious, dishonorable nature of their own actions. In general, he started with a characteristic vice or folly and chose a limited number of physical traits, gestures, or phrases to translate the mental state of its practitioners into a composite but concrete human form. By exaggerating and distorting the traits of this "type" character, Quevedo purposely destroyed any possible illusion of a factual point-for-point correspondence between the fictional world of his novel and the real world outside his novel. For this reason, it would be a mistake to view his characters as psychologically plausible individuals in realistic settings.

Rather than create fully rounded human personalities, Quevedo attempted to demonstrate that the hypocritical practitioner of any given vice or folly contains within himself the refutation of his own pretensions. In "Las zahurdas de Plutón," a devil figure exclaims, "bien mirado, en el mundo todos sois bufones" ("viewed properly you are all clowns").[6] In the *Sueños* and *El Buscón*, Quevedo himself created the perspective from which readers could recognize the absurdity of behavior regarded as perfectly normal in a corrupt society. By revealing what lies behind this behavior—a pride based upon ephemeral, ultimately worthless possessions or gratifications—he succeeded in portraying many of his fictional characters as clowns who hypocritically deny the true nature of their own actions. In another of Quevedo's *Sueños*, "El mundo por dentro," a wise old man declares that all men live on Hypocrisy Street, the main street of the world.

In *El Buscón*, every character is a clown living on Hypocrisy Street—a clown pursuing earthly vanities, ignoring the inevitability of his own death, and blinding himself to the responsibilities of his God-given place in society. The absurdity of a clown's actions is comic and provokes laughter; if Quevedo's technique is successful, readers will laugh, but they will also realize that the patently ridiculous behavior of his characters represents a symbolic condemnation of the moral blindness which permits entire classes of people to deny the truth about themselves and persist in their foolish, sinful activities. For example, Cabra's words and gestures suggest the psychological reality of many miserly schoolmasters, and the garrulous poet whom Pablos encounters on the road to Madrid stands for a whole class of incompetent versifiers. Within the context of Quevedo's work, caricature and morality are merely two different ways of expressing the same attitude toward life, because if Cabra and the poet are presented as ridiculous figures whose vices and follies are present in contemporary society, there must be an implicit standard according to which they are judged. This standard was Quevedo's conception of honor and religion, and it allowed him to present fictional characters as ingeniously contrived generalizations about whole classes of people. When Quevedo created ludicrous caricatures in *El Buscón* or associated hell with the dream-visions in his *Sueños*, he imparted a surrealistic quality to his writings—a quality not altogether different from the bizarre atmosphere in the paintings of Hieronymous Bosch, whom he greatly admired. Like Bosch, Quevedo used this quality to remind people of the religious and moral standards according to which his "clowns" could be considered both ridiculous and blind. In Quevedo's satiric works, belief and technique are inseparable, and the jokes in *El Buscón* are intimately linked with concerns of the utmost seriousness.

Within his frame of reference, noble birth and "limpieza de sangre" should have been reflected in people's behavior, but in reality conversos and commoners often attempted to pass as noble Old Christians, while true noblemen often neglected their proper roles in society. Fundamentally sound, the traditional values were thus being constantly undermined by selfishness, presumption, brutishness, and materialism. Although the religious views behind this attitude resembled those expressed by Alemán,

Quevedo's social attitudes were altogether different, and he undoubtedly wrote *El Buscón* at least partially in response to ideological assumptions implicit in picaresque novels like *Guzmán*, with which he was obviously familiar.[7] As an aristocrat who decried the loss of traditional values, the disintegration of a divinely ordained social hierarchy, and the presumptuousness of the lower classes, he attributed the material and social aspirations of conversos and commoners to an unwarranted dissatisfaction with their proper places in society. For this reason, he started with a character like Guzmán, but rather than treating his pícaro seriously, he exaggerated Pablos' dominant characteristics and reduced him to a one-dimensional, static figure whose ridiculous behavior stands for the psychological reality of a particular type of moral blindness—that of a buscón or pícaro.

The frequency with which words like "pícaro" and "picaresco" recur in Martí's *Guzmán* and Úbeda's *Justina* suggests that some authors and booksellers were attempting to take financial advantage of a rather strong popular interest in picaresque themes and subjects. In the *Sueños* Quevedo frequently applied the term "pícaro" to people who concealed their actual desires behind respectable masks, while placing inordinate value upon worldly goals and repressing an awareness of their inevitable deaths.[8] In the underworld slang of the period, a "buscón" was a petty thief or swindler. Quevedo himself used "buscona" as a synonym for prostitute and "buscón" for confidence man, but he also punned upon the word's radical association with "buscar" (to seek). In *El Buscón*, Quevedo's "pícaro" seeks money, sexual pleasure, and social position; however, in one of the *Sueños*, Quevedo contrasted "buscar" with "lograr" (to attain) in terms of wisdom, implying that a "buscón" has not attained and might never attain a knowledge of the truth. Within this context, Pablos can be viewed as a vulgar rogue who pursues false goals and ignores the truth about himself and his world.

In contrast to Guzmán, who experiences a religious conversion and tells his story from an "atalaya" of human life, Pablos travels across the sea and returns to Spain without having changed his "life and customs." Whereas Guzmán claims that he intends to fabricate a "perfect man" by writing his memoirs, the narrating Pablos only brings discredit upon himself by telling his story.[9] Whenever he is humiliated—confronted by the reality of his own disgraceful origins—Pablos flees from the place where he is known and goes elsewhere to assert his fraudulent claim to a higher social station than the one to which he is entitled by birth; however, all his attempts are doomed to failure because an inherently vulgar character is incapable of escaping his origins.[10] Unlike Lázaro and Guzmán, the narrating Pablos' personality does not plausibly evolve from his previous experiences; it is determined by his *converso* heritage and his blindness in refusing to acknowledge the truth about himself. He does undergo a series of initiations, but he gains no insight from them; he only assimilates the surface lesson of each experience and fails to grasp its more profound significance. Thus, unlike Lázaro and Guzmán, he is not using an account of his past to convince readers of his self-worth;[11] with the possible exception of the concluding aphorism, he himself never conceives of his life as the specific illustration of a general truth. In fact, the entire fictional world of *El Buscón* is perceived not from Quevedo's point of view, but through the eyes of a foolish, self-deluded *converso* who is following the "way of the world," the same broad highway that Quevedo satirized in "Las zahurdas de Plutón." For this reason, both the autobiographical perspective and the picaresque myth in *El Buscón* become negations of analogous structures in *Lazarillo* and *Guzmán*. Like Úbeda and Martí, Quevedo exploited the contemporary popularity of picaresque themes, but unlike them, he did not merely play with the surface meanings of words like "pícaro." He integrated them into a morally significant, ingeniously wrought novel which exposed the vulgarity of an ambitious, lower-class *converso* and undoubtedly amused the aristocratic audience for which it was intended.

The morally blind narrator of this novel is subjected to the same reductive technique which Quevedo applied to all the other characters in *El Buscón*, and the result is a totally different narrative texture from that of *Lazarillo* or *Guzmán*. The irony of Lázaro's mock naive correspondence with Vuestra Merced was not lost upon Quevedo, but rather than evoking a compassionate understanding for a character whose mentality has been warped in the socializing process, the author of *El Buscón* deliberately set out to eliminate the possibility of sympathy by making the narrator himself into a caricature of the picaresque personality. Written for readers who shared Quevedo's assumptions about the rightness of the established social hierarchy, *El Buscón* exposes the inherent absurdity of all vulgar but ambitious *conversos* like Guzmán.

The narrating Pablos seems to be confiding in Vuestra Merced and assuming that readers share the values which he himself applies to his story; however, this is a highly dubious assumption. Vuestra Merced and Quevedo's upper-class readers might have laughed at Pablos' witticisms, but they would also have laughed at him: his aspirations and his humiliations. For them, his attempt to curry favor with Vuestra Merced was itself presumptuous, and the disjointedness of the narrative reflects a vulgar character's inability to grasp the significance of the events which he is describing. Although his witticisms were capable of evoking laughter, Pablos himself was a type-figure with whom upper-class readers could not possibly empathize.

In essence he is an "other-directed" man, a materialistically inclined, fundamentally selfish conformist whose sensitivity to the expectations and preferences of others causes him to follow fashion rather than any discernible moral code.[12] Just as Pablos' previous behavior was modeled upon his conception of what he should do in order to gain approbation, the recording of his memoirs is a self-satisfied attempt to make a favorable impression upon someone from a socially superior class. Regarding his past disgraces as affronts to an exaggerated sense of importance, he can disregard their true significance by transforming them into jokes. Because he hopes to be judged, not as a morally responsible individual, but as a witty entertainer, he is even willing to place great emphasis upon his own most dishonorable actions. He never seems to realize that by revealing them he is actually condemning himself. Within Quevedo's frame of reference, the source of Pablos' misfortune is his own character. Ignoring the real cause of his sufferings, however, Quevedo's fictional narrator attributes them to the devil, fortune, society, or some other external force. In doing so, he demonstrates a continuing attachment to earthly vanities and a refusal to occupy his God-given place in society. Such moral blindness is further compounded by hypocrisy when he ridicules the bestial or ludicrous actions of others and then blithely recounts how he himself behaved in much the same way.

Because Pablos' self-image is based entirely upon his conception of what others might think about him, he readily imitates modes of behavior which, for Quevedo, reflected the selfishness and materialism responsible for the breakdown of traditional values; furthermore, Pablos is completely oblivious to the fact that genuine honor implies the integrity with which people actualize their inner convictions. For this reason, he never realizes that his own ambitions, actions, and afflictions—no matter how ingeniously he embellishes them—reveal him to be a vulgar, dishonorable fool. For example, he concludes his memoirs by philosophizing, "nunca mejora su estado quien muda solamente de lugar, y no de vida y costumbres" (280) ("one who only changes his location without changing his life and customs will never improve his condition").[13] From his perspective, this aphorism represents a clever way of ending his story; from Quevedo's point of view, however, Pablos is avoiding an awareness of his own blindness by taking refuge in a banal phrase which had once been a Latin commonplace. By accepting clichés in lieu of genuine wisdom, Pablos is again betraying a lack of taste and insight, but as in *Lazarillo*, the narrator's proverbial expressions are also appropriate in ways which he himself fails to recognize. For example, his concluding statement about a person who only changes places and not his life or customs identifies the dominant pattern in his own life. Attempting to rise in society, he must repeatedly flee from places where his vulgarity has become obvious, but because vulgarity is an innate part of his character, he never actually improves his own condition. The fact that his voyage to the New World fits this pattern is amply illustrated by the manner in which he distorts even the most serious considerations into jokes.

For Quevedo, the ultimate futility of worldly reputation and material possessions would be glaringly evident to anyone who recognized the inevitability of death. Pablos repeatedly mentions the word "death," but rather than yielding wisdom and self-awareness, his allusions are always calculated to produce laughter. This insensitivity toward the meaning of death is apparent in his descriptions of the starving students at Cabra's boarding school and the execution of his own parents, but it emerges most clearly when the rector of the university conducts a house-to-house search for swords which Pablos had stolen from the night watch. On this occasion, the buscón escapes detection by donning a shroud and feigning the "espectáculo" (spectacle) of his own death. His ruse succeeds, but although he fools the rector, he is also fooling himself: anything which he might obtain by his cleverness will ultimately be rendered meaningless by the death he so unconcernedly jokes about. In the final paragraph of his memoirs, he himself admits that he is not "tan cuerdo" (sufficiently prudent) to learn from experience; consequently, even when he is brought face to face with his own death, he fails to recognize that his attachment to false values is ludicrous within a context of inescapable mortality. In moral and psychological terms, the narrating Pablos is the same vulgar buscón he has always been.

In fact, Pablos could not possibly have changed his life and customs, because Quevedo placed him in a fictional world which operates to punish the buscón whenever he attempts to rise in society and to reward him whenever he abandons himself to overtly roguish behavior. Incapable of feeling genuine shame or learning the lesson implicit in his various initiations, Pablos never evolves or grows. No matter what he does, he is merely expressing the same corrupt mentality in different ways. Although this mentality reflects Pablos' vulgar heritage as well as the pervasive corruption in his society, Quevedo is actually placing his picaresque hero in a double-bind situation, in which there is no viable alternative. As long as he remains content to be a dissolute companion of university students or Sevillian thugs, he can lead "la mejor vida" (the better life), but when he pretends to be more noble or wealthy than he actually is, he is inevitably unmasked and disgraced. The picaresque or buscón personality of the protagonist does emerge in a series of immoral choices, but due to Quevedo's ideological assumptions about conversos and pícaros, Pablos' range of choice is limited to two equally condemnable alternatives: he can choose to be what he is, a vulgarian, or he can pretend to be what he is not, a nobleman and an Old Christian. But because he will be wrong whatever he chooses, *El Buscón* seems to lack the human dimensions of *Guzmán* and *Lazarillo.* Quevedo's elitist and anti-Semitic attitudes defined the sort of fictional world in which his pícaro was obliged to live, and the plan of his novel consisted in allowing this type-character to express his own absurdity by revealing what would occur when his corrupt mentality confronted external reality in a series of superficially different but fundamentally similar incidents.

The basic qualities of Pablos' personality are clearly delineated in the legacy which he inherits from his disreputable, pretentious parents. His father, Clemente Pablos, is a barber who steals from his customers and advises the buscón to become clever in the "arte liberal" (liberal art) of thievery. As a drunkard who encourages his wife's prostitution, Clemente has little claim to any genuine sense of honor, but he insists that people refer to him not simply as a barber, but as a shearer of cheeks and a tailor of beards. Pablos' mother, Aldonza de San Pedro, is a prostitute, procuress, and sorceress, but although her genealogy is less than respectable, she claims to be such an "Old Christian" that she is descended from the litany. Both parents desire Pablos to follow in their footsteps, but he has no intention of pursuing either profession—"yo, que siempre tuve pensamientos de caballero desde chiquito, nunca me apliqué a uno ni a otro" (18) ("I, who from earliest childhood had a caballero's thoughts, never applied myself to either one or the other"). Ironically, in rejecting their specific vocations, he unwittingly emulates their example, for like them he actually wants to be recognized for a quality which he possesses in name only.

Never does he think in terms of developing the mental or moral qualities of a genuine caballero. He is not even disturbed if the local schoolboys gossip ambiguously about his heritage, but when one of them openly calls him the son of a whore and witch, he hits the boy on the head with a rock. While recounting the incident to his mother, Pablos asks her about his own paternity; she replies by praising him—"bien muestras quién eres" (23) ("you show well who you are")—without giving him a direct answer to his question. Shamed by her equivocal response, he secretly determines to leave home. During every stage in this episode, Pablos fails to act as a genuine caballero would act: he admits that he wouldn't react to veiled insults, and when it becomes impossible to avoid humiliating allegations about himself, he discovers that he has no real honor to defend and can only escape insults by running away from them. For the rest of his life, Pablos will be "showing well who he is," because even in the attempt to deny his disreputable origins, he remains the prisoner of what he cannot change—his lower-class, picaresque, converso identity.

The first time that Pablos actually appears to occupy a position of superiority occurs during the "king of the cocks" episode. Chosen to represent the king in an annual carnival celebration, Pablos mounts proudly upon his steed (in reality a lame, half-blind, skeletal nag), but when it eats a cabbage from a vegetable-seller's stand, the market women and the schoolboys enter into a mock epic battle. During the ensuing confusion, Pablos and his nag fall into a pile of excrement and garbage, but rather than blaming his misfortune upon his own inability to ride horseback like an authentic caballero, he characteristically flees from the schoolboys (who know about his disgrace) by accepting an offer to accompany the noble don Diego to Cabra's boarding school. The pattern established in this episode recurs throughout the book, because each time that Pablos occupies a position to which he is not entitled by birth, he falls into the filth and slime which Quevedo associates with Pablos' inner corruption.[14]

It is precisely this internal corruption which, according to Quevedo's world view, Pablos can never escape. Ultimately, the buscón himself acquiesces in a mode of life which parallels that of his parents and his disgusting Uncle Ramplón. In the final section of the book he joins a group of Sevillian thugs in a drunken orgy reminiscent of an earlier party organized by Ramplón, but whereas Pablos had held himself aloof from

Fig. 10. Pablos' journey (map by Allen Bjornson)

his uncle's companions and watered his own wine to remain sober, he now welcomes the embrace of the thugs and shows no hesitation in drinking large quantities of unwatered wine. Like his father, Pablos rapidly develops a taste for wine, takes refuge in a cathedral to escape prosecution, practices the "liberal art" of thievery, and links his fate with a prostitute who resembles his mother. Like Guzmán, Pablos' life inscribes a circular pattern in which the pícaro returns to himself, but whereas Guzmán can choose between the corruption of the flesh and the perfection of the spirit, the morally blind and pretentious Pablos has no choice. The only possibility open to him is a way of life which corresponds to his vulgar character.

Before embracing the inevitable, Pablos alternately strives toward two seemingly contradictory goals. Sometimes he actively covets a higher social role than the one into which he was born; sometimes he throws himself into a life of petty thievery and coarse, physical pleasure. As an other-directed man, he lacks the qualities of a truly honorable or religious person and never expresses the slightest intention of acquiring them; he wants only the material possessions and social status conventionally linked with ideas of nobility and Old Christian blood. In real terms, he remains unconcerned about the fact that his actions are morally culpable and inappropriate to his place in society, but whenever the disparity between his self-image and his inherently vulgar character becomes obvious to others, he claims to feel a deep sense of shame. Yet even this shame has nothing to do with an awareness of his own guilt or folly. It merely reflects the culpability with which he was born and from which he cannot possibly escape.

Pablos' corruption is emphasized by a recurrent pattern of pretension and humiliation. When he assumes a higher social station than the one to which he is entitled, he stumbles into painful or humiliating situations, but rather than perceiving his disgrace for what it is—a symbolic punishment for picaresque, converso presumptuousness—he compounds his guilt by blaming his misfortunes on others or on forces outside himself. This pattern reaches a climax during Pablos' attempt to marry doña Ana. Because he cannot court a beautiful young noblewoman if he admits who he actually is, Pablos lies about his past and pretends to be a caballero who is perfectly at ease riding about town on horseback; however, his lies render him vulnerable to being unmasked as a fraud, incapable of sustaining the noble role he is attempting to play. A genuine caballero would be able to control a horse, but when Pablos rides ostentatiously in front of doña Ana's house, his horse bucks and the inexperienced Pablos falls into a mud puddle.

The incident echoes the earlier "king of the cocks" episode, but on this occasion the moral behind the experience is reinforced by subsequent events. Through an extraordinary coincidence doña Ana's cousin is Pablos' childhood companion don Diego, who unexpectedly appears in Madrid and penetrates the tissue of lies which Pablos had fabricated to support his masquerade as a caballero. To mark the presumptuous buscón for a prearranged ambush, don Diego exchanges capes with him, but the cos-

tume of a genuine nobleman subjects the hapless Pablos to two attacks:
one intended for the real owner of the cape and one arranged for him by
don Diego. Although Pablos cannot defend himself in a truly honorable
fashion (as an authentic nobleman might have done), he fails to understand
that the two beatings which he suffers result from his own dishonest
masquerade. In his eyes, don Diego was "totalmente causa de mi des-
dicha" (236) ("completely to blame for my bad luck"). As in the "king of
the cocks" episode, Pablos repeatedly alludes to the "vergüenza" (shame)
which he feels when his respectable mask begins to disintegrate under the
pressure of reality, but true shame implies an awareness of the culpability,
weakness, or inappropriateness of one's actions, and Pablos' attempt to
shift the blame for his disgrace to don Diego merely reveals his own
refusal to recognize who and what he is;[15] his "shame" is merely another
expression of his shamelessness.

The same quality emerges even more clearly in his choice to become a
"bellaco" (rogue). Because overt roguery is well suited to Pablos' inner
corruption, Quevedo portrays the pícaro as being perfectly happy among
the dissolute students of Alcalá and the disreputable thugs of Seville. It is
not that Quevedo approves of roguish behavior when practiced by rogues;
quite the contrary, he is demonstrating that Pablos is in his proper sphere
when he is engaged in petty thievery and bestial drunkenness. Only when
the buscón denies his natural condition and attempts to usurp an unmerited position is he punished in the temporal world; however, even while he
is enjoying his greatest successes as a "bellaco," a far more rigorous judgment awaits him after death.

Although he boasts about the material comfort resulting from his clever
and dishonest actions, Pablos sees himself only in terms of what others
think of him. As he is traveling toward Alcalá with don Diego, he observes
how a group of "bellacos" flatter and cajole his master into paying for their
dinners. When they arrive at Alcalá, Pablos is subjected to two revolting
initiations at the hands of "bellacos"—students who spit all over him and
servants who beat him and defecate in his bed. In each of these three cases,
"bellacos" pretend to be genuinely interested in befriending an appointed
victim in order to manipulate him for their own profit or amusement.
Pablos gains insight into this situation when he overhears the servants
laughing and joking about their part in his disgrace, and it is at this
moment that he decides, "'Haz como vieres' dice el refrán, y dice bien. De
puro considerar en él, vine a resolverme de ser bellaco con los bellacos, y
más, si pudiese, que todos" (74) ("'Do as you see others doing,' says the

proverb and says it well. By mere thinking about it, I resolved to be a rogue among rogues, and more roguish, if I could, than anyone else").

This decision permits him to both accumulate a small fortune and gain the approbation of others. For example, at one point he boasts about his cleverness in stealing a basket of raisins from a confectioner, but although his roguish companions appreciate his wittily told account of the affair, they don't believe his story. To convince them of his audacity and cleverness, he invites them to watch him perform another theft in the same shop. He shouts "Die," thrusts his sword next to the confectioner, and impales a box of sweets which he parades triumphantly in front of the admiring rogues while the uninjured shopkeeper, who believes himself to have been mortally wounded, lies moaning on the floor. The material profit from such a ruse is insignificant; the important thing is the approval of the onlookers. He himself admits that their praise prompted him to continue in this vein. "Yo, como era muchacho y oía que me alababan el ingenio con que salía destas travesuras, animábame para hacer muchas más" (84) ("I, being a young boy and hearing the cleverness of my tricks praised, stirred myself to do many more of them"). Thus, a mode of life which he had originally adopted as a means of protecting himself against further humiliation becomes a habitual pattern of immoral behavior, because his clever ruses and thefts are always rewarded with material wealth, the admiration of others, and the psychologically satisfying illusion that he is the master and not the victim of circumstances.

Pablos' happiness remains almost totally contingent upon the approval of others. From the beginning of his autobiography, he uses locutions of attribution like "dicen que" ("they say that"), "como todos dicen" ("as everyone says"), "malas languas daban en decir" ("evil tongues began to say"), "hubo fama que" ("it was well known that"), "unos la llamaban" ("some called her") and "sospechábase en el pueblo que" ("in the town people suspected that") in order to substantiate descriptions of his parents' disreputable activities. Even as a child, he seems to have been extremely sensitive to gossip; in fact, the impulse to reject his parents' vocations stems largely from a desire to dissociate himself from them and their bad reputations. When he parades as a caballero, he is seeking the advantages of a good reputation, but as he discovers in Alcalá, the acceptance of others can also be obtained by acting roguishly. In writing his memoirs for Vuestra Merced, he is trying to follow both paths at the same time. By manipulating language and turning everything into a joke, he hopes to entertain someone who could satisfy his ambition to see himself among caballeros, but he is also exercising the roguish wit which permitted him to enjoy wealth, reputation, and a sense of control over circumstances during his student days at Alcalá.

However, for readers who accept Quevedo's traditional values, the ultimate absurdity of these goals is mirrored in Pablos' own psychological reality, the very reality which distorts the perspective from which his own life is seen and judged. Because the buscón attaches supreme importance to earthly vanities and treats others as dehumanized objects to be manipulated for his own pleasure or profit, he fails to recognize the truth about himself and the potential humanity of others. Assuming that he is justified in doing anything which enriches him, enhances his reputation, or gives him pleasure, he deceives others when they possess something which he desires and flees from them when they threaten to unmask him. For example, in the "colegio buscón" episode, Pablos combines his roguish instincts and his noble pretensions by associating himself with a group of false caballeros who utilize deception and flattery to sustain noble façades while perpetrating ingenious confidence tricks upon unsuspecting people. The members of this pseudorespectable society are called "hermanos" (brothers), but when Pablos gains their confidence by contributing to the common treasury, he is actually disobeying their rules, because he withholds most of his money from them and eventually uses it to free himself from the fate inflicted upon them when the entire "colegio buscón" is arrested and thrown in jail. But whether Pablos is parading through town in his meticulously arranged rags or appearing to share his entire wealth with the "brothers," his relationship with others is predicated upon his attempt to project a self-image quite different from his true nature, and as long as he maintains this attitude, his life will be one of anxiety and solitude. Every mask will be torn from him; authentic communication, compassion, and community will be impossible; and everything he attains will prove valueless.

While developing this satiric portrait of a pícaro or buscón, Quevedo employed a technique exploited with consummate artistry in *Lazarillo*— the ironic reversal of meaning in words commonly associated with honor and religion. In *El Buscón*, Pablos and the other characters are continually trying to cloak themselves in respectable appearances, and Quevedo's ironically reversed terms constitute an important part of their hypocritical masquerades. Because the words themselves are code words signifying the absence or perversion of qualities with which they are generally associated, Quevedo was also subtly commenting upon a general disregard for truly noble and Christian values and a widespread debasement of language in which words no longer meant what they were commonly assumed to mean.

Throughout *El Buscón* there are repeated references to religious objects and practices, but without exception they are seen through the distorting perspective of Pablos' mentality. As a consequence, religion is always presented in physical rather than spiritual terms. Within the context of Quevedo's ideological assumptions, a converso like Pablos (or, by extension, Guzmán) could not escape the blemish of his Jewish origins. Thus, when he leaves his uncle a highly offensive letter in which he announces his desire to "negar la sangre que tenemos" ("deny the blood which we have in common"), he is engaging in what Quevedo must have considered an impossible undertaking. As a child in Segovia and as a student in Alcalá, Pablos publicly taunts New Christians with witticisms aimed at exposing the futility of their attempts to conceal their converso origins.[16] Assuming that he will be judged as a wit, Pablos overlooks a fact apparent to both Quevedo and Vuestra Merced: Pablos is mocking others for the folly of what he himself is doing. His jests at the expense of Ponce Aguirre or the "morisco" innkeeper are based upon his recognition of their attempts to conceal the truth about themselves, and yet Pablos himself is involved in a never-ending flight from his own converso origins.

In the Cabra and "colegio buscón" episodes, this incorrigible converso is introduced to a religion compounded of starvation and hypocrisy. Cabra himself is a "clerigo" (clergyman) who wears a cassock and a biretta; he sermonizes upon the virtue of temperance, brotherhood, and thrift, but his very speech is "ética," which means consumptive as well as ethical and suggests both his own fast-approaching death and the emptiness of his words. Under the tutelage of this antipriest, Pablos and don Diego partake of an eternal meal—eternal not because it provides spiritual food for their eternal souls, but because it is simply nonexistent, having neither beginning nor ending. The stomachs of the two boys seem to have been excommunicated, and after don Diego's father removes them from their purgatory, they eat instead of fasting during the forty days of Lent. The entire episode is based upon the ironic reversal of religious terminology: Cabra's name signifies goat (i.e., devil) and he conducts his disciples toward hunger and physical death rather than salvation and spiritual life. Because he values insignificant economies above life itself, he continues to pursue selfish, materialistic goals while remaining blind to the death which he is bringing upon himself and which actually occurs while Pablos is at the University of Alcalá.

During the "colegio buscón" episode, the brothers are referred to as "sacerdotes" (priests) who say an "oración" (prayer) as they don their vestments. After pretending to donate his fortune for the good of the community, Pablos himself becomes a "misacantano" (priest saying his first mass) who is introduced to his "diócesi" (diocese) by a "padrino" (pater spiritualis, an older priest who serves as the spiritual father and guide of a younger one). Like Cabra, however, the members of the "colegio buscón" actually practice a religion of hunger and deprivation. Don Toribio admits that they take great pains to avoid infringing upon each other's territory, because stomachs "andan . . . en celo" (are jealous). However, the phrase "en celo" suggests not only jealousy, but also devotion or piety, although it can also be used to describe an animal in heat. If stomachs are "in heat," they are ravenously hungry. Thus, by means of an ingenious, many-layered pun, religious belief is equated with hunger. Later, when Pablos expresses concern for the fate of his stomach, a street-corner vendor accuses him, "poca fe tienes con la religión y orden de los caninos" (176) ("you have little faith in the canine religion and its orders"). The word "canino" does refer to "dog," but it is also a slang term for extreme hunger, and just as he finally escapes from Cabra's "religious instruction," he eventually flees from the "brothers" in the "religious order" of the "colegio buscón."

But in fleeing from a religion of hunger and physical deprivation, Pablos abandons himself to a worldly faith in material wealth and brutish, animal pleasures, despite the fact that he describes his perverse religion in the same terms as those used by genuine practitioners of the true Catholic faith. Even the rosary and the sacraments take on ironically reversed meanings for him. Many brothers in the "colegio buscón" sport rosaries as part of their disguises, but like Pablos' mother and all the old-crone figures who resemble her, they are carrying rosaries not to indicate an authentic piety, but to deceive others and eventually dupe them. Always mentioned in conjunction with thieves, prostitutes, and witches, the rosary in *El Buscón* is a sign of false religion—a religion of selfish, materialistic goals.

Similarly, the communion becomes an ironically reversed ceremony in which Pablos symbolically accepts his own vulgar identity and repudiates all spiritual values. Although he refuses to participate in the anticommunion conducted by his Uncle Ramplón, he later wholeheartedly receives

Fig. 11. Jacques Caillot's "Beggar with Rosary,"
reflecting a principal motif in the "colegio buscón"
section of Quevedo's *El Buscón*

the bread and wine offered by the Sevillian thugs. At Ramplón's party,
bread is called the image of God, wine is consumed in great quantities,
and the meat pies are reputed to contain morsels of Pablos' recently executed father. Ramplón's companions asperge the meal with holy water and
recite a responsory from the requiem mass. In a parallel scene near the end
of the book, Matorral (the leader of the Sevillian thugs) refers to his bread
as the face of God and swears by it that the group should kill a policeman.
The perversion of the sacraments is complete when the other thugs lean
over the wine trough, drink, and pledge him their support. Just as
Ramplón's feast degenerates into a revolting cannibalism, the bread and

wine of the Sevillian thugs is transformed into an act of murder. In both instances, the sacramental wine deadens men's faculties and reduces them to their lowest, most bestial level. But whereas Pablos had rejected the embrace of Ramplón's friends, watered his wine, and mocked the vulgarity of his uncle, he welcomes the embrace of the Sevillian thugs, quaffs a half-gallon of wine, and goes down on his hands and knees to join the others at the wine trough. During the drunken festivities in Segovia, he had helped a "corchete" (policeman, constable) to his feet, but in Seville he assists his new brothers in murdering two "corchetes." By choosing to participate in this second anticommunion, Pablos acknowledges his resemblance to the disreputable Ramplón and acquiesces in a life of sin and degradation; he transforms the sacramental bread and wine into vehicles which impart spiritual death, not salvation.[17]

If Pablos' religion is actually a type of irreligion, his honor is a type of dishonor. According to Quevedo's world view, an authentic nobleman inherits a sense of honor and identity from his forebears. Lacking any such legacy in real terms, Pablos sets out to obtain the superficial appearance of it. When he learns about the death of his own parents and informs don Diego, he boasts, "si hasta ahora tenía como cada cual mi piedra en el rollo, ahora tengo mi padre" (94) ("If until now I like anyone else had my seat in the gallery, I now have my father"). Intending to imply that he is moving toward a more noble destiny, Pablos inadvertently admits that his inherited honor consists of material wealth and a disreputable mode of life, because in this context, the word "father" serves as a synechdoche for his father's money and his father's example. In addition, the phrase "tener la piedra en el rollo" signifies not only having a seat in the gallery; it can also mean "to be a man of honor." Thus, if he is willing to abandon a "piedra en el rollo" in order to take possession of his "padre," he is actually confessing his willingness to renounce the principles of honorable men.

The suggestion that Pablos conceives of honor in material terms is strengthened when he admits, "habia menester tapar primero la poca [honra y virtud] de mis padres, y luego tener tanta, que me desconociesen por ella" (108–109) ("First I need to collect the small amount [of honor and virtue] possessed by my parents, and then have so much that people will fail to recognize me on account of it"). Later, in the company of the Sevillian thugs, he again quantifies his "honor" by toasting it and drinking large quantities of wine. It is in this manner that he proves himself truly worthy of his father, for like Clemente Pablos, the buscón measures the family honor in terms of dishonestly acquired wealth and the wine which induces his drunken, brutish excesses.

Nevertheless, Pablos wants others to respect him as they would respect a genuine caballero, but just as the rosary and the communion signify an ironically reversed religion, the nobleman's collar becomes a recurrent symbol of his ironically reversed honor. As don Toribio explains, people who see a collar don't need to suspect that there is no shirt beneath the coat. In terms of Pablos' own attempt to pass for a nobleman, the collar or outward appearance of a caballero never guarantees the substance of nobility; in fact, every time that a collar is mentioned in *El Buscón*, it designates not honor but dishonesty, moral corruption, and ludicrous pretentiousness. Pablos himself sports an elaborate collar to impress doña Ana, but while he is walking in the park it becomes snagged in a low-hanging tree branch, symbolically signaling the weakness in his masquerade and suggesting a further analogy between Pablos' fate and that of his condemned father, who had placed a collarlike noose around his own neck. The hypocrisy behind honorable appearances becomes even more obvious when a notary, who has just accepted a bribe to extricate Pablos from prison, implicitly associates the buscón's future freedom with the straightening of his collar, or when Pablos himself unhesitatingly turns down his respectable collar as a sign of his initiation into the brotherhood of Sevillian thugs. But the prisoners in the Toledo jail also wear collars around their rectums to discourage the importunities of homosexuals, and during his apprenticeship in the "colegio buscón," Pablos is told that he must revolve like a sunflower in order to always present the front of his collar to passersby. Linked with pretense, hanging, homosexuality, and the mechanical turning of a sunflower, the outward symbol of Pablos' honor thus represents the total absence of any genuine sense of honor.

By allowing Pablos to characterize himself through the use of these ironically reversed words and phrases, Quevedo was not undercutting the traditional values of Spanish society.[18] On the contrary, he was attempting to reaffirm their validity by showing how terms associated with the two most important sanctions of social respectability—honor and the true faith of Old Christians—were reduced to empty words in the common parlance. Although Pablos mocks Cabra's and don Toribio's false religion, his laughter ironically reveals a profound blindness toward the similarity between their worldly values and his own. If he does become a caballero, it is only by distorting the true sense of the word into its opposite, for he voluntarily joins the other "caballeros de rapiña" (preying gentlemen) in the "colegio buscón," and when he boasts about his own "industria" (ingenuity)—a quality which don Toribio had called the philosopher's stone of his fraternity—Pablos unwittingly acknowledges another affinity with his false brothers. Like them, he is a "caballero de industria" (confidence man)—the only sort of caballero which a vulgar individual like him could ever hope to become.

Alemán and the anonymous author of *Lazarillo* had portrayed pícaros as victims of the tragic dehumanization imposed upon them and people like them by the socializing process. By parodying the structures and basic assumptions of these novels and particularly *Guzmán*, Quevedo was implicitly defending his own traditionalist, elitist opinions and providing upper-class readers with a palatable alternative to earlier portrayals of the pícaro's dilemma in a corrupt society. Reduced to a type-figure whose every word and gesture reveals the hypocrisy and moral blindness of characters like Guzmán, Pablos is capable of amusing socially elite readers at the very moment they are condemning him as irrevocably vulgar. In fact, Quevedo's reaction against the sympathetic portrayal of rogues endowed *El Buscón* with form and meaning, for in parodying the morally serious pseudoautobiographical perspective and the idea of character as process, he projected his own world view into the picaresque myth, and it was this world view which molded the novel's isolated anecdotes and ingenious repartee into an artistically unified, intellectually provocative commentary upon pícaros and the picaresque life.

6

THE WANING OF
THE SPANISH PICARESQUE:
El diablo cojuelo
AND
Estebanillo González

By the middle of the seventeenth century, popular interest in themes of picaresque life had diminished considerably, although Castillo Solórzano's picaresque adventure novels continued to appear during the 1630's and 1640's. Against a background of social decadence and debilitating foreign wars, the leisure-class Spaniards for whom most picaresque novels had been written were turning to other types of fiction, but they constituted precisely the audience addressed in two final picaresquelike novels—Luis Vélez de Guevara's *El diablo cojuelo* (1641) and the anonymous *Vida y hechos de Estebanillo González: Hombre de buen humor* (1646).

The influence of Quevedo is particularly strong in Vélez's work, which is filled with puns, paradoxes, wordplays, extended metaphors, distortions of commonplace proverbs, and even explicit allusions to *El Buscón*.[1] With reductive techniques and aristocratic assumptions similar to those of his predecessor, Vélez exploited the panoramic possibilities of the picaresque format to present a gallery of caricatured fools and sinners, but unlike Quevedo, he did not reduce his picaresque hero don Cleofás to the level of a dehumanized clown. Perhaps because his own experiences and preoccupations were reflected in the characterization of his central character,[2] he portrayed Cleofás as susceptible to illusion but quite capable of perceiving his own follies and attaining wisdom. Earlier picaresque novels are specifically mentioned in *Estebanillo*,[3] where many of their principal themes recur. As in *Lazarillo*, a poor young boy leaves home, travels, experiences hunger, learns that he cannot survive by acting morally or honorably, and ultimately records his memoirs to project a favorable image of himself in the hope of receiving some benefit from a powerful superior. Presented as a success story, his autobiography actually reveals the process by means of which he succumbs to dehumanizing social pressures. It is possible that Estebanillo actually lived and wrote these memoirs,[4] but if that was the case, life was beginning to imitate art, for by defining himself in terms of literary precedent, the narrator would have been reviving the tragic and pathetic dimensions of the *Lazarillo-Guzmán* model in a genuine autobiography.

Despite the fact that *El diablo cojuelo* and *Estebanillo González* were written for aristocratic readers, they reflect quite different attitudes toward the prevailing value system. Vélez allowed the limping devil (a traditional folklore figure) to guide Cleofás through a dreamlike chaos in which characteristically distorted actions and physical traits stand for the mental states of people who are seeking to gratify an assortment of vain desires. Observing this panorama from a position of security while fleeing from the consequences of his own folly (a romantic attachment to an unworthy, deceitful woman), Cleofás ultimately attains a heightened awareness of himself, his world, and the genuine noble principles according to which he should act.[5] *Estebanillo González* also appears to reaffirm ideological assumptions of the dominant classes in Spanish society, but beneath the surface of an allegedly "true account" of his adventures, Estebanillo reveals how society perpetuates and institutionalizes one form of self-degradation, and his unabashed renunciation of stereotyped heroic poses allows him to expose the pseudovalues, idealistic myths, and appalling cruelty of the very people for whom he was ostensibly writing.[6] Thus, whereas Vélez followed Quevedo in reaffirming the validity of stoic detachment and genuine nobility in a world where traditional values had lost currency, Estebanillo suppresses the anxiety and loneliness of a wretched existence behind a mask of "good humor" and the illusion that his story is as entertaining as those of literary pícaros. Seeking protection and financial support from his social superiors, he cannot openly challenge their most cherished values and privileges, but like the narrating Lázaro, his very frame of mind is an indictment of the society which engendered him.

Divided into ten "trancos" to suggest the strides or bounds of the limping devil, *El diablo cojuelo* is structured around two interrelated attempts to elude pursuers. A student from Alcalá, Cleofás is fleeing from the civil authorities in Madrid, where a hypocritical prostitute, doña Tomasa, had lodged a complaint against him for having supposedly insulted her. Seeking refuge in an astrologer's garret, he discovers the limping devil imprisoned in a vial and liberates him. While Cleofás and his new companion travel toward Seville, doña Tomasa persuades one of her many lovers to help her find and take vengeance upon the offending student; at the same time, Satan designates a subordinate devil, Cienllamas, to recapture the mischievous limping devil. Although obscured by the dizzying montage of grotesque caricatures encountered by the fleeing companions, an underlying unity derives from Cleofás' movement toward a higher level of consciousness.

Just as Cleofás is fleeing from Tomasa and her dubious demands for justice, the limping devil is attempting to evade Cienllamas and assert his independence from Satan's authority. However, both flights are unsuccessful: Cienllamas apprehends the limping devil and Cleofás is arrested in Seville on the basis of a warrant which Tomasa had obtained in Madrid. In practical terms, a preexisting order is reestablished: the limping devil is returned to his subordinate position in the infernal hierarchy, and Cleofás, extricated from his captors by the limping devil's final ruse, again becomes a student. Nevertheless, Vélez' picaresque hero undergoes a considerable change between the beginning and the end of the novel. The limping devil has shown him a broad spectrum of human vice and folly, and he himself has begun to perceive the absurdity of his infatuation for Tomasa. As the themes of flight and panoramic vision coalesce into this heightened awareness, the book's unity of focus becomes clear.

One of the implied assumptions behind Cleofás' loss of illusions is his acceptance of the fact that a man's identity should be defined in terms of his place in a rigidly stratified society. As in *El Buscón*, commoners who feign nobility are subject to caricature, but a positive standard also emerges in *El diablo cojuelo*, where authentic noblemen are always portrayed in a favorable light. In the third tranco, false noblemen are parodied adjusting their masks in mirrors and shopping for respectable names and relatives, but in contrast to the vanity and hypocrisy of these unnamed fools, numerous idealized portraits of named aristocrats are also presented. By devoting laudatory encomiums to each of them, Vélez was undoubtedly currying favor with potential patrons, but he was also acknowledging traditional sanctions of respectability in an established social order. The book's third-person narrator even employs two prologues: one to mock and repudiate the judgment of vulgar "mosqueteros" (uncultivated, lower-class men who occupied standing places in the pit of the Madrid theater) and another to establish a bond of mutual understanding with upper-class, cultivated readers who possessed the wit and intelligence to appreciate the morally serious dimensions of his narrative.

Within the fictional world of *El diablo cojuelo*, Cleofás ultimately abandons a false, romanticized conception of himself as Tomasa's lover, and when he returns to Alcalá to complete his studies, he is described as "desengañado" (disabused of illusions). Insofar as he recognizes the transitoriness and confusion of the material world, the folly of pursuing earthly vanities, and the wisdom of respecting true nobility, he has understood the significance of his own apparently chaotic perceptions and experiences; he is approaching the level of awareness presumably shared by the narrator and his imagined readers. This is accomplished not by giving a complete account of Cleofás' life, but by concentrating upon a crucial episode in his moral and psychological development. Described at the beginning as a "galán de noviciado" (novice gallant), he holds stereotyped romantic ideas about love and defines himself in terms of a noble self-image.

Even his name—don Cleofás Leandro Pérez Zambullo—suggests the nature of his folly. In Luke 24:18, Cleofás is a follower of Christ. After the crucifixion, he meets his resurrected master. Failing to recognize Him, Cleofás naively asks if He is the only person to remain ignorant of the recent events in Jerusalem. Leandro (or Leander) is the legendary hero who risks his life each night by swimming the Hellespont to see his beloved Hero. Pérez is one of the most commonplace names in Spain, and Zambullo is derived from "zambullir" (hid, conceal oneself). Cleofás' name thus characterizes him as one who remains blind to the truth while seeing himself as the gallant hero in an idealized romance; in reality, he is no different from the many commoners who bear the name Pérez, and he is obliged to conceal himself from those who desire to punish him for his temerity in wooing Tomasa. When he first encounters the limping devil, this poor "estudiante de profesión" (professional student) has naive and sentimental ideas about the confusing, deceptive reality in which he is living.

Under the guidance of his supernatural companion, however, he begins to perceive what lies beyond appearances, beneath the roofs of the city, and behind the happy masks of Fortune's followers. Like Quevedo, Vélez portrayed the material world as illusory, ever-changing and arbitrary. Because society conditions people to persist in the pursuit of ephemeral goals, they are effectively blinded to the fact that wealth, reputation, and sensual pleasures can at any moment be lost or rendered meaningless by death. Selecting a single gesture or situation to represent a particular vice or folly, Vélez identified and condemned various forms of moral blindness: a hypocritical obsession with virginity is suggested both by an ugly old woman mixing potions to restore a maidenhead and by an elderly marquis furtively entering a commoner's house to deflower a young girl; a perverse desire for respectability is represented by a starving and homeless couple who refuse to part with an extravagantly luxurious carriage; a monomaniacal concern for material possessions is symbolized by a miser who spends each night inside his own money chest. Society itself is a human boiling pot, a turbulent sea, a constant battleground where all the participants are pursuing their own selfish schemes. Because they all regard everyone else as potential enemies, they deliberately raise dust clouds of fraud and lies to deceive others, but in the process, the arbitrariness of nature is intensified and even the smallest grain of truth is obscured. These dehumanized caricatures exist in a dreamlike reality where actions and gestures are transformed into symbolic, visualizable equivalents of the psychological states in which vice and folly are perpetrated. As the limping devil presents these people to Cleofás, the young student begins to recognize that beneath their masks they are "sabandijas racionales" (rational vermin) and it is this insight which constitutes his first step toward heightened self-awareness.

For this new awareness to be personally relevant, however, Cleofás must also acknowledge and renounce the folly to which he himself is subject. His own moral blindness is rooted in his attitude toward Tomasa, whom he calls a saint and adores with what he believes to be an ardent, romantic love; in reality, she is a "doncella chanflona" (counterfeit virgin), and the narrator intimates that Cleofás is being pursued for tasting fruits which many others had already enjoyed. Her name echoes the verb "tomar" (to take), and the reader is assured that she lives up to her name by taking as much as she can. Thus, Cleofás' infatuation renders him as blind as any of the absurd caricatures in the houses or streets of Madrid. From the beginning, the limping devil is obviously aware of Tomasa's hypocrisy, and he promises to reveal many things about her. In the second tranco, he removes the roof of her house and shows her dressed in a nightshirt to receive another lover; in Seville, he informs Cleofás that she and her new lover have recently arrived in the city. Upon both occasions, the passionate student is overcome by a desire to attack the unfaithful woman, but shortly before the second incident, he still anxiously looks for her reflection in the magical mirror with which his companion is showing him the main street of Madrid—"que todavía la tenía en el corazón, sin haberse templado con tantos desengaños" ("for he still held her in his heart, his ardor untempered by so many disillusionments").[7] Only when she leaves for the New World does he fully relinquish his romantic idealization of her and of his own role as her lover. By the end of the novel, he resigns himself to losing her, abandoning his folly and returning to his proper place in society. In essence, his picaresque journey is a maturation experience which allows him to perceive realities behind a world of illusory appearances.

None of this would have been possible if Cleofás had not allied himself with the limping devil. While attempting to elude his pursuers in Madrid, he is compared to a helpless shipwreck victim who is guided to salvation by a starlike light in the astrologer's garret. The imprisoned devil whom he finds there does extricate him from a physically dangerous situation, but he also provides the perspective from which the young student can penetrate deceptive appearances and accept the loss of his own illusions. By maintaining a safe distance between Cleofás and the panorama of vice and folly, the limping devil permits his companion to grasp the significance of what he perceives and judge it dispassionately, for despite the absurdity of Cleofás' infatuation for Tomasa, he clearly possesses the potential for wisdom. He, not his guide, draws conclusions from what they see, and he is the one who remarks that madness and war are everywhere. When the two of them contemplate the starry sky or observe the astrologer's funeral in the limping devil's mirror, it is Cleofás who comments upon God's grandeur and the vanity of earthly things. In liberating the limping devil and expressing a willingness to serve him, Cleofás is voluntarily subjecting himself to one part of his own personality, the mischievous part which plays practical jokes upon innkeepers and merchants; however, this is also the insightful part which penetrates the dust clouds of hypocrisy and deception. The two companions might even be regarded as complementary aspects of the same personality, for only when catalyzed by a mocking, perceptive spirit can the intelligent but naive young man acquire self-knowledge in a world of chaos and illusion.

In *Estebanillo González*, this same confusing, deceptive world reappears, but as in *Lazarillo*, it is no longer viewed and judged by an individual who fully believes in the traditional system of values according to which he must appear to live. The book's wealth of historically verifiable details suggests that seventeenth-century readers accepted it as an authentic autobiography, and this impression is heightened by the fact that it is dedicated to Octavio Piccolomini, who was the most powerful nobleman in the Spanish Netherlands at the time and could easily have suppressed it if he felt that his own name was being misused in a work of fiction. Events and geographical locations are accurately depicted, but Estebanillo himself is essentially a buffoon, willing to transform everything—even himself— into a joke. His memoirs are introduced as a "libro de chanzas" (joke book), although he exhorts people to read his jokes to the end, for they are mixed with truths. Addressing the same socially elite audience for whom he had previously rehearsed tales of cowardice, drunkenness, gluttony, and shame, he does not hesitate to stress the most ludicrous aspects of his own life; he even deforms them to enhance their comic potential. To hold himself up to the ridicule of his upper-class readers, Estebanillo needs a certain strength of personality, a cynical resilience in the face of reiterated degradation, and by telling what purports to be a true story, he clearly reveals how his adult mentality evolves during a series of dehumanizing interactions with an irrevocably corrupt society. While bartering his self-respect for the good will and money of his audiences, he is not merely an entertainer; he is also a human being who suffers pain and humiliation. It is perhaps a truism to assert that beneath the comic gestures of a clown lie intimations of sadness and anxiety, but this truism has seldom been more poignantly illustrated than in the pathetic story of Estebanillo González.

From the beginning of his career, Estebanillo's own predispositions incline him toward vulgar hedonism and petty crime. By the time he is fifteen years old, he has already swindled a succession of masters, sailed as a kitchen boy in an expedition against pirates, enlisted in the French and Spanish armies, and traveled through Italy, Spain, Portugal, and southern France. In recounting his early wanderings, he generally projects himself as a happy-go-lucky pícaro, altering his own mask to correspond with those of the people whom he encounters along the way—"con el alemán soy alemán; con el flamenco, flamenco; y con el armenio, armenio" ("with the German, I am a German; with the Fleming, a Fleming; and with the Armenian, an Armenian").[8] His thefts are portrayed as clever jokes, his gambling, gluttony, and drunkenness as enjoyable pastimes. By following his natural inclinations, however, Estebanillo develops habits, and these habits provide him with gratifications and defenses which become indispensable in his later attempts to cope with a harsh and cruel world. During the expedition against pirates, for example, he escapes the terrors of a storm by drinking himself into a stupor. Having learned that drunkenness allows him to maintain a gay and carefree attitude vis-à-vis a hostile or terrifying reality, he customarily turns to alcohol whenever he desires to avoid an awareness of painful or frightening situations. Whether he breaks an arm or learns that he has been condemned to death, whether he hears the approach of a hostile army or believes that a generous master is dying, his response is always the same. He becomes drunk, and in his drunkenness he can no longer be held responsible for confronting that which he fears.

This drunkenness allows Estebanillo to sustain his illusion of "buen humor" and momentarily forget his loneliness and anxiety, but society itself reinforces his predispositions and renders him a prisoner of his own habits. It is society which offers him a well-defined role in harmony with his habitual modes of behavior and encourages, almost requires, him to adopt it. Very early in his career, he learns to profit by turning himself into an object of ridicule. At one point during the expedition against pirates, a clever rogue defrauds him of money belonging to his master. Having suffered a beating for his temerity in threatening the fellow who cheated him, Estebanillo fears that he might receive another one at the hands of his master, but when he returns to the ship and relates the humorous story of his own gullibility, everyone laughs; the lost money is forgotten, and he himself escapes punishment. Later, after being sentenced to death for having accidentally killed a fellow soldier in Barcelona, he receives a pardon from the Cardinal-Infante, who had been amused by his jokes and humorous self-parodies. Despite the obvious advantages of being judged as an entertainer rather than as a kitchen boy or soldier, Estebanillo still hesitates to accept the role of buffoon; in fact, he explicitly rejects the Cardinal-Infante's offer to employ him in that capacity. Only after experiencing the fear of battle and the instability of several sutlery enterprises does he settle in Antwerp and accept the financial security of this socially sanctioned but humanly degrading position.

Because buffoons are not judged according to traditional moral standards, Estebanillo no longer needs to conduct himself honorably. No one will blame him for turning his back upon a battlefield, losing his sutler's wagon, or arriving late with a royal message; quite the contrary, many of his most shameful actions will be recompensed with money and the protection of powerful masters, who reward him not for fighting bravely or delivering messages promptly, but for making them laugh. By providing the social and economic sanctions which render the clown's role attractive, society reinforces Estebanillo's natural inclinations toward drunkenness and practical joking, but when he is swept almost without realizing it into the chaos and confusion of the Thirty Years' War, he continues to repudiate what respectable men would consider to be a morally responsible attitude toward life. Supposedly the soldier's duty demands that he fight bravely in the defense of patriotic ideals, but inclination and social conditioning have caused Estebanillo to value wine, good food, and wit above heroism, and he feels no qualms about parodying "pious Aeneas" or boasting that "mi gusto es mi honra" ("my pleasure is my honor").[9] To survive in an environment dominated by brutality, hypocrisy, and death, he temporarily becomes a soldier, sutler, or royal courier, but for him the myths which sustain men in these social roles are false; life is more important than honor.

If buffoonery represents the only social role which corresponds to Estebanillo's temperament, it also provides him with an appropriate mode of expression for a highly developed entrepreneurial instinct. Nearly everyone in his world feigns allegiance to the accepted values—honor, religion, heroism—but Estebanillo knows that most people are motivated by self-interest and that those who have money obtain what they desire. Like Lázaro, Estebanillo recognizes the rules of the game and decides to adopt them. Early in life, he learns to buy things cheaply and sell them dearly. As a buffoon, he is reducing himself to a ludicrous object and selling it for its amusement value. In both Antwerp and Vienna, he risks his own capital to stage carnival skits, and on each occasion he receives large tips or "baratos" for having amused his noble patrons. In monetary terms, his investments yield an excellent return.

In human terms, however, his relationships with others become little more than business transactions. His noble patrons are not fellow human beings but potential sources of income, and he even develops a rudimentary social philosophy which justifies his right to accept their gifts: " . . . el ser señores no consiste en la nobleza del solar ni en la grandeza del título, sino en dar muestras de serlo, ayudando a los desvalidos y favoreciendo a los que poco pueden, y honrando generalmente a todos; que para no hacer esto, poco me importa a mí ni a nadie que sean grandes o que sean pequeños" ("Being a nobleman doesn't consist in the nobility of the house or the magnificence of the title, but in giving signs of being noble, succoring the helpless, protecting those who can do little and in general honoring everyone; for if they don't do this, it makes little difference to me or anyone else whether they are great or small").[10] Throughout his memoirs, Estebanillo repeatedly distinguishes between "grandes" and "pequeños," always implying that the former have an obligation to demonstrate their nobility by bestowing tangible signs of it upon others. Including himself among the "pequeños," he concludes that "mi oficio es de recibir, y no de dar" ("it is my business to receive and not to give").[11] Wealthy patrons make sport of him for their amusement, but he is also exploiting them for his profit. If he can convince himself that his self-esteem is engaged not in what he does or says but only in the amount of money which he receives, he can even respect himself as long as he continues to obtain substantial "baratos."

The same motivations which impel Estebanillo to practice buffoonery prompt him to write his autobiography. Tired of the many different roles which he has played (he lists eighty-three of them in the verse prologue), he wants to retire to Naples and open a gambling casino, but he needs the favor and financial backing of an influential patron if he hopes to realize his dream. For this reason, he dedicates his memoirs to Piccolomini, who as Duke of Amalfi exercises political authority in Naples. As a former master of the buffoon, Piccolomini could be expected to have some sympathy for the project, and Estebanillo plays upon this sympathy. Nearly everything in his autobiography is calculated to justify his appeal for sponsorship and money. He reiterates his contention that noblemen should give to the "pequeños" of this world, and he acknowledges a desire to please the entire nobility; as for himself, he only desires "cosa justa" (that which is just). Thus, willing to describe behavior which most people would be ashamed to admit, he encourages his noble readers to regard him as an object of amusement, because he is more concerned with obtaining his "barato" than projecting himself as an honorable or admirable man.

But Estebanillo's mask occasionally slips, revealing a profound sense of pathos behind his superficial good humor. Having renounced any claim to honor in the traditional sense, he implicitly licenses his patrons to humiliate and hurt him in return for their "baratos." He endures the disgrace of being accoutered in deer's antlers and paraded through the streets of Brussels, and he suffers the anxieties of a mock castration, because he realizes that such dramas reflect the caprices of gentlemen and are the price which those of his profession must pay; however, despite his apparent insouciance and the buffoon's exemption from any obligation to act in a morally responsible fashion, Estebanillo is not completely immune to the suffering and humiliation inflicted upon him. On one occasion, several courtiers denigrate his poetry as the product of a lower-class mentality, and he cannot refrain from pointing out that poor and humble people have the same human faculties as noblemen; the implication is, of course, that he too is capable of comprehending the truth and writing about it. Occasionally he himself admits the intensely personal significance of what is happening to him. When he believes that he is about to be executed or castrated, he momentarily becomes serious and perceives life in terms of his own inevitable death. When the friends of his prosperity abandon him in a time of need, he is obliged to recognize his utter loneliness. Usually he attempts to repress such insights, but he cannot completely overlook them, for they continually intrude upon his consciousness and breed a sense of anxiety within him.

During the final pages of his autobiography, Estebanillo becomes increasingly aware of the inherent instability of life. After an absence of twelve years, he returns to Naples and notices that young women have aged, former companions have died and even the city is no longer the same. As usual, he drinks heavily to avoid recognizing the meaning of what he sees, but upon this occasion he cannot escape a fear that he might be condemned to poverty and misery as he grows older; he himself admits that the thought of death is responsible for the melancholy tone of his concluding remarks. In the light of such comments, it is evident that Estebanillo is susceptible to human sentiments of fear and loneliness, although his own inclinations and the requirements of his social role make it impossible for him to take solace in the pity and understanding of others. Having acquiesced in a role which denies his humanity, he remains trapped in that role. He might desire to escape an awareness of death, loneliness, and mutability, but his entire autobiographical enterprise is undertaken to justify his request that Piccolomini support his plans to establish a Neapolitan gambling casino—the epitome of arbitrariness and mutability. Hoping to enjoy material wealth in serenity, Estebanillo ironically believes that his salvation lies in a profession which symbolizes the very fate he is so pathetically attempting to escape.

As in *Lazarillo* and *Guzmán*, *La desordenada codicia* and Luna's *Segunda parte*, *Estebanillo* reflects the assumption that character is formed or deformed in an interaction between the self and the external world. In Vélez' *El diablo cojuelo*, Cloefás ultimately recognizes and accepts his relatively low place in the social hierarchy; his maturation experience gives him a heightened awareness of his own nature. In *Estebanillo González*, the narrator's mentality results from an assimilation of dehumanizing behavior patterns practiced by the majority of people who proclaim their continuing attachment to honor, religion, and patriotism. Like Lázaro, Estebanillo desires material and psychological security, and the perverted mentality which derives from his pursuit of them constitutes a powerful indictment of society.

Before completely losing its vitality in Spain, the picaresque tradition yielded two final variations upon the *Lazarillo-Guzmán* model. Both were written for upper-class readers, but whereas *El diablo cojuelo* reaffirmed a traditionalist world view similar to that expressed in *El Buscón*, *Estebanillo González* implicitly adopted the idea of character as process. Like *Lazarillo*, it revealed the hypocrisy and cruelty of a society which conditions lower-class wandering characters to regard their own disgraces as salable commodities and to accept the resultant dehumanization as the legitimate price of survival—a society which encourages them to flee from themselves to avoid perceiving the falsity and sterility of their lives. Nearly one hundred years after the appearance of the first Spanish picaresque novel, the tradition itself had lost the vigor which it enjoyed at the midpoint of its Golden Age, but at the very moment of its decline, a novel purporting to be a genuine autobiography reinvigorated the socially critical perspective which had largely disappeared in works influenced by the *Lazarillo-Guzmán* model but written in conformity with upper-class tastes and ideological assumptions.

7

TRANSLATIONS
&
TRANSITIONS

By the mid-1640's when the last picaresque novels were appearing in Spain, *Lazarillo*, *Guzmán*, *El Buscón* and other works in the tradition had already been translated into most of the major European languages, although in foreign contexts they would be variously presented as jest books, language-instruction manuals, edifying tracts, comic novels, and criminal autobiographies. These translations imparted decisive impulses to French, English, and German novelists, whose works in turn became intimately linked with them. During this process of adaptation and assimilation, original texts were radically altered to bring them into conformity with indigenous literary conventions and world views, but in each country, works associated with the picaresque tradition contributed to breaking down the traditional separation of styles and establishing the legitimacy of considering vulgar characters as appropriate subjects for morally serious literary treatment. In a very real sense, they helped to shape the socio-literary context from which *Simplicissimus*, *Moll Flanders*, *Gil Blas*, and *Roderick Random* later emerged.

A gradual process, the transformation of the Spanish picaresque passed through many different guises, but even in the earliest translations of *Lazarillo* a modifying tendency was evident. Rendered into French by Jean Saugrain in 1560, the anonymous little novel also appeared in four different sixteenth-century English translations. The best and most popular of them was written by David Rowland of Anglesy in 1586. In Germany an accurate manuscript translation existed by 1614, but it was never published, and when *Lazarillo* became available to German readers three years later, it was in the form of another, less reliable version, which was bound together with Nicolas Ulenhart's *Die kurzweilige lustige und lächerliche Histori... von Isaak Winkelfelder und Jobst von der Schneid*, a free adaptation of Cervantes' *Rinconete y Cortadillo*.[1] Binding *Lazarillo* together with the "amusing, merry, and ludicrous" story of two rogues living in Prague

THE PLEASANT HISTORY OF

LAZARILLO de TORMES a Spaniard, wherein is contained his marvellous deeds and life.

With the strange adventures happened to him, in the service of sundry Masters.

Drawne out of Spanish by *David Rowland* of *Anglesey*.

The Third Edition, corrected and amended.

Accuerdo, Oluido.

LONDON,

Printed by *E.G.* for *William Leake*, and are to be fold at his shop in Chancery Lane, neere the Rols. 1639:

The Blinde Man.

Lazarillo.

Here i *Lazarillo's* birth and life,
His wily feats and honest wife,
With his feven mafters fhall you find,
Expreffing Spanyards in their kind

Fig. 12. Frontispiece and title page of an early English edition of *Lazarillo*

must have encouraged German readers to regard the anonymous novel as a witty collection of jokes in the tradition of *Till Eulenspiegel*. Saugrain and Rowland had attempted to cultivate the same impression when they assured their readers that the little book possessed a salutary power to banish melancholy. The title page of Saugrain's version actually characterizes it as the "fort plaisant et délectable" ("highly amusing and delightful") account of "gentil Lazare," whose story contains "faits merveilleux, . . . terribles avantures, . . . actes notables et propos facecieux" ("marvelous things, . . . terrible adventures, . . . notable deeds and jests").[2] As in early seventeenth-century Spanish editions, *Lazarillo* was presented to English, French, and German readers as a type of comic entertainment, a sophisticated jest book.

However, Saugrain and Rowland also suggested another reason for reading *Lazarillo*, when they asserted that it contained an instructive and accurate description of Spain. Probably working from Saugrain's translation, Rowland dedicated his "Pleasaunt Historie" to Sir Thomas Gresham, who would supposedly learn about "the nature and disposition of sundrie Spaniards" without having to inconvenience himself by visiting their country.[3] Like most people, Englishmen and Frenchmen tended to think of foreigners in terms of stereotyped images, and *Lazarillo* must have reaffirmed their preconceived notions about Spaniards, whom they invariably associated with excessive pride and a refusal to do manual work. One of the later French translations of *Lazarillo* even contained an introduction which contends that "tous les Espagnols sont de mesme, & mourront plustost de faim que de se mettre en quelque mestier" ("all Spaniards are the same and would rather die of hunger than take up some trade").[4] Those who relied upon comic works like *Lazarillo* for their impressions of Spanish manners and social conditions undoubtedly received a rather distorted picture of the country, but in the context of periodic hostilities with the Hapsburg monarchy, that was exactly the image which many French and English readers desired to cultivate.

Although Saugrain's translation was the first known version of *Lazarillo* to conclude with the opening chapter of the apocryphal 1555 Anvers continuation, it is probable that the French translator based his inclusion of the episode upon a lost Spanish edition.[5] Both William Phiston's English translation (1596) and the published German version follow the same practice, which tends to obscure the ironic symmetry of the central character's rise in society and decline in integrity. If Lázaro concludes his story with an account of his drunken escapades in the company of German soldiers, it becomes easier to view him as an insouciant, jovial storyteller than as the tragic victim of dehumanizing pressures in a corrupt society. In the German translation, the first tratado is divided into nine chapters and the episode with the soldiers becomes the twenty-eighth and final chapter. In this version, the anticlimactic final section serves an additional purpose, for by destroying the impression that Lázaro has succeeded in the world, it encourages readers to interpret the superficially entertaining story as an illustration of inconstancy and the vanity of earthly things. Like the 1573 "Lazarillo castigado" upon which it was based, the 1617 German translation was purged of all anticlerical allusions and puns upon the sacraments; the monk and pardoner episodes, the prologue and the addresses to Vuestra Merced are omitted; the archbishop becomes an elderly squire, or "Juncker zu Toledo," and even the chaplain for whom Lazarillo works as a water-seller is transformed into a shopkeeper. By removing all traces of satire against the Church, the translator made it possible to interpret *Lazarillo* as an orthodox Counter-Reformation narrative.[6]

Just as this German *Lazarillo* was linked with jest books like *Till Eulenspiegel*, Saugrain's version of the novel undoubtedly appealed to French readers as a particularly clever way of stringing together the humorous content and satiric commentary which they associated with indigenous collections of comic tales or "facetie" (jests), but it was in England where a widespread curiosity about low-life and criminal behavior coalesced with an impulse toward longer, more coherent prose structures to produce the first picaresquelike novels outside of Spain. Joke books like *Skoggin's Gests* (1567) and Skelton's *Merry Tales* (1566–1567) resemble *Lazarillo* in echoing traditional folklore anecdotes. The plays and cony-catching pamphlets of Nicholas Breton, Henry Chettle, Robert Greene, and Thomas Dekker contain rogue-heroes and low-life scenes. Idealized characters like the artful Long Meg of Westminster and Thomas Deloney's shrewd Jack of Newburie are capable of playing "merry pranks," but they are also identified with virtue and patriotism; Long Meg steals from the rich to give to the poor and so distinguishes herself at the Battle of Boulogne that Henry VIII grants her a pension, whereas honest Jack of Newburie equips a regiment at his own expense and proves his bourgeois integrity by refusing an offer of knighthood.

But the only English novel to approach the complexity and artistic unity of *Lazarillo* was Thomas Nashe's *Jack Wilton, or the Unfortunate Traveler* (1594). Appearing four years after Rowland's popular translation, *Jack Wilton* portrays a wandering protagonist who acts as a foil to the absurdities of supposedly "respectable" people. Nashe maintained the autobiographical perspective of a facetious, tongue-in-check narrator, but his picaresque hero is more of an idealized rogue than a lower-class victim of a hypocritical social order. Born a gentleman and educated as a page in the court of Henry VII, Wilton leaves the king's service to become a soldier of fortune and travel on the continent with the earl of Surrey. Eventually he returns to England with fame, wealth, and a beautiful wife. Throughout his adventures, he never loses his self-esteem, and his world never punishes him for presuming to kidnap a countess or impersonate his noble master. It is probable that the cosmopolitan Nashe knew *Lazarillo* in either the original text or in one of the extant translations; in fact, there must have been a general familiarity with the blind-beggar episode, for Shakespeare alluded to it or an incident based upon it in *Much Ado About Nothing* (1598).[7] Despite essential differences in the characterization of Lazarillo and Jack Wilton, late sixteenth-century English readers undoubtedly placed their fictional autobiographies in the same category of humorous literature; they wanted witty, entertaining stories, and that is what they apparently found in *Lazarillo* and *The Unfortunate Traveler*.

Outside of Spain, *Guzmán* too was appreciated as an entertaining narrative, but its value as a compendium of knowledge and as a philosophical treatise was not overlooked. One of the characters in the dialogue *Quaternio or a Fourefold Way to a Happie Life* (1633) by Thomas Nash ("Philopolites") takes the novel with him when he wants to "spend an houre merrily," although he also implies that there is much wisdom to be gained from it.[8] Within a year of its original publication in Spain, the first French translation of *Guzmán* had already been published by the royal secretary-interpreter Gabriel Chappuys, who was also responsible for French versions of the most important chivalric and pastoral romances. A few years later Barèzzo Barezzi issued a popular Italian translation, *Vita del picaro Gusmano d'Alfarace* (Part I, 1606; Part II, 1615), which influenced the style and the explanatory notes in many later English, German, and French editions.

The first of these was the drastically altered *Der Landstörtzer Gusman von Alfarache oder Picaro genannt* (1615) by the extraordinarily prolific Aegidius Albertinus, a Jesuit priest, court librarian, and secretary to the elector of Bavaria. Most of Albertinus' fifty-two known publications are either translations or encyclopedic compilations in the tradition of Vincent de Beauvais, but whether he was dealing with fact or fiction, his goal remained the same: he was a popularizer seeking to convince readers that an acceptance of orthodox Counter-Reformation dogma constituted the only true path to salvation.[9] For him, Alemán's novel provided the raw material for an argument in favor of his own theological position, and he felt no compunctions about omitting the original author's name from the title page or radically altering its structure to emphasize the impossibility of attaining salvation without the mediation of Catholic priests, doctrines, and sacraments. Whereas it is possible for Alemán's pícaro to achieve grace and independently become an "atalaya" of human life, Albertinus' Gusman cannot do so until he has received religious instruction from a representative of the church and symbolically accomplished the traditional three stages in the sacrament of confession—contrition, confession, and penitence.[10]

On the surface, Albertinus' theological assumptions resembled those of Alemán. In practice, they functioned in an entirely different manner. Orthodox Catholic doctrine and the experiences of an alienated outsider provided Alemán with rational arguments and specific examples to defend his underlying contention that a converso had as much right to existence and salvation as an Old Christian. In Albertinus' novel, the process is reversed. The sinful activities and reformation of a rogue are followed by the rational arguments of a priest. Together the narrative and the sermons culminate in Gusman's increased awareness, but within the context of Albertinus' assumptions, this heightened awareness implies a willing subordination to the legitimate authority of church and state.

To emphasize the necessity of obedience and illustrate the doctrine of "justification by works," Albertinus divided the novel into two sections. Besides new episodes set in Germany, Switzerland, and Austria, the first of these sections contains events taken from Alemán's Part I, Martí's apocryphal continuation, and Albertinus' own imagination. After a peripatetic career as innkeeper, pimp, usurer, merchant, novice in a Benedictine monastery, and itinerant actor, Albertinus' Gusman is sentenced to death for stealing, but when the queen intervenes to save him, he confesses and takes the sacraments. Alemán's interpolated tales and sermonizing digressions are omitted from this section, and the narrative itself is not told from a retrospective autobiographical perspective, for that would imply that the lower-class hero could understand the meaning of what he was relating and could therefore dispense with the instructions of a priest.

At the beginning of Part II, Gusman already recognizes the corruption of the world and regrets his past sinfulness. After three years in the galleys, he enters a forest, sits beneath a tree, and begins to contemplate what he has done and what he desires to do. At this moment a hermit speaks to him. Having detached himself from the pursuit of earthly vanities and attained a state of mind susceptible to the teachings of the church, Gusman has already undergone a religious conversion, but a conversion out of fear is not sufficient, and for that reason, the entirety of Albertinus' second section is devoted to Gusman's religious education—a series of sermons delivered by the hermit. By acknowledging his transgressions, regretting them, and receiving the priest's instructions, the "Landstörtzer" (vagabond, rogue) completes the first and second stages in the sacrament of confession. When he voluntarily offers to undertake a pilgrimage to Jerusalem as a penitence for his sinful life, he is promising to accomplish the third and final stage.

The division of *Gusman* into separate narrative and didactic parts emphasizes the role of the church in guiding men toward salvation, but the narrative itself also has several levels of allegorical significance. Writing in a tradition which can be traced back to Biblical exegesis, Albertinus allowed the story of one man to stand for every man's journey through an inconstant and illusory world, the soul's progression through various stages of sinfulness, and the evolution of the earthly city during a state of corruption. On each level, salvation is possible, but only within the confines of the church.[11]

Albertinus never wrote the promised account of Gusman's voyage to the Holy Land, but his book went through five editions in seven years and soon became the standard German example of picaresque fiction. This popularity prompted Martin Freudenhold to publish his own Part III of *Gusman* (1626) in which the well-intentioned pilgrim reverts to his old sinful ways and travels through the Near and Far East, South America, and much of Europe before retiring to a hermitlike existence. The final sections are more like a compendium than a fictional narrative, for like Martí in Spain, Freudenhold introduced numerous descriptive essays into the text, often borrowing them verbatim from previous writers; in his case, Thomas Garzoni's encyclopedic *Piazza Universale, das ist: Allgemeiner Schauplatz* (1585; German translation, 1619) was undoubtedly the most important single source of materials. There is, of course, ample precedent for a tendency to exploit the picaresque format as a means of stringing together expository pieces; for example, Part II of *Gusman* consists almost entirely of sermons composed by Albertinus and placed in the mouth of the priest, but whereas his Gusman serves as the central figure in an orthodox religious allegory, Freudenhold's almost completely secular Gusman recedes into the background and becomes little more than a pretext for displaying the author's knowledge on a wide range of subjects.[12]

In France and England, translations of Alemán's novel retained a greater fidelity to the original. Chappuys' version had existed since 1600, although it was generally regarded as inferior, and in 1619 the learned private tutor and later academician Jean Chapelain published a more accurate translation. Shortly thereafter James Mabbe, a fellow of Magdalene College and a secretary who had spent three years in Spain, brought out a sophisticated English version called *The Rogue* (1622–1623). In his preface, Chapelain admitted that *Guzmán* could satisfy a lively contemporary interest in the vulgar activities of "gueux" (rogues), but he also stressed Alemán's inventiveness, the variety of his learning, the truth of his philosophy, and the appositeness with which he depicted widespread evil practices. Mabbe emphasized the same rhetorical and encyclopedic qualities of the novel, but he also encouraged readers to view *The Rogue* as a reliable source of information about the customs and language of Spaniards. He himself was in Madrid when Covarrubias' *Tesoro de la lengua castellana* (1611) appeared, and in translating *Guzmán*, he did not hesitate to appropriate phrases, proverbs, and explanatory notes from the famous dictionary. Sometimes he acknowledged his indebtedness. More often he did not. For example, desiring to impress English audiences with his command of the original language, he composed a Spanish introduction but neglected to mention that many of his sentences were taken verbatim from Covarrubias. Throughout the novel, Mabbe added new figures of speech and rendered images more explicit and concrete, but in amplifying Alemán's ideas, defining words, or suggesting English equivalents for *Guzmán*'s numerous proverbs, he generally had recourse to the *Tesoro* or one of John Minsheu's foreign-language dictionaries.[13] In the text and in marginal notes partially dependent upon those of Barezzi's Italian translation, Mabbe drew attention to peculiarly Spanish customs and religious practices. All this—the use of authoritative reference works, the inclusion of explanatory notes, the emphasis upon characteristic modes of behavior—contributed to the impression that *The Rogue* was an accurate picture of Spanish life.

To a Protestant translator writing for English Protestant readers, the ostensibly orthodox dogma of *Guzmán* presented a potentially serious problem, because Englishmen tended to regard the doctrines of "popery" with extreme distrust. Mabbe circumvented this objection by implying that despite doctrinal differences the most profound concerns of Alemán and the Catholic mystics—the denunciation of earthly vanities, the contemplation of death, the emphasis upon introspection as a path to spiritual knowledge—resemble those of Protestants; in other words, the Catholic world view is presented as the insightful portrayal of universally accessible truths.

The situation is somewhat different for the German version of Úbeda's *Justina*. *Gusman* and *Lazarillo* had been published in Catholic Southern Germany, and both of them had been reconciled with orthodox Counter-Reformation doctrine. But when the well-known Protestant publisher Johann Friedrich Weiss brought out the anonymously translated *Die Landstörtzerin Justina Dietzin Picara genandt* (1620), it is quite possible that he succeeded in deceiving Frankfurt's Catholic censors and producing a book which could be read as a parody of the Catholic church and its lives of saints.[14] Working from Barezzi's considerably modified *Vita della picara Giustina Diez* (1615), the translator used only the first part of his Italian model as the "marvelous" life of a shameless "Landstörtzerin" who claims to have wandered through all the valleys and mountains of life. *Justina Dietzin* probably appealed to German readers as a miscellaneous collection of proverbs, rules of conduct, and amusing fables. Whatever the reasons for its relative popularity, however, it was not, as its Spanish predecessor had been, a hieroglyphic allegory composed for the amusement of a social elite; on the contrary, it was a facetiously told story capable of being comprehended by middle-class Protestant readers.

The only Spanish Protestant writer of picaresque fiction was Luna, whose sequel to *Lazarillo* first appeared in France. By 1622 Luna had moved to England, where a translation of this continuation, *The Pursuit of the History of Lazarillo de Tormes*, became, after Mabbe's *Rogue*, the most popular Spanish picaresque novel to appear in a seventeenth-century English translation.[15] In 1653 Paul Kuefuss translated *Segunda parte* into German and published it together with the 1617 version of *Lazarillo*. Just as most seventeenth-century English and French translations of *Lazarillo* contained the *Segunda parte*, subsequent German editions almost invariably included Kuefuss' translation. In all cases, this practice tended to obscure the original book's symmetry and its underlying assumption that a pícaro's warped character could result from the dehumanizing social pressures to which he was subjected. This tendency was strengthened by Luna's emphasis upon the "arbitrariness of fortune" theme, but whereas the English and French translations retained Luna's implicit criticism of prevailing social and religious institutions, Kuefuss removed an antiec-clesiastical, antiestablishment bias from the continuation and encouraged readers to view Lázaro's experiences as allegorical representations of false paths to orthodox Catholic truths. Like Albertinus' *Gusman*, the Kuefuss *Lazarillo* acquires a significance nearly opposite that of the Spanish original, for it too is called upon to illustrate the validity of church doctrine and indirectly support the state which embraces that doctrine. From novels of social criticism, *Lazarillo* and *Guzmán* were thus transformed by German translators into conformist admonitions to avoid sinfulness and to distrust the transitoriness of earthly things.

That is not to say that Kuefuss' edition of *Lazarillo* was no longer read as a jest book. Like its French and English counterparts, it undoubtedly appealed to German readers for its humor as well as for its sexual es-capades and satirical attacks upon religious hypocrisy. Toward the end of the century, the English *Pursuit* was reissued as *The Witty Spaniard* and bound together with an anonymous sequel, *The Life and Death of Young Lazarillo* (1688).[16] The final anticlerical chapters of the *Pursuit* were omit-ted from this edition, and replaced by a third-person account of Lazaro's death and the misfortunes of his young son. The sequel is little more than a randomly organized collection of humorous anecdotes inspired by *Lazarillo*, *Guzmán*, *El Buscón*, *Don Quixote*, and other "comic" works. An inveterate thief and prankster, the young Lazarillo is a stereotyped carica-ture of the hapless victim. In an incident reminiscent of Quevedo's "king of the cocks" episode, he drowns ignominiously when his Rocinante falls into a "bottomless privy." By diluting Luna's social commentary and further obscuring the original work's complex structure, *The Witty Spaniard* succeeds in reducing the composite story contained in it and the *Pursuit* to the level of the jest books in comparison with which *Lazarillo* had once represented a distinct advance in narrative technique.

In this respect, the fate of Quevedo's *El Buscón* is even more curious than that of *Lazarillo* and *Guzmán*. It has been suggested that the Sieur de la Geneste who authored the French translation *L'Aventurier Buscon* (1633) was actually the young Paul Scarron,[17] but even more important than the identity of the translator is the transformation which he effected in the characterization and plot structure of Quevedo's novel. In response to a French taste which permitted, among other things, a greater latitude in the portrayal of sexual encounters, La Geneste reworked *El Buscón* and transformed it into the sentimental adventure story of a spirited young man who ultimately achieves happiness. The panorama of representative vices and follies remains an integral part of the novel, but Quevedo's satiric condemnation of the pícaro's vulgarity and presumptuousness completely disappears. Although the resultant novel bears little resemblance to the original, it must have appealed to the French book-buying public, for not only did it become the most popular of all Spanish picaresque novels in French translation, it was republished more often during the seventeenth century than the Spanish original from which it was adapted.[18]

La Geneste's hero was a protean but attractive and noble-souled rogue, and the popularity of the French *Buscon* must have encouraged similar interpretations of other Spanish pícaros. One of the characters in Charles Sorel's *Histoire comique de Francion* (1623, 1626, 1633) asserts that people in general took a great deal of pleasure in reading the adventures of vagabonds and rogues like Lazarillo and Guzmán.[19] When Corneille's *L'Illusion comique* was first performed in 1635, its action centered on the handsome, talented Clindor, who served as a charlatan, secretary, clerk, carnival entertainer, poet, writer of novels, and valet, before succeeding magnificently as an actor and finding happiness with the beautiful Isabelle. Near the beginning of the play, however, the young man's father is worried about him and engages a magician to discover the whereabouts of his son. The magician concludes an account of Clindor's many occupations by remarking, "Enfin, jamais Buscon, Lazarille de Tormes, Sayavèdre et Gusman ne prirent tant de formes" ("In short, neither Buscon nor Lazarillo, neither Guzman nor Sayavedra ever took so many forms").[20] Since Buscon and Clindor are attractive, successful adventurers and Corneille associated them with Lazarillo and Guzmán, it appears that a reinterpretation of the Spanish pícaro was beginning to occur in France.

To a large degree, this new conception of the picaresque hero arose from an assimilation of the Spanish novels into indigenous French traditions. The translator Vital d'Audiguier admitted that Spaniards might be superior to Frenchmen in contriving "histoires" (stories), but he criticized them for their impure style and proposed to cloak the Spanish picaresque in a style more appropriate for French readers.[21] In his *Bibliothèque françoise* (1667), Charles Sorel included translations of Spanish picaresque fiction in his chapter on "romans comiques" (comic novels), but he objected to them because their unheroic characters were not entirely suitable to French taste; he himself obviously preferred the entertaining adventures of generous and noble-spirited protagonists.[22] La Geneste's *Buscon* seems almost to constitute a direct response to this preference, and Sorel himself had

Fig. 13. Charles Sorel (Lasne)

suggested that translators compose "selon la raison et selon la coustume" ("according to reason and custom").[23] What he actually meant was that the good translator must find the golden mean between fidelity to the original and conformity to the taste of the people for whom he is writing. If French versions of Spanish picaresque novels were to be considered "romans comiques," they would have to follow the implicit criteria for this type of fiction, and that was precisely what happened in La Geneste's *Buscon*.

To a certain extent, such a transformation had already begun to take place in regard to *Guzmán*, which Chapelain described as "une satyre bien formée sur les pas de Luciā et d'Apulée en leur Asne d'or, et plus im-médiatement sur ceux de Lazarille de Tormes que a esté son prototype" ("a well-formed satire modeled upon Lucian and Apuleius in their *Golden Ass* and more directly upon *Lazarillo de Tormes* which was its immediate prototype").[24] A forerunner of Boileau, Chapelain viewed the translator's task as the transformation of one country's genius into an idiom which corresponded to the genius of another country; by integrating *Guzmán* into a long literary tradition of vulgar characters whose low-life adventures served partially as pretexts for presenting a varied mixture of entertaining shorter pieces, he was effectively placing it in the same category as Sorel later did in discussing comic novels. Like Chapelain, Sorel believed that popular language and vulgar subjects were compatible with morally seri-ous literature because they conveyed a sense of reality; in fact, he praised both the Spanish picaresque novels and the French comic novels for their treatment of commonplace subjects. "Les actions communes de la Vie estans leur objet, il est plus facile d'y rencontrer de la Verite." ("Their object being the common activities of life, it is easier to discover truth in them.")[25] Because Sorel considered an awareness of truth indispensable to any valid moral judgment, he was implicitly criticizing literary works in which it was not readily discernible.

For him, this stricture applied specifically to the dominant forms of literary expression in early seventeenth-century France—works in the classical, humanistic tradition (associated with the academy) and the less respectable but more popular romances. In particular, the pastoral, chival-ric, sentimental, historical, and heroic romances tended to trace the excit-ing adventures of ideally attractive heroes in imaginary realms. Their moral and philosophical idealism tended to preclude the "commonplace activities" which Sorel thought necessary; in fact, his own comic novel *Francion* in one sense represented a reaction against the pretentiousness, improbability, and artificiality of the romances. His efforts were not without precedent. He himself admired and translated the works of Cervantes, whose *Don Quixote* served him as a model for the depiction of less elevated situations, a greater closeness to nature, and the satirical treatment of people and previous literature which had lost contact with reality.

The erotic, often scabrous details, low-life episodes, satiric perspective and echoes of common speech in *Francion* could also be found in Rabelais, Villon, and Noël du Fail as well as in the "libelles" (lampoons, vulgar satires) and "histoires gauloises" (stories in a semipornographic, semigallant French mode) sold along the quais of the Seine in Paris. By the time that *Francion* was published, the financially hard-pressed Sorel had already written several minor works for this market, and the remarkable popularity of his first novel suggests that there was more than a grain of truth in his contention that the book was so frequently attacked because it contained that which people most fervently desired.[26] By the early 1620's, the mixture of styles and the exploitation of vulgar subjects characteristic of *Francion* were already present in John Barclay's popular Latin novel *Euphormion* (1603–1607), Du Souhait's compilation of *Histoires comiques* (1612), the anonymous *Histoire comique de Fortunatus* (1615), and Theophile de Viau's unfinished *Fragmens d'une histoire comique* (1623; published, 1632), but it was Sorel's *Francion* which established the comic novel and gained public acceptance for it.

In subsequent years, Du Bail's *Gascon extravagant* (1637) was presented as the French equivalent of a Spanish picaresque novel. Like the sentimentalized lower-class protagonist in Tristan L'Hermite's melancholy, semiautobiographical *Le page disgracié* (1643), the Gascon perpetrates clever ruses, experiences the vicissitudes of fortune and travels extensively, permitting the author to include a panoramic overview of characteristic human follies. Although Furetière's *Roman bourgeois* (1666) and the Sieur d'Ouville's translation of Castillo Solórzano's *La Garduña de Sevilla* evince definite affinities with this tradition, the last significant picaresquelike comic novel was Scarron's *Roman comique* (1651, 1657), which achieved an even more resounding success than *Francion*. Well-read in Spanish literature and like Sorel a fervent admirer of Cervantes, Scarron frequently borrowed materials from Salas Barbadillo, Castillo Solórzano, and María de Zayas. On one occasion he even facetiously signed himself "Lazarillo de Tormes" in a letter to a friend, and it is possible that the inspiration for his portrayal of strolling actors in the *Roman comique* derived from a reading of Rojas' *El viaje entretenido*.[27] But despite his acquaintance with Spanish literature, Scarron treated his noble-hearted picaresque hero Le

Destin more like Francion or Clindor than Lazarillo or Guzmán; in fact, if he actually was La Geneste, he and his *Buscon* had already played a crucial role in the assimilation of Spanish pícaros into the French comic-novel tradition.

The writers and translators of comic novels tended to be eclectic, drawing inspiration from such disparate sources as jest books, folk anecdotes, satires, historical chronicles, travel accounts, and authentic autobiographies. Disregarding the classical separation of styles, they did not hesitate to fuse wit and humor with moral seriousness and claims to verisimilitude. Despite their objections to the artificial style and idealized content of the romances, however, they frequently retained stereotyped romance conventions and applied them to contemporary subjects in familiar settings. The obvious incongruity results in laughter, but as in *Don Quixote*, the open repudiation of romance in the comic novel obscures an actual transference of romance modes of characterization and plot construction to recognizably human actions and plausible settings. The heroes of these novels—Francion, Buscon, Le Destin—are endowed with inherent nobility of mind and soul. The hypocrisy and maliciousness of others may cause them to experience momentary setbacks or humiliations, but their own qualities allow them to rise in society and marry a paragon of beauty and virtue. The romances undoubtedly appealed to readers who desired to fantasize, to vicariously experience noble passions and virtuous ideals; by sentimentalizing the picaresque hero and combining elements of poetic justice with low-life language and themes, the comic novel contributed significantly to breaking down the traditional separation of styles and preparing the way for the subsequent evolution of the French novel.

Since the French translations of Spanish picaresque novels were closely identified with the indigenous comic novel, they too were regarded primarily as exciting and witty adventure stories. Hints of this development already existed in some of the Spanish novels. Marcos de Obregón had an inherently noble character and lived in a fictional world which rewarded virtue and punished vice; the picaresque adventurers of Salas and Castillo were often successful in their attempts to pass for noblemen, and Castillo's pícaras even succeeded in retiring to the peaceful enjoyment of their ill-gotten wealth. However, neither they nor Marcos were susceptible to the ennobling power of love, whereas Francion, the French Buscon, and Le Destin all achieve ultimate happiness in a romantic relationship to an idealized woman. In Spain pícaros never became the idealized heroes of romance plots, because rigid class distinctions, Inquisitorial censorship, and the book trade's dependency upon aristocratic patronage rendered such a portrayal both implausible for those who might read about it and impractical for those who might write about it.

In France the ideal social order was still generally assumed to be hierarchical, but unlike the upper-class Spaniards for whom most picaresque novels were written, the growing bourgeois reading public, to whom many French authors directed their work, tended to consider a person's place in that order to be properly determined by merit, not by the accident of birth. Because there was theoretically no impediment to prevent people from rising to positions consistent with their qualities of mind and soul, Frenchmen could conceive of a lower-class, wandering rogue who attained material well-being without compromising his sense of truth or identity. The assumption that everyone had an inherent nature and could legitimately rise to a corresponding place in society represented a significant modification of the aristocratic ideology of writers like Quevedo, but it continued to preclude the possibility of literary characters who developed in the interaction between themselves and the world outside themselves. Francion, Buscon, and Destin are all static characters who express their "âmes généreuses" (generous souls) or noble natures in a series of contacts with that world.

Although the modified conception of character and social order must have been appealing to bourgeois readers, it was not an exclusively bourgeois idea. For example, Sorel rejected a bourgeois dependency upon money as the primary determinant of social respectability. According to him, the ideal society would be one in which everyone recognized a natural hierarchy of merit; individual happiness and social justice would presumably result if all people were free to express their inherent natures. Because worthy men were born to low social stations and unworthy aristocrats or bourgeois to higher ones, money tended to pervert the natural order, and the existing social organization might actually prevent people from achieving their potential and living in harmony with others.[28] Under these circumstances, Francion can be seen as a noble-spirited individual born into low circumstances; before he can occupy a place in accord with his nature, he must overcome an existing false hierarchy.

In the preface to *Francion*, Sorel contended that men could liberate themselves from vulgar prejudices and live like gods if they would only exercise their reason and wit, gratify their desires for pleasure, and follow their generous impulses. As a poor relation among the wealthier "libertins" who clustered around Theophile de Viau before his arrest and im-

Fig. 14. A twentieth-century portrayal of Francion, illustrating the gallantry of the French picaresque hero and the influence of Sorel's portrait (van Maele, 1925)

prisonment in the early 1620's, Sorel was propounding the philosophical hedonism characteristic of the so-called "libertinage." Intensely aware of the same transitoriness which moved Spanish religious writers toward asceticism, the "libertins" advocated the cultivation of noble pleasures by noble individuals as the best possible life. The printer and bookseller most intimately linked with "libertinage" was the same Pierre Billaine who had published Chapelain's *Guzman*.[29] Not only did Billaine bring out the works of Theophile de Viau; *Francion* was one of his most successful publishing ventures. Besides La Geneste's *Buscon*, translations of Quevedo's *Sueños* and Úbeda's *Justina* also appeared under his imprint.

When one considers that both Vital d'Audiguier, who translated *Marcos* and *La desordenada codicia*, and his nephew Pierre d'Audiguier, who translated Luna's continuation, were also associated with the "libertins," one of the reasons for the link between Spanish picaresque novels and French comic novels becomes clear. Sorel wrote *Francion*, the first important comic novel, and defended the type of fiction which it represented; he was associated with the same movement as many of the people involved in the translation of picaresque novels, some of which had already been published by Billaine. When *Francion* proved successful, Billaine must have been willing to publish similar novels. The radically altered *Buscon* followed the same conventions as those adopted by Sorel, and it too proved enormously popular. In both of these works, as in the *Roman comique* and many lesser comic novels, the successful formulas include the use of an adventure-story plot in which noble-souled, picaresquelike heroes overcome obstacles separating them from their merited places in society.

The inherent nobility and eventual happiness of characters like Francion and La Geneste's Buscon permitted readers to feel reassured in the efficacy of sentimental love and the justice of a world which rewarded likable heroes for their qualities of mind and soul. Upon occasion Francion may be obliged to wear ragged and dirty clothes, but in contrast to weak-willed, cruel aristocrats or dull-witted bourgeois, he possesses an "âme véritablement généreuse" (truly generous soul) which encompasses good taste, generosity (or openness) and the stoic equanimity with which he counters the assaults of a hostile fortune. His very name suggests that he is a "français" (Frenchman) who is "franc" (open and honest, but also free) and the name of his beloved Nays (from the Greek Naiades, goddesses of calm water and poetic inspiration) portends lasting happiness for the hero when he finally marries her.[30]

Like La Geneste's Buscon and Scarron's Le Destin, Francion has an incorruptible sense of his own identity; for example, while courting Nays he refuses to adopt a false name, because that would be tantamount to admitting the lack of anything worthy of commendation in himself. This does not mean that he never adopts disguises. Francion is perfectly capable of donning a mask to deceive a jealous husband or to flatter an important personage, but he never has recourse to begging or thievery, because such activities would be unworthy of his noble nature. Indeed, at one point he admits, "Me deliberant de suivre en apparence le trac des autres, je fis provision d'une science trompeuse, pour m'acquerir la bienveillance d'un chacun. Je m'estudiay a faire dire a ma bouche le contraire de ce que pensoit mon coeur, et a donner les compliments et les loüanges a foison, aux endroits où je voyois qu'il seroit necessaire d'en user" ("Determining to make a show of following the common path, I supplied myself with the science of deception in order to acquire the good will of everyone. I took pains to have my mouth say the opposite of what my heart was thinking, and to pass out compliments and praises liberally in places where I saw that it would be necessary to make use of them").[31] When he proceeds to acknowledge his desire to find a "grand Seigneur" (great lord) who might secure his fortune, Francion is beginning to sound like the squire in *Lazarillo*, but unlike the squire, he placed a condition upon the nature of his future master; he will refuse to serve anyone unworthy of respect. The difference is crucial, because under these circumstances, it becomes possible for him to benefit from his master's patronage without renouncing his own integrity.

Francion's qualities entitle him to a noble station in life, and when external appearances fail to accord with his inner nature, a tension develops in the narrative, although this tension is always resolved by the introduction of a romance pattern that reestablishes the correspondence. Sometimes his vindication results from his own prowess, which on one occasion permits him to humiliate the pretentious Count Bajamond in a duel. Sometimes his fundamentally just fictional world operates to rectify the situation; for example, near the end of the novel, a more powerful judge intervenes to free him after a less powerful judge has unfairly convicted him. But at no time does his experience of the outside world modify his character. Immune to the socializing process which transforms Lazarillo and Guzmán into alienated outsiders, Francion liberates himself from vulgar opinion by demonstrating an ability to enjoy worldly pleasures without remorse, to perform valiant actions when necessary, and to maintain a stoic equanimity under duress. If he is unjustly imprisoned, he nourishes his spirit in contemplation. Condemned to death, he betrays not the slightest indication of fear. Because he possesses a capacity to "estouffer le desir des choses qui ne se peuvent" ("stifle the desire for impossible things"),[32] Francion can ally himself with an inherent tendency toward justice in his fictional world; as a consequence of the unimpeded interaction between his noble character and this tendency toward justice, a typical romance pattern repeatedly emerges to restore him to his proper place in the social hierarchy.

Despite his picaresquelike ruses and wanderings, Francion is a genuine hero who can impose his self-conception upon a society which initially denies the validity of his noble pretensions. He is able to do this because his fictional world operates according to the assumption that the truth behind deceptive appearances will eventually be revealed and that material rewards will be distributed to virtuous men who act according to their natures. As a truly noble-souled individual, Francion ultimately acquires wealth and marital bliss, and they transform him from a libertine into a mature and responsible individual. This happy ending is the logical outgrowth of ideological assumptions held by Sorel and much of his reading public. In the first place, it reflects a rudimentary poetic justice, which allows Francion to occupy a social station in accord with his noble nature, but it also reinforces a widespread desire to believe in social justice and earthly happiness.[33] The same pattern obtains in Scarron's *Roman comique*, in which a mysterious menace seems to be hanging over the troupe of strolling actors when they arrive in Le Mans. The menace is ultimately revealed to be the malicious Saldagne, who plans to abduct the beautiful and noble actress L'Estoille, but like the hero of *Francion*, the witty, generous-hearted Le Destin is ultimately united with his ideal woman when a higher judge rectifies the injustices perpetrated by a lower one.

In the French *Buscon*, there is also a happy ending, but it is achieved in a curious fashion. By omitting Pablos' implication with the Sevillian thugs and his marriage to a prostitute, La Geneste allowed Buscon and his friend Alistor to become servants in a wealthy household, where they convince the beautiful and wealthy bourgeois Rozelle that Buscon is of noble birth. After they are married, she forgives him his deception, and when her uncle perishes in a shipwreck, the young couple inherit both his fortune and that of Rozelle's mother.

From the beginning, Buscon is portrayed as a clever, handsome man capable of genuine friendship with Alistor; Quevedo's puns upon converso origins as well as Pablos' humiliations with the jailor's daughter, doña Ana, and the nuns of Toledo disappear from La Geneste's version. Like Francion, Buscon devises clever ruses and enjoys sensual pleasures, but because he is basically an "honneste homme" who opposes a stoical equanimity to the arbitrariness of fortune, he can experience the ennobling power of love and take advantage of the opportunity to marry an idealized woman. Rozelle's money and love recompense Buscon's noble nature and render him happy, but in order to prove his worthiness and deserve his happiness, he must renounce the youthful excesses of his earlier life and adopt a more socially responsible attitude. This is precisely what happens, but to make it happen, La Geneste revised José Camerino's novella "El pícaro amante" (1624) and substituted it for the final section of Quevedo's novel.[34] Such modifications unquestionably betrayed the spirit of the original, but they also reflected the taste and ideology of many potential readers in seventeenth-century France; without them, *Buscon* could not have repeated the success of *Francion*, and this was undoubtedly one of Billaine's primary considerations when he decided to publish it.

The attractiveness of this modified picaresque format is even reflected in a Spanish novel written in France by an exile converso—Antonio Enríquez Gómez' "Vida de don Gregorio Guadaña," the fifth and dominant section of his *El siglo pitagórico* (1644). Like Luna and García, Enríquez Gómez fled to France after suffering Inquisitorial persecution in Spain,[35] but whereas the *Segunda parte* and *La desordenada codicia* portrayed a socializing process which unfairly deprived alienated outsiders of their right to a decent human existence, his *Siglo pitagórico* was primarily concerned with the arbitrary exclusion of worthy individuals from the honors and wealth to which their noble natures entitled them. For this reason, he adopted a narrative form which resembles *Francion* and the French *Buscon* more than *Lazarillo* or *Guzmán*. His don Gregorio is a picaresque adventurer who is headstrong and hedonistic but ultimately superior to the respectable people who look down upon him. One example from his story illustrates this point rather well. After traveling from Seville to Madrid, don Gregorio seduces the noble but quite willing doña Angela. Confronted by her relatives, he is accused of having besmirched the "antiguo blason y ilustre sangre de los Bracamontes" ("ancient escutcheon and illustrious blood of the Bracamontes," a well-known aristocratic Portuguese family).[36] They offer him a choice between marrying her and going to prison. The hypocrisy of the respectable family becomes obvious in their disregard for doña Angela's complicity in the affair and their own willingness to ally themselves with him by marriage, but don Gregorio refuses the dishonor of living in their house, even though his integrity may cost him his liberty. By juxtaposing such a noble-souled picaresque hero with a highly respected but less honorable family, Enríquez Gómez was implicitly questioning the traditionalist assumptions about aristocratic, Old Christian blood, but he was also avenging himself upon a society which had unjustly persecuted him.

Like García and Alemán, Enríquez Gómez openly espoused orthodox Catholic doctrine to demonstrate that the persecution of conversos was not only unreasonable, but also un-Christian. Although *El siglo pitagórico* is based upon the fiction that a soul is recounting its various incarnations, Enríquez Gómez assured his readers that he didn't believe in the "false doctrine" of the transmigration of souls. And when he asked, "¿Quien se puede librar de la mancha commun del pecado?" ("Who can free himself from the common flaw of sinfulness?")[37] he was implying that everyone is subject to temptations of the flesh and that all people will be judged according to their transgressions. If this is true, honor based upon anything other than virtue and merit is ridiculous and detrimental to public morality. Even in its modified form, the picaresque novel proved capable of expressing the anxiety and resentment of exile conversos.

A secondary concern in *El siglo pitagórico* was the presentation of satiric portraits in the style of Quevedo. It is perhaps ironic that the converso Enríquez Gómez should draw inspiration from the anti-Semite Quevedo, but the gallery of caricatures was also a characteristic feature of the French comic novels. In his preface to *Guzman*, Chapelain identified the picaresque novel with Latin satire. To define the comic novel, Sorel in his *Bibliothèque françoise* made the same association. In both cases, the link was based primarily upon a diversity of styles and a clever unmasking of representative vices and follies. For Scarron as well as for Sorel and the French translators of Spanish picaresque novels, these goals were achieved through caricature and the interpolation of sentimental tales; for example, the *Roman comique* includes adaptations of four Spanish novellas which illustrate various aspects of the same love and justice theme which lie behind Le Destin's ultimate union with L'Estoille,[38] but Scarron's novel also contains the memorable burlesque caricatures of La Rancune, La Rappinière, Madame Bouvillon, and the hapless dwarf Ragotin.

Similar "original" characters appear in Tristan's *Le page disgracié* and nearly all the other comic or picaresque novels of the period, but it is in *Francion* that the adventure-story plot is most intimately fused with caricatural technique. If the world has deviated from its ideal form and become dominated by hypocritical, prejudiced individuals, it confronts the noble-souled hero with a wall of false masks. As a frank, generous individual, Francion considers it his duty to penetrate these masks and expose the genuine values upon which a truly just social hierarchy might be based: "Mon coustumier exercice estoit de chastier les sottises, de rabaisser les vanités et de me mocquer de l'ignorance des hommes. . . . Il me sembloit que comme Hercule, je ne fusse né que pour chasser les monstres de la terre" ("My customary exercise was to chastise follies, humble vanities and mock the ignorance of men. . . . It seemed to me that like Hercules, I was born for the sole purpose of chasing monsters from the earth").[39] Besides his function as a sentimentalized hero, Francion thus serves as a wandering practical satirist, revealing the foibles of an ignorant peasant, a miserly nobleman, and the pretentious pedant Hortensius.

In all these satiric portraits, the gulf between what people are and what they think they are becomes apparent; for example, Hortensius' latinate French, his visionary social ideas, and his willingness to believe that he has been elected king of Poland reflect an almost total lack of contact with reality, and this impression is confirmed when he actually conducts a love affair on the principles of romances which he branded too dangerous for his own students to read. Like the caricatures of La Geneste or Scarron, Sorel's portrayal of Hortensius is based upon the assumption that everyone is endowed with a noble or ignoble nature. Since the fictive worlds of the comic novels and the translations associated with them are posited upon the belief (or hope) that appropriate rewards and punishments will be distributed to these various natures, the caricatural distortion of secondary characters and the hero's happy ending represent complementary facets of the same impulse toward poetic justice.

Spanish picaresque works certainly exercised an important influence upon the French comic novel, but because they were read and translated according to French genius and taste, they themselves came to be regarded as comic novels in which typically picaresque panoramas of representative vices and follies were superimposed upon romance patterns and adventure-story plots. It was in this form that many of them were introduced to English and German audiences. Rather than the Spanish originals, John Davies of Kidwelly translated La Geneste's *Buscon* (1657) and Scarron's adaptation of Salas Barbadillo's *La hija de Celestina* (ca. 1660); the anonymous author of *The Life and Death of Young Lazarillo* even bears witness to an English fusion of comic and picaresque novels, for he placed "Guzmanic, Busconic and Scarronic writers" in the same category.[40] A popular German *Francion* was published in 1662, and the success of a 1671 translation of La Geneste's *Buscon* triggered the development of an entire tradition of adventurer novels.[41]

Like the *Buscón*, the first English edition of Quevedo's *Sueños* was translated from La Geneste's French version. Although it reappeared in numerous editions, its popularity failed to stimulate much interest in Davies of Kidwelly's *Buscon*, which was reprinted only once—twenty-six years later in an abridged version. However, the success of Mabbe's *Rogue* did call forth a spate of imitations and spurious sequels. Borrowing heavily from D'Audiguier's French translation of García's *La desordenada codicia*, William Melvin linked Andrew, the hero of his *Sonne of the Rogue* (1638), with Guzmán, but because the book sold poorly, it was rebound and sold under various other names: *Lavernae, or the Spanish Gypsy* (1650), *Guzman, Hinde and Hannam Outstript* (1657), and *A Scourge for a Den of Thieves* (1659). The fate of Melvin's pastiche failed to deter the publication of novels like *English Gusman* (1652), *French Rogue* (1672), *The Dutch Rogue, or Guzman of Amsterdam* (1683), and *Teague O'Dively, or the Irish Rogue* (1690), or plays like Roger Boyle's *Guzman* (1669) and Thomas Duffet's *The Spanish Rogue* (1672–1673).[42]

By far the most successful of these imitations was *The English Rogue Described in the Life of Meriton Latroon* (1655, 1668, 1671), which the hack writer George Head began and the bookseller-publisher Richard Kirkman later continued. Both men had written criminal biographies for middle- and lower-class readers, and it seems plausible to assume that *The English Rogue* was intended for the same audience; in fact, the vulgar, joking tone

The Globe's thy Study er, for thy boundless mind
In a less limit cannot be confind .
Gazing; I here admire: thy very lookes
Show thou art read as well in men, as bookes.
He that shall scan thy face, may judge by it,
Thou hast an Headpeece that is throngd with wit.

I·F

THE

English Rogue:

Deſcribed in the Life

Of Meriton Latroon,

A WITTY

EXTRAVAGANT:

Comprehending the

Moſt Eminent Cheats

OF

BOTH SEXES.

By —— Head

Read, *but don't* Practiſe; *for the Author finds,*
They which live Honeſt, *have moſt quiet minds.*

LONDON,
Printed for *Francis Kirkman*, and are to be Sold by
William Rands in *Duck-lane*, 1680.

Courtesy of the Newberry Library, Chicago

Fig. 15. Frontispiece and title page of *The English Rogue*

and criminal personalities characteristic of the *Rogue* novels which appeared in the wake of Mabbe's *Guzman* indicate that an impulse which originated in the Spanish picaresque novel was gradually being assimilated into an indigenous English tradition. Principal structural elements of the Spanish picaresque novels reappear in *The English Rogue*, and individual episodes are borrowed from them (in particular from García's *La desordenada codicia*), but Head and Kirkman also introduced literary conventions and ideological assumptions which were not present in the earlier picaresque or comic novels.

Preoccupied with enumerating concrete details and creating the illusion that their narrative was factually accurate, Head and Kirkman rationalized the portrayal of criminal activity on the basis of its value as a negative moral example, but like Defoe's later novels, *The English Rogue* reveals a profound disjunction between its overt condemnation of illicit behavior and the morality implied in the narrative—the morality which allows a rogue to both repent and retain the profits of his former dishonest enterprises. The son of a Protestant pastor killed in an Irish revolt, Meriton Latroon is forced unto the road at an early age. After suffering numerous unmerited beatings, he gradually learns what he must do in order to survive. Later he becomes a highwayman who taunts his victims by leaving them sarcastic visiting cards. A life of crime and commerce is followed by repentance and marriage to an obedient Indian woman who agrees to take care of all his domestic needs. At the end of the novel, he drowns any regrets which he might have in a small glass of Canary wine and advises his readers to "save and be prosperous."

As in Defoe's *Moll Flanders* and *Colonel Jacque*, this sort of happy ending doesn't completely resolve the latent contradiction in the authors' Protestant ethic of materialistic pragmatism. In *The English Rogue*, the social world is a battlefield where everyone is competing against everyone else. If the acquisition of wealth is a moral good, each person has the duty to increase his possessions. Stealing is condemned, but in practical terms, the greatest thieves are admired as long as they escape detection. In such an environment, it is only prudent to distrust others and disguise one's true feelings, because that is the only way to obtain the "credit" needed to accumulate wealth and defend oneself against the attacks of others. Just as others betray Meriton, he has no qualms about betraying them.

Acquisitiveness and mask-wearing are the natural concomitants of his and every person's struggle for survival and success. If the result is solitude and universal distrust, it is best to accept them, and that is what Meriton does. Even when he obtains sufficient wealth to renounce his previous crimes and live comfortably, he remains isolated from others, but his isolation is portrayed as natural in a harsh world of inevitable competition; in fact, his acceptance of it is one aspect of a mentality which evolves during the socializing process. A similar set of ideological assumptions would reappear in Defoe; thus, the idea of character as process (evident in both *Lazarillo* and *Guzmán*) would be reinvented for lower- and middle-class English Protestant audiences after writers in the comic-novel tradition had abandoned it in favor of the static characterization which appealed to French bourgeois readers.

But whatever the specific consequences in individual countries, the presence of large and increasingly influential middle classes in England, France, and Germany proved highly significant for the subsequent evolution of European picaresque fiction. In Spain the bourgeoisie was numerically insignificant, and it remained virtually impossible for individuals from the lower classes to enter the petty nobility. This dilemma was exacerbated for conversos and channeled into particular modes of literary expression by the likelihood of Inquisitorial persecution. In the picaresque novel, for example, Spanish writers tended to assume that the vulgar character was *a priori* excluded from respectability and, by extension, the ennobling power of honor or love. When the pícaro did rise in society, his success demanded compromise—the renunciation of any claim to intellectual honesty or deeply felt human emotions.

In France, Germany, and England, the middle classes served as a buffer between the lower classes and the aristocracy; the ambitious commoner could and very often did rise in society by marrying advantageously or accumulating wealth. Within this context, the lower-class, wandering individual was potentially included within the boundaries of respectable humanity, and this difference is clearly reflected in both the translations of Spanish picaresque novels and the indigenous literature associated with them. Vulgar heroes in these novels and later ones by Grimmelshausen, Defoe, Lesage, and Smollett do improve their stations in life or attain wisdom, and their successes do not necessarily imply a sacrifice of emotional or intellectual values. With a decline in the importance of noble patronage and an improvement in the technology of printing, it is not surprising that booksellers desirous of expanding their trade encouraged the publication of picaresque works which responded to the tastes and social assumptions of bourgeois readers; in fact, this is undoubtedly one of the most important reasons for the redirection and reorientation of the Spanish picaresque when it was transplanted north of the Pyrenees.

8

THE UNIVERSALITY OF THE PICARESQUE: VISIONS OF TRUTH IN GRIMMELSHAUSEN'S

Simplicissimus

Elements of the picaresque tradition reached Hans Jakob Christoffel von Grimmelshausen in several different forms. He had almost certainly read *Francion*, the German *Lazarillo*, Albertinus' *Gusman* and Kuefuss' version of Luna's *Segunda parte*, and it was at least partly by following precedents established by them that he was able to forge a highly complex artisic unity from the more than one hundred fifty popular and literary sources upon which he drew in creating his own *Der abentheuerliche Simplicissimus Teutsch* (1668).[1] In *Satyrischer Pilgram* (1667), Grimmelshausen praised *Francion* for its truthful picture of life; Sorel's comic novel might well have served him as a model for the fusion of romance and satire which characterize his portrayal of a generous-hearted individual whose picaresque wanderings culminate in a peaceful tranquility, but whereas Sorel conceived of his happy ending in terms of material wealth and marital bliss, Grimmelshausen depicted the height of Simplicissimus' happiness as an ascetic withdrawal from society. Like Sorel, Grimmelshausen must have had ambiguous feelings about his own ties with the rising bourgeoisie, which provided the principal market for his writings. In *Proximus und Lympida* (1672), he polemicized against the simplistic notion that high birth has anything to do with virtue, because virtue implies conscious choice, while nobility is no more than a superficial external attribute; however, he himself repossessed the nobiliary "von Grimmelshausen" many years after his bourgeois grandfather had abandoned it. His own ambivalence was undoubtedly reflected in his characterization of Simplicissimus, whose concealed noble origins endow him with a particular nature, although this nature is presented as a quality attainable by everyone, not as an inherent trait entitling him to an elevated position in society.

In the sense that Simplicissimus' life illustrates orthodox Counter-

Reformation theology, it resembles the German translations of Spanish picaresque novels. In Albertinus' *Gusman*, the literal meaning of the hero's picaresque journey serves as a vehicle for several allegorical levels of spiritual significance, and an emphasis upon the inconstancy of fortune in a world of illusory appearances is evident in all these works. They even provide ample precedent for Simplicissimus' hermit existence and his belief that permanent satisfactions can only be found in the realm of the spirit.[2] But like the Spanish converso Alemán, Grimmelshausen was applying orthodox doctrine in a much broader sense than the one normally sanctioned by the church. Born and educated in Protestant Hessia, he spent most of his adult life in Southern Germany and only converted to Catholicism rather late in life. In contrast to Albertinus, Grimmelshausen openly eschewed the ponderous "theological style," and he allowed his picaresque hero to discover the path to salvation without the intermediary of the church or its priests. It is in this manner that he reconciled Catholic assumptions about the universal accessibility of God's grace with a characteristically Protestant attitude toward the independent, personal seeking of God.

Just as Grimmelshausen's moral vision reveals a tendency to harmonize opposing ideologies, the style of *Simplicissimus* reflects the fusion of conventions adopted from romance, satire, history, emblem books, religious allegory, and astrological tracts. Grimmelshausen himself had written idealized romances, satires, and popular almanacs. In the multi-layered, serio-comic *Simplicissimus*, elements from all these literary forms are woven into a highly complex narrative unity. As in Alemán's *Guzmán*, the picaresque myth is transformed into an allegorical representation of the human condition. Viewed from the "atalaya" of a wise narrator who retrospectively condemns his own participation in a corrupt society, the experiences of an individual picaresque hero become illustrations of truths which everyone is capable of knowing. But the narrative structure of *Simplicissimus* is far more complex than that of *Guzmán*, for by granting Simplicissimus the spiritual enlightenment which Guzmán admittedly could not sustain, Grimmelshausen fosters the illusion that the numerological or astrological symbolism, the fourfold allegory of Biblical exegesis, and the emblematic techniques which unify the novel's bewildering diversity of materials are actually expressions of his fictive narrator's penetrating insight.[3]

Grimmelshausen once claimed that *Simplicissimus*, the *Continuatio* (1669), *Die Landstörtzerin Courasche* (1670), *Der seltzame Springinsfeld* (1670), and the two parts of *Das Wunderbarliche Vogelnest* (1672, 1675) comprise a ten-part "simplician" cycle, but because the central character's story is largely contained in the original novel and the continuation, which were generally bound together after 1669,[4] it seems plausible to assume that these two sections of the narrative belong together and should be read as a single work. In fact, the *Continuatio* provides a plausible explanation for the existence of Simplicissimus' autobiography and establishes the only valid basis for understanding the point of view from which it was supposedly written. After being shipwrecked on an uncharted island in the Indian Ocean, Grimmelshausen's hero perceives the "truth" (defined in terms of orthodox Counter-Reformation doctrine) and devotes his life to works of piety. Among them is the recording of his life story. Ensconced in a dark cave and working by the light of mysterious little boxes, he composes his memoirs on palm leaves, which are ultimately carried back to civilization by a Dutch sea captain who lands on the island after his ship has been blown off course.

The autobiographical form of the novel obliges readers to at least nominally accept the illusion that the allegorical, symbolic, and emblematic levels of meaning are introduced into the narrative by Simplicissimus, whose avowed goal is the expression of truth as he perceives it. Because this truth involves a belief in the existence of a divinely ordained, beneficent harmony beneath fleeting, chaotic appearances, he regards the events of his life—whether experienced or imagined—in the same way that he views the physical objects on his island. Just as they contain symbolic levels of meaning and must be interpreted to be understood, his own apparently arbitrary course through life follows patterns, the existence of which can only be grasped by a similar process. Rather than attempting to justify his past behavior or establish a factually accurate account of what happened to him, the narrating Simplicissimus is primarily concerned with presenting his experiences as representative illustrations of the world view which he presently holds.

The nature of this world view and his manner of revealing it are suggested by the well-known satyr frontispiece at the beginning of the original work as well as by emblemlike episodes in the *Continuatio*. Both offer clues to the metaphysical and aesthetic principles upon which the entire work is based; in addition, they exercise readers in the discernment of these principles behind the literal meaning of a scene or an event.[5] Successful interpreters of the frontispiece or of the emblemlike episodes in the *Continuatio* should also be able to recognize the enlightened point of view from which Simplicissimus is writing and to interpret the symbolic significance of the story itself. A good example of Grimmelshausen's technique occurs in the *Continuatio* when sailors from the Dutch ship ransack Simplicissimus' hut, eat the fruit of a local plum tree, and go mad. The ship's officers light torches and pursue Simplicissimus into the dark cave, where he has taken refuge from the depredations of the crew, but their torches are suddenly extinguished, and they themselves become disoriented. Only when Simplicissimus gives them the mysterious light boxes and guides them to the surface can they escape the overwhelming darkness. In a gesture of forgiveness, he nurses the sailors and cures them by making them eat the pits of the plums which had originally caused their madness.

This episode contains an allegorical representation of three primary levels of awareness. The first is that of the sailors, who gain a rudimentary knowledge of physical reality through their senses; however, they remain incapable of genuine understanding because their selfish impulses—unchecked by rational or spiritual considerations—imprison them in the never-ending pursuit of pleasurable sensations or superficial satisfactions. They had originally gone mad when they ate only the sweet flesh of the plum (the deceptively attractive appearance of things), and they are cured when they digest the hard, bitter pits of the same plums (the inner reality of desired things). The second level of awareness is that of the ship's officers, whose rational faculties allow them to avoid the excesses of the crew and penetrate into the cave by the light of torches (reason). The third and highest level of awareness is that which governs Simplicissimus' withdrawal into the dark cave. If others attempt to force their way into this realm with the torches of reason, they inevitably lose their way and can only find it again by the light of Simplicissimus' mysterious little boxes (spiritual illumination). Having plumbed the depth of his own being and achieved true wisdom, he is capable of guiding the officers and curing the sailors, but just as the radiance of the boxes is gradually diminished by the light of the sun, divine inspiration tends to be obscured by the "sunlight" of rational activity and mundane preoccupations as soon as one leaves a state of introspection and meditation. By this time, Simplicissimus has become a wise man or, as the ship's chaplain admiringly exclaims, "so weit kombt ein Mensch auff dieser Welt und nicht höher" (573) ("in this world a man comes thus far and no higher").[6] It is this level of awareness which permits the generous hermit to grasp the deeper significance of all things and guide readers through the labyrinth of his own life, proffering the

169

light boxes of spiritual illumination to enable them to perceive a divinely ordained stability and harmony beneath the apparent confusion and randomness of the narrative.

In Grimmelshausen's aesthetics, the light or wisdom emanating from the mysterious boxes is the equivalent of poetic inspiration, and it allows Simplicissimus to transmute everything—objects, dreams, his own previous experiences—into symbolic expressions of spiritual truths. In effect, he becomes a poet who contrives images that mediate between the tangible physical world (which readers can perceive with their senses) and the ineffable realm of the spirit (which they cannot). Because events which never actually took place can embody truth as well as those which did occur, the factual accuracy of Simplicissimus' descriptions is less important to him than their symbolic value. By filling his autobiography with fantastic episodes—a flight to the witches' sabbath, a descent into the realm of sylphs beneath the waters of Mummelsee, an entire sequence of bizarre experiences on his island—he himself contributes to the impression that the narrative is not literally true. In the *Continuatio*, he even hints that things which he recounted as fact in the first five books were actually fictions: elements from the catalogue of waters and springs are repeated verbatim from the Mummelsee episode but introduced as examples of the lies which he invented to satisfy the curiosity of friendly people who offered him hospitality, and he admits never having seen a miraculous plant which he previously claimed to have eaten in Russia.[7] For him, the crucial factor in his autobiography does not involve correspondence with empirically verifiable facts, but the communication of a mental attitude in which events and objects are apprehended. With the aid of spiritual insight, Simplicissimus has composed a story which permits readers to grasp what he considers to be the "truth" behind appearances. Those who fail to perceive it might enjoy a "kurzweilige Histori" (entertaining story; the phrase also appears in the title of the German *Lazarillo*) but, like the sailors on the island, they are only eating the "Hülse" (hull or husk) and ignoring the "Kern" (core)—the wisdom which he is offering them.

An initial clue to the mode of thought necessary for a proper understanding of the narrative is provided by the novel's frontispiece, which was probably designed by Grimmelshausen himself (Fig. 16).[8] This copper engraving utilizes the conventions of a well-established German tradition of emblems, stylized pictorial representations accompanied by a motto which places the portrayed object in a context of figurative meaning, and a "subscriptio" which elaborates upon its significance. Grimmelshausen knew this tradition and occasionally even borrowed materials

Fig. 16. Frontispiece to Grimmelshausen's *Simplicissimus* (1668)

from emblem books like Wilhelm Zincgref's *Sapienta picta* (1624).[9] In these works, the picture is a potential which can only be realized by the individual who perceives it with his senses, puts it in a context of meaning with his reason, and comprehends its deeper significance with the aid of spiritual insight. In Grimmelshausen's emblematic frontispiece, the narrating Simplicissimus is depicted as a composite satyr-Phoenix-bird-fish gesturing obscenely toward a picture book and trampling upon seven masks. By allegorical extension, the figure also represents man, who possesses human features (reason and a soul) while remaining imprisoned in a beastlike body subject to desire, decay, and death.

The satyr's picture book contains images of earthly vanities and objects associated with Simplicissimus' life. It even resembles Simplicissimus' autobiography in that it portrays visualizable physical realities which can trigger an awareness of spiritual truth; however, readers tend to see reflections of their own states of mind in everything. In *Springinsfeld*, an elderly Simplicissimus, having returned from his island, exhibits a "Gaukelbuch" (book of illusions) in the marketplace at Strasbourg. The pages of the book remain blank until a bystander blows upon them; at that moment, pictures appear—pictures which correspond to the individual's own dominant preoccupations. For one man, the book becomes filled with swords and guns; for another with money; for still another with the heads of fools and donkeys. Just as these people lack Simplicissimus' divinely inspired "light" and fail to comprehend the meaning of what they have seen, readers might regard the events in Simplicissimus' autobiography without understanding their true significance.

To assist readers in the interpretative process, the poet-narrator becomes like the satyr in the frontispiece. Although the popular etymology which traced "satire" to "satyr" is demonstrably false, the association was conventionally employed by seventeenth-century satirists.[10] In Grimmelshausen's frontispiece, the satyr's enigmatic smile, obscene gesture, and pointed sword all suggest the manner in which satire mocks false appearances and stereotyped ideas. Traditionally the satyr adopts many masks and believes in none of them. Like him, the narrating Simplicissimus has worn many disguises, and he is now describing them in an attempt to strip the façade of respectability from all the vices and follies of men. From his perspective, the entire world is a theater of masks: everyone wears them, and each person wears many different ones during a lifetime. Any individual's place in society is determined largely by historical accident, and as Simplicissimus' own experiences demonstrate, the same person can be master or servant, victimizer or victim. Capable of deceiving the mask-wearer as well as those whom he encounters, these masks are doubly harmful, and anyone who prides himself on his social role reveals a profound ignorance about himself. Such people are trapped in what Grimmelshausen called the "verkehrte Welt" (reversed world),[11] where everyone blindly pursues transitory, superficial pleasures and ignores the consolation of spiritual insight.

In a sense, these people are subject to a moral blindness, and when Grimmelshausen had the maxim "Der Wahn betrügt" ("Delusion deceives") inscribed in all authorized editions of his later works, he was making a double-edged indictment of those who inhabit the reversed world and wear masks to fool others. They might succeed, but if delusion implies a dependence upon sensual gratifications and material possessions, their own sanity is actually madness, and what they regard as perfectly normal (drinking, gambling, whoring, waging war) is the utmost folly. By the same token, the "madness" of a simple hermit, a rude farmer, or a court fool is actually the height of sanity. The poet-narrator-satyr perceives these masks (and the states of mind which they represent) from an enlightened perspective. To communicate his awareness of their falsity, he transforms the people who wear them into one-dimensional characters whose words and gestures represent a characteristic type of moral blindness. Although such people might appear to prosper, they are deceiving themselves, because their attachment to the reversed world imprisons them in states of mind which exclude any meaningful contact with themselves, other people, or the realm of spiritual truth.

In the reversed world, delusion deceives, but the satyr or the scorpion (in his picture book) are traditionally considered antidotes to the moral sickness of those who adopt worldly values and succumb to false appearances. To expose the intricacy of their deceptions, the narrator (whose name, like that of Francion, suggests openness and frankness) serves as a foil to their follies and vices. Tested against the "simplicity" of his world view, their moral blindness, pride, and selfishness lose the protective shield of social convention and appear as what they actually are. Because a "simple" is also a herbal medicine, the narrator could be regarded as one who collects and compounds "simples" (the various elements of his story) to facilitate the spiritual cure of his readers.[12] For example, the mad Jupiter, who attaches himself to Simplicissimus after being captured along the road near Dorsten, conceives of himself as an Olympian deity and prophesies the advent of a new golden age, when an "authentic German hero" will appear and impose a "German peace" upon the world. Overlooking the most elementary physical realities and waging his own fiercest battles against the fleas in his pants, Jupiter appears to be an utter fool, but delusion deceives: beneath his madness is a strong impulse toward harmony, order, and justice. Within the context of the Thirty Years' War, his idealistic notions make more sense than the predatory barbarity of nearly everyone who is considered "sane" by respectable members of society; his very madness protects him, for even when Jupiter is captured, no one bothers to harm him. Another example of Grimmelshausen's technique involves Courasche, who embodies all the principal qualities of the reversed world. When she plants her maid's illegitimate child on Simplicissimus' doorstep, she believes that she is deceiving him, but because Simplicissimus had been having an affair with the maid, the deceiver is actually deceiving herself. Her own punishment is particularly appropriate, for in pursuing sexual pleasure, she becomes syphilitic and sterile.[13] Later she tells her own story to avenge herself upon Simplicissimus for his allegedly disparaging remarks about her, but in doing so she reveals herself to be far worse than she had appeared in his account of her. By revealing the sanity behind apparent madness and the madness behind the illusory, transitory satisfactions to which most people attach such great importance, the narrating Simplicissimus is showing those who read his memoirs with comprehension how to "repudiate folly and live in peace," as he says in the eight-line "subscriptio" of the frontispiece.

But the satiric perspective is destructive, corrosive. In order to "live in peace" readers also need to recognize the positive elements of Simplicissimus' world view, and it is in communicating them that the novel's astrological symbolism plays a crucial role. If God's plan is orderly, it is presumably reflected in the organization of the cosmos, and anyone who possesses sufficient wisdom and insight to "read" the stars will be able to perceive the principles which govern its operation; it is for this reason that Simplicissimus' hermit-father, the elder Herzbruder, and the prophetess of Soest can accurately predict future events. As an enlightened narrator, Simplicissimus himself is adept at reading the stars. The frontispiece of the *Continuatio* depicts Pegasus soaring above the earth and contains the motto "ad astra volandum" (Fig. 17). Because he possesses the spiritual illumination which permits him to fly above the illusory appearances of the reversed world and discern the divinely ordained harmony of the universe, the narrator himself is like a winged horse "flying toward the stars."[14]

Fig. 17. Emblem from the
title page of Grimmels-
hausen's *Continuatio* (1669)

Adopting a reversal and slight distortion of the Chaldaic planetary system, Grimmelshausen's fictive narrator divides his life into phases during
which he is successfully exposed to the dominant influences of Saturn
(associated with peasants, hermits, loneliness, nearness to nature, magic,
fraud, intrigue); Mars (soldiers, war); Jupiter (fools, madmen, wisdom,
hunting, eloquence, fame); the sun (brightness, wealth, honor, rational
intelligence); Venus (beauty, love, eroticism, music); Mercury (medicine,
charlatanry, liars, thieves); the moon (water, dreams, transitoriness); and
Saturn once again.[15] Depending upon its constellation with other planetary forces, the dominant influence of any planet can be either positive or
negative, and many planets exert modifying influences outside their dominant phases. Indicated by the presence of characters, objects, or relationships defined in terms of their astrological connotations, the influence of
each planet impinges upon Simplicissimus' life and momentarily determines his chief character traits as well as his primary spheres of activity.[16]
In essence, the planetary structure of Simplicissimus' autobiography
functions as a symbolic representation of order and harmony beneath
fleeting, illusory appearances; what at first appears to be an arbitrary
concatenation of fragmentary materials is thus transformed into a clear
illustration of meaningful form.

Simplicissimus' story might even serve as Grimmelshausen's paradigm
for human existence, suggesting the degree to which human fate is determined by forces beyond the individual's control. In his almanacs, Grimmelshausen insists that the stars cannot compel people to perpetrate evil,
although he admits that astrological influences can predispose them to
clear or unclear vision, weak or strong will.[17] This of course does not
resolve the problem of whether or not they are free to influence their own
fates through an exercise of will, but it clearly implies that they are subject
to external forces. In *Simplicissimus*, these forces (symbolized by the suc-

cessive dominant influences of the "planets") and fortune (the inconstancy of worldly things as explained to the hero by the incessantly changing statue Baldanders) are subordinate to the will of God, but together they provide a context within which the individual makes choices (Fig. 18). According to this world view, Simplicissimus or anyone else remains responsible not for events governed by unstable, arbitrary fortune or divinely ordained external forces, but for the attitude with which he exercises his will.

Because the narrating Simplicissimus' attitude has been determined by a single fundamental choice which enables him to regard all things in their true light, he tends not to regard time as a linear progression. From his perspective, people do not evolve toward the truth; they merely live through a succession of eternally recurring stages characterized by varying degrees of ignorance or insight. While experiencing the events and fantasies of his past, Simplicissimus lacked the awareness to fully comprehend their significance, because he had not yet made the fundamental choice to live in the realm of spiritual truth. During each stage of his career, he wears a mask which represents one form of moral blindness and corresponds to his state of mind at that moment. Just as the satyr tramples upon seven masks in the frontispiece, the poet-narrator is repudiating the roles governed by the seven "planets" during his own life—a life in which each successive mask is tried and proved false. Each of these masks or stages illuminates the same truth in a different fashion; taken together, they translate the poet-narrator's spiritual awareness into an allegorical representation of the human condition.

In effect, the cumulative impression of Simplicissimus' past experience functions like an emblem. Just as a motto places the emblem within a context of figurative meanings, a consistent series of astrological and al-

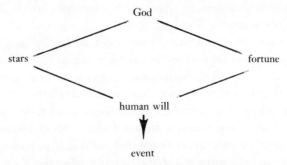

Fig. 18. Grimmelshausen's view of the relationships
among forces affecting human fate

legorical clues establishes the basis for a narrator-reader communication beyond the literal facts of the story. As a consequence the entire narrative exists in an implicit dialectic between the constant, stable perspective of the fictive narrator and the shifting, impermanent states of mind associated with the roles he assumes in the reversed world. There is of course movement from one role to another, but Simplicissimus does not regard his life as a process during which an individualized personality evolved through the interaction between a self and the external world.[18] Throughout his autobiography he makes little attempt to create the illusion of psychological continuity; for example, his previous dreams or visions of truth have no effect upon his subsequent awareness, and when he adopts a new role, he seldom does anything to indicate that he is the same person who played earlier roles. If there is unity of characterization in *Simplicissimus*, it is provided not by the developing consciousness of the novel's hero but by the enlightened perspective from which the story is told.

It is this perspective that unifies the narrative episodes identified with planetary influences and the intercalated fantasies which heighten the hero's kaleidoscopic perceptions into visions of truth. As an untutored boy on his Knan's farm and a naive companion to his hermit-father, Simplicissimus engages in activities which fall primarily under the influence of Saturn; however, the soldiers who pillage the farm and the hermitage already mark the growing dominance of Mars, which imposes itself in the "social tree" dream, culminates in the Battle of Wittstock (Book II), and never completely disappears from the background of the novel. Like everyone else, Simplicissimus is born ignorant and subject to illusion, but the errors of his naiveté are (in the poet-narrator's mind) closer to the truth than the socially sanctioned roles which characterize his later life. For example, when he describes his Knan's farm as if it were a paradise or a nobleman's castle,[19] educated and respectable people might be tempted to laugh at his simplicity, and when he regards Swedish soldiers on horseback as four-legged wolves, he is obviously making a foolish error. In real terms, his folly is ironically appropriate: the uncomplicated lives of peasants are in some ways more noble and edenic than the lives of those who actually live in castles, and the predatory marauders are very much like the wolves against which his Knan had warned him. By implicitly comparing the real value of things with the value accorded them by social convention, the enlightened narrator is inviting readers to reflect upon how delusion deceives in the reversed world.

He himself was first exposed to this perspective during the three years he spent with his hermit-father. After the destruction of his Knan's farm by the Swedish soldiers, Simplicissimus wanders for three days in the woods; in the midst of his darkest despair, he hears the hermit's nightingale song and observes the morning star. They evoke in him a sense of peacefulness and harmony, suggesting a divine order and contrasting sharply with the human cruelty symbolized by the cries of tortured peasants and the flames which are consuming their homes.[20] The nightingale is a traditional symbol for beauty, humility, and comfort in solitude or despair, and when Simplicissimus feels a natural impulse to join in the hermit's song, he is experiencing the attraction of everything which the hermit has to teach him—of everything which ultimately becomes a part of his own spiritually enlightened world view.

Having liberated himself from the world of false masks, Simplicissimus' hermit-father has withdrawn from society and sought to place himself in harmony with the divinely sanctioned order of the universe. Although his self-imposed poverty and the chains with which he voluntarily burdens himself appear to imprison him, they actually reflect a free choice of the attitude with which he confronts the world—an emancipation from blind attachment to sensual pleasures and material possessions. Throughout the narrative, the hermit's state of mind functions as a touchstone, which reveals the moral blindness behind Simplicissimus' later roles in the reversed world. Although the young boy profits from the older man's example, he doesn't yet comprehend its meaning, and he adopts virtuous behavior patterns by imitation. After the hermit's death, he puts on a hair shirt, not to humble himself before God but to emulate his mentor's appearance and to keep warm. Ultimately Simplicissimus will choose a similar mode of life on his island, but by that time he will have experienced the attraction of earthly vanities; he will know what he is renouncing. Compressed into three simple maxims—know thyself, avoid bad company, and remain "beständig" (constant)—the hermit's wisdom will not be fully appreciated until the young boy recognizes its validity in terms of his own experience. Although he cannot impose an enlightened perspective upon his son, the hermit does provide a theological framework within which Simplicissimus' movement away from rural simplicity and back to it can be understood as an alienation from and return to himself.

These early experiences on the farm and in the hermit's company are governed by positive aspects of Saturn, but in both instances the harmony and peacefulness of a rustic existence are abruptly shattered by the intrusion of marauding soldiers or, in astrological terms, the influence of Mars. In a symbolic sense, war constitutes the projection of human greed and cruelty onto an entire physical setting, for it is a self-destructive expression of society's pursuit of earthly vanities. It is also an intensified form of the arbitrariness and instability characteristic of life in the reversed world. But if everything which occurs is part of God's plan, as the poet-narrator contends, even the most horrible events might have beneficent consequences. Simplicissimus himself would never have received a moral education from his hermit-father if war had not separated him from his Knan's farm. And the instructions of the recently deceased hermit would have remained hidden if soldiers had not pillaged the hermitage and thrown down the book which contained them. Thus, in a larger context, war could even be regarded as God's way of obliging people to confront the truth about themselves.

This is precisely what the poet-narrator is attempting to communicate in the "social tree" dream, which occurs just after the soldiers have ransacked the hermitage. Compressing and intensifying the images of cruelty and suffering which Simplicissimus has already seen, the dream permits readers to conceptualize laws of organization and interaction in a society dominated by greed and moral blindness. If properly understood, Simplicissimus' own perceptions could reveal the nature and cause of war, but at this point, the young boy lacks sufficient understanding to interpret what he has seen, and the details of of his experiences and dreams remain fragmentary and disordered. It is only within the consciousness of the fictive narrator that they coalesce into a meaningful and harmonious pattern.

By the late seventeenth century, the tree had become a commonplace symbol for the healthy hierarchical order of a peaceful society;[21] however, in Simplicissimus' mind the real trees around his father's devastated hermitage are transformed into symbolic images with diametrically opposed connotations. At the summit of each tree sits a nobleman; its upper branches contain army officers, who are separated from the mercenary soldiers in the lower branches by an unscalable slippery spot. The tree's entire weight rests upon workers and peasants at its roots. Sighs, tears, blood, money, and bone marrow are squeezed from them, and the officers shortsightedly use the knife of "contribution" to carve physical well-being from the roots which sustain their own elevated positions. Whenever money rains upon the tree, the higher officers reserve most of it for themselves, while the lower branches die for lack of sustenance. Rogues circulate among the roots to joke, whore, and plunder. Occasionally, when others fall from the tree, they even manage to clamber into its lower branches.

In general, there is a great clutching from below. Everyone hopes for the fall of his superiors and craves a higher spot for himself, but no matter how well people climb, they can never scale the slippery spot between the upper and lower branches; it can only be ascended with the aid of a silver ladder called "Schmiralia" (bribery), which is let down from above. Everything is buffeted by incessant motion: people rise and fall. Their relationships change. The trees themselves begin to move and gradually blend into a single enormous tree, which is so shaken by the winds of jealousy, hatred, pride, and avarice that it looks like an emaciated skeleton. Whether they occupy high or low positions in this social hierarchy, people desire more than they have. In its most intense and self-destructive form, this mentality of wanting more expresses itself in war. Ironically, those whose acquisitiveness and ambition motivate them to participate in the resultant chaos fail to perceive that their struggles produce only anxiety and dissatisfaction for themselves, suffering and injustice for everyone. By contributing to the arbitrariness and inconstancy already inherent in the reversed world, they reveal themselves to be far more "simple" or foolish than the naive young boy in whose mind the dream is taking place.

Because he lacks his hermit-father's secure sense of self, however, Simplicissimus is vulnerable to pressures exerted upon him by a society which apportions rewards to those who conform and punishments to those who do not. Failing to grasp the implicit lesson of the "social tree" dream, he plunges further and further into the chaos and confusion of the reversed world during the Jupiter, sun, and Venus phases of his career. He achieves considerable worldly success, but in order to become the daring hunter of Soest or the gallant Beau Aleman, he must be willing to wear masks and engage in the pursuit of what he would later consider to be earthly vanities. When his pride and selfishness cause him to lose sight of the simple spiritual wisdom to which his hermit-father had exposed him, he himself becomes (from the narrator's perspective) the greatest of fools. During the initial episodes, he had been simple in the sense of uneducated, and that is why the hermit had baptized him "Simplicius." After leaving the woods and entering Hanau, he demonstrates a virtuous "simplicity" by intuitively recognizing the folly of many commonly accepted social practices, but the sophisticated townspeople laugh at his naiveté, and the military governor transforms him into a court fool, registered in the regimental roles as "Simplicissimus." From the narrator's point of view, the true simpletons are the mask-wearing, morally blind individuals who mock the innocent boy, but Simplicissimus himself later adopts their modes of behavior, becoming just as "simple" or "mad" as they had been; in fact, his entire life is a movement from one "simplicity" to another and a return to the original one.[22]

The crucial turning point in Simplicissimus' attitude toward role-playing and worldly pursuits takes place at the winter solstice and involves a cruel hoax perpetrated upon him by the governor of Hanau. Conducted to a subterranean "hell" where the governor's drunken commissaries keep him awake for three days and finally blanket-toss him, he is subsequently transported to a richly furnished bedroom, a "heaven" where three disguised laundrywomen bathe and care for him. After falling asleep, he wakes up and discovers that he is dressed in a ridiculous calfskin and confined to a filthy goosepen. Forewarned by a friendly pastor, Simplicissimus knows that his journeys to "heaven" and "hell" were contrived to mock his simplicity, but for the first time in his life, he consciously disguises his true sentiments to cope with deceptive, hypocritical people. By pretending to accept their lies and masks, he even enjoys a certain immunity to laugh at those who believe that they are laughing at him. A propensity to calculate his own advantage allows him to survive, but it also represents a first step away from the hermit's teachings, for this newfound pragmatism engenders his own first mask and prepares him to accept those which follow. The respectable townspeople who envision heaven in terms of soft beds, gluttony, and material comfort are precisely the sort of bad company against which his father had warned him. Viewed from the poet-narrator's perspective, their heaven is actually a type of hell, and the hero's acceptance of their value system represents a type of bedevilment.

The high point of Simplicissimus' worldly career is reached during the "hunter of Soest" episode, but experiences which appear to reflect his greatest freedom turn out to represent his most complete subjugation to the delusions of the reversed world, and this insight is rendered explicit by a series of devil images which dominate the central portion of his autobiography. In all Grimmelshausen's "simplician" writings, an attachment to earthly vanities is symbolically equated with being under the devil's influence. In *Simplicissimi Galgen-Männlein* (1674), an elderly Simplicissimus advises his son that the pursuit of anything less than one's spiritual well-being constitutes the worship of false gods and the renunciation of one's own humanity. The worst sin is idolatry, he claims, and the worst form of

181

idolatry is devotion to the devil, who has the power to create the illusion of Venusberg before men's very eyes.

In *Simplicissimus*, "bedevilment" symbolizes the mental attitude of people who attach supreme importance to earthly vanities while ignoring their own spiritual needs. Framed by the heaven-hell sequence in Hanau (39–40 chapters from the beginning of Book I) and the Mummelsee episode (39–40 chapters from the end of the *Continuatio*), Simplicissimus' enslavement to the devil begins with an imitation of Satan and a flight to the witches' sabbath (50–51 chapters from the beginning), and it ends with his "conversion" after the devil speaks directly to him from the body of a possessed man in Einsiedeln (50–51 chapters from the end). As the hunter of Soest he dresses in green and again imitates the devil when he steals bacon from a pastor (65 chapters from the beginning)—the same sort of activity in which he participates when he joins the Merode Brothers (65 chapters from the end). By reinforcing the idea that worldly success precludes spiritual awareness, the symmetry of this "bedevilment" sequence provides another illustration of the poet-narrator's attitude toward the reversed world.

Blinded by selfishness and pride, the young Simplicissimus places great value upon his reputation as the hunter of Soest, wealth he accidentally discovers in a "haunted" house, and the sexual pleasures enjoyed in Lippstadt and Paris, but in each of these situations he is merely imitating roles he had observed others playing. After being victimized by marauding soldiers, he becomes a marauding soldier; after being a page and fool to the governor of Hanau, he acquires a page and the fool Jupiter; after condemning the polite customs of Hanau and the carnal activities of young lovers, he himself becomes a gallant and a lover. Furthermore, everything upon which he bases his pride proves ephemeral: the hunter is captured, his money is stolen by a Cologne merchant, and he himself is tricked into marrying a retired colonel's daughter. Like everyone else in the reversed world, the Simplicissimus of these episodes is worshiping false gods, and by doing so he is subjecting himself to the anxiety of unquenchable desire and continuous insecurity. No matter how much money, reputation, or sensual gratification he receives, he will always want more. No matter how secure he may appear to be, his self-esteem is constantly threatened by the possible loss of the insubstantial things upon which it feeds.

After apparent successes in the Jupiter, sun, and Venus phases of his life, Simplicissimus succumbs to the influence of Mercury and Mars be-

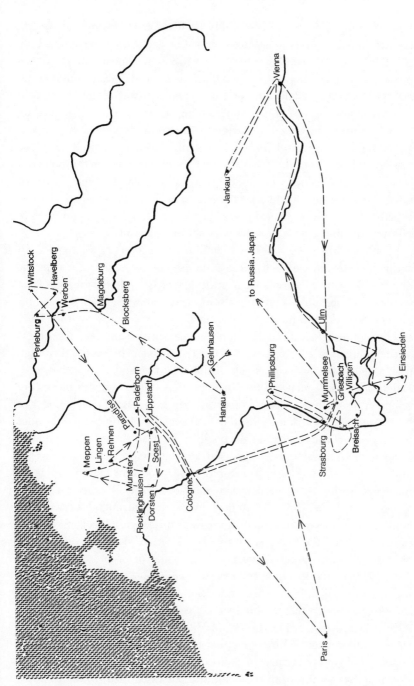

Fig. 19. Simplicissimus' journey (map by Allen Bjornson)

fore regaining a Saturnian tranquility on his island. Having lost wealth, reputation, and physical attractiveness (his face has been scarred by smallpox), he still remains subject to delusion and inconstancy. At one point, he supports himself by peddling quack medicines to gullible villagers. At another he falls into the Rhine, and it plays with him like a ball, eventually placing him in the embarrassing situation of being rescued by the very ship he had been preparing to attack. In both instances, he was attempting to deceive others, while actually deceiving himself. No false mask could preserve him from the ravages of smallpox or the powerful currents of the Rhine, and by an ironic twist of circumstance, his own safety becomes dependent upon the good will of his intended victims. Whether he succeeds or fails in deceiving others, however, he continues to act upon assumptions which the poet-narrator regards as false.

Simplicissimus does experience definite inclinations toward good and antipathies toward evil, but because he has not yet achieved insight, he remains incapable of the change in attitude which would liberate him from the prison of deceptive, constantly shifting appearances. The nature of his attitude is strikingly illustrated during parallel encounters with Olivier and the younger Herzbruder who introduce negative and positive aspects of the dominance of Mercury.[23] From the moment he first meets them near Magdeburg, he instinctively dislikes Olivier and feels attracted to Herzbruder. Both men call him brother, but whereas Olivier repeatedly stands in his way and seems to represent an exaggerated development of his own proclivity toward worldliness and moral blindness, Herzbruder pledges eternal friendship and always aids him in adversity. As the hunter of Soest, Simplicissimus is plagued by a counterfeit double known as the hunter of Weil. The impersonator proves to be Olivier, and to avoid further confusion between himself and a man who acted more cruelly and viciously than he did, the hunter of Soest confronts his rival and humiliates him. Near the end of Book IV, Olivier again blocks Simplicissimus' path, and the two men engage in a lengthy, inconclusive struggle, after which they agree to collaborate in a life of crime. Although he distrusts his new companion and feels uncomfortable with him, Simplicissimus does not openly repudiate him. Similarly, after marauding soldiers have killed Olivier and Simplicissimus has appropriated the dead man's money, he encounters Herzbruder in Villingen and agrees to accompany him on a pilgrimage to Einsiedeln, not because he feels a sincere religious impulse, but simply because he desires to help a needy friend. Even when a devil speaks to him from the body of a possessed man, Simplicissimus converts out of fear rather than the positive conviction which, according to orthodox Catholic doctrine, would have been necessary for salvation. Herzbruder too is mortally wounded in battle, but like Olivier, he momentarily serves as Simplicissimus' alter ego, provoking him into revealing both his basically sound impulses and his lack of commitment in following them.

That he possesses courage and a willingness to seek the truth is demonstrated when he literally plunges beneath the unstable surface appearances of Mummelsee (associated with the lunar phase of his life). There are three major fantasy episodes in *Simplicissimus*—the "social tree" dream in Book I, Jupiter's plans for social reform in Book III, the Mummelsee episode in Book V—and there is a discernible progression among them. The "social tree" dream identifies the nature and cause of chaos in the reversed world at war; Jupiter's monologue advances the possibility of imposing peace, justice, and harmony upon such a world; and the Mummelsee episode reveals the potentiality for such peace in the natural world. In the first of these episodes, men are acting like the sailors who ransacked Simplicissimus' hut on the island; they are blindly and selfishly pursuing what their senses have taught them to desire. In the second, Jupiter's plans resemble the strategy of the ship's officers, for they reflect his ability to reason. In the third, Simplicissimus encounters the sylphs, "Elementargeister" (nature spirits) who speak a universally comprehensible language and possess a perfect knowledge of all objects in the physical universe.[24] Like the Houyhnhnms in *Gulliver's Travels*, they live in a rational, harmonious social order; they neither sin nor suffer sickness, and when they die they accept death stoically, without anxiety, but they lack souls and remain incapable of the spiritual awareness attained by the poet-narrator. As the sylphs themselves realize, the potentiality for spiritual awareness distinguishes human beings from all other creatures; thus, each of the three fantasy episodes contains an allegorical statement about a progressively higher level of consciousness.

In none of these cases does the experiencing Simplicissimus fully grasp the significance of what he sees or hears, for he has not yet attained the enlightened perspective which he later enjoys. For example, the stable world beneath the turbulent waves of lakes and seas is traditionally associated with wisdom, and one who enters it usually gains insight or fulfills a wish. Both are offered to Simplicissimus, although he is not yet ready to take advantage of them. The society of the sylphs reflects divinely ordained harmony in a form uncorrupted by human selfishness, and if he could have comprehended this situation, he would have learned the true value of worldly possessions. Against the background of the peaceful existence of the sylphs, his own previous life clearly illustrates the ultimate valuelessness of anything which he might obtain by mask-wearing, but when they give him an opportunity to describe the reversed world, he denies the ugliness and chaos of social life as he has experienced it; in other words, he lies to create a favorable impression on his hosts. As creatures with a perfect understanding of all natural phenomena, they of course recognize his falsehoods, and when Simplicissimus receives a magical stone with the power to fulfill his desire for wealth by producing a spa at the point where it first contacts the earth, the king of the sylphs expresses the ambiguous wish that his guest will be recompensed "als du mit Eröffnung der Wahrheit umb uns verdient hast" (432) ("as you, through disclosure of the truth, have deserved of us"). After returning to solid ground, Simplicissimus loses his way and falls asleep. The stone drops from his pocket and locates the valuable spring inaccessibly in the middle of the forest. His reward is indeed proportionate to the degree of truth contained in his descriptions of life in the reversed world. By continuing to covet material possessions like an income-producing spa, Simplicissimus demonstrates not only failure to comprehend his vision of harmony and order, but also the ongoing moral blindness of someone who becomes the prisoner of a worldly role to which he attaches supreme importance.

After having passed through all the representative stages of human life, Simplicissimus ultimately returns to the enlightened world view of his hermit-father. The cyclical completeness of his journey is suggested by the reappearance of Saturn's dominance, but when Simplicissimus voluntarily repudiates the society of men and devotes his life to understanding and praising the works of God, he is no longer merely imitating another person's behavior, as he had been doing after the hermit's death. At the end of Book V, he begins to live in the wilderness and read edifying books, and by the time he resigns himself to an ascetic life on his island, he has actually created his own hermit ideal. His mode of life on the island becomes a direct expression of what he himself believes to be true. As his own autobiography demonstrates, he now perceives order behind what had previously appeared to be chaos. By choosing to adopt a state of mind which conforms to his hermit-father's teachings, Simplicissimus is achieving the highest possible level of human awareness, and he is also returning to himself, for only within the context of his own experience does his mentor's example acquire its full meaning and personal relevance.

Simplicissimus thus ends where it began, moving from a simple, natural existence to worldly success and back again. In the beginning, Simplicissimus experiences poverty, but he is also exposed to a vision of spiritual truth. Because his naive acceptance of this truth is not based upon a knowledge of the reversed world, he remains vulnerable to its temptations, and after the hermit's death he tries on a series of increasingly successful masks until he attains the summit of his worldly career as the hunter of Soest—an episode which spans the two central chapters of the book. At this moment, he is also furthest from self-knowledge and an awareness of the divine plan behind deceptive, insubstantial appearances. In either direction from the middle, parallel episodes trace Simplicissimus' movement toward and away from blind confidence in social masks and the values which they represent. In conjunction with the planetary symbolism, the inverse relationship between physical comfort and spiritual well-being in this symmetrical structure serves as another illustration of the order and harmony which the poet-narrator perceives beneath the delusion and instability to which everyone is subjected.

Behind the bewildering diversity of materials in *Simplicissimus*, there is order, and although that order is obviously imposed by the author Grimmelshausen, the book's primary unifying principle derives from the illusion that its symbolic-satiric style is a direct expression of the mature narrator's world view. During the ongoing dialectic between his insight into the stable harmonious order of "God's plan" and the experiencing Simplicissimus' subjection to fleeting, illusory, chaotic appearances, there emerges an impression of universality and an implicit conviction that all people can follow their own paths to the enlightened perspective from which the story is told. In the "subscriptio" to the original novel's frontispiece, the poet-narrator-satyr claims to have been born like a Phoenix out of fire (made aware of his rationality during his journey to "hell" in Hanau), flown through the air without being lost (traveled to the witches' sabbath without losing his soul), wandered through water (descended into Mummelsee) and traveled across land (experienced the reversed world in many different places). He observed that which often afflicted and seldom delighted him, and recorded it all in "this book" (wrote his memoirs). Admirably equipped to travel through the traditional four elements (earth, air, fire, and water), he functions as a symbolic everyman who, having passed through every possible realm of experience, views all human life from the spiritually enlightened perspective which endows his memoirs with unity and universality.

9

THE AMBIGUOUS SUCCESS OF
THE PICARESQUE HERO IN DEFOE'S

Moll Flanders

Like Grimmelshausen, Daniel Defoe was writing in a tradition which translations and imitations of Spanish picaresque novels had helped to establish. A representative of the ambitious and rising English bourgeoisie, he too attacked certain elements of traditional aristocratic ideology, while integrating others into his own world view. As in *Simplicissimus*, the impression of coherence in his *Fortunes and Misfortunes of the Famous Moll Flanders* (1722) depends upon the sustained illusion that an enlightened narrator is recounting and interpreting a characteristically picaresque journey through a hostile, deceptive world; however, in both aesthetic and moral terms, Moll functions quite differently from the protagonist in Grimmelshausen's novel.

Simplicissimus is a seer who shapes the various episodes of his life into a symbolic expression of truth; Moll is an autobiographer whose memory is self-serving and selective and whose comprehension of her own life is limited and partial. Simplicissimus is defined in terms of a static human nature; she is portrayed as a highly individualized character whose personality evolves in the interaction between self and environment. In the sense that Moll's consciousness represents the culmination of a socializing process, she resembles the narrating Lázaro, but whereas *Lazarillo* is an implicit condemnation of the dehumanized value system which this process conditions people to accept, *Moll Flanders* reflects the assumption that it is a perfectly natural phenomenon which perpetuates the necessary techniques of survival. For Defoe as for Head and Kirkman, however, a paradoxical situation arises when social pressures oblige a lower-class, wandering character to adopt modes of behavior which conform to necessity but conflict with generally accepted standards of morality. This very problem is encountered but never fully resolved in *Moll Flanders*, where ambiguity is compounded by the difficulty of determining whether Defoe or the fictive narrator should be considered the source of any irony which exists in the narrative.

Every interpretation of *Moll Flanders* is based upon some (often unstated) standard for distinguishing between the world view implicit in Defoe's portrayal of his fictive narrator and the attitudes which she herself expresses in telling her story.[1] Because many of Moll's judgments are made in conformity with principles enunciated elsewhere by Defoe, the dividing line is often blurred and tenuous, but an awareness of Defoe's artistry as a consummate creator of masks can contribute to a better understanding of the way in which narrative perspective is manipulated in the book. In a 1704 letter to his political patron Robert Harley, Defoe quoted the apostle Paul's account of becoming "all things to all Men" and praised dissimulation. Two years later, while working for Harley as a secret agent in Scotland, he alluded to the same Biblical passage and admitted, "I am all to Every one that I may Gain some."[2] In his polemical tracts, Defoe frequently adopted personae and allowed them to speak for themselves. As early as *A Poor Man's Plea (1698)*, his advocacy of moral reform among the upper classes was couched in the homely, unsophisticated speech of a simple but honest lower middle-class Englishman. In *The Shortest Way with the Dissenters* (1702), his parodistic impersonation of an imaginary high-church Anglican was so successful that the tract was considered seditious, and Defoe himself was placed in the pillory. Like Grimmelshausen, he identified these satirical writings as the plain speech of the "satyr"; he clearly depended upon readers to penetrate the artifice and recognize the fictive narrator's biases.

If a reader is expected to pass judgment upon Defoe's narrators and people like them, he must perceive the class or category to which they belong, and this presupposes the validity of drawing general conclusions from specific cases. In the preface to *Moll Flanders*, Defoe insists that the book has a profoundly moral intention and can be applied to "vertuous and religious uses" (4).[3] As a representative thief or sinner, Moll has didactic value, and her story reveals how anyone in her circumstances could succumb to temptation and embrace corrupt behavior patterns. Within a larger context, her fictional life illustrates basic conflicts between good and evil—conflicts which all people ultimately face. At the same time, *Moll Flanders* is constructed around the illusion that Moll is a highly individuated character whose life and personality are unique.[4] As a real-seeming individual with ascertainable motivations and preconceptions, she presents herself as a repentant sinner confessing past transgressions

THE

FORTUNES

AND

MISFORTUNES

Of the FAMOUS

Moll Flanders, &c.

Who was BORN in

NEWGATE,

And during a Life of continu'd Variety for Threeſcore Years, beſides her Childhood, was Twelve Years a *Whore*, five Times a *Wiſe* (whereof once to her own Brother) Twelve Years a *Thief*, Eight Years a Tranſported *Felon* in *Virginia*, at laſt grew *Rich*, liv'd *Honeſt*, and died a *Penitent*.

Written from her own MEMORANDUMS.

The Third Edition, Corrected.

LONDON:

Printed for JOHN BROTHERTON, at the *Bible* in *Cornhill*, againſt the *Royal Exchange*. MDCCXXII.

Courtesy of the Newberry Library, Chicago

Fig. 20. Title page of *Moll Flanders*

and witnessing to the Providential occurrences which brought about her reform, but she also reveals herself as a person who still practices deceptions upon her closest relatives, regards her husband's jovial indolence as the height of gentility, prides herself on the sincerity of her "conversion" while casuistically defending her former illicit activities, and remains at least partially blind to her own inconsistencies and evasions.

Because she is a limited and biased observer of her own past, Moll's opinions cannot represent an ultimate standard of truth and moral value in the book, and the author clearly distances himself from her by claiming that she is "not so extraordinary a penitent as she was at first" (7) or "as she afterwards pretends to be" (3). By depicting a narrator who honestly describes her own dishonesty, Defoe exploits the pseudoautobiographical perspective to favorably dispose readers toward Moll, but by casting suspicion upon the strength of her religious convictions, he alerts them to possible misrepresentations of her own past. Because the standards for evaluating her comments are not clearly established in the author's preface, the moral significance of Moll's example remains unclear, and readers are left in the ambiguous position of sympathizing with a character whose unreliability they have been warned against but whose arguments often seem to coincide with those of the author and the implied reader.[5]

Throughout his writings, Defoe recognizes how fear and poverty drive men to sin and crime: "Necessity is above the power of human nature, and for Providence to suffer a man to fall into that necessity is to suffer him to sin. . . . Necessity makes the highest crimes lawful, and things evil in their own nature are made practicable by it."[6] Defoe himself had experienced difficult circumstances, engaged in questionable business practices, and defended the idea that England would prosper if it eliminated the "necessity" which drove people to follow their natural impulses for self-preservation by resorting to criminal activities. If a character like Moll is confined to a rigidly structured society which offers few if any legitimate avenues to survival and prosperity, it is perfectly natural for her to adopt illegal means of obtaining what she needs and desires.

One of the secondary characters in *Roxana* (1724) states the principle succinctly when she declares, "as to honesty, I think honesty is out of the question, when starving is the case," and she later adds, "Comply and live, deny and starve."[7] Because all people naturally seek physical survival and psychological well-being, they will adopt corrupt behavior patterns if there are no other ways for them to obtain these ends. Defoe himself repeatedly excoriates self-righteous individuals who condemn others when their own virtue has never been tested, and he frequently portrays criminals who act virtuously as soon as they find themselves in an environment where they need no longer resort to unlawful activities to pursue their needs and desires. Just as the hero of *Colonel Jacque* (1723) proves honest and industrious when transportation to the colonies accords him the opportunity to accumulate wealth honestly, Moll appears perfectly content to lead a calm and virtuous life whenever "necessity" is relaxed as the result of an advantageous marriage or a resettlement in the New World.

Within the context of Defoe's Protestant tradesman ethic, those who achieve social status through the exercise of their own talents and energies are deserving of praise, and this is precisely what Moll accomplishes. Displaying the same inventiveness, entrepreneurial skill, and resiliency which Defoe admired in the successful English businessman, Moll succeeds (or appears to succeed) in economic and spiritual terms, enjoying the comforts of material wealth as well as the psychological satisfaction of repenting her previous sins and refusing to allow a preoccupation with them to disturb her present feelings of virtue. Her brother-husband faints and attempts to commit suicide when he learns of their incestuous marriage, and her banker husband despairs and finally dies under the weight of bankruptcy, but Moll never relinquishes her intense desire to survive and prosper.

In this respect she is quite similar to the two people with whom she has the closest ties during her adult life—the governess and Jemy. Despite many reverses of fortune, the governess always "stood upon her legs" (171), and when Jemy discovers that he has spent everything he owns to win Moll's nonexistent fortune, he cheerfully resigns himself, "I must try the world again; a man ought to think like a man. To be discouraged is to yield to the misfortune" (130). Among all the individuals whom Moll encounters, these are the only ones whose stories, Defoe hints, merit a more complete recording. Like most of the characters who interest him, they possess physical attractiveness, vitality, ambition, and a talent for inventing disguises. In a world where the common welfare derives, in Defoe's opinion, from granting all people the freedom to exercise their will and resourcefulness in the enlightened pursuit of self-interest, characters like Moll and her companions reflect a redefinition of the romance hero in terms of bourgeois ideological assumptions about the individual and society.[8]

When Defoe alludes to the stereotyped image of life as a storm-tossed boat at sea, he does not employ it (as Alemán and Grimmelshausen had done) to illustrate the individual's powerlessness in a chaotic world, but rather to justify the hero's attempt to render his boat seaworthy and guide it toward a "safe harbor." According to him, the most effective way of achieving this goal involves the same basic principles employed by a successful tradesman; reduce everything to quantifiable terms, rationally balance alternatives and consequences, regard all other people as potential competitors and relate to them primarily on a contractual basis. If the Protestant conception of "calling" is modified slightly and reinterpreted in a secular context, Moll's final happiness could be viewed as a reward for adhering to her vocation and actualizing the potentialities of her existence and her environment through an exercise of will.

To a certain extent (but only to a certain extent) Moll adopts a world view like that of Defoe. She justifies her former dishonest activities on other occasions, and she ultimately adopts a characteristically Protestant attitude toward a fortune which she could never have obtained if she had not acquired initial capital for her New World investments by engaging in thievery and prostitution. From outside Moll's frame of reference, her "conversion" at Newgate prison and her subsequent financial success are morally ambiguous, but by couching her autobiography in terms reminiscent of authentic religious works, she obscures discrepancies between what she describes and how she interprets it. Like a genuine spiritual autobiography, her memoirs do impose meaning upon the chaos and apparent arbitrariness of her life, but this meaning does not always fit the facts as she reports them, and insofar as readers perceive the divergence, they can recognize the fears and desires which motivate Moll to distort the truth in attempting to mislead them.[9]

For example, Moll evaluates her own previous experiences and concludes that if "honest employment" or a "good husband" were available, she would prefer them to a life of prostitution and crime; however, such protestations of virtuous intention are somewhat hypocritical in light of her willingness to relinquish the dependable income from her needlework when a more profitable scheme occurs to her, or to abandon a potentially "good husband" like the banker when the possibility of a more advantageous match attracts her attention. When she finally marries the banker, she claims to abominate her wicked past, rationalizing her actions by asserting that she would have been happy if she had been "wife to a man of so much honesty and so much affection from the beginning!" (158). What she neglects to mention at this point is that she had been married to such a man at the beginning. Although her first husband, Robin, had been both honest and affectionate, she repaid him by indulging in adulterous fantasies with his elder brother during the entire five years of their marriage.

Throughout the narrative, Moll contrives numerous ways of deflecting the reader's attention from her own culpability: her thefts are presented as object lessons to her victims; she boasts about not having lied when she merely allows others to persist in their mistaken impressions of her; she condemns an action but not herself for having performed it; she focuses upon external details and quantifiable measurements to give the impression of honesty, when she is acting in a quite dishonest fashion; she emphasizes the evil alternative which she rejected in order to palliate the evil alternative which she chose; she shifts the blame from herself to the devil, an ignorance of the facts, "necessity," or the foibles of others. For stealing from a burning house, prostituting herself, embracing Catholicism, or abandoning her children, she develops sophistical self-justifications; thus, although she admits her crimes and openly blames herself, she always describes them in such a way that their seriousness will be attenuated, if (as she assumes) the reader agrees with her interpretation of events.[10] In essence, she is admitting that she is, in Lázaro's terms, "no more saintly" than her neighbors, but like him, she is also implying that they are no more saintly than she is. By assuming that under similar circumstances anyone would have acted as she did, Moll is cultivating approbation by effectively challenging readers to condemn her for what they themselves are capable of doing. In the process, however, she sidesteps the issue of her own guilt or innocence.

The question of moral responsibility is also circumvented by a blurring of distinctions between the accurate recording of details and the honest evaluation of their significance. By paying scrupulous attention to physical details, Moll projects herself as an honest person, but by encouraging readers to assume that her honesty carries over into her considerations of ethical matters, she is confusing factualism with integrity. Objects, people, and events are named, measured, and placed in categories; frequently they are reduced to their monetary value or profit-making potential. This tendency may create the impression that Moll is portraying her past objectively, dispassionately; in actuality, her calculations reflect the subjective processes of an isolated individual attempting to reconcile an awareness of her sinful past with a conviction of her own inner worth. In her eyes this show of truthfulness establishes her virtue and palliates her previous guilt.[11]

The blurring of distinctions also characterizes another of Moll's ploys to draw attention away from her morally culpable actions. At the end of the novel, she is enjoying the fruits of behavior which she retrospectively condemns, but because her newfound wealth is dissociated from its origins and interpreted as an appropriate reward for her inherent qualities and present virtue, she obfuscates the real contradiction between her condemnation of criminality and her willingness to enjoy a fortune founded upon the profits of criminal activities. In essence, she is implying that her own success story illustrates the existence of a rudimentary poetic justice in her fictional world. When she first marries Jemy, neither of them has the fortune which they encouraged the other to believe they possessed, but although they are victims of a mutually inflicted fraud, they feel drawn toward each other, and Moll even suggests that they travel to America, where it would be possible for them to obtain sufficient wealth to "live like our selves" (137). Although the proposal is not acted upon at that time, the two of them meet again in Newgate, and after they take up residence in the New World, Moll does everything to gratify Jemy and "make him appear, as he really was, a very fine gentleman" (295). Overwhelmed by his good fortune, Jemy too becomes a penitent, truly convinced that he has not been disappointed in his earlier expectations of gaining a fortune by marrying her. Behind Moll's portrayal of this "happy ending"—behind the fulfillment of her desire to "live like our selves" or make Jemy appear "as he really was"—lies the assumption that both of them are by nature gentlefolk. Part of Moll's motivation for dressing her husband fashionably is a selfish desire to give substance to her own pretensions; if she is married to a gentleman, she obviously must be a gentlewoman. By securing the outward trappings of gentility, she is merely obliging the rest of the world to accept her for what she has always considered herself to be.

Just as Moll's commentary upon her life includes logical contradictions and blurred distinctions, there are discrepancies between the facts she reports and the conventional meanings (spiritual autobiography, poetic justice) she attempts to impose upon them. From outside Moll's frame of reference, her manner of telling the story reveals that she is firmly convinced of her inherent worth and that she has a pronounced talent for presenting herself in the most favorable possible light; however, until she repents, her life is a perfect expression of the picaresque myth as delineated in *Lazarillo* and *Guzmán*. Born at Newgate, she is the daughter of an unknown father and a mother who is a convicted thief; after a sobering initiation she adopts the selfish, dehumanizing value system of a competitive society and abandons herself to a life of sin, fraud, and petty crime. As the dominant social attitudes are inculcated into her, she suffers the same consequences as Lázaro, but since these attitudes are not implicitly contrasted with traditional ideals of compassion, friendship, and intellectual honesty, her successful assimilation of them is portrayed as the acceptance of inescapable reality, not as the perversion of a potentially humane consciousness.

Even after her conversion and during her greatest prosperity, Moll remains a solitary character whose morality is based upon mask-wearing and the enlightened pursuit of her own economic self-interest. She lies to her son, conceals assets from her husband, and continues to exploit personal relationships for their profit-making potential, but all these actions are regarded as natural. In Defoe's eyes, it is plausible for a lower-class, wandering character to rise in English society and achieve physical well-being without compromising her self-esteem, because there is no necessary conflict between what Moll must do to cope with a hostile world and what she would have to do if she desired to believe in her own virtue and inner worth. By incorporating this assumption into her fictional world, Defoe is reinforcing a fundamentally bourgeois justification for upward social mobility and signaling a profound difference between his world view and that of Alemán or the anonymous author of *Lazarillo*, for by sanctioning the consequences of the socializing process, he removes his picaresque hero from the double-bind situation to which Lázaro and Guzmán had been subjected. However, by adopting the idea of character as process, Defoe is also undermining Moll's contention that she possesses an inherent gentility, which is appropriately rewarded by a respectable, physically comfortable place in society.

Self-serving and often misleading, Moll's version of reality nevertheless provides readers with sufficient information to recognize the process during which she learns the rules of the game and develops the very self-image expressed in her interpretation of events. The crucial stages in this process are initiation, assimilation, and conversion, although Moll's conversion is largely an extension of the preceding stage, involving as it does the application of a heightened clarity of vision to goals and principles internalized earlier. Early in life she is introduced to her "vocation" and shocked into an awareness of what she must do in pursuing it. After her mother's transportation to the New World, she is ultimately registered as a ward of the city in Colchester and cared for by a nurse-schoolteacher who educates her pupils "as mannerly as if [they] had been at the dancing school" (11).

It is at this stage in her career that Moll embraces the idea of becoming a gentlewoman and first experiences an obsessive fear of servitude and destitution.

Both her desire and her anxiety derive from a deeply felt need for security, and already she instinctively realizes that whatever she wants is contingent upon the possession of money. Modeled upon the apparent freedom and security of a well-dressed local prostitute, her aspirations essentially reflect a commonsense preference for physical comfort, but even the expression of her desire to be a gentlewoman proves profitable, for when respectable Colchester families learn of her ambition, they indulgently humor her improbable fantasies and give her money. By convincing the nurse-schoolteacher that she can support herself by needlework and teaching, Moll herself avoids the usual fate of orphans, who were put to service at an early age. Indeed, her entire stay with the older woman represents a rudimentary business deal. In return for the money which Moll earns or receives from the respectable townspeople, the nurse-schoolteacher guarantees her a modicum of security and independence.

When her protectress dies, Moll fears being "turn'd out of doors to the wide world" (17) and deprived of the relative comfort which she enjoys. As a consequence, she overcomes her distaste for servitude and readily engages herself as a chambermaid and young ladies' companion in one of the upper middle-class families which had shown an interest in her. As an orphan with neither money nor expectations, Moll is apparently quite unrealistic in her dreams of becoming a gentlewoman, but she soon learns that she is more beautiful and talented than the daughters of the respectable Colchester family; why shouldn't she aspire to the same material well-being which they are presumably destined to enjoy? Her pride convinces her that she is entitled to it, and for the rest of her life, her efforts will be directed toward procuring the genteel life-style which, in her eyes, she deserves.[12]

But Moll has not yet fully assimilated the rules of the game, and because she so ardently longs for gentility and freedom, she remains vulnerable to the schemes of anyone who appears to offer her what she desires. Thus, when the elder brother in the Colchester family entreats her to become his mistress and promises to marry her, she is "taken up only with the pride of [her] beauty, and of being belov'd by such a gentleman" (25). All her "solid reflections" are silenced, and she accedes to his solicitations, because she is still living in a sentimental fantasy world where without striving she hopes to receive the physical and emotional satisfactions of having both money and a handsome gentleman husband; in reality, the elder brother has no intention of marrying her; his promises are merely part of his strategy to seduce an attractive young chambermaid. To rationalize his enjoyment of her favors, he is continually giving her money—five guineas after he first speaks to her of his passion, a hundred guineas just before he seduces her, and five hundred pounds when he convinces her to marry his younger brother. In effect, he is paying her for her services, and because he has paid her quite well, he feels no qualms about discontinuing the relationship when it is no longer in his interest to maintain it. Although she was as fascinated with the money as she was with her lover—"I spent whole hours in looking upon it; I told the guineas over a thousand times a day" (25)—she associates it with emotional attachment and assumes that the hundred guineas which he calls an "earnest" of his affections are given "in earnest." Duped by his mask of sincerity, she fails to comprehend that for him an earnest is no more than a money payment, a substitute for emotional engagement.

Her sentimental expectation of obtaining emotional security through love, and gentility through money, is shattered by the elder brother's disavowal, and the illness which follows her disappointment reflects the impact of her initiation into the "wickedness of the times." In theory society does not sanction misrepresentation and seduction; in practice most people act as the elder brother has acted. In pursuing self-interest, they mask their true desires and attempt to outwit others. At first Moll refuses to engage in this sort of behavior, as she would be doing if she accepted the younger brother's proposal of marriage, but as at the moment of the nurse-schoolteacher's death, Moll fears being "turn'd out of doors" (31) if she perseveres in her rejection of a prudent but personally repug-nant course of action. Despite her vow never to commit the "unnatural" act of marrying her lover's brother, she ultimately opts for the lesser of two evils, pretends to be a virgin and resigns herself to drawing some advantage from the situation. Like Lazarillo after his experience with the stone bull or Guzmán after his experiences at the various inns on the road to Madrid, Moll perceives that she is alone in the world and must adapt herself to its ways if she hopes to survive and prosper. Realizing that she has been exchanging sex for money, she resolves to play society's game according to its rules. The fact that she ultimately achieves the sort of marriage which she had envisioned when she first yielded to the impor-tunities of the elder brother indicates the fundamental difference between her fictional world and that of the two Spanish pícaros; whereas they are dehumanized in the socializing process, she acquires a knowledge of both her vocation and the most effective means of pursuing it.

From this point on, Moll never completely trusts anyone's words; she has been "trick'd once by that cheat call'd love" (53), but she resolves never to be fooled again. By eliminating sentimental considerations from her pursuit of security, she signals her acceptance of a world in which everyone inevitably acts out of self-interest, and acts best when acting rationally. In such a world, it behooves people to enter into agreements with others when some form of cooperation can serve their mutual self-interest. This contractual approach to human relationships breeds a suspicious, exploitive attitude, but as the shrewd Quaker William in *Colonel Jacque* contends, "I would as soon trust a man whose interest binds him to be just to me, as a man whose principle binds himself."[13] If one's primary allegiance is to self-interest, it becomes possible to remain honest while misleading others and refusing to communicate openly and honestly with them. It is in precisely this fashion that Moll is honest about her own dishonesty.

For a woman in seventeenth-century England, the most promising contractual relationship was an advantageous marriage. As a beautiful and talented chambermaid without a dowry, Moll rises in society by accepting the younger brother's marriage proposal, and after his premature death she determines "to be married or nothing, and to be well married or not at all" (53). In her eyes, marriage has become a business deal in which she exchanges sexual favors and fidelity for security and respectability. In retrospect, she doesn't regret having lost her virginity to the elder brother; she simply regrets that her own sentimentality had blinded her to its real value and prompted her to sell it far too cheaply. In all her subsequent liaisons and marriages, she suppresses emotional considerations and seeks to obtain the highest possible price for her consent. Her attitude represents the only "prudent" course of action in a world where all people are naturally motivated by self-interest.[14]

The commercial attitude, which demands that everything and everyone be regarded in terms of their profit-making potential, reduces all human relationships to the cash nexus and fosters solitude and insensitivity toward others, but this is the price of survival in a society of omnipresent masks. Because all Defoe's major characters are intent upon surviving and prospering, they even learn to consider this lack of genuine communication as an advantage. Moll exclaims, "Oh! what a felicity is it to mankind . . . that they cannot see into the hearts of one another!" (158). And the bourgeois narrator of *Journal of the Plague Year* (1722) discovers that isolation and emotional independence can provide protective barriers against the infections and dishonest schemes of other people; one might even consider loneliness the inevitable consequence of a prudently managed life, as Robinson Crusoe does when he declares that "life in general is, or ought to be, but one universal act of solitude."[15] Within this context, Moll's assimilation of selfish and deceptive modes of behavior becomes the opposite of what it had been for Lazarillo and Guzmán. Rather than dehumanizing her, the socializing process prepares her to cope with reality and fulfill her dreams of gentility.

Even after her conversion she demonstrates the same shrewd business sense which had been honed to perfection during her earlier career of prostitution, thievery, and marriages of convenience. Like every other successful character in Defoe's fiction, she recognizes the need to develop a strategy and establish her "credit." Because she often lacks sufficient capital or social standing to justify the gentility for which she yearns, she must pretend to be more respectable, wealthy, or trustworthy than she actually is; in other words, she must assume a mask which will deceive others into accepting her for what she is not. These masks allow her to profit from the ignorance of others and protect herself from people whose self-interest may conflict with her own, for as she admits to the banker, "I had never met with a man or woman yet that I could trust, or in whom I could think my self safe" (116). At the very moment when she admits her distrustful attitude, her behavior toward the banker demonstrates how this attitude can be translated into action. On her second visit to him, she fears that he might accompany her home and, knowing where she lives, inquire into her character and circumstances, but upon reflecting that her neighbors don't know the truth about her disreputable past, she becomes reassured and concludes that the reader can easily perceive "how necessary it is for all women who expect any thing in the world to preserve the character of their virtue, even when perhaps they may have sacrifiz'd the thing itself" (120). If she hopes to exchange her sexual favors and extremely modest income for the genteel life-style which the banker could provide, she must maintain the appearance of a virtue which she does not possess, and this is particularly important, since the banker is already unhappily married to a woman whom he calls a "whore."

In collaborating with other thieves, Moll always conceals her identity and her place of residence; on several occasions, this prudence effectually safeguards her from danger, because when her companions are arrested, they cannot identify her, although they might be willing to betray her in bargaining for lighter sentences. Even at the moment of telling her story, Moll refuses to reveal her actual name, because criminal charges remain outstanding against her at Old Bailey. From her point of view, masks constitute ways of exploiting her limited resources and protecting herself. The masks of others are like snares, and she must continually avoid being trapped by them. During her initiation, she had been fooled by the elder brother's mask-snare, but after the rude shock of being repudiated by him, she perceives how she must act, and for the rest of her life she continues to manipulate appearances and set snares for others.

The crucial point at which Moll's story diverges from those of the earliest Spanish pícaros involves the religious "conversion" which takes place at Newgate prison and supposedly transforms her from a sinner to a penitent. Until this point, her actions have been evaluated according to two different sets of values, and although they are compatible in Defoe's world view, they yield quite different judgments of Moll's character. From a perspective dictated by the need to struggle for survival in a world of economic competition, she is engaged in the justifiable pursuit of self-interest; from a religious point of view, her increasing dependence upon immoral and illegal actions makes her the central character in a history of spiritual degeneration. Before her "conversion" Moll lacks the one quality—religious feeling—which according to Defoe allows people to reconcile economic individualism with "honest" role-playing. Without religious feeling, she is incapable of rationally pursuing true self-interest, because she ignores the powerful influence of Providence in all human affairs, overlooks the self-blinding dominance of pride and greed in her own character, and suppresses the horror of stealing from those who are as unfortunate as she is. Under these circumstances she is subject to a state of mind in which reason, applied only to the calculation of her apparent short-term self-interest, actually prevents her from obtaining the freedom and security which she desires.

All her dishonest activities are merely outward manifestations of this false consciousness. The narrating Moll admits that people like the elder brother or the governess "reason'd me out of my reason" (51, 150), but although others might reinforce her impulses toward evil, her own power of reasoning will be subverted as long as she remains in this "harden'd" state of mind, as another of Defoe's major characters realizes: "a vicious inclination removed from the object is still a vicious inclination, and contracts the same guilt as if the object were at hand. . . . All motions to good or evil are in the soul. Outward objects are but second causes."[16] To become virtuous, Moll needs not only to eschew thievery and prostitution, she must alter her fundamental attitude toward life, but only when an external event catalyzes her potential for insight does she begin to suspect the flaws in her outlook. When she is arrested and imprisoned in Newgate for attempting to steal a trifling amount of cloth, her worst fears are realized, but in one sense Newgate—that "emblem of Hell"—is merely the symbolic equivalent of the anxiety and lack of freedom which a "harden'd" attitude had already imposed upon her.

Newgate itself is a disgusting, noisome, filthy place which breeds criminals rather than reforming them, and although it at first sickens Moll, she soon becomes accustomed to it and even feels "as naturally pleas'd and easy with the place as if indeed [she] had been born there" (242), which of course she had. As on many previous occasions, she succumbs to habit, which conditions people in a "harden'd" state of mind to accept things which at first appeared revolting and unnatural. After accommodating herself to the thought of marrying her lover's brother and later to abandoning her own children, she reaches the final stage of moral corruption when she resigns herself to the unnatural ugliness of Newgate; as she herself admits, the worst of all human conditions involves the willing acceptance of evil without realizing that it is evil.

At this physical and spiritual nadir of her career, she sees Jemy being brought into the prison. Because she can empathize with the gentleman thief who had once exhausted his own modest resources to gain her nonexistent fortune, she for the first time reflects seriously upon the consequences of her previous deceptions—"conscious guilt began to flow in my mind. In short, I began to think, and to think indeed is one real advance from hell to heaven; all that harden'd state and temper of soul . . . is but a deprivation of thought; he that is restor'd to his thinking is restor'd to himself" (245). Shocked into a new state of consciousness by the appearance of Jemy and the exemplary but unexpected conversion of the governess, Moll begins to perceive her illicit activities in their true light and to recognize how unreasonable it had been for her, a woman with over £700, to steal two relatively insignificant pieces of cloth. Moll's heightened vision of reality resembles a spiritual rebirth. Ironically, this rebirth occurs at the very place where she had been born sixty years earlier and initiates a series of experiences which parallel those of her own mother—a woman who had been imprisoned at Newgate for a similar crime before being transported to America, where she became a respectable penitent and a wealthy gentlewoman.

From the vantage point created by this new awareness, Moll perceives what she considers to be the true significance of events which she had not understood while experiencing them. Modeling her confession upon spiritual and devotional works of the period, she recognizes patterns of "hardening" and "providential" intervention behind the random, apparently chaotic episodes of her life.[17] Because Defoe believed that the divine operates through natural phenomena, he was convinced that close scrutiny of any experience could reveal the working of Providence. For this reason, he himself was willing to expend considerable effort in trying to compile a definitive account of the particularly violent storm which devastated London in 1703.[18] By an extension of this principle, anyone can further his knowledge of divine order by seeking to comprehend what Robinson Crusoe calls the "allusive allegorical history" of one's own life. For example, at first glance Crusoe's shipwreck and Moll's imprisonment appear to be unmitigated catastrophes, but within a larger frame of reference, they are actually providential, because they provoke a cognizance of the divine plan and an attitude in which the rational pursuit of one's long-term self-interest becomes possible. Moll's detailed record of her own past thus becomes both an interpretation of previous events from a postconversion perspective and an attempted expression of the wisdom implicit in that perspective.

Within this context, her previous experiences are regarded as a progression from moral blindness and rebellion against God to the development of habits which harden her against an awareness of Providence. At first, motivated by "necessity," she is aware that her actions are immoral or illegal, but as she acquires a small fortune she becomes increasingly motivated by vanity and greed. In this perverted state of consciousness, she perpetrates the same abuses which had been perpetrated upon her. Originally horrified at the prospect of marrying her lover's brother, she eventually marries her own brother and inflicts a similar horror upon him. Originally seduced by a wealthy gentleman who overcame her reservations, she herself seduces a banker who prides himself on being able to sleep with her in the same bed without making love. Such reversals of roles suggest Moll's growing insensitivity toward the nature of her own actions, and the narrator, taking her cue from contemporary religious works, integrates them into the characteristic hardening process which would undoubtedly have been familiar to contemporary readers.

From her supposedly enlightened perspective, Moll portrays her previous impulses toward vice as promptings from the devil and her impulses toward virtue as signs of special Providence. It is the devil, she says, who prompts her to take the bundle from an apothecary's shop and suggests that she murder a little girl from whom she steals a necklace; the devil carries her out to look for booty and prevents her from abandoning a life of crime when she has sufficient wealth to live comfortably. She might resist the "wicked impulse" or "evil counsellor within" (168), as she does in regard to the child or when she momentarily resolves to mend her ways, but habit and initial success deaden her fear of being apprehended. At the same time, she remains susceptible to insights which, if properly understood, are capable of bringing about her reform. For example, when her savings reach £200, she contemplates a comfortable retirement, and it is at this point that she visits an unfortunate former colleague who has been imprisoned at Newgate. Although the young woman's fate graphically illustrates the revolting punishment from which no criminal is immune, Moll turns her back upon its meaning and discontinues her visits because the place of her own birth nauseates her. In the narrator's eyes, her serious reflections constituted a "blessed hint" and took place in a "happy minute" (176); they were, in other words, impulses from Providence. Like the promptings of the "devil," these impulses can be efficacious only if she chooses to heed them, but in neither case do Moll's descriptive terms emerge directly from the events of her story; on the contrary, they form parts of a pattern being imposed upon those events by a woman who conceives of herself as a repentant sinner and employs a traditional religious vocabulary to project herself as one.

It is in this light that Moll's depiction of her final happiness must be understood. She claims to experience joy at having reconciled her psychological and material needs by conducting her affairs prudently and placing herself in harmony with Providence, but the fact remains that she is the one who attributes her propitious circumstances to divine intervention. Even her descriptions of the weather seem to reflect the change in her state of consciousness. When she unwittingly marries her half-brother, accompanies him to America, and returns to England, she experiences two extremely tempestuous crossings, but when she and Jemy become "new people in a new world" (264), their journeys there and back take place in the calmest possible weather. In fact, the entire concluding section of *Moll Flanders* is posited upon a series of ideological assumptions which cause Moll's fictional world to actually reflect the principles of a poetic justice to which she herself attributes her final happiness. As soon as her conversion allows her to perceive her self-interest more clearly, her dreams of gentility and emotional security are fulfilled. It is true that the pastor who visits her at Newgate advises her to "improve" the additional time granted her by the reprieve, and she does conduct the business of life so skillfully that she attains a "zenith of good fortune," but it is also true that when she arrives in America she receives a small fortune from her mother's estate to compensate her for a total lack of inheritance at the moment of her original birth at Newgate. If her sinful behavior originates in "necessity," physical well-being in a less structured society frees her to act virtuously and recognize what is presumably best and most true about herself.

In Moll's eyes, her autobiography is a success story which culminates in a happy ending. By accepting an imperfect society on its own terms, she believes that she can survive and prosper without forfeiting her right to salvation, and by acquiring the wealth and gentility toward which she has always aspired, she is fulfilling a dream which has sustained her since her earliest childhood experiences in Colchester. Her emotional security assured by the presence of an affectionate husband and her physical well-being by a substantial sum of money, she feels confident in linking her material success with her moral virtue. All such links have been rendered suspect by Defoe's cautionary comments in the preface, but he himself created Moll's fictional world, and it is an open one, full of potential for lower-class, wandering individuals who desire to rise in society without relinquishing a good opinion of themselves. In contrast to Lazarillo, Moll need never choose between prosperity and self-esteem, respectability and her conception of virtue.

By acknowledging the inevitability of selfishness and solitude and by according a positive spiritual value to mask-wearing and the accumulation of wealth, she succeeds where Lazarillo fails, and in this success lies one of the reasons for the popular appeal of *Moll Flanders* in eighteenth-century England. In the preface, Defoe distances himself from the fictive narrator, but he never calls the fact of Moll's material success into question, nor does he denigrate the vitality with which she undertakes risky enterprises, rebounds from defeat, and ultimately obliges a recalcitrant environment to grant her what she desires. In essence, Moll is a disarmingly congenial individual who attains her dream after overcoming numerous hardships and temptations. Because her visions of prosperity, respectability, and marital felicity corresponded to those of many middle- and lower-class Englishmen, it is hardly surprising that her success story appealed to them.

Unlike his contemporaries Pope and Swift, Defoe was not writing for an intellectual or social elite, and the "plain style" of his novels reflects the tastes of a rapidly growing nonaristocratic book-buying public—a public which tended to prefer useful books written in a clear, morally serious fashion and dealing with facts and practical problems.[19] This public was largely middle class, but all Defoe's novels were reprinted in cheap, unauthorized editions which became quite popular among servants, apprentices, and other literate people from the lower classes. Although the literary establishment looked askance at the vulgarity of such writings, it was Defoe who succeeded in drawing together themes and techniques from disparate sources (criminal biography, social and scientific tracts, religious writing, sensationalist journalism) and fusing them into internally coherent, imaginative works which stand at the beginnings of the English novel tradition. Like the anonymous author of *Lazarillo*, Defoe skillfully manipulated the pseudoautobiographical perspective as a unifying device in a narrative based upon the assumption that even the most vulgar character's life is worthy of morally serious literary treatment, because it illustrates the process by means of which everyone assimilates commonly accepted values and modes of behavior. But there is a clear disjunction between Lázaro's attitudes and the implicit world view in *Lazarillo*, whereas Moll's ideas frequently overlap with the standards according to which she is presumably judged. In this difference and in the diametrically opposed endings of the two novels are reflected both the rise of bourgeois ideology and the ambiguity of bourgeois attitudes toward success.

10
THE PICARESQUE HERO ARRIVES:
SENTIMENT AND SUCCESS IN
LESAGE'S
Gil Blas

For eighteenth- and nineteenth-century European readers, the most familiar example of picaresque fiction was undoubtedly Alain-René Lesage's *Histoire de Gil Blas de Santillane* (1715, 1724, 1735),[1] but although Lesage borrowed extensively from the Spanish picaresque tradition, *Gil Blas* has relatively little in common with *Lazarillo*, *Guzmán*, and *El Buscón*. By the early eighteenth century, a generally accepted link between French comic novels and translations of Spanish picaresque novels had already established a conventional image of the picaresque hero as a noble-souled adventurer who achieves secular happiness after having perceived the world's hypocrisy and injustice and demonstrated his own integrity, honesty, and wit. By adapting this convention to the tastes of a growing bourgeois reading public without completely repudiating aristocratic ideological assumptions, Lesage continued to receive an annual pension from his noble patron, while attracting a sufficiently large popular audience to become the first French novelist capable of supporting himself by the sale of his books.[2]

During the quarter century which preceded the first publication of *Gil Blas*, France experienced a marked resurgence of interest in picaresque literature, and as the translator of numerous Spanish works, Lesage recognized that a potential market existed for the further exploitation of materials drawn from this tradition. In 1678 Abbé Jean-Antoine de Charnes had retranslated *Lazarillo* into the polite style of an adventure story, replacing the original narrator's cynicism with an air of gallantry; this edition was reprinted five times between 1690 and 1721. In 1696 Gabriel de Brémond brought out a popular new translation of *Guzmán* and two years later Sieur Raclot published a new version of *El Buscón*. Between

1700 and 1709 *Marcos de Obregón* was reissued more times than it had been during the previous eighty years.[3]

With the exception of his enormously popular *Le diable boiteux* (1707; revised 1726), a free adaptation of Vélez de Guevara's *El diablo cojuelo*, Lesage completed his versions of Spanish picaresque novels—*Guzman d'Alfarache* (1732) and *Histoire d'Estévanille Gonzalez* (1734; revised 1741)—after *Gil Blas* had already established the popularity of the narrative formulas which he later imposed upon them. Precisely for that reason, his modifications of the Spanish texts clearly reveal the principles according to which he composed his own picaresque fiction and the reasons why his versions surpassed the originals in popularity.[4] Like the earlier comic novels, Lesage's adaptations of Spanish picaresque novels focus upon a handsome, congenial young man who experiences a series of adventures and, despite low birth and the pervasive corruption of society, moves toward a state of peace and temporal harmony in which he accepts the world's imperfections and enjoys (or anticipates) a realizable earthly happiness.

Lesage's Guzman and Cleofas do not actually achieve this happiness, but they are so similar in character and outlook to characters like don Chérubin in *Le Bachelier de Salamanque* (1736, 1738) and Estévanille Gonzalez, who do acquire wealth and bourgeois respectability, that readers would have no difficulty imagining such a conclusion; in fact, when he revised *Le diable boiteux*, Lesage modified the ending to heighten the suggestion that Cleofas will soon enjoy a felicitous marriage with the beautiful, wealthy Seraphina, who has become enamored of him as a consequence of the limping devil's efforts in his behalf. Alemán and Vélez had employed picaresque themes to unmask the deceptiveness of earthly vanities; Lesage adopted them to entertain readers whose entire system of values was posited upon a belief that wealth, pleasure, and reputation could provide happiness for a person who did not attach supreme importance to them.

By naming Vélez' anonymous limping devil "Asmodeus" and fusing him with "Cupid," Lesage transformed him into the spirit who presides over successful love affairs as well as foolish and dishonest ones. It is in this capacity that Asmodeus relates two intercalated tales (a third was added in 1726) in which sentimental love triumphs over pride or opposing loyalties and culminates in marriage. Like the successful lovers in these tales, Cleofas is susceptible to errors of judgment, but he is also capable of wit, generous sentiments, and a modicum of control over his environment.

Fig. 21. Lesage's Cleofas meets the limping devil
(Johannot, 1842)

Before escaping from dona Thomasa's apartment, he fought valiantly against her four bullies, and because his fictional world operates to reward him for his possession of innately noble qualities, he has the satisfaction of seeing her arrested and imprisoned when Asmodeus-Cupid casts dissension among the bullies. The panoramic vision of society which passes before his eyes serves not to disabuse Cleofas of illusions about love but to inculcate him with a resigned acceptance of what he cannot change—the vices and follies of his fellowmen. Ultimately it is this attitude which renders him worthy of the happy ending promised by the 1726 conclusion. In a corrupt world, Lesage implies, a harmonious, peaceful existence remains possible for individuals who are endowed with the intelligence, common sense, generosity, good taste, and basic integrity to deserve it.

To make Alemán's *Guzmán* conform to his pattern, Lesage was obliged to deviate even more drastically from the letter and spirit of the original text. Nearly everything associated with the "desengaño" and "converso" themes was omitted. In Alemán's novel, the hero's revolting experiences represent physical equivalents of the mental states in which people attach supreme importance to worldly goals. Lesage suppressed these episodes, but he was not satisfied with simply omitting the offensive account of Guzmán's humiliations while courting a young woman in Saragossa, for he insisted upon including a footnote to characterize the incident as being in such poor taste that it was inappropriate for translation. In addition, Lesage removed the fictive narrator's asides to the reader, shifting the focus away from overtly moral concerns and toward the actual experiences of the protagonist. Although he severely criticized Brémond's translation, Lesage worked directly from it, and many passages near the end of his *Guzman* are taken verbatim from the earlier version. When Brémond diverged from the original narrative, Lesage usually followed, but whereas Brémond retained the sermonizing digressions and even added some of his own, Lesage found them objectionable in a work of entertainment and felt justified in purging the novel of what he called its dogmatic air and superfluous moralities. In his introduction to *Guzman*, he contended that the comic potential and entertaining nature of the original would emerge more clearly if the action were presented in a continuous, uninterrupted narrative to provide readers with material for reflection, reserving to them the secret pleasure of discovering the work's underlying morality. But the implicit morality of these experiences is itself considerably modified in Lesage's version of the novel. Even the hapless Guzman becomes capable of successfully consummating his love affairs, and although he is still in the galleys at the end of Lesage's narrative, he is calmly awaiting a pardon which will permit him to enjoy the more reasonable life he has resolved to lead. Because neither Guzman's character nor his fictional world presents insurmountable obstacles to marital felicity and a materially comfortable existence, it becomes perfectly plausible to imagine him living like don Chérubin or Estévanille Gonzalez in a gentlemanly retirement—an ending just as improbable within Alemán's context of values as La Geneste's conclusion to the *Buscon* would have been within the framework of Quevedo's ideological assumptions.

Whatever their distinguishing characteristics may have been in the original texts, Lesage's Cleofas, Guzman, and Estévanille Gonzalez all become attractive, talented adventure-story heroes who experience innate impulses toward virtue, enjoy amorous conquests without being thrust into humiliating circumstances, and finally achieve the prospect of a destiny appropriate to their natures. The basically similar plot structures which characterize all these novels perhaps reflect the influence of the Persian and Turkish tales which Lesage published in collaboration with Pétis de la Croix.[5] In many of these tales, a prince reduced to poverty travels extensively, but he overcomes all obstacles, regains the position which he merits, marries a beautiful woman, and devotes the rest of his life to the pursuit of wisdom. The obstacles which prevent him from occupying his rightful position in society serve as interest-provoking pretexts to prolong a story that will end when secular happiness is assured. By setting his picaresque novels outside France and placing Spanish characters at the center of them, Lesage could adapt similar narrative patterns to the more ordinary adventures of nonaristocratic heroes without completely losing the exotic appeal of unfamiliar places and foreign peoples.

In the novels of Lesage, however, this exotic appeal is always balanced by a sequence of events which eighteenth-century French readers could accept as real. All his characters exist within historically and geographically plausible environments. In adapting Boiardo's *Orlando amoroso* he admitted, "J'ai substitué à ces pays imaginaires des royaumes marqués sur la carte, et les rois qui se trouvent devant Albraque n'y sont point en dépit du bon sens ni de la géographie" ("For these imaginary countries I substituted kingdoms which can be found on the map, and the kings who are in front of Albrac are not there in defiance of either common sense or geography").[6] By replacing Boiardo's fabulous realms with real countries and modifying the action to exclude impossible or improbable events, Lesage cultivated the same impression which he sought in his adaptations of Spanish picaresque fiction; he was trying to create the illusion that his characters were real people whose adventures could be traced upon real maps. To achieve this, he frequently had recourse to historical or geographical source materials; and in his picaresque novels, he heightened the illusion of verisimilitude by explaining local customs and including an occasional Spanish word.[7]

His limping devil even loses the supernatural elements with which Vélez had endowed him. *Le diable boiteux* sustains a commonsense level of plausibility, because it is presented as a dream or vision which might have occurred to Cleofas one night while he was preoccupied with thoughts of love. When he first sees the limping devil, he acknowledges having been in Asmodeus-Cupid's service for a long time, implying that this particular spirit appeared to him because he was continually involved in amorous affairs. More than half the limping devil's "tableaux" are devoted to follies committed in the name of passion or gallantry. Together with his stories of sentimental love, these scenes are calculated to provide Cleofas with "une parfaite connaissance de la vie humaine" ("a perfect knowledge of human life").[8] Asmodeus-Cupid himself admits that he can do instantaneously only what nature accomplishes more slowly; the implication is that Cleofas could have obtained the same "perfect knowledge of human life" over a longer period of time by simply paying attention to what happened around him. The dream suggestion is enhanced by the fact that Lesage compressed the entire action of the novel into a single night and obliged Asmodeus-Cupid to obey the irresistible summons of his magician-master at the dawning of a new day.

This penchant for plausibility is also reflected in Lesage's characterization of the picaresque heroes in his novels. Although calculated to evoke a sense of vicarious excitement, characters like Estévanille, Guzman, and Cleofas are nevertheless portrayed as if they were average Frenchmen whose aspirations and moral values resemble those of Lesage's assumed reader. No longer concerned with an attempt to overcome his converso origins, Lesage's French Guzman is neither particularly virtuous nor entirely corrupt. If he does not undergo a religious conversion, he also does not betray the mutineers, as Alemán's Guzmán had done. When reduced to poverty, he does not despair, because he realizes that a more favorable situation will evolve in the normal course of events, and he feels confident that, when it does arise, he will possess the talent and genius to take advantage of it. Although he never completely loses the attractive qualities which he shares with Lesage's other picaresque heroes and which entitle them to happiness, he remains sufficiently flexible to adapt himself to the various milieux through which he travels.

Despite low or questionable birth, Cleofas, Estévanille, don Chérubin, and even Guzman can successfully integrate themselves into a hierarchically organized society in which they are free to rise. Their eventual happiness is not contingent upon aristocratic birth; it is attributable to innate qualities. More like the heroes of Sorel's *Francion*, La Geneste's *Buscon*, and Scarron's *Roman comique* than Moll Flanders or the Spanish pícaros, they are rewarded not for any specific actions which they perform, but for the noble nature which expresses itself in those actions. For Lesage, Spanish picaresque novels constituted a storehouse of incidents and situations, but he embellished them so skillfully that he transformed his disparate materials into adventure stories admirably suited to the tastes and sensibilities of a rapidly growing French reading public. By portraying the picaresque hero as if he were the protagonist of a romance set in a real-seeming, concrete, nonheroic world and by endowing him with the average Frenchman's standards of common sense and decorum, Lesage succeeded in captivating large numbers of readers, because he fulfilled their yearning for vicarious escape and their demands for plausibility without repudiating either the aristocratic assumption of inherent nobility or the bourgeois dream of upward social mobility.

The enormous and enduring popularity of *Gil Blas* is at least partially comprehensible in these terms, but despite the novel's success, its impulse to reconcile two different world views in the characterization of a picaresque hero is not without contradiction. On the one hand, Gil Blas is a noble-souled adventurer whose fictional world operates in such a way that he is ultimately rewarded for his innate qualities of soul and mind; on the other, he is a rather average individual whose protean flexibility permits him to survive and prosper by adapting himself to a series of morally corrupt environments. Whereas the first type of characterization implies that an individual's personality and fate are determined by his nature, the second suggests the importance of the socializing process. Within the autobiographical format of the novel, the latent contradiction between these two conceptions of character is overcome in the mind of Lesage's relatively unobtrusive narrator. Filtered through the good-humored, ironic detachment of his consciousness, the events of Gil Blas's past life and the satirical portraits of secondary characters conform to patterns of poetic justice in which people's supposedly true natures are revealed. As in *Simplicissimus* and *Moll Flanders*, the unifying principle of *Gil Blas* is the perspective of a fictive narrator who presents his previous experiences as illustrations of his present attitudes. If his story is morally instructive, as he insists that it is, the morality is perhaps to be found in his ability to smile indulgently at his own transgressions and at the perversity of others. In actuality he could never have attained prosperity and marital bliss without participating in the activities of a corrupt society, but from his point of view, moral compromise and mask-wearing are merely instruments for coping with that society, whereas his present happiness represents an appropriate reward for his inherently noble nature.

Written at widely separated intervals during a twenty-year period, *Gil Blas* reflects shifts in the author's dominant preoccupations, but continuity is maintained in that the same ideological assumptions and conceptions of character are applied to each stage in the protagonist's variegated career. When Lesage finished the first six books of *Gil Blas* in 1715, he undoubtedly conceived of it as a completed novel; however, its popular success prompted him to add three books in 1724 and three more in 1735. Each of these three sections has a happy ending which could function as a plausible conclusion, but whenever Lesage resurrected his picaresque hero, he carefully knit the new section to the old one by developing strands of action which had been merely adumbrated previously.

Modeled to a large extent upon Vicente Espinel's *Marcos de Obregón,* the first six books describe Gil Blas's young manhood. He serves many masters and learns what he must do in order to survive; the happy ending is assured when he is appointed steward on don Alphonse's country estate. After experiencing the "small world," Gil Blas like Goethe's Faust enters the "great world" of archbishops, prime ministers, and kings. Characters from the first section reappear in the second one, and events correspond to those recorded in history books. In this section, Gil Blas experiences a precipitous rise in social status, while suffering a decline in moral sensitivity. The parallel development culminates in his fall from the duke of Lerma's favor, but although his imprisonment in the Tower of Segovia at first appears to be a catastrophe, it actually serves as a catalyst which awakens him to the threatened disintegration of his basically decent character. The final sections of the novel demonstrate that the emotionally mature hero can occupy responsible positions without losing his sense of virtue; after twenty years of service to the Count-Duke Olivares, he retires to his own country estate at Lirias, marries a beautiful noblewoman, and resolves to lead a life of philosophical resignation.

The quality which renders him worthy of this happiness is variously attributed to his "âme généreuse" (generous soul), his "génie" (cleverness, intelligence), his "bon naturel" (good nature) or his sense of personal honor, but the implication is always the same: from birth Gil Blas is endowed with an inherently noble nature. No matter how much he compromises his integrity while accommodating himself to a corrupt society, this nature functions as an indestructible kernel of selfhood, and as long as he maintains a humble, intellectually honest attitude, his noble character will ultimately be rewarded by an appropriate place in the social hierarchy. Gil Blas learns much about generally accepted modes of behavior in society, but in the final analysis, what he learns is less important than who he is. Like Marcos de Obregón, he is the son of poor but respectable parents who give him good advice: "Ils m'exhortèrent... à vivre en honnête homme, à ne me point engager dans de mauvaises affaires, et, sur toutes choses, à ne pas prendre le bien d'autrui" (I,5) ("They urged me... to live like an honest man, never to become engaged in dishonest activities, and above all things, not to take the possessions of others").[9] His intelligence is recognized quite early and cultivated by a generous uncle, who gives him enough money to begin his studies at the university. Because his trip to Salamanca is interrupted by highwaymen who take him prisoner, Gil Blas never receives the education which might have enabled him to become a clergyman like his uncle, but he does something much more exciting; he experiences a series of adventures which sharpen his intellect and introduce him to the inevitable corruption of life in society. As a naive, talented young man whose inheritance includes legitimate birth, money, and good advice, he might adopt the ways of that society, but he also possesses a sufficiently strong sense of identity to avoid becoming totally corrupted by it.

The qualities which comprise this incorruptible sense of identity—intelligence, wit, good humor, honesty, and an ability to communicate openly on a sentimental level with like-minded individuals—are sufficiently generalized that they might be associated with both bourgeois and aristocratic values. Like an ambitious bourgeois, Gil Blas employs wit and ingenuity pragmatically to improve his position in the social hierarchy; like a noble-spirited adventurer, he also uses them to extricate himself from difficulties—to escape from the robbers' dens into which chance precipitates him. In general, his intelligence is tempered by a good-natured equanimity. Knowing that everything changes, the narrator believes that under adverse circumstances a reasonable man needs only exercise his patience and take advantage of more propitious conditions when they arise. Whenever he takes himself too seriously and loses the ability to laugh at himself, misfortune overtakes him, but misfortune is always temporary, and in retrospect he realizes that it was just as foolish of him to despair when imprisoned in the Tower of Segovia as it had been for him to exult during his earlier good fortune under Lerma. He now knows that it would have been better to maintain an attitude of calm resignation, for in a world of constantly changing realities, such an attitude will allow him the greatest latitude to exercise his own wit and intelligence.

Another aspect of Gil Blas's noble nature is his conscience. Never is he completely free from the "reste d'honneur et de religion" ("remnant of honor and religion") which causes him to repudiate thievery and vulgarity. During his exemplary service to the Count-Duke Olivares, he is perhaps not sufficiently virtuous to reject all immoral actions, but he is incapable of committing them without remorse; for example, after reluctantly agreeing to provide a mistress for the king, he brings the beautiful young Lucrèce to Madrid. Mortified by the role she is expected to play, Lucrèce retires to a convent where she dies of sorrow, and Gil Blas himself becomes so disgusted with his part in this melodramatic tragedy that he asks to be excused from similar duties in the future.

Gil Blas's ability to empathize with others—to feel and honestly communicate sentiment—is perhaps the most important index of his acceptance or rejection of his own noble nature. Usually open and generous, he weeps in sympathy for his friends in distress; he even feels compassion for characters like Lorença Sephora and Raphaël, who had been directly responsible for some of his own past difficulties. During his service to Lerma, however, Gil Blas becomes blinded by the importance of his own position and succumbs to a pride so exaggerated that it threatens to destroy every vestige of his basically decent character. Despite his considerable wealth, he even refuses to succor his indigent parents and the uncle to whom he was indebted for his start in life. When Fabrice admonishes him for the artificiality of his manners, Gil Blas would rather break off their long-standing friendship than listen to the truth.

Only after his illness and imprisonment in the Tower of Segovia does he return to himself and regret having treated others so shamefully. Because his faithful valet Scipion salvages several trunks of money and secures his master's freedom, Gil Blas receives a second chance, and in the last three books of the novel, he systematically makes amends to all those whose trust he had betrayed during his service to Lerma. He visits his parents and repairs his previous neglect. He renews his friendship with Fabrice, and rather than burying his sentiments beneath a mask of self-importance, he treats his old friend with frankness and generosity. When Olivares falls from favor, Gil Blas even follows the minister into exile, although he himself would not have been obliged to leave government service. Having regained an ability to establish relationships on the basis of sentiments like generosity, loyalty, and sincerity, he clearly demonstrates a capacity for decent behavior in elevated circumstances, and it is in this way that he proves himself worthy of the happiness which he claims to be experiencing at the end of the novel.

Although Gil Blas must adopt an appropriately detached attitude toward his wealth before he can properly enjoy it, his success is portrayed primarily as a function of his inherently noble characteristics. In Lesage's fictional world, virtue is neither learned nor contingent upon aristocratic birth—a fact amply illustrated by the autobiographies of secondary characters whose lives are implicitly compared with that of Gil Blas. Of the four highwaymen who tell their stories in the robbers' den, the first had wealthy parents and an expensive education, the second a brutal lower-class father and no education, and the third lower-class parents and a noble education, while the fourth had been trained as a priest in an ascetic order. The son of an actress, Raphaël had also received a good education after being adopted by a well-situated family. All these men become criminals; Gil Blas does not.

The reason for this is relatively simple; they lack an inherent quality which Gil Blas possesses. In Lesage's fictional universe, there are "génies" (clever, intelligent, witty people) and "sots" (stupid fools), but although ingenuity has positive connotations, it is a morally neutral quality, and the greatest rogues can be the most extraordinary "génies." As consummate role-players, Raphaël and Rolando (the leader of the bandits) represent what Gil Blas might have become if he had been unable to resist temptations to which they succumbed. After cleverly abetting a woman who desires to make a young nobleman fall in love with her, he himself admits, "si je voulais me mettre dans le génie, je deviendrais un habile fourbe" (I, 234) ("If I had wanted to exercise my ingenuity, I would have become an artful rogue"). And the duke of Lerma himself expresses astonishment that bad examples had not completely corrupted the young man whom he characterizes as a bit of a pícaro. After listening to Gil Blas's story, Lerma concludes, "Combien y a-t-il d'honnêtes gens qui deviendraient de grands fripons, si la fortune les mettait aux mêmes épreuves!" (II, 88) ("How many honest men would have become great rogues if fortune had subjected them to the same tests!") Gil Blas possesses the same "génie" as Rolando or Raphaël, but although he does suffer occasional lapses of moral sensitivity, he differs from them in precisely the manner implied by Lerma; a personal sense of honor prevents him from abandoning himself completely to the corrupt behavior patterns which he sees in others.

In Lesage's novel, characters either possess a predisposition toward honesty and decency or they do not. Like Gil Blas, Scipion and don Alphonse are exposed to the same opportunities as Rolando and Raphaël. Having previously engaged in dishonest activities, Scipion readily accommodates himself to the graft characteristic of Lerma's court, but certain types of action revolt him, and his loyalty is illustrated by a solicitude for his master's possessions and a willingness to share his master's imprisonment when Gil Blas falls from the minister's favor. Don Alphonse participates in a theft of 3,000 ducats from the wealthy Jew Samuel Simon, but he later repays the money. Like him, Gil Blas feels vaguely uneasy about participating in the theft, and when don Alphonse entrusts him with 3,000 ducats, he conscientiously returns the entire sum to Samuel Simon, although he could have kept it without running the slightest risk of detection. As he himself boasts, he acquitted himself like a "garçon d'honneur" (honorable young man). Taken together with his own story, the autobiographical accounts of these secondary characters provide a broad spectrum of possible reactions to the corrupt world. As an "honorable young man" with honest sentiments, Gil Blas instinctively repudiates Raphaël and Rolando, whereas he feels a strong elective affinity for don Alphonse, Scipion, and other noble-souled individuals like himself. Ultimately, it makes little difference whether an individual is born an aristocrat or a commoner, whether he is well or poorly educated; the crucial factor is the presence or absence of an innate inclination toward virtuous behavior.

Despite his inherently noble qualities, Gil Blas is not a heroic character who places absolute demands upon himself and his environment; in fact, within the context of an inevitably corrupt society, a refusal to feign compliance with its rules would be foolish and self-defeating. Very early in life, he learns the art of role-playing, for as one of the minor characters in the boy barber's tale contends, "le monde n'est guère vertueux que de cette façon. Il en coûte trop pour acquérir le fond des vertus: on se contente aujourd'hui d'en avoir les apparences" (I, 119) ("the world is hardly virtuous, except in this fashion. It costs too much to acquire real virtues: today people content themselves with having the appearances of them"). In such a world, Lesage's picaresque hero learns to do what everyone else is doing, and because he is among the "génies," he does it more skillfully and successfully. In a very real sense, his life is a series of roles adopted in response to the milieux through which he passes. When he is with thieves, he steals; when he serves the pretentious doctor Sangrado, he becomes an absurd doctor; when he is the valet of a dandy, he emulates the foppishness of his master. But none of these roles modify his basically decent character; they are simply justifiable, practical ways of coping with society.

The early episodes in *Gil Blas* are all adapted from *Marcos de Obregón* and constitute the protagonist's initiation into the world of masks. After being gulled by a flattering freeloader, he reflects upon his parents' advice and recognizes its limitations—"loin de m'exhorter à ne tromper personne, ils devaient me recommander de ne pas me laisser duper" (I, 10–11) ("far from urging me not to deceive others, they should have advised me not to allow myself to be deceived by others"). Gil Blas never completely loses the conscience or basic sense of honesty inculcated in him by his parents, but if he hopes to survive and prosper in a society comprised of deceivers and deceived, he realizes that it is necessary to avoid being among the deceived.

His subsequent experiences reinforce this lesson and suggest how he must act in situations where he cannot expect others to deal honestly with him. Deceived by a mule-driver's strategem to spend some time alone with a beautiful young woman, Gil Blas flees from the inn at Cacabelos and falls into the hands of Rolando and his men, from whom he escapes by lying and appropriating money from their coffers. Because he is wearing clothes stolen by the robbers, he is arrested and imprisoned by policemen who prove more mercenary than the highwaymen. Eventually set free, he is compensated for his loss of money by the thousand ducats given to him by a wealthy widow whom he had saved from the robbers' den, but blinded by his newfound wealth, he succumbs to the masquerade of a well-dressed young woman who claims to be the widow's cousin; in actuality, Camille and her two accomplices are swindlers who abscond with all his earthly possessions.

This series of experiences clearly establishes the basic premises of Gil Blas's mature world view. The freeloader, the mule-driver, the highwaymen, the policemen, and Camille all appear to be different from what they actually are, and Gil Blas suffers as a consequence of his failure to penetrate their masks. At first he is depressed at being "buried alive" in the robbers' den and again in the prison, but he leaves them, and his means of escape illustrate two of the most important recurrent patterns in the novel. In fleeing from the highwaymen, he does to them what the freeloader and the mule-driver had done to him: he dissimulates his true desire (freedom) beneath a mask (willingness to join the highwaymen). By adjusting his behavior to the demands of those who are more powerful than he is, he obtains what he desires. In contrast, when he leaves the prison and receives money from the wealthy widow, he is being rewarded for his ingenuity and basic decency in helping her to escape from her abductors. Unlike Moll Flanders, he did not earn the money by hard work or shrewd investment; he simply deserved it, and his fictional world operates in such a way that he receives what he deserves. On the one hand, he must involve himself in a corrupt world, and involvement implies compromise; on the other, he must retain a sense of personal honor, and if he acts accordingly, he will be rewarded for doing so. The loss of his small fortune to Camille and her accomplices illustrates the same lesson which he learned in more modest circumstances with the freeloader and which he will be obliged to relearn under more opulent ones in the duke of Lerma's service: whenever an overblown sense of one's own importance outweighs intelligence and a sense of proportion, one becomes particularly vulnerable to the deceptions of others.

Having assimilated the implicit lessons of this initiatory period, Gil Blas accepts the first in a series of increasingly important but always subordinate positions: after hiring himself out to a canon and a doctor, he successively engages himself to serve members of the lesser nobility, actors, wealthy noblemen, don Alphonse, the archbishop of Grenada, the duke of Lerma, and finally the Count-Duke Olivares. His constant need to have a master above him reflects his resignation to what he regards as a necessarily hierarchical organization of society,[10] but by assimilating the rules of the game, he learns to control by indirection situations upon which he could never directly impose his will.

Fabrice enunciates the principle and identifies it as the hallmark of a perfect servant. "Un génie supérieur qui se met en condition... entre dans une maison pour commander plutôt que pour servir" (I, 66). ("A man of superior intelligence who becomes a servant... enters a household to command rather than to serve.") Like the squire in *Lazarillo*, Fabrice indicates that a man of superior intelligence must appear to respect what he knows to be false, because by flattering a master's weaknesses, he can outwit those who are more powerful than he is and obtain what he could never obtain if he attempted to realize his desires without dissimulation. So well does Gil Blas cultivate this "perfect servant" mentality that Fabrice later congratulates him, "Que de talents vous réunissez en vous! ou plutôt... vous avez l'outil universel, c'est-à-dire vous êtes propre à tout" (II, 117) ("What talents are united in you! or rather... you have the universal tool; that is to say, you are capable of anything"). Compounded of Gil Blas's adaptability and the facility with which he pleases his masters, this "universal tool" presupposes a mentality which can reconcile an overlay of moral scruples with the enjoyment of material advantages that can only be obtained by compromising one's integrity.

Whenever Gil Blas fails to humor his masters, he suffers. Don Luis Pacheco dismisses him because he doesn't want to believe his valet's accounts of a young mistress's infidelity, and the archbishop of Granada discharges him for honestly appraising the quality of the man's sermons, as he had been requested to do. But if he totally devotes himself to currying favor, he runs the danger of losing a necessary sense of proportion; for

Fig. 22. Gil Blas, Count Galiano, and the sick monkey
(Smirke, 1809)

example, he exhausts himself catering to a pet monkey for which Count
Galiano has an exaggerated affection, but when Gil Blas himself falls ill,
Galiano abandons him without the slightest recognition of his services.

During his first stay at court, Gil Blas emulates the dominant behavior
patterns and amasses a large fortune by accepting bribes, selling influence,
and procuring mistresses for the young prince, but despite his success in
pleasing Lerma, the minister is unwilling to prevent or alleviate the misery
to which his former secretary is subjected in the Tower of Segovia. Only
when Gil Blas becomes fully aware that his artificial or immoral roles are
merely means of coping with a corrupt society can he perform them
without endangering either his own integrity or the physical well-being

which by extension depends upon it. In a world where prime ministers beguile kings by furnishing them with amusing pastimes, his own position depends upon a willingness to please Olivares by procuring a mistress for Philip IV. Because he remains sensible to the repugnant nature of what he has done, he presumably does not deserve to be punished, as he had been during his service to Lerma when he failed to recognize the immorality of his actions. In Lesage's fictional world, success demands compromise, but as long as an individual realizes the true nature of his actions, it is apparently legitimate for him to disavow moral responsibility for them.

For this reason, what Gil Blas does is not as important as the attitude with which he does it. Only when he adopts a good-natured detachment from wealth and power does his fictional world grant him security in the form of a relatively permanent position under Olivares. Only when he ceases to attach supreme importance to the amenities of life can he fully enjoy Lirias, the peaceful country estate which both expresses and rewards the nobility of his character. The wealth which he amasses under Lerma is not inherently evil, but when an obsession with it impairs his ability to feel pangs of conscience or authentic human sentiments, he no longer possesses his wealth; it possesses him. Actually, the turning point in Gil Blas's attitude is reached during the serious illness which he suffers after devoting all his energies to the care of Galiano's pet monkey. When the count abandons him, Gil Blas reflects, "Je ne pouvais plus, comme autrefois, envisager l'indigence en philosophe cynique" (II, 80) ("I could no longer, as formerly, face indigence like a Cynic"). Fearful that he might forfeit the amenities to which he had become accustomed while serving the archbishop of Granada and Galiano, he single-mindedly pursues them when he enters the service of Lerma. On the verge of losing his usual gaiety, his balanced perspective, and his sense of humanity, Gil Blas experiences a second turning point during his illness at the Tower of Segovia. Rather than reinforcing his obsession with wordly possessions, however, this illness awakens him to the necessity of dealing honestly with himself and others, and it occasions his desire to purchase a thatched cottage where he could enjoy a peaceful retirement from the corrupting influences of the court. Although don Alphonse's gift of Lirias permits him to fulfill this wish, the death of his first wife prompts Lesage's picaresque hero to return to the court, where he demonstrates his ability to withstand temptations which had previously triumphed over his basic sense of decency.

Gil Blas's experiences might make him wary of deceptive appearances and blinding obsessions, but they also reinforce the idea that, despite the invariably hypocritical and foolish behavior of others, the existing social order is fundamentally just, because it allows virtuous, talented people to rise to positions commensurate with their natures. In addition, it actually apportions the perquisites of a noble life-style to people like Gil Blas, whose resigned, good-natured reasonableness enables him to enjoy a materially comfortable existence without sacrificing either a sense of proportion or an ability to feel and express sentiment. This principle could be equally well illustrated by the lives of don Alphonse and Scipion—those directly above and below him in the harmonious social order which obtains at the end of the novel. It is to don Alphonse that Gil Blas owes both his first major step upward in the social hierarchy (from servant to steward) and the landholding where he retires; similarly, he is the one who underwrites Scipion's highly profitable voyage to the New World and provides the dowry which enables Scipion's daughter to marry a nobleman. Like the thousand ducats given to Gil Blas by the wealthy widow, these gifts correspond not to specific services, but to honest, good-natured, loyal natures, which manifest themselves in generous actions and prove exceedingly congenial to potential benefactors.

In essence, all three characters are rewarded for what they are rather than for what they do. Although Gil Blas's relationships to don Alphonse and Scipion are based upon sentiments of true friendship, don Alphonse is clearly his social superior, just as Scipion remains subordinate to him; however, in Lesage's fictional world, there is no stigma attached to service, because nearly everyone in the social hierarchy is simultaneously master and servant.[11] Even the powerful Lerma and Olivares are servants to the king. Lesage's fiction is governed by a poetic justice which assures that talented, virtuous servants will receive appropriate rewards, and that is exactly what happens to don Alphonse, Gil Blas, and Scipion, when they retire to country estates and begin to enjoy wealth, marital bliss, and the expectation of many truly noble descendants (don Alphonse was the illegitimate son of a nobleman, Gil Blas was ennobled by Olivares, and Scipion's son-in-law is a nobleman). At the end of the novel, Lesage simply creates a new nobility.

The sentimental equation of character and fate undoubtedly has moral significance, but there is also another type of moral commentary in Lesage's novels, as he himself indicates in reference to *Estévanille Gonzalez*, a book in which "on ... trouve des caractères et des leçons de morale cachées sous des images riantes" ("one ... finds characters and lessons of morality

Fig. 23. The happy ending: Gil Blas and his family
(Smirke, 1809)

hidden beneath pleasant images").[12] The word "character" suggests La
Bruyère's well-known *Les Caractères*, a collection of literary portraits in
which representative human types (often identified with specific contemporary personages) were satirized. Quite familiar with La Bruyère's work,
Lesage adopted a similar approach in *Le diable boiteux;* in fact, even *Gil Blas*
was read and appreciated as a satiric "roman à clef."[13] With the aid of
slight distortions wittily introduced into the portrayal of secondary
characters, readers were privileged to laugh at hypocritical and affected
roles like those which were being performed with utmost seriousness in
real eighteenth-century French society. The moral and ideological assumptions behind these distortions are the same as those which underlie
the protagonist's final happiness: people are either noble or ignoble, and

although the pleasure, honor, and wealth which they enjoy are not necessarily evil, commonly accepted attitudes toward them may be perverse; noble individuals sometimes adopt such attitudes and ignoble individuals often appear to succeed, but from the perspective of the fictive narrator's serene detachment, everyone's true nature ultimately emerges.

The "moral lessons" which Lesage mentions in his introduction to *Estévanille Gonzalez* are thus never explicitly stated, but they do constitute the structuring principles behind Lesage's fictional universe; they determine what will happen to major characters and how traits in the satirized portraits will be distorted. In the author's preface to *Gil Blas*, Lesage announces that he intends to portray "la vie des hommes telle qu'elle est" (I, 1) ("the life of men such as it is"). From the beginning of his career, Lesage desired to be recognized as a dramatist. He admired Molière, was thoroughly acquainted with the drama of Golden Age Spain and succeeded in having several of his own plays produced at the Comédie Française, although most of his work was done for the more popular boulevard theaters. As in *Le diable boiteux*, the artificial reality of *Gil Blas* resembles an enormous comic stage, where all the characters are playing roles in a kaleidoscopic sequence of scenes which reconcile the audience's sentimental expectations of poetic justice with its demands for verisimilitude.

By satirizing individual eccentricities and implying that a generous lower middle-class hero who appreciates the amenities of life without being dependent upon them is the sort of person who deserves to possess them, Lesage simultaneously flattered bourgeois aspirations for upward social mobility and reinforced aristocratic assumptions about inherent nature and the hierarchical ordering of society. Reconciling the implicit demands of these two audiences was made somewhat easier by the tendency of successful bourgeois to model their ideas of taste and sensibility on those of the lower nobility. Reflecting these ideas and corresponding to what Lesage himself frequently referred to as "le génie français" (the French spirit), the clarity, smoothness, concrete descriptiveness, moderation, and good humor of Lesage's writing is reminiscent of the style cultivated by Sorel and Scarron in reaction to the pretension and artificiality of the romances. In his foreward to *Le diable boiteux*, he contended that because French readers instinctively prefer naturalness of expression and exact descriptions, they would not appreciate Vélez' bizarre images and figures of speech. Of all the Spanish picaresque novels, the only one which approximated Lesage's definition of "le génie français" was *Marcos de Obregón*, and he had no qualms about reducing Vélez' wordplays and compressed symbolism or Alemán's rhetorical, involuted, and often abstract constructions to the same pleasant, readily comprehensible style which he associated with Espinel's novel. Lesage was a consummate artisan, but he imposed the same criteria of good style upon all his narratives, and as a consequence all his picaresque heroes seem to be cast in the same mold.

Like the similarities of plot and characterization in all Lesage's picaresque fiction, the recurrence of this style reflects an impulse toward the creation of a narrative form capable of appealing simultaneously to several different audiences. As entertaining adventure stories in which congenial protagonists overcome a series of obstacles before achieving the freedom to live "generously," Lesage's novels satisfied a dream shared by the aristocracy and the upper middle classes in eighteenth-century France. Lacking any productive function in society, many aristocrats were sorely in need of bourgeois financial resources, whereas many bourgeois yearned for the social respectability of the aristocracy; members of both classes desired to occupy positions in which they could enjoy material wealth as something they deserved for merely being themselves.

The picaresque format adopted by Lesage was admirably suited to portray the fulfillment of this desire without contradicting conventional laws of plausibility, because characters like Gil Blas were granted both an innate nobility of mind and an opportunity to seek the social station in which they could freely express their generous souls. Like Moll Flanders, Gil Blas succeeds, and his ability to circumvent the double-bind situation confronted by many Spanish pícaros is traceable in part to a world view influenced by bourgeois individualism, but whereas Defoe cast suspicion upon Moll's ideas of inherent gentility and allowed readers to perceive that her success derived from the practice of a shrewd tradeswoman's ethic, Lesage followed an essentially aristocratic model in attributing Gil Blas's rise in society to a virtue which he possessed from birth.

During the seventeenth century, French comic novels had contributed to breaking down the traditional separation of styles, but they never completely gained the approbation of either respectable society or the contemporary literary establishment; in contrast, Lesage's novels were almost universally accepted as entertaining, instructive, and skillfully contrived fictions. Different classes of readers could be pleasurably entertained by the adventures of a picaresque hero whose bourgeois flexibility allows him to survive and whose noble nature entitles him to happiness. By popularizing this conception, Lesage like many of his predecessors in the picaresque tradition helped to legitimize the novel's characteristic mixture of comic and serious styles and to establish it as an accepted, morally serious form of literary expression.

11

THE PICARESQUE HERO AS
YOUNG NOBLEMAN: VICTIMIZATION
AND VINDICATION IN SMOLLETT'S
Roderick Random

Tobias Smollett admired Lesage. He translated *Gil Blas* and *Le diable boiteux*, and when he had his portrait painted in 1756, he was holding a copy of *Gil Blas*.[1] In his preface to *The Adventures of Roderick Random* (1748), he even acknowledged that his own novel was "modeled" upon the "plan" of *Gil Blas*. Echoes of Lesage's pseudoautobiographical perspective, adventure-story format and generous-hearted picaresque hero do reappear in *Roderick Random*, but within the context of Smollett's preoccupations and ideological assumptions, elements of the picaresque myth are reinterpreted and endowed with a significance nearly opposite that of *Lazarillo* and *Guzmán*. The novel itself has often been faulted for its lack of unity and in particular for its failure to reconcile the sentimental aspects of Roderick's life with the caricatural distortion of secondary characters,[2] but like most previous authors in the picaresque tradition, Smollett imposed a certain unity and coherence upon his novel by fostering the illusion that everything in it had been perceived and recorded by the same fictive narrator. In *Roderick Random*, this narrator is relatively unobtrusive, but after overcoming numerous obstacles and learning what to expect from mankind, he plausibly adopts the perspective from which he recounts his own adventures and describes secondary characters. Functioning as a screen through which objective reality is filtered, his consciousness is a device by means of which satire and sentiment become complementary expressions of the same world view.

Based on a nostalgia for justice and stability in an apparently chaotic world, this consciousness imposes self-justificatory patterns upon Roderick's experiences and satiric distortions upon the descriptions of others. Both tendencies reflect an underlying desire to see good people rewarded and evil people punished. In his preface to *The Adventures of Ferdinand*,

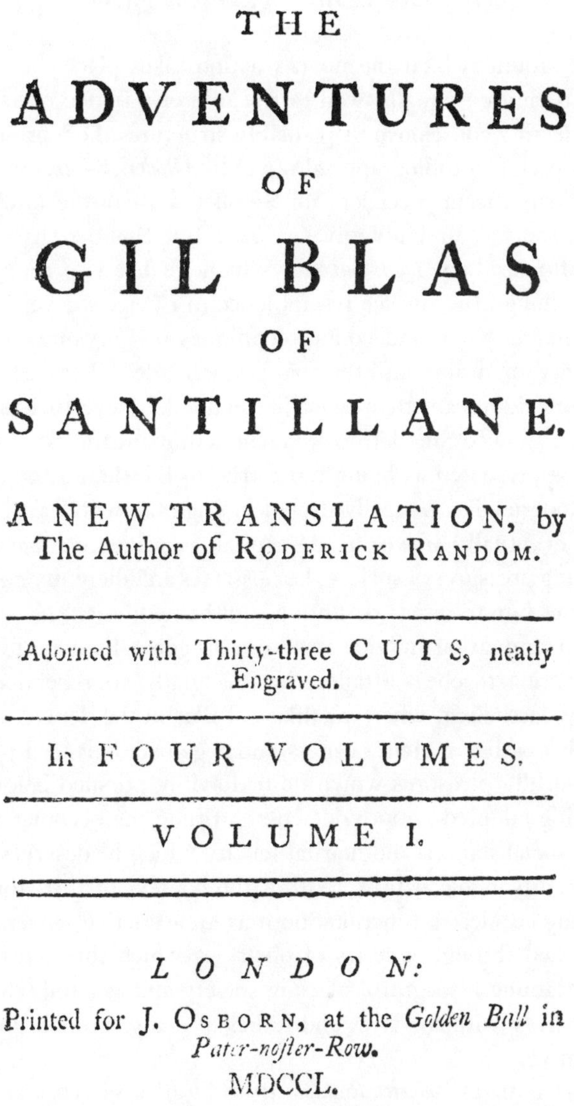
THE

ADVENTURES

OF

GIL BLAS

OF

SANTILLANE.

A NEW TRANSLATION, by
The Author of RODERICK RANDOM.

Adorned with Thirty-three CUTS, neatly
Engraved.

In FOUR VOLUMES.

VOLUME I.

LONDON:
Printed for J. OSBORN, at the *Golden Ball* in
Pater-noster-Row.
MDCCL.

Courtesy of the Newberry Library, Chicago

Fig. 24. Title page of Smollett's translation of *Gil Blas*

Count Fathom (1753), Smollett defined the novel as a loose unrestrained structure which achieves coherence because it imitates nature in a meaningful fashion and focuses upon a major character whose presence integrates narrative and satiric elements of the text into a unified sequence of events. He was undoubtedly thinking of the protagonist's function as a center around which the novel's action takes place, but one could apply this definition equally well to the role of a fictive narrator whose shaping, selecting consciousness plausibly structures the representation of reality in a pseudoautobiographical novel like *Roderick Random.*

The most significant precedent for Smollett's use of the autobiographical perspective was undoubtedly *Gil Blas*, but Smollett had also been strongly influenced by *Don Quixote*, which he likewise translated into English. Although the surface resemblance to Lesage's novel is more obvious, the moral vision and comic techniques of Cervantes had a more lasting impact upon him, and the changes he made in Lesage's "plan" are perhaps more significant than what he retained.[3] Nevertheless, it is this "plan" which allowed Smollett to reconcile sentiment and satire in a narrative which is presented as being more true to life than a romance. Like Gil Blas, Roderick is a basically decent young man who leaves his native village and eventually arrives in the capital. Repeatedly subjected to the dehumanizing pressures of society, he possesses an inherently noble nature which enables him to resist corruption, but being human, he occasionally succumbs to temptation and deviates from his generally honest demeanor. After attempting to cheat a tailor, he is actually apprehended and imprisoned at Marshalsea, where he (like Gil Blas in the Tower of Segovia) renounces his earlier pretentiousness and regains a balanced perspective upon the worldly pleasures which he had avidly pursued before his disgrace. Having adopted a more detached attitude, he becomes worthy of the wealth, social station, and marital felicity which he deserves by virtue of his inherently noble nature. Within the context of this story and its happy ending, Roderick functions both as an attractive, adventure-story hero conducted through a series of obstacles which threaten to prevent him from attaining his rightful place in society and as a foil whose virtue contrasts sharply with the vices and follies of many secondary characters in the narrative.

What differentiates *Roderick Random* from *Gil Blas* is a sense of outrage at the cruelty and hypocrisy of people who undeservedly occupy positions of authority—positions which allow them to perpetrate injustice upon everyone under their control. With an urbane sense of humor, Lesage's hero resigns himself to the inevitability of social corruption. For him, moral compromise and role-playing become the legitimate price of social advancement. Although Roderick's "impetuous passions" are supposedly calmed by his marriage to the peerless Narcissa, his refusal to compromise absolute moral principles remains intact, and even from the vantage point

Courtesy of the Newberry Library, Chicago

Fig. 25. Illustration from Smollett's
translation of *Gil Blas*

of his final happiness, he continues to feel a smoldering resentment at the injustice to which he and other decent people have been subjected. Undoubtedly a reflection of Smollett's own attitude, the narrating Roderick's pride and sense of injured innocence govern both the portrayal of his own experiences and the description of the caricatured individuals whom he meets.

Like Cervantes, Smollett believed that an ideal social organization would promote the happiness of all its members, protect their rights, and redress their wrongs, but he recognized that cruel and selfish people often prosper at the expense of honest, generous individuals, and he knew that such arbitrary tyranny often cloaked itself in hypocritical protestations of virtue and justice. He himself admitted that *Roderick Random* was expressly designed "to animate the reader against the sordid and vicious disposition of the world" (xvii),[4] and the epigraph which he chose to introduce *Ferdinand, Count Fathom* reflects an attitude not altogether different from that of Cervantes:

> Materiam risus, invenit ad omnes
> Occursus hominum.
> Ridebat curas, nec non et gaudia vulgi;
> Interdum et lachrymas fundebat.
>
> (Food for laughter he found in all his
> Meetings with men.
> He laughed at the worries and even at the joys of the rabble;
> At the same time he shed tears.)[5]

In reacting against the pretension and artificiality of chivalric romances, Cervantes did not reject the moral absolutism and traditional ideals embodied in them; in fact, the serio-comic life and adventures of Quixote reflect the melancholy sadness of an idealist whose hopes for a better and more just world have been repeatedly disappointed. It is precisely this attitude which emerges in the epigraph to *Ferdinand, Count Fathom* and permeates much of Smollett's own work. Unlike Gil Blas, Quixote refuses to smile good-naturedly at a ubiquitous breakdown of moral values or to accept socially sanctioned but perverse patterns of behavior. In this respect, Roderick is far more of a Quixote than a Gil Blas.

Smollett and the readers whom he addressed in the preface wanted to believe, as Roderick's generous friend Morgan passionately declares, that "there is such a thing as justice" (196), and the fictional world of the novel allowed them to do so. The cast of characters in *Roderick Random* is divided into good people—Roderick, Strap, Bowling, Ratlin, Morgan, Thompson, and Mrs. Sagely—and villains or fools like Oakhum, Mackshane, Crampley, Gawky, and Captain Weazel. The most important single quality shared by people in the first group is an honesty of sentiment which permits them to deal openly and generously with each other. It is this trait which places Roderick in conflict with devious, scheming characters and allows him to establish sincere relationships with decent people like himself. Even when he is experiencing the utmost misery and destitution, he remains capable of feeling and expressing compassion for others. The unfortunate Nancy Williams deceives him and infects him with venereal disease, but he forgives her and helps her to regain her

Fig. 26. Strap's misfortune in the dining cellar, an early London experience
(Cruikshank, 1831)

health, and during his imprisonment at Marshalsea, he commiserates with the ill-treated poet Melopoyn. At times his own sentimentality might appear naive; for example, he weeps at the sorrows of the heroine on a London stage. The fops and coquettes who frequent the theater would feel perfectly justified in laughing at his simplicity, but this very show of

Fig. 27. Captain Weazel and Miss Jenny Romper (Rowlandson, 1805)

emotion indicates that he possesses a "generous soul" which they lack. Roderick's friends and patrons have a similar ability to feel and communicate honest human emotion, and just as he succors Melopoyn at Marshalsea, he is in turn revived by the loyalty of Strap (as Gil Blas had been revived by the loyalty of Scipion) and liberated by the benevolent intervention of Bowling.

In contrast to these generous-hearted individuals are the numerous characters whose inability to communicate openly and honestly with others is often reflected in their physical features, gestures, and speeches. Such people sometimes gain momentary ascendency over Roderick and other virtuous people in the novel, but they are invariably punished, and one of the ways in which they are punished involves the caricatural distortion imposed upon them by the narrator.[6] But even more important is the humiliation or disgrace which they inevitably suffer, and which represents an appropriate punishment for their previous injustice and moral blindness. Perhaps the best example of this technique involves the characterization of the protagonist in *Ferdinand, Count Fathom*. Fathom is a clever rogue who calculates his potential profit before undertaking any action; he wears a succession of masks and manipulates others for what he believes to be his own material self-interest, but unlike Defoe's Moll Flanders or Colonel Jacque, Fathom fails to rise in society as a consequence of assimilating socially sanctioned behavior patterns.

Fathom's disgrace, like Roderick's success, reflects an underlying poetic justice which ultimately recompenses virtuous individuals with happiness in a social station appropriate to their inherent qualities, while denying wealth and position to those who lack birth or merit. Behind this narrative pattern lies the basically aristocratic assumption that every person has an inherent nature which corresponds to his place in the social hierarchy. Anyone is capable of expressing decent human emotions, but in Smollett's novels, virtuous characters always implicitly recognize their proper place and establish fitting relationships with others. Even Fathom can be redeemed as soon as he relinquishes his ambition and learns to feel love, friendship, and compassion, for when he retires to the countryside, it is quite possible, as we discover in *The Expedition of Humphry Clinker* (1771), for him to become a modestly prosperous apothecary.

In *Roderick Random* the protagonist's ability to feel and communicate honest human sentiment is linked with noble birth, but because Roderick is unjustly deprived of his inheritance, he is thrust into a world where people like Fathom frequently dominate. Within the context of the author's world view (and the fictive narrator's resentment), these people serve two functions: their schemes to harm or defraud Roderick are obstacles which separate him from the earthly happiness he deserves, and their distorted features or ironically appropriate punishments serve as a "satire upon mankind," as Smollett himself declared in a letter to one of his Scottish friends.[7] The first of these two functions is also a means of engaging readers' sympathies and sustaining their interest before satisfying their implied desire to see justice emerge. For this reason, the entire narrative and nearly all the individual episodes in it evince a fundamentally similar victimization-vindication sequence: malicious people deprive the hero of what rightfully belongs to him and subject him to suffering or humiliation, but his character is tempered by hardship, and with the aid of honest, loyal friends and his own resiliency, he regains his sense of wellbeing and his enemies are punished. Always the eventual outcome vindicates the hero's faith in his own sense of martyred innocence.

The second function of the evil or foolish secondary characters in *Roderick Random* implies reference to a reality outside the novel. Although Smollett includes specific caricatures of his own enemies, the gallery of satiric portraits also represents a commentary upon the general nature of eighteenth-century English society—a society of "baboons" (one of Smollett's favorite metaphors) or "bears," a dehumanized society in which men prey upon one another and proclaim their own degradation as a positive standard of value. By introducing an attractive, basically decent young man into a corrupt milieu where he falls victim to its snares, Smollett admittedly hopes to arouse people against a pervasive iniquity and hypocrisy in his own society, but all reader responses—indignation at Roderick's unmerited suffering, laughter at satirized vices and follies, satisfaction at the hero's triumph and the defeat of his enemies—are posited upon the fictive narrator's belief in (and their own hopes for) earthly justice. At least in Smollett's eyes, sentiment and satire are reconciled on the level of the novel's implicit moral vision.

If the poetic justice which governs the outcome in all Smollett's early novels reflects a sentimental desire for peace and harmony in an apparently chaotic, unjust world, a real problem arises when Smollett, attempting to convey the impression that genuine human emotions are involved, has recourse to a conventional language of clichés.[8] Cervantes also used banal expressions, but whereas Dulcinea's beauty and virtue exist largely in Quixote's imagination, Roderick's beloved Narcissa is presented as an actual woman who interacts with other characters and yet remains a "pattern" of earthly perfection, a divine creature, a kind nymph, a delightful object. Her lips are like cherries or "the dewy rosebud just bursting from the stem," and she arouses all the standard symptoms of lovesickness in Roderick, whose tenderness and affection are usually marked by the welling of tears in his eyes. In the marriage bed, the previously chaste Narcissa becomes "a feast a thousand times more delicious than [his] most sanguine hope presaged!" (463). It is perhaps appropriate that the earthly happiness which rewards him for being a generous-hearted, honest young man is crowned by a "feast," but even though Narcissa is ostensibly perceived through the fictive narrator's biased account of his own ecstatic happiness, these stereotyped descriptions prevent readers from considering her and Roderick's emotions for her as plausible aspects of a real-seeming relationship between them.

The situation is quite different in earlier sections of the novel. During a series of violent, physically repulsive episodes which contrast sharply with Lesage's ideas of good taste and decorum, Smollett's hero demonstrates the inherent nobility of his mind and character while absorbing a practical education in the ways of the world. For example, as an impetuous young man with a basically decent character, he must remain loyal to his own feelings and values, and he must resist the temptation to confuse the way men act with the way they should act. Because circumstances invariably vindicate him, he learns the wisdom of exercising patience in adversity. Having traveled to London in hopes of receiving a naval commission as a surgeon's mate, he obtains the proper certification but not the desired position. The commission is only available to those who have enough money to bribe the authorities. Without a source of income, Roderick cannot obtain a position, and without a position, he has no source of income. Ironically, this double-bind situation is resolved for him when he is abducted by a press gang and delivered to the warship *Thunder*, where his talents become obvious and he is actually designated surgeon's mate.

Attainment of the original desire justified Roderick's conviction of his own merit, but it hardly protects him from further victimization. A microcosmic version of the corrupt society ashore, the *Thunder* is governed by the vain, ignorant Captain Oakhum and the cowardly, hypocritical Doctor Mackshane. Even before the voyage begins, their arbitrary system of justice becomes evident when Oakhum declares that there are no sick men on his ship and peremptorily orders all those in the infirmary to report on deck. As a result of this inhuman treatment, five gravely ill sailors die, and Oakhum himself suffers for his folly, for he is severely pummeled by a madman whom he has ordered released as sane. During the entire voyage of the *Thunder*, similar tyrannical abuses of authority cause Roderick considerable unmerited suffering. Within a larger context, the senseless slaughter of poorly trained troops at the Battle of Carthagena and the even more deadly plague which follows are catastrophes which could have been avoided if the English general staff had been less incompetent and more humane. As a result of their decisions, the sea clogged with bloody carcasses becomes a grotesque symbol of human depravity. Under these circumstances, Roderick himself falls ill, and because he has been portrayed as an innocent victim, readers can be expected to empathize with him and repudiate the malice of his tormentors.

A model for the anticipated reader reaction is furnished by Roderick's own responses to similar sufferings inflicted upon others. The thumbnail autobiographies of Melopoyn and Nancy Williams illustrate the same truths as his own story: in general, people are hypocritical, selfish, and stupid. Although he is suffering misery and poverty on both occasions, he listens sympathetically as his fellow sufferers recount their misfortunes, and he becomes indignant at the "sordid and vicious disposition" of the men who had treated them so unjustly. His emotions are engaged in their causes, and this is precisely the reaction prescribed in the preface for readers of *Roderick Random*.

The same principle applies to the happiness of Smollett's virtuous characters. If readers are favorably disposed toward Roderick, they presumably feel gratified when, after refusing to subordinate himself to cruel and hypocritical men, he triumphs over them and ultimately enjoys the utmost contentment in his peaceful country retirement. The effect is the same as it had been in *Gil Blas*, but there is a crucial difference. Whereas Lesage's picaresque hero rises in society to occupy a social station in harmony with his merit, Roderick is a born nobleman returning to a heritage which had been unjustly taken from him. After Bowling liberates him from Marshalsea and stakes him to a profitable voyage, Roderick discovers his father in the person of a rich South American plantation owner; together the two men return to Scotland, where they purchase and refurbish the familial estate, thus legitimizing their title to a landholding which profligate relatives had usurped from them.

Although occasionally impelled by pride or ambition to commit actions unworthy of his noble nature (he mistreats his faithful friend Strap, courts the hideously deformed Miss Snapper for her wealth, and attempts to defraud his tailor), Roderick has a generous, compassionate nature, and by the end of the novel he places himself in harmony with it, recognizing that simple human values—friendship, love, trust—provide the only viable basis for a satisfying existence. Throughout the novel, he is an inherently noble individual, but without money he remains subject to the arbitrariness and tyranny of unjust authority. From the vantage point of the worldly-wise narrator, Roderick's encounters with boorish, egocentric, or cruel individuals test his worthiness to occupy a social station commensurate with his noble birth while obliging him to undergo a rudimentary moral education; at different points in the narrative his father, his uncle, Mrs. Sagely, Nancy Williams, and he himself all remark that undeserved suffering has improved his understanding, developed his sentiments, or tempered his constitution. Rather than succumbing to the dehumanizing pressures of society, he benefits from them by learning to recognize the usual wickedness and indifference of people. By menacing his existence or tempting him to conform, these pressures give him the opportunity to demonstrate that he can live in a corrupt environment without becoming totally depraved. When he finally gains his independence from this society and occupies his rightful place, he knows how to exercise prudence and cherish the company of a few honest friends.

The ending appears to reinforce the idea that although honest sentiment is more important than wealth or reputation, material benefits will ultimately accrue to people who have proved themselves worthy of possessing them. For example, after futilely seeking to marry rich women for their money, Roderick finds true happiness with Narcissa only because he is willing to accept her without a dowry; however, he eventually does recover the full inheritance from her self-indulgent, insensitive brother. His imprisonment at Marshalsea brings him to the realization that the money and social status which had preoccupied him before his arrest must be subordinated to genuine human feelings, but once he has placed his earlier desires in proper perspective, his fictional world operates in such a way that he actually acquires them.[9]

However, it is possible to suggest an alternative explanation of these situations: if Roderick is noble throughout the novel, his noble qualities are really useless to him until he obtains the wealth which frees him from arbitrary, unjust authorities. Smollett himself must have been aware of this underlying ambiguity when he placed the following motto on the title page of *Roderick Random:* "Et genus & virtus, nisi cum re, vilior alga est" ("Without material possessions, high birth and character are worth less than the weeds of the sea").[10] Taken from Horace's second sermon, the passage expresses Ulysses' rationale for desiring to accumulate a fortune before returning to Ithaca—a rationale formulated in response to Tiresias' advice that he return for the intrinsic value of the homecoming. Within Smollett's frame of reference, the motto is undoubtedly intended ironically, for Roderick's character is worth more than the weeds of the sea, and it is because he has a virtuous character that readers empathize with him and take pleasure in his final happiness; nevertheless, by implying that the intrinsic rewards of Roderick's homecoming can only be enjoyed if he possesses sufficient wealth to secure his independence from a corrupt society, Smollett seems to be suggesting that there is more than a little merit in Ulysses' argument.

Unlike Ulysses, however, Roderick is rather inept at role-playing. He claims that he could adopt a thousand different schemes, "without forfeiting the dignity of [his] character beyond a power of retrieving it, or subjecting [himself] wholly to the caprice and barbarity of the world" (161), but in actuality he lacks what Lesage would have called "génie." When he contemplates a career in public administration, he ultimately rejects the idea because he feels incapable of precisely the activities which Gil Blas dutifully performed for Lerma and Olivares—flattering important people, procuring mistresses, writing hypocritical propaganda. Even when he accepts Strap's offer to outfit him as a gentleman so that he can beguile a rich heiress into marrying him, one of his London acquaintances comments, "You are too honest and too ignorant of the town to practise the necessary cheats of your profession and detect the conspiracies that will be formed against you" (313). In effect Roderick never succeeds as a confidence man because he is incapable of being anyone other than himself.

That which sustains him is neither the "génie" which permits Gil Blas to adapt himself to various milieux, nor the sense of humor which allows Lesage's hero to laugh at his own weaknesses; it is rather a strong sense of pride which enables him to resist the socializing process and retain his integrity even under the most adverse circumstances. During his youth, he is mistreated by an ignorant schoolmaster, and on board the *Thunder* he is cruelly tied to a bulkhead during the Battle of Carthagena, after Oakhum and Mackshane supposedly "prove" that the anodyne Greek notations in his diary are coded plans for a mutiny. On numerous occasions Roderick is subjected to similar treatment, but in every case his noble breast becomes filled with a justifiable anger which strengthens his will to live and prevents him from succumbing to despair. After a dishonest, lascivious priest steals his money and leaves him penniless on the highway to Paris, Roderick himself admits, "It was happy for me that I had a good deal of resentment in my constitution, which animated me on such occasions against the villainy of mankind and enabled me to bear misfortunes otherwise intolerable" (270). Within the context of Smollett's world view, Roderick's anger is a perfectly normal manifestation of his healthy passion and his innate sense of justice. As an adventure-story hero seeking to express his independence and lust for life, he may commit evil acts, but they are always portrayed as excusable on the grounds of momentary blindness or sheer impetuosity. In contrast, his enemies are characterized by their perverse, selfish motives, and when they are appropriately chastized, Roderick gains a nobleman's revenge over them and what they stand for.

Born into a Scottish aristocratic family, he instinctively rebels against unjust authority and moral compromise, and his attitude is clearly vindicated by the novel's happy ending. Because he is finally occupying the social station which he should have inherited at birth, his triumph is actually a reaffirmation of aristocratic privilege. The attitude of his loyal friend Strap is particularly instructive in this regard. Strap marries Nancy Williams and retires to a small farm given him by Roderick's father. Although Strap is rewarded for his ability to feel and express genuine human sentiment, he remains in his place. As a reformed prostitute, Nancy Williams lacked the moral perfection necessary to reward Roderick for his inherent nobility, even though she had once been his mistress. Nevertheless, she is considered an appropriate match for the commoner Strap, who is so intent upon keeping his distance that he even refuses to dine at the same table with Roderick and his father. By maintaining class distinctions and by depicting his protagonist as an authentic nobleman whose adventures culminate in a return to his proper place, Smollett effectively integrates aristocratic conceptions of character and social justice into the narrative perspective from which Roderick's life is recounted and implicitly interpreted.

Combined with a sentimental belief in (or desire for) peace and harmony, these ideological assumptions govern the novel's circular movement from noble birth in Scotland to unmerited suffering in other places and back to a noble social station in Scotland, but they are also reflected in the epicycles of victimization and vindication which recur in nearly every episode. For example, the situation on the *Thunder* is virtually identical to the one which Roderick confronts as a schoolboy in Scotland. In both

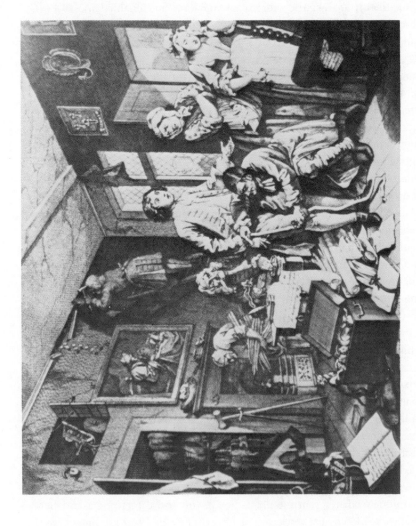

Fig. 28. The first plate in Hogarth's *Rake's Progress* (ca. 1735), which may have influenced Smollett's portrayal of the picaresque hero

cases arbitrary authority is exercised by a tyrant (his grandfather, Oakhum), and he himself is placed under the direct supervision of a cowardly sycophant (Syntax, Mackshane); his allies include a loyal friend (Strap, Thompson) and a generous-hearted patron (Bowling, Morgan). During his schooldays, he is flogged for having been a passenger on a sinking ferryboat, beaten for having been run over by a horse cart, and scourged for having been bitten by the baker's dog; on the *Thunder* he is convicted of sedition on the basis of Mackshane's false accusations and tied to a bulkhead during a battle in which he is besplattered with the brains of a decapitated officer and covered with the entrails of an unfortunate drummer. Just as the schoolmaster's arbitrary punishments create a situation in which Roderick is obliged to develop a strong body and to exercise the "uncommon genius" which enables him to become the best student at the school, he later survives the Battle of Carthagena and the subsequent epidemic thanks to a strong will to live and the solicitude of his friends; by the time he returns to England, he even manages to acquire a modest fortune in wages and gifts.

Rather than attempting to please the authorities who exercise a socially sanctioned power over him, Roderick sustains himself by an absolute conviction of injured innocence. In the first instance, he gains his revenge when Bowling arrives and administers a well-deserved flogging to the schoolmaster; in the second, his vindication occurs later, when it is revealed that Oakhum has died and Mackshane is languishing in prison, after both have been found guilty of embezzlement. Even if Roderick is not strong enough to combat the authorities who victimize him, and must therefore vent his resentment in impotent anger, he does possess the internal strength to survive their persecutions, and his fictional world operates in such a way that his virtue and their perfidy ultimately receive appropriate recompense.

Within the larger framework of the entire narrative, Roderick is deprived of his birthright by a heartless grandfather, but after overcoming all obstacles and learning what to expect from the society of men, he regains privileges associated with the familial estate and becomes, as Morgan announces in *The Adventures of Peregrine Pickle* (1751), the father of a flourishing family. In light of a prophetic vision recorded at the beginning of *Roderick Random*, this detail is particularly significant. Before Roderick was born, his mother dreamed that she gave birth to a tennis ball. Although batted out of sight by the devil, the ball is returned with equal force to a place near her feet, where a "goodly tree covered with blossoms" (21) springs up. The fulfillment of the dream's implicit prophecy is the final vindication of the hero's injured innocence. Roderick's happiness represents a young nobleman's victory over the general wickedness of the world, rather than, as is the case with Gil Blas, the climax of an older man's long career of faithful service in subordinate positions. Where Gil Blas succeeds, Roderick Random triumphs, and in the difference lies a profound modification of Lesage's "plan."

Simplicissimus, Moll Flanders, and *Gil Blas* reflect an assimilation of the picaresque format to the expression of a bourgeois world view influenced to varying degrees by aristocratic ideological assumptions; *Roderick Random* constitutes a reaffirmation of the traditional association between noble birth and high social station. Smollett feared that England's cultural heritage and moral values were being undermined by the rise of the bourgeoisie and the popularity of "hack writers" like Defoe, whose *Robinson Crusoe* and *Colonel Jacque* are mentioned in *Roderick Random* as examples of works which lack literary merit but achieve financial success because they pander to the "vulgar tastes" of the rabble. Although Defoe's novels were popular among the literate lower classes, he himself identified with the commerical bourgeoisie; middle-class aspirations for upward social mobility are reinforced in his picaresque narratives, and a middle-class Protestant value system dominates his entire work. In contrast, Smollett distrusted the commercial classes and their tradesman ethic; he conceived of himself as writing for a more educated, respectable audience, and it is for this reason that he chose to model his picaresque narratives not upon Defoe's works, but upon the picaresque adventure novels of a French writer who respected rules of good taste and decorum.

The Spanish picaresque did exert a discernible influence upon English literature, but if Defoe followed well-established precedent in associating criminal biography with elements of picaresque fiction, Smollett's conception of the picaresque was mediated by its association with French traditions of literary expression. But even in the process of following Lesage's "plan," Smollett transformed the picaresque hero into a genuine nobleman momentarily separated from the elevated social station he deserves. By allowing this hero to triumph over a hostile world, the author simultaneously decried a widespread loss of respect for traditional values and reinforced his readers' belief in (or hope for) the efficacy of earthly justice. For Smollett, the picaresque format offered an opportunity to place a noble hero in contact with a corrupt world. As that hero proved himself worthy, he also illustrated the aristocratic assumption that one's nature is determined at birth and ought to govern one's place in a static social hierarchy. Some Spanish writers had based picaresque fiction upon similar ideological assumptions, but in general they did not endow their protagonists with a concealed nobility like that of Roderick Random. Like Cervantes, Smollett was affirming the necessity of pursuing an ideal at the same time that he illustrated the difficulty of ever attaining it. During its two-hundred-year evolution, the picaresque novel underwent numerous changes, but when Smollett modified literary conventions developed in Spain and adapted to French taste, he succeeded in transforming the characteristically picaresque sequence of events and giving it a meaning just the opposite of that which it had borne in the earliest Spanish novels.

NOTES
INDEX

NOTES

1 For a provocative discussion of this idea, see Alexander A. Parker, *Literature and the Delinquent: The Picaresque Novel in Spain and Europe 1599–1753* (Edinburgh: University Press, 1967), pp. 1–27.

2 The term "double bind" was first defined in Gregory Bateson, Don D. Jackson, Jay Haley, and John H. Weakland, "Toward a Theory of Schizophrenia," *Behavioral Science* 1 (1956), 251–264; rpt. in Bateson, *Steps to an Ecology of Mind* (New York: Ballantine, 1972), pp. 201–227. Originally developed to explain the development of schizophrenic symptoms in some family situations, a double bind occurs when a person feels obliged to choose in a situation where there are no viable alternatives.

3 A complete bibliography of scholarly works on the picaresque novel would occupy many pages; a checklist is contained in Joseph Laurenti, *Bibliografía de la literatura picaresca: Desde sus orígines hasta el presente* (Metuchen, N.J.: Scarecrow, 1973). Convenient overviews of this criticism can be found in Joseph Ricapito, *Bibliografía razonada y anotada de las obras maestras de la novela picaresca española* (Madrid: Castalia, 1976), which is a revised and updated version of his "Toward a Definition of the Picaresque: A Study of the Evolution of the Genre Together with a Critical and Annotated Bibliography of *La Vida de Lazarillo de Tormes*, *Vida de Guzmán de Alfarache*, and *Vida del Buscón*," Diss. UCLA, 1966, and in Ulrich Wicks, "Picaro, Picaresque: The Picaresque in Literary Scholarship," *Genre*, 2 (1972), 153–216. Essays on the subject are collected in *Pikarische Welt: Schriften zum europäischen Schelmenroman*, ed. Helmut Heidenreich (Darmstadt: Wissenschaftliche Buchgesellschaft, 1969), and *Knaves and Swindlers: Essays on the Picaresque Novel in Europe*, ed. Christine J. Whitbourne (London: Oxford University Press, 1974), University of Hull Publications.

4 Credit for establishing the existence of a coherent picaresque subject matter must be accorded to Frank W. Chandler for his descriptive overview of thirty-four Spanish picaresque novels in *Romances of Roguery* (New York: Macmillan, 1899). Chandler's list was revised and augmented by Helmut Petriconi, "Zur Chronologie und Verbreitung des spanischen Schelmenromans," *Volkstum und Kultur der Romanen*, 1 (1928), 324–342, but it was Angel Valbuena Prat who created a virtual picaresque canon when he published twenty-three narratives in his comprehensive anthology *La novela picaresca española* (Madrid: Aguilar, 1943). Despite the fact that it is primarily concerned with English literature, Chandler's two-volume *The Literature of Roguery* (Boston: Houghton Mifflin, 1907) provides the first systematic attempt to identify a corpus of picaresque

fiction written outside Spain, although early nineteenth-century critics like Sainte-Beuve had applied the term to *Gil Blas*, just as Ballantine had used it in 1810 when alluding to the works of Defoe. More recent scholarly attempts to place the picaresque novel in a European context include Robert Alter, *Rogue's Progress: Studies in the Picaresque Novel* (Cambridge: Harvard University Press, 1964); Stuart Miller, *The Picaresque Novel* (Cleveland: Case Western Reserve University Press, 1967); Parker, *The Delinquent;* and Frederick Monteser, *The Picaresque Element in Western Literature* (University, Alabama: University of Alabama Press, 1975).

5 Considerable controversy has developed over whether the word "picaresque" should be reserved for a limited number of sixteenth- and seventeenth-century Spanish novels, or whether it can be used in reference to a type of fiction which is capable of appearing at any time and in any place. In general, hispanists apply the term only to Spanish Golden Age novels, and some of them restrict its use to a very small number of examples: *Guzmán* is the archetype of the genre for Samuel Gili Gaya, "Apogeo y desintegración de la novela picaresca," in *Historia general de las literaturas hispánicas*, ed. Guillermo Díaz-Plaja (Barcelona: Barna, 1953), III, iii-xxv; *El Buscón* for H. Peseux-Richard, "A propos du *Buscón*," *Revue hispanique*, 43 (1918), 43–58; *Marcos de Obregón, Estebanillo González, El diablo cojuelo*, and the work of Gracián for José Castro Calvo, *Valores universales de la literatura española* (Barcelona: Sayma, 1961), pp. 91–139. Among those who would apply the term more broadly, Jakob Ulrich includes Sanskrit novellas in his anthology *Romanische Schelmennovellen* (Leipzig: Deutsche Verlagsaktiengesellschaft, 1905) and contends that the picaresque novel could evolve independently and everywhere. Similar views have been expressed by D. J. Dooley, "Some Uses and Mutations of the Picaresque," *The Dalhousie Review*, 37 (1957–58), 363–377; Alter, *Rogue's Progress;* Miller, *The Picaresque Novel;* Alexander Blackburn, "The Picaresque Novel: A Literary Idea 1554–1954," Diss. Cambridge, 1963; R. W. B. Lewis, *The Picaresque Saint* (Philadelphia: Lippincott, 1959); W. M. Frohock, "The Idea of the Picaresque," *Yearbook of Comparative and General Literature*, 16 (1967), 43–52; and many others. In establishing his canon of picaresque novels, Chandler displayed a propensity for categorizing which caused him (as Parker points out) to propagate many facile generalizations about picaresque fiction; however, Parker himself attempts to define the picaresque in terms of a single constituent element (delinquency), which in turn becomes his touchstone for determining whether or not a novel belongs to the genre; for a critique of Parker's thesis, see Fernando Lázaro Carreter, "Glosas Críticas a *Los pícaros en la literatura* de Alexander A. Parker," *Hispanic Review*, 41 (1973), 469–497, and for a sympathetic commentary upon Lázaro Carreter's description of the picaresque, see Gonzalo Sobejano, "*El coloquio de los perros* en la picaresca y otros apuntes," *Hispanic Review*, 43 (1974), 25–41. One of the more promising attempts to obtain a broader perspective upon the problem is contained in Ulrich Wicks, "The Nature of Picaresque Narrative: A Modal Approach," *PMLA*, 89 (1974), 240–249. Drawing primarily upon the critical theory of Robert Scholes, Wicks locates the picaresque mode on the lower end of a scale which descends from

romance (in which the hero and the fictional world are vastly superior to the reader and the actual world) through history (in which they are roughly equivalent) to satire (in which they are vastly inferior). Combining this approach with structural and generic considerations, Wicks discusses the picaresque in terms of individual works which evince characteristic elements of his abstract model. The applicability of this model to the analysis of specific contemporary novels is demonstrated in Wicks, "Onlyman," *Mosaic*, 8 (1975), 21–47. If, as Wicks contends, the picaresque hero can be regarded as an archetypal example of the solipsistic protagonist who is not at home in a disordered universe, themes and techniques of earlier picaresque fiction naturally tend to recur in twentieth-century novels which portray the individual as an alienated exile in a hostile, fallen world. The weakness of Wicks's approach lies in his failure to consider the socio-cultural contexts in which the earlier picaresque novels emerged and interacted in a historically verifiable process. A convincing attempt to combine historical factors with a valid conceptual model appears in Claudio Guillén, "Toward a Definition of the Picaresque," in *Literature as System: Essays Toward the Theory of Literary History* (Princeton: Princeton University Press, 1971), pp. 71–106. This essay is a revised version of a similarly titled paper in *Proceedings of the IIIrd Congress of the International Comparative Literature Association* (The Hague: Mouton, 1962), pp. 252–266.

6 These views are expressed respectively in Blackburn, "The Picaresque Novel"; Sherman Eoff, "The Picaresque Psychology of Guzmán de Alfarache," *Hispanic Review*, 21 (1953), 107–109; Mireya Suárez, *La novela picaresca y el pícaro en la literatura española* (Madrid: Imprenta Latina, 1923); J. F. Montesinos, "Gracián o la picaresca pura," *Cruz y Raya*, 1 (1930), 37–63; Gustave Reynier, *Le roman réaliste au 17ème siècle* (Paris: Hachette, 1912); Lewis, *The Picaresque Saint;* J. Frutos Gómez de las Cortinas, "El antihéroe y su actitud vital," *Cuadernos de literatura*, 7 (1950), 97–143; Domingo Pérez Minik, *Novelistas españoles de los siglos XIX y XX* (Madrid: Guadarrama, 1957); and Marcel Bataillon, "Introduction," in *Le roman picaresque* (Paris: La Renaissance du Livre, 1931), pp. 1–39.

7 The term "picaresque myth" is employed by Guillén in "Toward a Definition of the Picaresque." The "picaresque mode" is discussed by Wicks in "The Nature of Picaresque Narrative."

8 For discussions of the anonymous author's indebtedness to traditional folklore materials, see Marcel Bataillon, "Introduction," in *La vie de Lazarillo de Tormes* (Paris: Editions Montaigne, 1958), pp. 19–34, and *Novedad y fecundidad del "Lazarillo de Tormes"* (Salamanca: Anaya, 1968), pp. 27–45; María Rosa Lida de Malkiel, "Función del cuento popular en *Lazarillo de Tormes*," in *Actas del Primer Congreso Internacional de Hispanistas*, eds. Frank Pierce and Cyril Jones (Oxford: Dolphin, 1964), pp. 349–359; Francisco Rico, "Introducción," in *La novela picaresca española* (Barcelona: Planeta, 1967), pp. xxx–xliv; and Fernando Lázaro Carreter, *"Lazarillo de Tormes" en la picaresca* (Barcelona: Ariel, 1972). The relationship between Masuccio Salernitano's *Il Novellino* and the fifth "tratado" (chapter) of *Lazarillo* is discussed by Lida de Malkiel and Lázaro Carreter as well as by Joseph Ricapito in *"Lazarillo de Tormes* and Masuccio's Fourth

Novella," *Romance Philology*, 23 (1970), 305–311. Lida de Malkiel suggests a sort of negative borrowing when she points out that Lazarillo's birth in the river might constitute a conscious parody of *Amadís de Gaula;* the ramifications of this allusion are discussed in Hans Gerd Rötzer, *Picaro-Landstörtzer-Simplicius* (Darmstadt: Wissenschaftliche Buchgesellschaft, 1972), pp. 8–10. One of the most popular works in fifteenth- and sixteenth-century Spain was Petrarch's *De remediis utriusque fortunae,* and it has recently been suggested that the author of *Lazarillo* borrowed situations (ignoble birth, poverty, service to cruel masters, marriage to an unfaithful wife) from the second part of this work, parodying Reason's advice for overcoming such adversities through the exercise of "virtus" (virtue) and adopting the format of self-justificatory speeches associated with the "de vera nobilitate" tradition; see R. W. Truman, *"Lazarillo de Tormes,* Petrarch's *De remediis adversae fortunae,* and Erasmus' *Praise of Folly,"* *Bulletin of Hispanic Studies,* 52 (1975), 33–53. The theme of the wandering trickster hero has many analogues in classical and medieval literature, and before the publication of *Lazarillo* lower-class characters had appeared in the Italian novella, *La Celestina, The Canterbury Tales,* and many other works.

9 Guillén ("Toward a Definition," p. 100) employs the term "half-outsider" in his discussion of the picaresque myth. Wicks ("Onlyman") regards exclusion or exile as a precondition and result of the essential picaresque situation, which for him involves birth into a broken or abnormal family situation, ejection into a hostile world, and a "Sisyphus" rhythm of experience.

10 Translated into Spanish by the Erasmian Diego López de Cortegana in 1513 and reissued three times by the mid-sixteenth century, *The Golden Ass* provides one of the few precedents for the use of the pseudoautobiographical perspective as an organizing device in *Lazarillo;* for a discussion of the possible relation between these two novels and the importance of the anonymous author's innovative use of first-person perspective, see Lázaro Carreter, *"Lazarillo de Tormes,"* pp. 28–40.

11 This feature of picaresque fiction has long been recognized; for example, in *The Literature of Roguery,* Chandler clearly identifies its "two poles of interest—one, the rogue and his tricks; the other, the manners he pillories" (I, 5).

12 The question is discussed in Francisco Ayala, *Experiencia y invención* (1950; rpt. Madrid: Taurus, 1960), pp. 149–157; Gonzalo Sobejano, "De la intención y valor del *Guzmán de Alfarache," Romanische Forschungen,* 71 (1959), 267–311; Edmond Cros, *Mateo Alemán: Introducción a su vida y a su obra* (Salamanca: Anaya, 1971), pp. 173–183; and Donald McGrady, *Mateo Alemán* (New York: Twayne, 1968), pp. 60–66.

13 An excellent discussion of this linkage is contained in Claudio Guillén, "Genre and Countergenre: The Discovery of the Picaresque," in *Literature as System,* pp. 135–158. This essay is an expanded version of "Luis Sánchez, Ginés de Pasamonte y los inventores del genero picaresco," in *Homenaje a Rodríguez-Monino, estudios de educación que le ofrecen sus amigos o discípulos hispanistas norteamericanos* (Madrid: Castalia, 1966), I, 221–231. It is also perceptively treated in Lázaro Carreter, *"Lazarillo de Tormes,"* pp. 193–229.

14 The modifications in the French *Buscon* are perceptively discussed in Andreas

Stoll, *Scarron als Übersetzer Quevedos—Studien zur Rezeption des pikaresken Romans "El Buscón" in Frankreich (L'Aventurier Buscon, 1633)*, Diss. Frankfurt/M, 1970; Dieter Reichardt, *Von Quevedos "Buscón" zum deutschen "Avanturier"* (Bonn: H. Bouvier, 1970), Studien zu Germanistik, Anglistik und Komparatistik, Vol. 7; and Cecille Cavillac, "'El pícaro amante,' de José Camerino et *L'Aventurier Buscon* de La Geneste: Étude d'un cas de médiation littéraire," *Revue de littérature comparée*, 47 (1973), 399–411. If Stoll's thesis is correct, La Geneste was actually a pseudonym for the young Scarron.

15 Miguel de Unamuno, *Niebla (Nivola)* (Buenos Aires: Espasa Calpe, 1943), p. 101.

16 The novel in general and the picaresque novel in particular are discussed in these terms by Ralph Freedman, "The Possibility of a Theory of the Novel," in *The Disciplines of Criticism: Essays in Literary Theory, Interpretation and History*, eds. Peter Demetz, Thomas Greene, and Lowry Nelson (New Haven: Yale University Press, 1968), pp. 57–77.

17 Parker (*The Delinquent*) develops the thesis that the picaresque novel is by definition a serious study of delinquency.

18 In the late nineteenth century, critics like Chandler, Garriga, Deleito y Piñuela and Morel Fatio interpreted picaresque fiction as a direct mirroring of social realities in Golden Age Spain; this approach has been recently revived in a rather simplistic fashion by Monteser in *The Picaresque Element*. In a more sophisticated treatment, the picaresque novel has been viewed as a less direct but nevertheless accurate representation of contradictions inherent in Spanish society by Alberto del Monte, *Itinerario de la novela picaresca española* (Italian, 1957; revised Spanish edition, Barcelona: Lumen, 1971). A more doctrinaire socialist-realist approach is advocated in Oldřič Belič, *Spanelský pikareskní román a realismus* (Prague: Universita Karlowa, 1963), Acta Universitatis Carolinae, Philologica, No. 4; and "La novela picaresca como orden artístico" (Prague: Universita Karlowa, 1963), Acta Universitatis Carolinae, Philologica, No. 3, pp. 5–35. Belič heralds the picaresque novel as the beginning of critical realism and discusses the pícaro's rootless, wandering, difficult existence as a reflection of the commoner's struggle for integration into a relatively undeveloped bourgeoisie. The pícaro is linked to a long tradition of "new men"—men who succeeded in bettering their social condition—in R. W. Truman, "Lazarillo de Tormes and the 'Homo Novus' Tradition," *Modern Language Review*, 44 (1969), 62–67. The idea that this "new man" can be identified with a world view which emerged during the Renaissance and became associated with the rising bourgeoisie is expressed in Rosario Rexach, "El hombre nuevo en la novela picaresca española," *Cuadernos hispanoamericanos*, No. 275 (1973), pp. 367–377. The picaresque novel is treated as an early manifestation of individual destiny in a society where the feudal order is disintegrating and being replaced by a naissant capitalism in Felix Brun, "Pour une interpretation sociologique du roman picaresque," in *Littérature et société: Problèmes de méthodologie de la littérature*, eds. Lucien Goldmann, Michel Bernard, and Roger Lallemand (Brussels: Institut de Sociologie de l'Université Libre de Bruxelles, 1967), pp. 127–135. The relationship between "realism" in the novel and the rise of a bourgeois

reading public is discussed in Ian Watt, *The Rise of the Novel: Studies in Defoe, Richardson and Fielding* (London: Chatto and Windus, 1957). Watt's thesis is critically reviewed in David H. Hirsch, "The Reality of Ian Watt," *Critical Quarterly*, 2 (1969), 164–179, and somewhat more concrete criteria for discussing the relationship between realism and bouregois value systems are advanced by English Showalter in *The Evolution of the French Novel, 1641–1782* (Princeton: Princeton University Press, 1972), pp. 69–74.

19 This world view is described in C. S. Lewis, *The Discarded Image: An Introduction to Medieval and Renaissance Literature* (Cambridge: University Press, 1964). That Lewis' syncretistic medieval "Model of the Universe" was not universally accepted becomes apparent when one considers the accounts of egalitarian "revolutionary millenarianism" contained in Norman Cohn, *The Pursuit of the Millennium* (1957; revised and expanded, London: Temple Smith, 1970). Cohn discusses movements which developed among the rootless, alienated poor of the towns and cities—movements often led by semiintellectuals or petty noblemen who appealed to the commoners' dreams of ameliorating their condition and their fantasies of apocalyptic destruction. Despite the "salvationism" of these movements, they tended to be revolutionary in the sense that they were dedicated to the eradication of existing social hierarchies. The history of the "chain of being" concept is traced in Arthur O. Lovejoy, *The Great Chain of Being* (1936; rpt. Cambridge: Harvard University Press, 1964).

20 During the Middle Ages, there was considerable literature on "estates." In general, the satiric representation of all classes and their characteristic vices dealt with stereotypes and was based upon the assumption that individuals were morally obliged to content themselves with their social station; see Jill Mann, *Chaucer and Medieval Estates Satire: The Literature of Social Classes and the "General Prologue" to the "Canterbury Tales"* (Cambridge: University Press, 1973), esp. pp. 1–16, 203–206. In this respect, it is interesting to note that all three estates are represented by the blind beggar, the priest of Maqueda, and the squire in the first three tratados of *Lazarillo*.

21 There is a considerable literature on the rise of a European bourgeoisie and its attitudes toward social mobility. See Elinor G. Barber, *The Bourgeoisie in Eighteenth Century France* (Princeton: Princeton University Press, 1955), esp. pp. 55–74, 99–140; Louis B. Wright, *Middle-class Culture in Elizabethan England* (1935; rpt. Ithaca: Cornell University Press, 1958); José Antonio Maravall, *Estado moderno y mentalidad social* (Madrid: Reviste de Occidente, 1972), esp. I, 401–477, and II, 3–47; Jean Dulumeau, *La civilisation de la Renaissance* (Paris: Arthaud, 1967), esp. pp. 317–336; Ferdinand Braudel, *La Méditerranée et le monde méditerranéen à l'époque de Philippe II* (Paris: Armand Colin, 1966), esp. II, 1–71; and Arnold Hirsch, *Bürgertum und Barock im deutschen Roman* (1934; revised, Cologne: Böhlau, 1957), esp. pp. 5–39.

22 Cecile Cavillac, "Les équivalents du mot 'bourgeois' dans la traduction espagnol de *Gil Blas*," *Revue de littérature comparée*, 43 (1969), 448–459.

23 This point is made by Antonio Domínguez Ortiz, "Historical Research on Spanish Conversos in the last 15 Years," in *Collected Studies in Honour of Américo Castro's Eightieth Year*, ed. M. P. Hornik (Oxford: Lincomb Lodge Research

Library, 1965), pp. 63–82; and Francisco Márquez Villanueva, "The Converso Problem: An Assessment," in *Collected Studies*, pp. 317–333. See also Márquez Villanueva, "Conversos y cargos concejiles en el siglo XV," *Revista de archivos, bibliotecas y museos*, 63 (1957), 503–540. In late sixteenth-century Portugal, commerce was almost entirely controlled by the third of the population which was Jewish or New Christian, and for this reason the terms "bourgeois" and "New Christian" were virtually synonymous; see Frédéric Mauro, "La bourgeoisie portugaise au XVIIᵉ siècle," *XVIIᵉ Siècle*, No. 40 (1958), pp. 235–257.

24 Márquez Villanueva, "The Converso Problem," p. 322.

25 A good example of this phenomenon is discussed by Carroll B. Johnson, "*El Buscón:* D. Pablos, D. Diego y D. Francisco," *Hispanófila*, 17 (1974), 1–26.

26 In many parts of Spain, the word "Portuguese" was virtually equivalent to "New Christian"; the crucial role played by this influx of Portuguese merchants into Spain is discussed in I. S. Révah, "Les marranes," *Revue des études juives*, 118 (1959–1960), esp. 36–40.

27 The seminal work on the converso problem is Américo Castro, *España en su historia: Cristianos, moros y judíos* (Buenos Aires: Losada, 1948), esp. pp. 470–586; Castro's ideas are revised and expanded in *La realidad histórica de España* (Mexcio City: Porrua, 1954), esp. pp. 443–561, and *De la edad conflictiva* (Madrid: Taurus, 1961). In addition to Révah, "Les marranes," and the essays by Domínguez Ortiz and Márquez Villanueva in *Collected Studies*, see Julio Caro Baroja, *Los judíos en la españa moderna y contemporanea* (Madrid: Arión, 1962), 3 vols.; Domínguez Ortiz, *La clase social de los conversos en Castilla en la edad moderna* (Madrid: CSIC, 1955), and *Los judeo-conversos en España y América* (Madrid: ISTMO, 1971), esp. pp. 193–217; Albert Sicroff, *Les controverses des status de "purité de sang" en Espagne du XVᵉ au XVIIᵉ siècle* (Paris: Didier, 1960); Márquez Villanueva, *Investigaciones sobre Juan Alvarez Gato: contribución al conocimiento de la literatura castellana del siglo XV* (Madrid: 1960), Anejos del Boletín de la Real Academia Española, No. 4; Antoine van Beysterveld, *Repércussions du souci de la purité de sang sur la conception de l'honneur dans la "comedia nueva" espagnole* (Leiden: E. J. Brill, 1966); Stephen Gilman, *The Spain of Fernando de Rojas: The Intellectual and Social Landscape of "La Celestina"* (Princeton: Princeton University Press, 1972); and Juan I. Gutiérrez Nieto, "La estructura castizo-estamental de la sociedad castellana del siglo XVI," *Hispania: Revista española de história*, No. 125 (1973), pp. 519–563. For general discussions of the converso problem in picaresque literature, see Marcel Bataillon, "Les nouveaux chrétiens dans l'essor du roman picaresque," *Neophilologus*, 4 (1964), 283–298, and Castro, "Perspectiva de la novela picaresca," in *Hacia Cervantes* (1957; revised, Madrid: Taurus, 1967), pp. 118–142. A Spanish translation of Bataillon's essay appears in *Pícaros y picaresca: "La pícara Justina"* (Madrid: Taurus, 1969), pp. 215–243.

28 Joseph Silverman, "Some Aspects of Literature and Life in the Golden Age of Spain," in *Estudios de literatura española ofrecidos a Marcos A. Morínigo* (Madrid: Insula, 1971), pp. 165–167.

29 Evidence for his possible converso origins remains circumstantial; the first to suggest that he might be a converso was Américo Castro in *Hacia Cervantes*, pp. 143–166. Others who have discussed the possible converso allusions in the

book include Gilman in "The Death of Lazarillo de Tormes," *PMLA*, 81 (1966), 150, and Francisco Márquez Villanueva in *Espiritualidad y literatura en el siglo XVI* (Madrid: Alfaguara, 1968), pp. 95–99.

Chapter 2. The Birth of the Picaresque: "Lazarillo de Tormes" and the Socializing Process

1 The earliest known editions of *Lazarillo* were published in 1554 at Burgos, Antwerp, and Alcalá. Their nearly simultaneous appearance has led some critics to suspect the existence of an earlier text (possibly 1553), and it is possible that holograph copies of the novel circulated for many years before its actual publication; in fact, the existence of different manuscript versions could explain variants in the 1554 editions. After a careful review of all extant sixteenth-century editions of the novel, José M. Caso González ("La primera edición del *Lazarillo de Tormes* y su relación con los textos de 1554," in *Studia hispanica in honorem R. Lapesa* [Madrid: Gredos, 1972–75], I, 189–206) posits the existence of a 1550 Antwerp *princeps* written by a rich nobleman who believed that the newly rich had no appreciation of hereditary (traditional) values and that nobility without concrete wealth to support it was pitiable. According to Caso González, this edition was based upon a *Lazarillo primitivo* (a lucianesque novel of social satire) and variously modified by subsequent editors. See also Aristide Rumeau, "Sur le *Lazarillo* de 1554: Problème de filiation," *Bulletin hispanique*, 71 (1969), 476–501. The novel's original composition has been dated as early as 1525 and as late as 1553. Its author has been variously identified as don Diego Hurtado de Mendoza, Fr. Juan de Ortega, Sebastián de Horozco, Juan de Valdés, Pedro de Rhua, Lope de Rueda, an unidentified converso, and a Flemish Jew influenced by Erasmian anticlericalism. However, questions involving authorship and date of composition will probably not be resolved with any degree of certainty unless new materials are discovered; for a survey of scholarly opinions on the subject, see Francisco Rico, "Introducción," in *La novela picaresca española* (Barcelona: Planeta, 1967), I, ix-xxv. The anonymous author's borrowings are discussed in Chapter 1, note 8. Even when there is no identifiable antecedent, an episode might reflect a folktale motif, and many of the characters are well-known *topoi*, as Fernando Lázaro Carreter indicates in *"Lazarillo de Tormes en la picaresca* (Barcelona: Ariel, 1972), pp. 63–65. Marcel Bataillon ("Introduction," in *La vie de Lazarillo de Tormes* [Paris: Éditions Montaigne, 1958], pp. 19–25; and *Novedad y fecundidad del "Lazarillo de Tormes"* [Salamanca: Anaya, 1968], pp. 27–45) supports the idea that Lazarillo himself was a traditional folklore figure, but María Rosa Lida de Malkiel ("Función del cuento popular en *Lazarillo de Tormes*," *Actas del Primer Congreso Internacional de Hispanistas*, ed. Frank Pierce and Cyril Jones [Oxford: Dolphin, 1964], pp. 349–359) contends that the main character's name associates him more closely with the Biblical Lazarus figures than with Spanish folklore. Rico ("Introducción," pp. xxvi-xxvii and xxxix) views Bataillon's thesis as suggestive but unproven. As evidenced by the hundreds of entries in the Laurenti and Ricapito

bibliographies, the secondary literature on *Lazarillo* is voluminous. The artistic unity of the work has been perceptively discussed in the above-mentioned essays by Rico, Bataillon, and Lázaro Carreter as well as in F. Courtney Tarr, "Literary and Artistic Unity in *Lazarillo de Tormes*," *PMLA*, 42 (1927), 404–421; Claudio Guillén, "La disposición temporal del *Lazarillo de Tormes*," *Hispanic Review*, 25 (1957), 264–279; Raymond Willis, "Lazarillo and the Pardoner: The Artistic Necessity of the Fifth Tractado," *Hispanic Review*, 27 (1959), 267–279; Rico, *La novela picaresca y el punto de vista* (Barcelona: Seix Barral, 1970), pp. 15–55; Lázaro Carreter, "Construcción y sentido del *Lazarillo de Tormes*," *Ábaco*, 1 (1969), 45–134 (rpt. in *"Lazarillo,"* pp. 59–192). Other suggestive treatments of the novel include Stephen Gilman, "The Death of Lazarillo de Tormes," *PMLA*, 81 (1966), pp. 149–166; Francisco Ayala, *"El Lazarillo": Nuevo examen de algunos aspectos* (Madrid: Taurus, 1971); Hans Gerd Rötzer, *Picaro-Landstörtzer-Simplicius* (Darmstadt: Wissenschaftliche Buchgesellschaft, 1972), pp. 1–27; Victoria Windler, "'Alienación' en el *Lazarillo de Tormes:* La fragmentación del 'yo' narrativo," *Estudios filológicos*, No. 8 (1972), pp. 225–253; Josette Blanquat, "Fraude et frustration dans *Lazarillo de Tormes*," in *Culture et marginalités au XVIᵉ siècle* (Paris: Klincksieck, 1973), Documents et travaux de l'équipe de recherche culture et société au XVIᵉ siècle, I, 41–73; and Howard Mancing, "The Deceptiveness of *Lazarillo de Tormes*," *PMLA*, 90 (1975), 426–432. Many critics have written perceptively on the first-person perspective in *Lazarillo*. Among others, see Guillén, "La disposición temporal"; Hans R. Jauss, "Ursprung und Bedeutung der Ich-Form im *Lazarillo de Tormes*," *Romanistisches Jahrbuch*, 8 (1957), 290–311; Horst Baader, "Noch einmal zur Ich-Form im *Lazarillo de Tormes*," *Romanische Forschungen*, 76 (1964), 437–446; Lázaro Carreter, "La ficción autobiográfico en el *Lazarillo de Tormes*," in *Litterae Hispanae et Lusitanae: Festschrift zum 50 Jährigen Bestehen des Ibero-Amerikanischen Forschungsinstituts der Universität Hamburg*, ed. Hans Flasche (Munich: Hueber, 1966), pp. 195–213 (rpt. in *"Lazarillo"*, pp. 13–57); Lázaro Carreter, *"Lazarillo"*, pp. 69–79, 172–177; Rico, *La novela picaresca y el punto de vista*, pp. 15–55; and Aubrey Bell, "The Rhetoric of Self-Defense of 'Lázaro de Tormes,'" *Modern Language Review*, 68 (1973), 84–93. Lázaro Carreter suggests that the autobiographical form of *Lazarillo* derives from a well-developed tradition of semipublic memoir-letters, whereas Robin McAllister (*"Lazarillo de Tormes* and Rhetorical Paradox," paper delivered at MLA Symposium, "Literature of the Renaissance and Golden Age," 27 December 1974) discovers a closer affinity with the "rhetorical paradox" (a formal defense of an unexpected, unworthy, or absurd position in order to call commonly accepted opinions into question), although he concludes that *Lazarillo* is actually a mixed form with elements of the mock oration, mock epistle, and confessional autobiography.

2 The idea of Lázaro's spiritual death is developed in Gilman, "The Death," pp. 149–166. The linguistic family to which the word "laceria" belongs is discussed by Yakov Malkiel in "La familia léxica lazerar, laz[d]rar, lazeria," *Nueva revista de filología*, 6 (1952), 209–276.

3 Most critics have found this episode either psychologically or structurally unsatisfying. In "Algunas notas sobre el 'tractado tercero' del *Lazarillo de Tormes*,"

in *Studia hispanica*, III, 507–517, Domingo Ynduráin summarizes their views and suggests a justification based upon Lazarillo's relationship to the squire.

4 *La vida de Lazarillo de Tormes y de sus fortunas y adversidades* in *La novela picaresca española*, ed. Francisco Rico (Barcelona: Planeta, 1967). All subsequent references to *Lazarillo* will appear between parentheses in the text and refer to pages in this edition.

5 The ramifications of this verbal echo are discussed by Rico in *La novela picaresca y el punto de vista*, p. 36.

6 Lázaro Carreter ("*Lazarillo*," p. 148) discusses the squire's interest in Lazarillo's past and points out Lazarillo's solicitude for the squire's feelings when the older man apologizes for not having any wine to offer his servant.

7 There is some indication that Lazarillo may be a New Christian, for his admission that the bread was carried in "el arca de su seno, do no se le podia pegar mucha limpieza" (49) ("in the chest of his chest, where not much purity could have stuck to it") may be a punning allusion to his own "impurity" of blood; this suspicion is furthered by his reference to himself as a "mozo nuevo," while he watches his master court the two women by the riverbank. For a discussion of Lázaro's phrase "criar de nuevo" in this context, see Américo Castro, "La 'novedad' y los 'nuevas,'" *Hispanic Review* 20 (1952), 149–153; rpt. in *Hacia Cervantes* (1957; revised, Madrid: Taurus, 1967), pp. 149–154.

8 María del Carmen Carlé, *Del concejo medieval castellanoleones* (Buenos Aires: Instituto de Historia de España, 1968), pp. 70–80. The ironic reversal of terms associated with "bien" and "bueno" is discussed in C. B. Morris. "Lázaro and the Squire: Hombres de Bien," *Bulletin of Hispanic Studies*, 40 (1964), 238–241; Bruce Wardropper, "El trastorno de la moral en el *Lazarillo*," *Nueva revista de filología hispánica*, 15 (1961), 441–447; Rötzer, *Picaro*, pp. 11–13; and Windler, "Alienación," pp. 230–231.

9 The colloquial speech of the time was permeated with such usages according to Victor G. de la Concha in "La intención religiosa del *Lazarillo*," *Revista de filología española*, 55 (1972), 247–250. He counts eighty-two mentions of "Dios" or "Señor" in *Lazarillo*. Gilman ("The Death," pp. 156–158) discusses the function of these allusions and perceptively refers to God as the "seminal commonplace" in the book.

Chapter 3. The Dissemination of the Picaresque: "Guzmán de Alfarache" and the Converso Problem

1 Actually only Part I (1599) could be considered a best seller. Within two years it went through sixteen printings, and in his eulogy to Part II (1604), Luis de Valdés mentions twenty-six printings and 50,000 copies sold during its first five years of publication. In his inaugural address to the Real Academia Española, Francisco Rodríguez Marín stated: "No creo que haya memoria en nuestra patria de libro que en el año de su publicación y en el siguiente inmediato se reimprimiera tantas veces" (cited in Guzmán Álvarez, *Mateo Alemán* [Buenos Aires: Espasa-Calpe, 1953], p. 80).

2 In his *Misteriosas andanzas atunescas de "Lázaro de Tormes"* (San Sebastián: Izaira, 1969), Máximo Saludo Stephan contends that the "fish" story was written by Pedro de Medino in defense of the defrocked Mallorcan commendador of the Order of Malta (Antonio Fuster; Licio in the story). According to Stephen, the tuna fish are either Turks or Christians who lack genuine belief; Medino's Lázaro may be a converso, but by drinking the wine, he becomes able to survive in the salt water of true faith. Like the "cuttle-fish with eight tongues," Knights of the Order of Malta would be at home in such a sea. Lázaro's final retreat to a "rock by the sea" becomes in this interpretation the symbolic equivalent of a retirement to Malta and a discovery of the truth. As reconstructed by Stephen, this allegory of Lázaro's experiences in the divine world parallels the original Lazarillo's experiences in the earthly realm. Marcel Bataillon (*Novedad y fecundidad del "Lazarillo de Tormes"* [Salamanca: Anaya, 1968], pp. 83–85) also discusses the 1555 sequel and suggests that transformation into a "tuna fish" stands for an abjuration of the true faith. The continuation is viewed as a veiled commentary upon abuses in government, courtly life, and military orders in Richard Zwez, *Hacia la revalorización de "La segunda parte del Lazarillo"* (Valencia: Albatros, 1970).

3 Both Hans Gerd Rötzer (*Picaro-Landstörtzer-Simplicius* [Darmstadt: Wissenschaftliche Buchgesellschaft, 1972], pp. 29–31) and Bataillon (*Novedad*, pp. 72–73) discuss these modifications in the "Lazarillo castigado."

4 Claudio Guillén (*Literature as System: Essays Toward the Theory of Literary History* [Princeton: Princeton University Press, 1971], pp. 137–142) discusses in detail the early editions of *Lazarillo*.

5 Fernando Lázaro Carreter (*"Lazarillo de Tormes" en la picaresca* [Barcelona: Ariel, 1972], pp. 206–222) discusses Alemán's attitude toward *Lazarillo;* he suggests that Alemán saw possibilities in the short novel's form and points out that Guzmán's service with the innkeeper is characterized as a worse condition than that of a blind man's servant. Other possible parallels are discussed in Donald McGrady, *Mateo Alemán* (New York: Twayne, 1968), pp. 60–66.

6 The seminal work on the miscellany qualities of *Guzmán* is Edmond Cros's *Protée et le Gueux: Recherches sur les origines et la nature du récit picaresque dans "Guzmán de Alfarache"* (Paris: Didier, 1967), but Franklin Brantley's "Baroque Structure and Innovation of *Guzmán de Alfarache*" (Diss. Tulane, 1967) and Barbara Davis' "An Analysis of the Structure and Style of Mateo Alemán's *Guzmán de Alfarache*" (Diss. Columbia, 1969) also approach the novel from this point of view. A summary of Cros's views appears in his *Mateo Alemán: Introducción a su vida y a su obra* (Salamanca: Anaya, 1971), pp. 75–93, and part of Davis' argument is reproduced in "The Style of Mateo Alemán's *Guzmán de Alfarache*," *Romanic Review*, 66 (1975), 199–213. Alemán's specific borrowings have been traced to many sources. The intercalated tales have been linked to Heliodorus' "Ethiopian History" and the novellae to Salernitano, Boccaccio, and Bandello. Brantley ("Baroque Structure," pp. 85–86), McGrady (*Mateo Alemán*, p. 74), del Monte (*Itinerario*, pp. 82–84) and Cros (*Mateo Alemán*, pp. 163–165) discuss the question of influence and provide lists of analogues and possible sources. Francisco Rico ("Introducción," *La novela picaresca española*

[Barcelona: Planeta, 1967], I, clxv-clxxx) compares the 1599 edition of *Guzmán* with the 1602 revised edition and clearly demonstrates Alemán's meticulous attention to style; Alonso de Barros' and Luis de Valdés' respective eulogies to Parts I and II of *Guzmán* as well as Baltasar Gracián's laudatory comments in his *Agudeza y arte de ingenio* (1642; first published edition 1648) indicate that the novel was greatly admired for the same varied and eloquent style which characterized the traditional miscellanies. Cros (*Protée*, pp. 48–48) discusses the history of Alemán's "atalaya de la vida humana" subtitle.

7 McGrady, *Mateo Alemán*, p. 119. Both McGrady and Cros (*Mateo Alemán*) provide readable accounts of Alemán's life and indicate numerous parallels between the fictional life of Guzmán and the real life of the author.

8 The possibility that the book's narrative and sermonizing sections are unified by Alemán's didactic purpose is advanced by Enrique Moreno Báez in his "¿Hay una tesis en el *Guzmán de Alfarache?*" *Revista de la Universidad Buenos Aires*, 4 (1945), 269–910; *Lección y sentido del "Guzmán de Alfarache"* (Madrid, 1948), *Revista de filología española*, Anejo 40; and in an article of the same title in *Arbor*, 4 (1948), 377–394. Essentially Moreno Báez attempts to show that Alemán is primarily concerned with the defense and illustration of orthodox Catholic teachings about original sin, free will, grace, and individual responsibility. According to him, *Guzmán* demonstrates that salvation is possible even for the most miserable of men; unfortunately, Moreno Báez overlooks the importance of Guzmán's converso heritage. Alemán's own converso background was first pointed out in Francisco Rodríguez Marín, "La casa de Mateo Alemán," in *Burla burlada: menudencias de varia, leve y entretenida erudición* (Madrid: Tip. de la *Revista de archivos*, 1914), pp. 135–140; and *Documentos referentes a Mateo Alemán y a su deudos cercanos (1546–1606) hallados por Francisco Rodríguez Marín* (Madrid: Tip. de Archivos, 1933), p. 6. The suggestion that *Guzmán* illustrates a Counter-Reformation world view is disputed in J. A. van Praag, "Sobre el sentido del *Guzmán de Alfarache*," in *Estudios dedicados a Menéndez Pidal* (Madrid: CSIC, 1954), V, 283–306. Van Praag believes the book to be dominated by a converso's cynical attitude toward Catholicism. Alexander A. Parker (*Literature and the Delinquent: The Picaresque Novel in Spain and Europe 1599–1753* [Edinburgh: University Press, 1967], pp. 31–45, 138–142) attempts to refute van Praag and demonstrate that Alemán was a sincere Catholic; however, the crucial role of the converso problem has been more or less firmly established in studies like Joseph Silverman, "Some Aspects of Literature and Life in the Golden Age of Spain," in *Estudios de literatura española ofrecidos a Marcos A. Morínigo* (Madrid: Insula, 1971); Edward Nagy, "El anhelo del Guzmán de Alfarache de 'conocer su sangre,' una posibilidad interpretiva," *Kentucky Romance Quarterly*, 16 (1970), 75–95; Carroll B. Johnson, "Dios y buenas gentes en *Guzmán de Alfarache*," *Romanische Forschungen*, 84 (1972), 553–563; Richard Bjornson, "*Guzmán de Alfarache*: Apologia for a 'Converso'," *Romanische Forschungen*, 85 (1973), 314–329; Victorio G. Agüera, "La salvación del cristiano nuevo en *Guzmán de Alfarache*," *Hispania*, 66 (1974), 23–30; and M. N. Norval, "Original Sin and the 'Conversion' in the *Guzmán de Alfarache*," *Bulletin of Hispanic Studies*, 51 (1974), 346–364.

9 Although the universally similar nature of all people is explicitly defined in the Tridentine profession of faith, it was not entirely safe for Spaniards to openly defend such ideas, as the denunciation of Fr. Luis de León illustrates; see Chapter 1, note 28.

10 Mateo Alemán, *Guzmán de Alfarache*, in *La novela picaresca española*, ed. Francisco Rico (Barcelona: Planeta, 1967). All subsequent citations will refer to pages in this edition and appear between parentheses in the text. One might well compare Guzmán's statement with the Tridentine doctrine: "Per unum hominem peccatum intravit in mundum et per peccatum mors, et ita in omnes homines mors pertransiit, in quo omnes peccaverunt" (*Sacros: Concilium Tridentum*, 1564; rpt. Antwerp, 1963, p. 14).

11 *Sacros*, p. 47.

12 Alemán's attachment to the emblem is suggested by his repeated allusions to it and the fact that he had it and the Latin motto, "Ab insidiis non est prudencia," printed in the upper right-hand corner of his portrait in all approved editions of *Guzmán* and *San Antonio de Padua*.

13 Agüera ("Salvación," p. 24) discusses this passage and similar ones at great length.

14 The entire Sayavedra episode constitutes Alemán's allegorical version of the manner in which his original manuscripts for Part II had been stolen from him and published by a Valencian law professor, Dr. Juan José Martí. By transforming the counterfeit Guzmán into a weak and base-spirited Sayavedra who has an irresistible urge to impersonate the genuine Guzmán, Alemán condescendingly recognizes the 1602 apocryphal continuation as an inferior work. Those who knew anything about the situation would undoubtedly have identified Sayavedra's suicidal leap into the sea with Martí's own death in 1604 and Pompeyo's duplicity with that of Pedro Mey, the printer of Martí's *Guzmán*. McGrady (*Mateo Alemán*, p. 119) discusses the affair and points out that Pompeyo is actually an anagram for Pedro Patricio Mey.

15 Norval ("Original Sin," esp. pp. 347–348) discusses this episode in terms of the Sisyphus myth and the weakness of the flesh; she ultimately concludes that there is no possibility of true grace in the novel. By paying particular attention to the earlier episodes in Guzmán's life, Johnson ("Dios y buenas gentes") and Agüera ("La salvación") arrive at a similar conclusion.

*Chapter 4. In the Wake of "Guzmán": Variations on the
Picaresque-Life Theme*

1 The origins of "pícaro" remain obscure, and during the past seventy years scholars have proposed many different etymologies for the word. Among them are "picar" (to pick, pierce, or mince; it also has slang connotations of snatching or stealing), "picardo" (a man from Picardy), "pica" (the lance carried by soldiers), "pikharte" (a follower of the excommunicated twelfth-century heretic Pedro de Valdo) and Arabic, Greek, English, and Basque loanwords. Convenient summaries of the arguments for and against these derivations can be

found in Alberto del Monte, *Itinerario de la novela picaresca española* (Barcelona: Lumen, 1971), pp. 11–13, and in Yakov Malkiel, "El núcleo del problema etimológico de 'pícaro'-'picardía' en torno al proceso del préstamo doble," in *Studia hispanica in honorem R. Lapesa* (Madrid: Gredos, 1972–75), II, 307–342. Numerous articles on the subject are listed in Joseph Laurenti, *Bibliografía de la literatura picaresca: Desde sus orígenes hasta el presente* (Metuchen, N.J.: Scarecrow, 1973), pp. 7–10. Annotations for most of them are provided in Joseph Ricapito, "Toward a Definition of the Picaresque," Diss. UCLA, 1966, pp. 74–87; rpt. and expanded in *Bibliografía razonada y anotada de las obras maestras de la novela picaresca española* (Madrid: Castalia, 1976). When the word "pícaro" first achieved currency in the late sixteenth century, it apparently signified a deceitful or shameless person of vulgar birth and without a fixed occupation. Its first confirmed appearance occurred in the 1540's, and some idea of its meaning is suggested in the *Carta del Bachiller de Arcadia al Capitán Salazar* (1548), where a "pícaro" is placed in opposition to a courtier. By the late sixteenth century, it must have already become a generally accepted term. It appears frequently in an epic poem composed between 1587 and 1598 by a soldier who apparently fought in Flanders during the early 1570's; he even employs "pícaro" to clarify the meaning of the French "gueuz" (rogue) for his Spanish readers; see F. González-Ollé, "Nuevos testimonios tempranos de *pícaro* y palabras afines," *Ibero-romania*, 1 (1969), 56–58. In dictionaries compiled by Christoval de las Casas (1570) and Diego de Guadix (1593), the "pícaro" is defined as a vulgar, poorly dressed man who lacks a sense of honor. Somewhat later and after *Guzmán* had become commonly known as "El Pícaro," Covarrubias' *Tesoro de la lengua castellana* (1611) still emphasizes the "pícaro's" willingness to perform vulgar tasks, but it also alludes to a characteristic freedom from duty and responsibility. Both Alemán and Covarrubias at one point equate "pícaro" with "esportillero"—a young boy who carries a basket, stations himself in a public place, and offers to carry anything for anyone. This willingness to accept any employment is perhaps symbolic of the "pícaro's" protean flexibility of character, but the essential meaning of the word seems to have remained associated with ideas of dishonor and vulgarity. It appears as a pejorative term for a low-spirited cheater of women in Salas Barbadillo's *La hija de Celestina* (1612), a dishonest jailor in Vicente Espinel's *Marcos de Obregón* (1618), a cowardly servant in Castillo Solórzano's *Teresa de Manzanares* (1632), and a roguish social climber in his *El bachiller Trapaza* (1637). Both popular and literary usages of the word during the seventeenth century are undoubtedly reflected in the *Diccionario de la Academia* (1737) definition of a "pícaro" as one who employs deception and lacks honor.

2 According to Donald McGrady (*Mateo Alemán* [New York: Twayne, 1968], p. 26), at least fifteen editions of the apocryphal *Guzmán* appeared before Alemán's own version was published in 1604, whereas Alemán's Part II went through only five editions in the two years after its first publication.

3 H. Petriconi, "Zur Chronologie und Verbreitung des spanischen Schelmenromans," *Volkstum und Kultur der Romanen*, 2 (1928), 324–342; rpt. in *Pikarische*

Welt: Schriften zum europäischen Schelmenroman, ed. Helmut Heidenreich (Darmstadt: Wissenschaftliche Buchgesellschaft, 1969), esp. pp. 73–74.

4 For an excellent detailed discussion of this phenomenon, see Claudio Guillén, "Genre and Countergenre: The Discovery of the Picaresque," in *Literature as System: Essays Toward the Theory of Literary History* (Princeton: Princeton University Press, 1971), esp. pp. 145–158.

5 "¿Que Guzmán de Alfarache o Lazarillo de Tormes tuvieron más amos ni hizieron más enredos?" Agustín de Rojas, *El viaje entretenido*, ed. John V. Falconieri (Salamanca: Anaya, 1965), p. 22.

6 "... es tan bueno... que mal año para *Lazarillo de Tormes* y para todos quantos de aquel género se han escrito o escribieren," Miguel de Cervantes Saavedra, *Don Quixote de la Mancha*, in *Obras completas* (Madrid: Aguilar, 1964), p. 1115.

7 Alemán, *Guzmán*, p. 261.

8 For discussions of two unpublished picaresque novels of the period, see Paul Langeard, "Un roman inédit: *El Guitón Honofre* (1604) de Gregorio Gonçález," *Revue hispanique*, 80 (1930), 718–722; and J. A. van Praag, "*Vida y costumbres de la Madre Andrea*," *Revista de literatura*, 14 (1958), 111–169. A critical edition of the former has recently been published as Gregorio Gonçález, *El Guitón Honofre (1604)*, ed. Hazel G. Carrasco (Madrid: Castalia, 1973), Estudios de Hispanófila, 25. Picaresquelike characters also appear in Lope de Vega's *El gran duque de Moscovia* (1617) as well as in plays by Tirso de Molina, Salas Barbadillo, and Castillo Solórzano. A. Bonilla y San Martín edited two of the most interesting picaresque poems: "Testamento del pícaro pobre," which appeared in *Anales de la literatura española* (Madrid: Tello, 1904), pp. 64–75, and "La vida del pícaro," which he published in *Revue hispanique*, 9 (1902), 295–330. For a discussion of the evolution of the word "pícaro," see note 1 above.

9 Textual parallels which establish the extent of Martí's borrowings from writers like Alonso de Cabrera, López Pinciano, Alejo Venegas, Pérez de Herrera, and Juan Gutiérrez are cited in Bernadette Labourdique and Michel Cavillac, "Quelques sources du *Guzmán* apocryphe de Mateo Luján," *Bulletin hispanique*, 81 (1969), 191–217.

10 Vicente Espinel, "Ad Guzmanum Alfarachie, Vicentii Spinelli Epigramma," in Alemán, *Guzmán*, p. 100.

11 The epithet "mozo de muchos amos" ("servant of many masters") in the book's subtitle was frequently applied to Lazarillo and Guzmán, and although many of Alonso's proverbial locutions were popular commonplaces, he was clearly alluding to Lazarillo's revenge upon the blind beggar when he claimed to have "smelled the post." The sermonizing passages in *Alonso* contain verbal parallels to Alemán's *Guzmán*, and the encyclopedic tendency obviously mirrors an important aspect of the earlier novel. Even individual incidents from *Guzmán* are transparently echoed in *Alonso;* for example, when Alonso gives a full purse to a famous preacher in order to gain a reputation for honesty, he is obviously imitating one of Guzmán's final ruses. The conversational setting, the moral tone, and many individual anecdotes reflect the influence of *Marcos*. When Alonso catches a thief by making all the suspects believe that a stick would

grow longer if held by the guilty man, he is essentially doing what Marcos had done with a bell that supposedly rang if a guilty man placed his hand in a dish of red ochre. Even in cases where events are not based upon specific analogues in previous picaresque literature, they often represent the mere reelaboration of commonplace narrative situations: initiation at the university, Algerian captivity, service to women blinded by their vanity.

12 In *Vicente Espinel and "Marcos de Obregón": A Life and its Literary Representation* (Providence, R.I.: Brown University Press, 1959), George Haley shows that *Marcos* was probably read as a rather transparent autobiographical allegory by contemporary readers; he concludes that it contains both the author's actual memories and his wish-dreams of prowess. Relatively little is known about Martí, but a readable account of Alcalá Yáñez' life is contained in Mañuel González Herro, "Jeronimo de Alcalá Yáñez," *Estudios segovianos*, 7 (1955), 57–135. Upon the basis of González Herro's facts, the case for Alcalá Yáñez' bourgeois mentality is made in Angel Valbuena Briones, "Burguesía y picaresca en *Alonso, Mozo de muchos amos*," *Arbor*, 8 (1972), 31–37.

13 Vicente Espinel, *Vida de Marcos de Obregón* (Madrid: Espasa-Calpe, 1959), I, 277–278.

14 Espinel, *Marcos*, I, 173.

15 Espinel, *Marcos*, II, 310.

16 The idea that the narrative perspective in *Marcos* reflects stream-of-consciousness technique is advanced in Vance Y. McConnell, "Antithetical Expression and Subconscious Conflict in Vicente Espinel's *Vida de Marcos de Obregón*," Diss. Arizona, 1966. McConnell contends that the narrating Marcos is unsuccessfully striving to dissipate the guilt and anxiety of a divided psyche by interspersing long, apologetic passages in the account of his life. A detailed discussion of the novel's ideological assumptions and recurrent narrative situations is contained in Richard Bjornson, "Social Conformity and Justice in *Marcos de Obregón*," *Revista de estudios hispánicos*, 9 (1975), 285–307. A somewhat different view is presented in Adrian G. Montoro, "'Liberated cristiana': Relectura de Marcos de Obregón," *Modern Language Notes*, 91 (1976), 213–230. Using "myth" in the sense popularized by Roland Barthes, Montoro suggests that *Marcos* is a veiled attack upon the then-current social myths of external honor and "limpieza de sangre." According to him, Marcos is not a conformist, but a hero who opposes his own patience and inner liberty to a gossiping, cruel, unjust world; the only difficulties with this interpretation involve its heavy reliance upon the equivocal interpretation of a renegade Christian as Marcos' alter ego and its failure to consider that the practical consequences of Marcos' actions help to maintain a corrupt *status quo*.

17 Espinel, *Marcos*, I, 143.

18 Espinel, *Marcos*, II, 173.

19 Jeronimo de Alcalá Yáñez y Ribera, *El donado hablador Alonso: Mozo de muchos amos*, in *La novela picaresca española*, ed. Angel Valbuena Prat (Madrid: Aguilar, 1943), p. 1250.

20 Alcalá Yáñez, *Alonso*, p. 1148.

21 Alcalá Yáñez, *Alonso*, p. 1258.

22 Justina refers to her servant as "mi lazarillo" and to herself as "la Guzmana de Alfarache." Her insistence upon never having been in the galleys is an obvious allusion to Guzmán's fate, and in a passage which echoes one of Lazarillo's tricks upon the blind beggar, she describes how her mother choked to death on a sausage. Among many expressions similar to those in *Lazarillo* are "donde una puerta se cierra, ciento se abren" ("where one door closes, a hundred open") and "pan, que es cara de Dios" ("bread, which is the face of God"). Improvisations upon "pícaro" include "picaral," "picardía," "picaresco," and "apicarada."

23 Like Lázaro, the narrating Pablos composes a detailed account of his life in hopes of receiving some favor or benefit from "Vuestra Merced," an unnamed social superior who has apparently expressed a desire to hear the "varios discursos" (various discourses; the term is possibly based upon the use of tratados in *Lazarillo*) of his life. Traits of the priest of Maqueda and the squire reappear in Quevedo's schoolmaster Cabra and the false "caballero" don Toribio, and Cabra's school bears a distinct resemblance to the squire's enchanted house. Like Guzmán, the narrating Pablos has converso origins, leaves home to escape the disgrace of being associated with disreputable parents, consciously chooses to become a rogue, avenges himself upon his uncle, falls from a horse while parading pompously in front of respectable townspeople, and ultimately "marries" a prostitute before committing a series of crimes in Seville and undertaking a sea voyage. Some of these parallels are discussed in Lázaro Carreter, "Glosas críticas a *Los pícaros en la literatura* de Alexander A. Parker," *Hispanic Review*, 41 (1973), 486, but the most complete discussions can be found in a series of articles by Victorio G. Agüera: "La salvación del cristiano nuevo en *Guzmán de Alfarache*," *Hispania*, 66 (1974), 23–30; "Nueva interpretación del episodio 'Rey de Gallos' del *Buscón*," *Hispanófila*, 49 (1973), 33–40; and "Notas sobre las burlas de Alcalá de *La Vida del Buscón llamado Pablos*," *Romance Notes*, 13 (1972), 503–506.

24 Marcel Bataillon has written extensively upon the *Pícara Justina*; all his important essays on the subject are collected in *Pícaros y picaresca: "La pícara Justina"* (Madrid: Taurus, 1969). For a discussion of the relationship between Úbeda and Calderón, see pp. 91–121 of this work.

25 Francisco López de Úbeda, *La pícara Justina*, ed. J. Puyol y Alonso (Madrid: Fortanet, 1912), Sociedad de Bibliófilos Madrileños, II, 299.

26 Úbeda, *Justina*, I, 159.

27 Bataillon (*Pícaros y picaresca*, pp. 123–127 and *passim*) identifies allusions to many subjects which absorbed the attention of people in attendance at Philip III's court. There are a great number of unusual words (e.g., *giroblera*, *ciclana*, *daifises*, *carispitis*) which, although they do not appear in any other work of the period, might have been recognizable to the courtiers for whom Úbeda was writing.

28 Úbeda, *Justina*, II, 272.

29 Alonso de Castillo Solórzano, *La niña de los embustes, Teresa de Manzanares*, in *La novela picaresca española*, ed. Valbuena Prat, p. 1351.

30 Castillo Solóranzo, *Aventuras del bachiller Trapaza, quinta esencia de embusteros y maestro de embelecadores*, in *La novela picaresca española*, ed. Valbuena Prat, p.

1504. An interesting contrast to this situation is provided by the contemporary short-story writer Doña María de Zayas y Sotomayor, whose picaresquelike stories show the failure of ruses played by female rogues and the success of ones played by men. In "Amar sólo por vencer," the roguish don Esteban successfully defrauds a gullible young noblewoman, whereas Isidora in "El castigo de la miseria" ends her life in destitution after duping a well-to-do but miserly former page.

31 Robert S. Rudder, "La segunda parte de *Lazarillo de Tormes:* La originalidad de Juan de Luna," *Estudios filológicos,* 6 (1970), 111. In addition to Rudder's article, details of Luna's life can be found in Jean-Marc Pelorson and Hélène Simon, "Une mise au point sur l'*Arte Breve* de Juan de Luna," *Bulletin hispanique,* 71 (1969), 218–230; and Joseph L. Laurenti, *Vida de Lazarillo de Tormes: Estudio crítico de La segunda parte de Juan de Luna* (Mexico City: Studium, 1965).

32 For an excellent discussion of García's background, see Jean-Marc Pelorson, "Le Docteur Carlos García et la colonie hispano-portugaise de Paris (1613–1619)," *Bulletin hispanique,* 71 (1969), 518–576. Additional information is contained in Giulio Massano, "*La desordenada codicia de los bienes ajenos* by Carlos García: A Critical Edition," Diss. Catholic U., 1974.

33 A somewhat incomplete discussion of picaresque novels placed on the Index is contained in Gerhard Moldenhauer, "Spanische Zensur und Schelmenroman," in *Estudios eruditos in memoriam de A. Bonilla y San Martín (1875–1926)* (Madrid: Viuda e Hijos de Jaime Ratés, 1927), I, 223–239.

34 Laurenti (*Vida*) and Valbuena Prat (*La novela picaresca*) criticize Luna for distorting the original, whereas he is treated as a perceptive reader and interpreter of *Lazarillo* by Horst Baader in "Lazarillos Weg zur Eindeutigkeit oder Juan de Luna als Leser und Interpret des anonymen *Lazarillo de Tormes,*" in *Interpretation und Vergleich: Festschrift für Walter Pabst,* eds. Eberhard Leube and Ludwig Schrader (Berlin: Erich Schmidt, 1972), pp. 11–33.

35 Gabriel Laplane, "Les anciennes traductions françaises de *Lazarillo de Tormes,*" in *Hommage à Ernst Martinèche: Études hispaniques et américaines* (Paris: Éditions d'Artrey, 1937), p. 151.

36 Juan de Luna, *Segunda parte de Lazarillo de Tormes,* in *La novela picaresca,* ed. Valbuena Prat, p. 47.

37 Carlos García, *La desordenada codicia de los bienes ajenos: Antigüedad y nobleza de los ladrones,* ed. Fernando Gutiérrez (Barcelona: Selecciones Bibliofilas, 1959), p. 76.

38 García, *Desordenada codicia,* p. 86.

39 Luna, *Segunda parte,* p. 40.

40 The fortune theme is discussed in both Rudder, "*La segunda parte,*" and Hans Gerd Rötzer, *Picaro-Landstörtzer-Simplicius* (Darmstadt: Wissenschaftliche Buchgesellschaft, 1972), pp. 31–35.

41 In doing this, Bonfons was following a practice probably inaugurated by printers in the Netherlands; see Chapter 7, note 5.

42 Luna, *Segunda parte,* p. 39.

43 Luna, *Segunda parte,* p. 45.

Chapter 5. *"El Buscón": Quevedo's Annihilation of the Picaresque*

1 *El Buscón* must have been written long before 1626, when a Saragossa bookseller, Robert Duport, published it without Quevedo's permission; manuscript
versions of the novel probably circulated for years among court and literary
circles until Duport obtained a possibly defective copy. Quevedo's political
enemies may have been involved in the unauthorized publication of *El Buscón*,
for the 1626 Madrid edition was brought out by Alonso Pérez, whose son Pérez
de Montalbán collaborated with Pacheco de Narváez and P. Niseno in scheming to have all of Quevedo's works banned by the Inquisition in 1628. Quevedo
himself neither revised *El Buscón* nor included it in his complete works, although he had the opportunity to do so, and he did revise other banned works.
In the preface to a 1631 revised edition of the *Sueños*, he complained about the
"foreigners" (i.e., those like Duport from outside the realm Castile) who
printed his youthful works without allowing him to revise them. Thus,
Quevedo never claimed to have written *El Buscón*, and he apparently didn't
consider it worthy of revision; he also never denied having written it, and no
one has ever seriously questioned his authorship. The book itself was a publishing success, and eleven editions had been printed by 1648, according to Harry
Sieber, "The Narrative Art of Quevedo in *El Buscón*," Diss. Duke, 1967, p. 3.
For the most complete discussion of the *Buscón* manuscripts, see Fernando
Lázaro Carreter's "Estudio preliminar" to his masterful critical edition, *La vida
del Buscón llamado don Pablos* (Salamanca: Universidad, 1965), pp. xi-lxxviii.

2 There has been considerable controversy over the moral seriousness and artis-
tic unity of *El Buscón*. The seminal study is unquestionably Leo Spitzer's "Zur
Kunst Quevedos in seinem *Buscón*," *Archivum Romanicum*, 11 (1927), 511–580,
rpt. in Spitzer, *Romanische Stil- und Literaturuntersuchungen* (Marburg a. Lahn:
N. G. Elwertsche Verlagsbuchhandlung, 1931), II, 48–125. Spitzer discusses
Pablos as an archetypical pícaro and finds the book's central organizing principle in the "desengaño" theme. Although he perceives an underlying tension in
Pablos' pursuit of earthly vanities (a realistic impulse toward life) and the
author's implicit rejection of them (an ascetic fleeing from life), he concludes
that Quevedo fails to integrate his materials into a coherent narrative
framework; for that reason, individual episodes remain essentially isolated,
separate entities. An entirely different view of the novel was advanced thirty
years later in Alexander A. Parker, "The Psychology of the Pícaro in *El Buscón*," *Modern Language Review*, 42 (1947), 58–69. For Parker, *El Buscón* is an
artistically unified work of art with moral purpose and psychologically plausible characterization. According to his interpretation, Pablos was both the
product of his environment and an autonomous moral agent whose tragedy
emerges from the fact that pride impels him to escape a deep sense of shame by
fleeing into an imaginary world. Three years later, this line of interpretation
was revived in Peter Dunn, "El individuo y la sociedad en *La vida del Buscón*,"
Bulletin hispanique, 52 (1950), 375–396, and in T. E. May, "Good and Evil in
the *Buscón*: A Survey," *Modern Language Review*, 45 (1950), 319–335. Dunn

argues that in condemning the morally weak and perverse individuals who comprise society, Quevedo portrays Pablos as a person who freely and knowingly chooses a life of roguery. Declaring that Quevedo associates reality and appropriateness with moral virtue, May views the novel as illustrating the manner in which Pablos' immoral choices lead him into unreality and implicitly contrast with the experiences of Christ. The suggestion that *El Buscón* is "grotesque" in its totality was made in Fritz Schalk, "Über Quevedo und seinem *Buscón*," *Romanische Forschungen*, 74 (1962), 11–30. Schalk also points out that Pablos, who recognizes "unreality" in others, fails to perceive that he is continually dreaming himself out of his own real but limited sphere into an unreal one. By this time, critics whose "conditioned reflexes" caused them to place *El Buscón* into neatly defined categories had already been attacked in Fernando Lázaro Carreter, "Originalidad del *Buscón*," in *Studia philologica: Homenaje ofrecido a Damaso Alonso por sus amigos y discípulos con ocasión de su 60 aniversario* (Madrid: Gredos, 1960–1963), II, 319–338. According to Lázaro Carreter, the young Quevedo had merely adopted the popular picaresque-novel format to display his own wit by contriving clever caricatures and wordplays. In his eyes, the book is essentially a "libro de ingenio" in which isolated jokes are arranged like beads on a string; thus, he concludes that Quevedo's originality lies totally in the ingenuity of his "agudezas" and not in any imagined aesthetic structure, moral ideas, or social criticism. Despite Lázaro Carreter's strictures against the sort of criticism practiced by Parker, Dunn, and May, their major premises were adopted by Cyril B. Morris in his *The Unity and Structure of Quevedo's "Buscón"* (Hull: University of Hull, 1965). For him, artistic unity is assured by the recurrence of motifs which imply that, while Pablos repeatedly attempts to flee from his past, he only succeeds in reenacting it over and over again. In *Literature and the Delinquent: The Picaresque Novel in Spain and Europe 1599–1753* (Edinburgh: University Press, 1967), Parker reiterates his thesis, whereas Lázaro Carreter's objections to it are convincingly presented in "Glosas Críticas a *Los pícaros en la literatura* de Alexander A. Parker," *Hispanic Review*, 41 (1973), 469–497. Essential agreement with Lázaro Carreter's basic position is expressed in Marcel Bataillon, *Novedad y fecundidad del "Lazarillo de Tormes"* (Salamanca: Anaya, 1968), p. 105; Raimundo Lida, "Pablos de Segovia y su agudeza: Notas sobre la lengua del *Buscón*," in *Homenaje a Casalduero: Crítica y poesía* (Madrid: Gredos, 1972), pp. 285–298; Lida, "Sobre el arte verbal del *Buscón*," in *Hispanic Studies in Honor of Edmund de Chasca*, ed. Curt A. Zimansky, *Philological Quarterly*, 51, No. 1 (1972), 255–269; and Francisco Rico, *La novela picaresca y el punto de vista* (Barcelona: Seix Barral, 1970). The controversy over *El Buscón* thus appears to reduce itself to two diametrically opposed views of the work: Parker and his school insist that it is a psychologically plausible and well-structured "libro de desengaño," whereas Lázaro Carreter and his supporters contend that it is an entertaining and witty "libro de ingenio." The book's attraction to seventeenth-century readers must have been largely based upon its jokes, puns, and caricatures; to the extent that Lázaro Carreter recommends a similar reading of the book, his interpretation has a certain historical validity, but the contemporary reception of any work seldom reflects the full range of its possible meanings, and elements of psychological coherence, moral significance and artistic unity are not incompatible with Quevedo's ingenious wordplays and caricatures.

3 Quevedo, Letter to Justus Lipsius, 1604, in *Epistolario completo*, ed. Luis Astrana Marín (Madrid: Reus, 1946), p. 6. The exchange of letters with Lipsius was crucial in the evolution of Quevedo's world view. For a full discussion of Seneca's influence upon Quevedo's stoicism, see Henry Ettinghausen, *Francisco de Quevedo and the Neostoic Movement* (Oxford: University Press, 1972).

4 Quevedo, "Visita de los Chistes," in *Los Sueños*, ed. Julio Cejador y Frauca (1916; rpt. Madrid: Espasa-Calpe, 1967), I, 213.

5 Quevedo, "El mundo por dentro," *Sueños*, II, 20.

6 Quevedo, "Las zahurdas de Plutón," *Sueños*, I, 115.

7 For a listing of parallels between *El Buscón* and the two earliest picaresque novels, see Chapter 4, note 23 above. In addition to the articles cited there, see Victorio G. Agüera, "Dislocación de elementos picarescos en el *Buscón*," in *Estudios literarios de hispanistas norteamericanos dedicados a Helmut Hatzfeld con motivo de su 80 aniversario*, eds. Josep M. Sola-Solé, Alessandro Crisafulli, and Bruno Damiani (Barcelona: Hispam, 1974), pp. 357–367; and Jenaro Taléns, "Para una lectura del *Buscón* de Quevedo," *Cuadernos de filología* (December 1971), pp. 83–97. Among the first to suggest that Quevedo was parodying the earlier picaresque tradition was Segundo Serrano Poncela, "¿El *Buscón*— Parodía picaresca?" *Insula*, 12, No. 154 (1959), 1 and 10.

8 In "Visita de los Chistes," "picarones" are men whose punishment awaits them after death, despite the fact that in this world they are commonly regarded as saints. In the introduction to "La hora de todos y la Fortuna con seso," Quevedo characterizes a "pícaro" as one who fails to understand the warning implicit in the subsequent dream-vision.

9 This parallel is pointed out in Michel and Cecile Cavillac, "A propos du *Buscón*, et de *Guzmán de Alfarache*," *Bulletin hispanique*, 75 (1973), 114–131.

10 This idea is discussed at length in Constance H. Rose, "Pablos' Damnosa Heritas," *Romanische Forschungen*, 82 (1970), 94–101.

11 On this point, see Agüera, "Dislocación," pp. 364–365.

12 For a discussion of the term "other-directed," see David Riesman, *The Lonely Crowd* (1952; rpt. New Haven: Yale University Press, 1964), pp. 3–10, 20–25.

13 Francisco de Quevedo, *La vida del Buscón llamado don Pablos*, ed. Lázaro Carreter (Salamanca: Universidad, 1965). All subsequent references to *El Buscón* will refer to pages in this edition and appear between parentheses in the text. The object of considerable debate, this aphorism is discussed in Edward M. Wilson and José Manuel Blecua, "Los aforismos de las *Lagrimas* y *La vida del Buscón*," in Quevedo, *Lágrimas de Hieremías Castellanas*, eds. Wilson and Blecua, *Revista de filología española*, Anejo 55 (1953), cxxviii-cxxvi; Dale Randall, "The Classical Ending of Quevedo's *Buscón*," *Hispanic Review*, 32 (1964), 101–108; Lida, "Pablos de Segovia," pp. 255–169. During the early seventeenth century, clichés were often used in their radical sense as stylistic devices. Quevedo's own disdain for banalities is well known and clearly emerges in the *Prématica*, where he lists several pages of proverbs which ought to be banished from the lan-

guage, and in "Discurso de todos los diablos," where he parodies a picaresque poet who speaks in clichés. One of the best discussions of Quevedo's use of such stylistic techniques is contained in Ilse Nolting-Hauff, *Vision, Satire und Pointe in Quevedos Sueños* (Munich: W. Fink, 1968).

14 In "Salvación," "Nueva interpretación," and "Notas," Agüera contends that the "king of the cocks" episode constitutes a parody of Guzmán's ostentatious promenades on horseback in Part I, Book II, Chapter 8 of Alemán's novel. He points out that Pablos' fall into the garbage heap during the carnival celebrations and Quevedo's puns on "sucio" have converso connotations, particularly since "sucio" literally means "dirty" but also connotes Pablos' lack of "limpieza de sangre."

15 Parker ("The Psychology of the Pícaro"; *The Delinquent*), May ("Good and Evil") and others have suggested that don Diego is an exemplary standard of noble, Old Christian virtue. In actuality, his name is identified with that of a well-known New Christian family from Segovia. He too is being parodied in *El Buscón*, as has been convincingly established in Carroll B. Johnson, *"El Buscón: D. Pablos, D. Diego y D. Francisco," Hispanófila*, 17 (1974), 1–26.

16 There are numerous puns upon "limpieza," "cristiano nuevo," and other words associated with Pablos' converso heritage. For detailed discussions of them, see Agüera, "Dislocación," esp. pp. 360–367, and Lida, "Pablos de Segovia."

17 Although his Christ parallels seem rather fanciful, Morris (*Unity and Structure*) does deserve credit for drawing attention to the similarity between what he calls these two "Last Supper" scenes.

18 For a discussion of Quevedo's attitudes toward traditional values, see Doris L. Baum, *Traditionalism in the Works of Francisco de Quevedo y Villegas* (Chapel Hill: University of North Carolina Press, 1970), University of North Carolina Studies in the Romance Languages and Literatures, No. 91.

Chapter 6. The Waning of the Spanish Picaresque: "El diablo cojuelo" and "Estebanillo González"

1 In addition to Vélez' identification of Pablos' demented swordsman as Luis Pacheco de Narváez and his borrowing of terms like "linea recta" and "angulo obtuso," he structured at least one episode (a student who awakens all the guests at an inn by shouting "fire") upon an incident in Quevedo's novel (Pablos provokes a similar disturbance while composing a play about a bear).

2 The semiautobiographical nature of *El diablo cojuelo* is suggested by the fact that, like his fictional hero, Vélez was known to have been a poor student with a noble name, a servant to several wealthy masters, a disillusioned lover, and the president of a literary academy. At one point, Cleofás recites a poem which he allegedly composed for one of the king's masked balls; Vélez read the identical poem at a similar event in 1637, according to Francisco Rodríguez Marín, "Prólogo," in Luis Vélez de Guevara, *El diablo cojuelo* (1918; rpt. Madrid: Espasa-Calpe, 1967), p. 187, n. 1.

3 Estebanillo compares his memoirs to *Lazarillo, Guzmán*, and *Justina*, implicitly

placing all four works in the same category. Twice he refers to himself as "Lazarillo de Tormes," and repeatedly as a "pícaro"; he even concludes that the only life is the life of a pícaro.

4 For discussions of *Estebanillo*'s historical accuracy, see Willis Jones, *"Estebanillo González*, a Study with Introduction and Commentary," Diss. Chicago, 1927, and *"Estebanillo González," Revue hispanique*, 79 (1929), 201–245; Arthur Bates, "Historical Characters in *Estebanillo González," Hispanic Review*, 8 (1940), 63–66; and Ernest Moore, "Estebanillo González's Travels in Southern Europe," *Hispanic Review*, 8 (1940), 24–45.

5 Two of the most insightful interpretations of *El diablo cojuelo* are contained in comparative studies of Vélez' novel and Lesage's adaptation of it: Charles Aubrun, *"El diablo cojuelo* et *Le diable boiteux:* Deux définitions du roman," in *Melanges à la mémoire de Jean Sarrailh* (Paris, 1966), I, 57–73; and Uwe Holtz, *Der hinkende Teufel von Guevara und Lesage: Eine literatur- und sozialkritische Studie* (Wuppertal: Henn, 1970).

6 The best recent studies of *Estebanillo* include Idalia Cordero de Bobonis, *"La vida y hechos de Estebanillo González:* Estudio sobre su visión del mundo y actitud ante la vida," *Archivum*, 15 (1965), 168–189; Juan Goytisolo, "Estebanillo González, hombre de buen humor," in *El furgón de cola* (Paris: Ruedo Iberico, 1967), pp. 57–76; and Nicholas Spadaccini, *"Estebanillo González* and the New Orientation of the Picaresque Novel," Diss. NYU, 1971. As in his studies of *Justina*, Marcel Bataillon ("Estebanillo González, buffon 'pour rire'," in *Studies in Spanish Literature of the Golden Age Presented to Edward M. Wilson*, ed. R. O. Jones [London: Tamesis, 1973], pp. 25–44) marshals an impressive collection of historical facts to support his conjecture that *Estebanillo* was an in-palace *tour de force*, possibly modeled on the career of a rather unreliable courier, Esteban Gamarra (registered as "Stefaniglio" in Piccolomini's account books), and written by Piccolomini's confidant, Geronimo de Bran, for an elite circle of readers at the court in Brussels. For a discussion of previous criticism, see Richard Bjornson, *"Estebanillo González:* The Clown's Other Face," *Hispania*, 60 (1977), forthcoming.

7 Luis Vélez de Guevara, *El diablo cojuelo*, ed. Francisco Rodríguez Marín (1918; rpt, Madrid: Espasa-Calpe, 1960), p. 165.

8 *La vida y hechos de Estebanillo González: Hombre de buen humor, compuesta por él mismo*, ed. Juan Millé y Giménez (1927; rpt. Madrid: Espasa-Calpe, 1956), I, 61.

9 *Estebanillo González*, II, 34.

10 *Estebanillo González*, II, 229.

11 *Estebanillo González*, II, 221.

Chapter 7. *Translations and Transitions*

1 The early French editions of *Lazarillo* are discussed in Rolf Greifelt, "Die Übersetzungen des spanischen Schelmenromans in Frankreich im 17. Jahrhundert," *Romanische Forschungen*, 50 (1936), 51–84; and Gabriel Laplane, "Les anciennes

traductions françaises de *Lazarillo de Tormes*," in *Hommage à Ernst Martineche: Études hispaniques et américaines* (Paris: Editions d'Artrey, 1937), pp. 143–155. For a treatment of the English translations, see Dale B. Randall, *The Golden Tapestry: A Critical Survey of Non-Chivalric Spanish Fiction in English Translation (1543–1657)* (Durham, N.C.: Duke University Press, 1963), pp. 57–68. The first German edition of *Lazarillo* is described in E. Herman Hespelt, "The First German Translation of *Lazarillo de Tormes*," *Hispanic Review*, 4 (1936), 170–175. In 1951 Hermann Tiemann edited a facsimile edition of this work, which was subsequently discussed in Hans Schneider, "La primera traducción alemana del *Lazarillo de Tormes*," *Clavileño*, 4 (1953), 46–58. German translations of *Lazarillo* are perceptively treated in Hans Gerd Rötzer, *Picaro-Landstörtzer-Simplicius* (Darmstadt: Wissenschaftliche Buchgesellschaft, 1972), pp. 35–46.

2 *Les faits merveilleux, ensemble la vie du gentil Lazare de Tormes, et les terribles avantures a luy avenues en divers lieux, livre fort plaisant et delectable* (Lyon: Jean Saugrain, 1560), title page.

3 *The Pleasaunt Historie of Lazarillo de Tormes a Spaniard, wherein is contained his marueilous deedes and life* (London: Abell Jeffes, 1586).

4 *La vida de Lazarillo de Tormes y de sus fortunas y aduersidades/ La vie de Lazarille de Tormes, et de ses fortunes et aduersitez. Traduction nouvelle* (Paris: Adrian Tiffaine, 1616), p. 82.

5 Laplane ("Les anciennes traductions," p. 149) points out that the first Spanish editions to follow this practice (1595, 1602) were also published in Antwerp; therefore, he considers it likely that Saugrain was translating from a lost Antwerp edition.

6 For a detailed discussion of this translation, see Rötzer, *Picaro*, pp. 39–46.

7 In Act II, scene 1, Benedict cries out, "Ho! now you strike, like the blind man; 'twas the boy that stole your meat, and you'll beat the post." William Shakespeare, *Much Ado About Nothing*, in *Comedies*, ed. Peter Alexander (London: Collins, 1966), p. 279.

8 Cited in Louis B. Wright, *Middle-Class Culture in Elizabethan England* (Ithaca, N.Y.: Cornell University Press, 1935), p. 407.

9 For discussions of Albertinus, see Karl von Reinhardstöttner, "Aegidius Albertinus, der Vater des deutschen Schelmenromans," *Jahrbuch für Münchner Geschichte* 2 (1888), 13–86; Judith Peters, "The Spanish Picaresque Novel and the Simplician Novels of Hans Christoffel von Grimmelshausen," Diss. Columbia, 1968; Charlton Laird, "Aegidius Albertinus and Antonio de Guevara," Diss. California, 1957; Rötzer, *Picaro*, pp. 94–120.

10 An excellent discussion of Albertinus' use of this symbology appears in Rötzer, *Picaro*, pp. 105–113.

11 The traditional four levels of allegorical significance are described in Dante's famous letter to Can Grande della Scala. For discussions of its importance as a German literary convention, see Rötzer, *Picaro*, pp. 116–120, and Hansjörg Büchler, *Studien zu Grimmelshausens Landstörtzerin Courasche* (Bern: Herbert Lang, 1971).

12 Freudenhold's continuation is discussed in Hubert Rausse, "Zur Geschichte

des spanischen Schelmenromans in Deutschland," *Münstersche Beiträge zur neuren Literaturgeschichte,* 8 (1908), 33–39, and Rötzer, *Picaro,* pp. 120–127.

13 Ernest J. Moncada, "An Analysis of James Mabbe's Translation of Mateo Alemán's *Guzmán de Alfarache,*" Diss. Maryland, 1966, pp. 59–65.

14 Ulrich Stadler, "Parodistisches in der *Justina Dietzin Picara:* Über die Entstehungsbedingungen und zur Wirkungsgeschichte von Úbedas Schelmenroman in Deutschland," *Arcadia,* 7 (1972), 158–170.

15 Eight editions of *The Rogue* and seven of *The Pursuit* appeared during the seventeenth century. Although such a record did not place them high on the list of all books published in this period (Lewis Bayly's devotional book *Practice of Piety* [1613] went through more than fifty editions in the century following its first publication), they were among the more frequently reprinted works of prose fiction.

16 *The Life and Death of Young Lazarillo* is reprinted in *Lazarillos raros,* ed. Richard Zwez (Valencia: Albatross, 1972), pp. 93–116.

17 Andreas Stoll, *Scarron als Übersetzer Quevedos—Studien zur Rezeption des pikaresken Romans "El Buscón" in Frankreich (L'Aventurier Buscon, 1633),* Diss. Frankfurt/M., 1970, pp. 365–447.

18 Dieter Reichardt, *Von Quevedos "Buscón" zum deutschen "Avanturier"* (Bonn: H. Bouvier, 1970), Studien zu Germanistik, Anglistik und Komparatistik, Vol. 7, pp. 47 and 157, n. 3. Reichardt points out that there were nineteen French editions of La Geneste's *Buscon* in the seventeenth century, whereas there were sixteen of *Guzman* and four of *Marcos.*

19 Charles Sorel, *Histoire comique de Francion,* in *Romanciers du XVIIe siècle,* ed. Antoine Adam (Paris: Gallimard, 1968), pp. 180 and 1380.

20 Corneille, *L'Illusion,* in *Théâtre choisi de Corneille,* ed. Maurice Rat (Paris: Garnier, 1961), p. 559.

21 Vital D'Audiguier, "Préface," in *La fouyne de Seville ou l'hameçon des bourses* (Paris: Pierre Billaine, 1661).

22 Charles Sorel, *La bibliothèque françoise* (Paris: Compagnie des Libraires du Palais, 1667), pp. 188–200.

23 Sorel, *Bibliothèque,* p. 238.

24 Jean Chapelain, "Introduction," in Mateo Alemán, *Guzman d'Alfarache* (Paris: Pierre Billaine, 1619–1620), p. iiii.

25 Sorel, *Bibliothèque,* p. 188. Sorel's critical assumptions are discussed in Jean-Pierre Leroy, "Réflexions critiques de Charles Sorel sur son oeuvre romanesque," XVIIe *Siècle,* No. 105 (1974), pp. 29–47.

26 Sorel, *Bibliothèque,* p. 194. Although Sorel's claim that *Francion* had been reprinted sixty times before 1667 seems somewhat exaggerated, it did go through at least twenty-two editions before the end of the century.

27 Letter to Marigny, May 8, 1659, in *Dernières oeuvres de Scarron* (Paris: David, Durand, Pissot, 1752), p. 47. The possible influence of Rojas is suggested in Paul Verdovoye, "La novela picaresca en Francia," *Clavileño,* 6 (1935), 30–37, and further developed in Henri Bénac, "Introduction," in Paul Scarron, *Le romant comique* (Paris: Société des belles-lettres, 1951), pp. 7–88.

273

28 For perceptive discussions of Sorel's social and economic ideas, see Frank E. Sutcliffe, *Le réalisme de Charles Sorel: Problèmes humaines du XVIIᵉ siècle* (Paris: Nizet, 1965), and Jean Serroy, "Francion et l'argent, ou l'immoraliste et les faux monnayeurs," *XVIIᵉ Siècle*, No. 105 (1974), pp. 3–18.

29 A good account of Billaine's publishing activities can be found in Reichardt, *Von Quevedos Buscón,*" pp. 47–50.

30 For a discussion of the names in Sorel's novel, see Michael Griffiths and Wolfgang Leiner, "Some Thoughts on the Names of the Characters in Charles Sorel's *Histoire Comique de Francion,*" *Romance Notes*, 15 (1974), 445–453.

31 Sorel, *Francion*, p. 245.

32 Sorel, *Francion*, p. 244.

33 A somewhat different emphasis is placed upon this conclusion in Jean Serroy, "D'un roman à métamorphoses: La composition du *Francion* de Charles Sorel," *Baroque*, No. 6 (1973), pp. 97–103. For Serroy, Francion's primary motivating impulse is a desire for freedom; by submitting himself to the discipline of marriage to Nays, he supposedly achieves his greatest liberty, because her beauty symbolizes all female beauty, and in enjoying her he is enjoying all women.

34 Cecille Cavillac, "'El pícaro amante' de José Camerino et *L'Aventurier Buscon* de La Geneste: Étude d'un cas de médiation littéraire," *Revue de littérature comparée*, 47 (1973), 399–411.

35 Earlier accounts of Enríquez Gómez' life contained glaring inaccuracies, but these have been corrected in I. S. Révah, "Un pamphlet contre l'Inquisition d'Antonio Enríquez Gómez: La seconde partie de la *Politica angélica,*" *Revue des études juives*, No. 121 (1961), pp. 81–168. Additional details have been supplied by Constance H. Rose, "Antonio Enríquez Gómez and the Literature of Exile," *Romanische Forschungen*, 85 (1973), 63–77.

36 Antonio Enríquez Gómez, *El siglo pitagórico, y la vida de don Gregorio Guadaña* (Madrid: Antonio Espinosa, 1788), p. 212.

37 Enríquez Gómez, *Siglo pitagórico*, p. 186.

38 The best and most recent study of these novellas is Frederick A. de Armas, *The Four Interpolated Stories in the "Roman Comique": Their Sources and Unifying Function* (Chapel Hill: University of North Carolina Press, 1971), University of North Carolina Studies in the Romance Languages and Literatures, No. 100. In "The Narrative Stance in Scarron's *Roman comique,*" *French Review* 47, Special Issue 6 (1974), 18–30, Peter Conroy contends that the narrator of Scarron's novel is actually its central character and that his presence unifies the narrative and the intercalated stories.

39 Sorel, *Francion*, p. 252.

40 *Life and Death of Young Lazarillo*, in *Lazarillos raros*, p. 99.

41 The early German editions of *Francion* are discussed in Manfred Koschlig, "Das Lob des *Francion* bei Grimmelshausen," *Jahrbuch der deutschen Schillergesellschaft*, 1 (1957), 30–73. For the impact of the *Buscon* translation in Germany, see Reichardt, *Von Quevedos "Buscón,"* pp. 75–133.

42 Randall, *Golden Tapestry*, pp. 183–184, 191–192.

Chapter 8. *The Universality of the Picaresque: Visions of Truth in Grimmelshausen's "Simplicissimus"*

1 General surveys of Grimmelshausen's indebtedness to previous writers can be found in Arthur Bechtold, "Zur Quellengeschichte des *Simplicissimus*," *Euphorion*, 19 (1912), 19–66, 491–546; Günther Weydt, *Nachahmung und Schöpfung im Barock: Studien um Grimmelshausen* (Bern: Francke, 1968), pp. 47–240, 393–419. Grimmelshausen's borrowings from Garzoni's encyclopedic *Allgemeiner Shauplatz* are enumerated in Jan H. Scholte, *Zonagri Discus von Waarsagern* (Amsterdam: J. Müller, 1921). The question of Sorel's influence is treated in Manfred Koschlig, "Das Lob des *Francion* bei Grimmelshausen," *Jahrbuch der deutschen Schillergesellschaft*, 1 (1957), 30–73, while Grimmelshausen's familiarity with Spanish picaresque novels is discussed in Weydt, *Nachahmung und Schöpfung*, pp. 393, 418–419; Weydt, *Hans Jakob Christoffel von Grimmelshausen* (Stuttgart: Metzler, 1971), pp. 51–57; and Hans Gerd Rötzer, *Picaro-Landstörtzer-Simplicius* (Darmstadt: Wissenschaftliche Buchgesellschaft, 1972), pp. 128–137. One aspect of Luna's possible influence upon Grimmelshausen is identified in María Navarro de Adicenses, "La continuación del *Lazarillo* de Luna y la aventura del Lago Mummel en el *Simplicissimus*," *Romanistisches Jahrbuch*, 12 (1961), 242–247.

2 Picaresque wanderings that culminate in a hermit existence are discussed by Rainer Schönhaar, "Pikaro und Eremit: Ursprung und Abwandlungen einer Grundfigur des europäischen Romans vom 17. ins 18. Jahrhundert," in *Dialog: Literatur und Literaturwissenschaft im Zeichen deutsch-französischer Begegnung*, ed. Rainer Schönhaar (Berlin: Erich Schmidt, 1973), pp. 43–94.

3 A somewhat exaggerated case for Grimmelshausen's use of numerology is contained in Siegfried Streller, *Grimmelshausens Simplicianische Schriften: Allegorie, Zahl und Wirklichkeitsdarstellung* (Berlin: Rütten & Loening, 1957). Credit for discovering and elaborating upon the astrological symbolism in *Simplicissimus* undoubtedly belongs to Günther Weydt for works which include his "Planetensymbolik im barocken Roman," *Doitsu Bungaku*, 36 (1966), 1–14; *Nachahmung und Schöpfung*, pp. 243–301; *Grimmelshausen*, pp. 60–71; and "Grimmelshausen in der Tradition: Zu Ausmass und möglicher Relevanz der Planetensymbole," in *Traditions and Transitions: Studies in Honor of Harold Jantz*, eds. Lieselotte Kurth, William McClain, and Holger Homan (Munich: Delp, 1972), pp. 70–77. Balanced interpretative essays on the subject can also be found in Helmut Rehder, "Planetenkinder: Some Problems of Character Portrayal in Literature," *The Graduate Journal* (University of Texas), 8 (1968), 69–97; and Kenneth Negus, *Grimmelshausen* (New York: Twayne, 1974), pp. 73–82. An excellent detailed study of astrological levels of meaning in the book is contained in Klaus Haberkam, *"Sensus Astrologicus": Zum Verhältnis von Literatur und Astrologie in Renaissance und Barock* (Bonn: Bouvier, 1972). Among the first to indicate that *Simplicissimus* could be interpreted according to the principles of Biblical exegesis was Clemens Heselhaus, "Grimmelshausen. *Der abentheurliche Simplicissimus*," in *Der deutsche Roman vom Barock bis zur Gegenwart: Struktur und*

Geschichte, ed. Benno von Wiese (Düsseldorf: A. Bagel, 1963), I, 15–63. This system is applied to *Courasche* in Hansjörg Büchler, *Studien zur Grimmelshausens Landstörtzerin Courasche* (Bern: Herbert Lang, 1971), and Mathias Feldges, *Grimmelshausens "Landstörtzerin Courasche": Eine Interpretation nach der Methode des vierfachen Schriftsinnes* (Bern: Francke, 1969), Basler Studien zur deutschen Sprache und Literatur, Heft 38. For a discussion of Grimmelshausen's emblematic technique, see Dietrich Jöns, "Emblematisches bei Grimmelshausen," *Euphorion*, 62 (1968), 385–391. The unity of a technique based upon the narrator's capacity to imply the universal significance behind particular events and to fuse the entertaining with the instructive is discussed in Jürgen H. Petersen, "Formen der Ich-Erzählung in Grimmelshausens Simplicianische Schriften," *Zeitschrift für deutsche Philologie*, 93 (1974), 481–507, and Uwe Böker, "Erzählerischer Realismus und Barockstil in Grimmelshausens *Simplicissimus Teutsch*," *Neuphilologische Mitteilungen*, 75 (1974), 332–348.

4 Weydt, *Grimmelshausen*, p. 18.

5 In regard to the *Continuatio*, this thesis has been provocatively advanced in Hubert Gersch, "Ein Sonderfall im Zeitalter der Vorreden-Poetik des Romans; Grimmelshausens vorwortloser *Simplicissimus*," in *Rezeption und Produktion zwischen 1570 und 1730: Festschrift für Günther Weydt zum 65. Geburtstag*, eds. Klaus Haberkam, Hans Guelen, and Wolfdietrich Rasch (Bern: Francke, 1972), pp. 267–284, and *Geheimpoetik: Die "Continuatio des abentheurlichen Simplicissimi" interpretiert als Grimmelshausens verschlüsselter Kommentar zu seinem Roman* (Tübingen: M. Niemeyer, 1973).

6 Hans Jakob Christoffel von Grimmelshausen, *Der Abentheurliche Simplicissimus Teutsch und Continuatio des abentheurlichen Simplicissimi*, ed. Rolf Tarot (Tübingen: Max Niemeyer, 1967). All subsequent references to *Simplicissimus* will appear between parentheses in the text and refer to pages in this edition.

7 Gersch, "Sonderfall," pp. 16–31.

8 Walter E. Schäfer, "Der Satyr und die Satire: Zu Titelkupfern Grimmelshausens und Moscheroschs," in *Rezeption und Produktion*, p. 184.

9 For discussions of the emblem-book tradition, see Albrecht Schöne, *Emblematik und Drama im Zeitalter des Barock* (Munich: C. H. Beck, 1964), and Dietrich Jöns, *Das "Sinnen-Bild": Studien zur allegorischen Bildlichkeit bei Andreas Gryphius* (Stuttgart: Metzler, 1966), pp. 3–58. The best modern collection of emblems is contained in Arthur Henkel and Albrecht Schöne, *Emblemata: Handbuch zur Sinnbildkunst des XVI. und XVII. Jahrhunderts* (Stuttgart: Metzler, 1967). Grimmelshausen's indebtedness to the emblem tradition is specifically discussed in Jöns, "Emblematisches bei Grimmelshausen," although this indebtedness is disputed in Karl-Heinz Habersetzer, "'Ars Poetica Simpliciana': Zum Titelkupfer des *Simplicissimus Teutsch*," *Daphnis*, 3 (1974), 60–82. Habersetzer contends that the primary inspiration for the satyr frontispiece and its implicit aesthetic philosophy can be traced to Horace's *Ars poetica*.

10 A satyr figures prominently in the frontispiece of Moscherosch's *Gesichte Philanders von Sittewald* (1643) as well as in three of Grimmelshausen's own works: see Schäfer, "Der Satyr und die Satire," pp. 197–202, 207–208, 219.

11 The "mundus inversus" (upside-down world) *topos* involves a reversal of the

accepted order of things. It is a common satiric technique and can be traced back to Greek comedy; see Ernst Robert Curtius, *Europäische Literatur und lateinisches Mittelalter* (1948; rpt. Bern: Francke, 1954), pp. 104–108; Ian Donaldson, *The World Upside-Down* (Oxford: Clarendon, 1970), esp. pp. 21–23; and Klaus Lazarowicz, *Verkehrte Welt: Vorgeschichte zu einer Geschichte der deutschen Satire* (Tübingen: Max Niemeyer, 1963), pp. 290–292 and nn. 113 and 114. The term "verkehrte Welt" was popularized in Germany by Moscherosch's *Gesichte*, a free adaptation of Quevedo's *Sueños*. Grimmelshausen employed it frequently in his almanacs and even adopted it as the title of a "simplician" pamphlet; see Bechtold, "Zur Quellengeschichte," pp. 23–30; and Weydt, *Grimmelshausen*, pp. 54, 82. In the present context, "reversed world" is generally used to indicate the social world in which people attach supreme importance to material goals and possessions while overlooking spiritual concerns. For examples of this theme in popular literature, see William A. Coupe, *The German Illustrated Broadsheet in the Seventeenth Century* (Baden-Baden: Heitz, 1966), I, 197–204, and II, plates 126–130.

12 J. M. Ritchie, "Grimmelshausen's *Simplicissimus* and *The Runagate Courage*," in *Knaves and Swindlers: Essays on the Picaresque Novel in Europe*, ed. Christine J. Whitbourne (London: Oxford University Press, 1974), University of Hull Publications, p. 65; and Heselhaus, "Grimmelshausen," pp. 15–16.

13 This point is discussed in Ulrich Stadler, "Das Diesseits als Hölle: Sünde und Strafe in Grimmelshausens 'Simplicianischen Schriften,'" in *Europäische Tradition und deutscher Literaturbarock*, ed. Gerhart Hoffmeister (Bern: Francke, 1973), pp. 351–369.

14 Attention is drawn to this emblem by Jeffrey Ashcroft, "Ad astra volandum: Emblems and Imagery in Grimmelshausen's *Simplicissimus*," *Modern Language Review*, 68 (1973), 843–862.

15 The order is that adopted by Rehder and Negus; Weydt places the sun before Jupiter, and Haberkam seems to agree with him, although he points out basic elements of agreement in Weydt's and Rehder's interpretations of the Jupiter phase.

16 Individual episodes in *Simplicissimus* are convincingly analyzed in terms of astrological conjunctions by Haberkam in *"Sensus astrologicus,"* pp. 12–61, 204–257.

17 Haberkam, *"Sensus astrologicus,"* pp. 294–307.

18 Since the 1920's there has been considerable debate over whether or not *Simplicissimus* is a "Bildungsroman." The integrity and coherence of the central character's personality is denied in Paul Gutzwiller, *Der Narr bei Grimmelshausen* (Bern: Francke, 1959), Basler Studien zur deutschen Sprache und Literatur, No. 20; and Günther Rohrbach, *Figur und Charakter: Strukturuntersuchungen an Grimmelshausens "Simplicissimus"* (Bonn: Bouvier, 1959), but it is reaffirmed in Lothar Schmidt, "Das Ich im *Simplicissimus*," *Wirkendes Wort*, 10 (1960), 215–220; and Werner Hoffmann, "Grimmelshausens *Simplicissimus*—Nicht doch ein Bildungsroman?" *Germanisch-Romanische Monatsschrift*, 17 (1967), 166–180. The problem is essentially one of definition; if a "Bildungsroman" necessarily involves a psychologically plausible portrayal of character development resulting

from an uninterrupted series of interactions between the self and its environment, *Simplicissimus* is obviously not a "Bildungsroman," but if "Bildung" implies "education" in the broadest sense of the word, *Simplicissimus* might be
considered a novel in which the hero achieves a heightened level of consciousness.

19 For a perceptive discussion of the paradise allusions in the novel, see Walter
Müller-Seidel, "Die Allegorie des Paradieses in Grimmelshausens *Simplicissimus*," in *Medium aevum vivum: Festschrift für Walter Bulst*, eds. Hans R. Jauss
and Dieter Schaller (Heidelberg: C. Winter, 1960), pp. 253–278.

20 This contrast is suggested in Urs Herzog, "Trost der Nacht: Zum Nachtigal-
lenlied in Grimmelshausens *Simplicissimus*," *Wirkendes Wort*, 23 (1973), 101–
110.

21 The "social tree" motif is discussed in Paul Böckmann, *Formgeschichte der
deutschen Dichtung* (Hamburg: Hoffmann und Campe, 1967), pp. 459–460. He
points out that the "social tree" image was generally employed to depict a
healthy social order and that Grimmelshausen reversed its traditional connotations. Several popular contemporary depictions of the "social tree" image are
discussed and reprinted in Coupe, *The German Illustrated Broadsheet*, I, 175–179,
and II, plates 101–105.

22 A similar pattern, moving from "simplicitas" to "stultitia" and back to
"simplicitas," is discussed in Gutzwiller, *Der Narr*, pp. 18–19.

23 A detailed discussion of their astrological significance is contained in Haberkam, "*Sensus Astrologicus*," pp. 238–257.

24 Grimmelshausen's use of "Elementargeister" and Paracelsian imagery is dis-
cussed in Harry Mielert, "Der paracelsische Anteil an der Mummelsee-
Allegorie in Grimmelshausens *Simplicissimus*," *Deutsche Vierteljahrsschrift für
Literaturwissenschaft und Geistesgeschichte*, 20 (1942), 435–451. See also Werner
Burkhard, *Grimmelshausen: Erlösung und barocker Geist* (Frankfurt/M: Dies-
terweg, 1929), p. 53.

*Chapter 9. The Ambiguous Success of the Picaresque Hero
in Defoe's "Moll Flanders"*

1 Since Dorothy van Ghent's essay "On *Moll Flanders*" in *The English Novel: Form
and Function* (New York: Holt, Rinehart and Winston, 1953), pp. 33–43, there
has been considerable controversy over the irony in Defoe's novel. The problem has been discussed perceptively by Maximilian Novak on numerous occasions in "Conscious Irony in *Moll Flanders*: Facts and Problems," *College English*, 26 (1964), 198–204; "Defoe's Theory of Fiction," *Studies in Philology*, 61
(1964), 650–668; "Defoe's 'Indifferent Monitor': The Complexity of *Moll Flanders*," *Eighteenth Century Studies*, 3 (1970), 351–365; and "Defoe's Use of Irony,"
in *Stuart and Georgian Moments: Clark Library Seminar Papers on Seventeenth and
Eighteenth Century English Literature*, ed. Earl Miner (Berkeley: University of
California, 1972), pp. 189–220. Other critics who have taken a position in the

debate include M. A. Goldberg, "Moll Flanders: Christian Allegory in a Hobbesian Mode," *University Review*, 33 (1966), 267–278; Howard Koonce, "Moll's Muddle: Defoe's Use of Irony in *Moll Flanders," Journal of English Literary History*, 38 (1971), 397–410; Wayne C. Booth, *The Rhetoric of Fiction* (Chicago: University of Chicago Press, 1961), pp. 321–323; J. D. Needham, "Moll's 'Honest Gentleman,'" *Southern Review* (Adelaide), 3 (1969), 366–374. James Sutherland also contributes to the discussion in *Daniel Defoe: A Critical Study* (Cambridge: Harvard University Press, 1971) and "The Relation of Defoe's Fiction to His Non-Fictional Writings," in *Imagined Worlds: Essays on Some English Novels and Novelists in Honour of John Butt*, eds. Maynard Mack and Ian Gregor (London: Methuen, 1968), pp. 37–50. Both Everett Zimmerman (*Defoe and the Novel*, Berkeley: University of California Press, 1975) and Paula Backscheider ("Defoe's Women: Snares and Prey," in *Studies in Eighteenth-Century Culture*, ed. Ronald C. Rosbottom [Madison: University of Wisconsin Press, 1976], V, 103–120) point out that Moll's behavior and attitudes resemble those condemned by Defoe in his popular conduct books. Although this would seem to indicate that the author is also condemning his heroine, it hardly explains the actual similarities between Moll's pragmatic, materialistic world view and that of Defoe.

2 Daniel Defoe, *The Letters of Daniel Defoe*, ed. George Healey (Oxford: Clarendon Press, 1955), pp. 43, 159.

3 Daniel Defoe, *Moll Flanders*, ed. James Sutherland (Boston: Houghton Mifflin, 1959). All subsequent references to *Moll Flanders* will appear between parentheses in the text and refer to pages in this edition.

4 For a discussion of individuation in Defoe's characterization of Moll, see Leo Braudy, "Daniel Defoe and the Anxieties of Autobiography," *Genre*, 6 (1973), 76–97. Moll's presence at the center of a real-seeming confession is treated as the novel's major organizing principle in Ralph Rader, "Defoe, Richardson, Joyce and the Concept of Form in the Novel," in *Autobiography, Biography and the Novel*, eds. William Matthews and Ralph Rader (Los Angeles: University of California, 1973), Papers Read at a Clark Library Seminar, pp. 39–44. Zimmerman (*Defoe and the Novel*) also develops this idea, while John J. Richetti (*Defoe's Narratives: Situations and Structures*, London: Oxford University Press, 1975) succeeds in placing the discussion of Moll's individuality in a somewhat different framework by focusing upon an existential dialectic between the self (which aspires to autonomy and serves as a touchstone of real-seemingness) and the other (which negates the self or rather combines with it to form a new self). According to Richetti's provocative interpretation, Moll's autobiography demonstrates that the self can survive in this process. Having "become herself" by confronting the negating pressures of the other, she is actually reasserting her original desire for independence, although the very nature of her freedom reflects the severely limited possibilities for self-expression in early capitalistic society.

5 One possible solution to this dilemma is suggested in John Preston, *The Created Self: The Reader's Role in Eighteenth-Century Fiction* (London: Heinemann, 1970),

pp. 1–37. Discussing the ironic experience of "created readers," Preston contends that because their sympathies are engaged in Moll's favor, they can be shocked into an awareness of what they would be condoning if they accepted the bond of implied complicity she offers them.

6 Daniel Defoe, *Serious Reflections of Robinson Crusoe*, in *Romances and Narratives*, ed. George A. Aitken (London: J. M. Dent, 1899), III, 35–36.

7 Daniel Defoe, *Roxana*, in *Novels and Miscellaneous Works* (London: G. Bell, 1899), IV, 22 and 95.

8 The standard treatment of Defoe's economic theory is Maximilian B. Novak, *Economics and the Fiction of Daniel Defoe* (Berkeley: University of California, 1962), University of California Publications, English Series, No. 24. See also his *Defoe and the Nature of Man* (London: Oxford University Press, 1963); Ian Watt, *Rise of the Novel* (1957; rpt. London: Penguin, 1963) pp. 62–139; and Hans H. Andersen, "The Paradox of Trade and Morality in Defoe," *Modern Philology*, 39 (1941), 23–46. Some of the romance elements in Defoe's novels are discussed in James Walton, "The Romance of Gentility: Defoe's Heroes and Heroines," in *Literary Monographs*, ed. Eric Rothstein (Madison: University of Wisconsin Press, 1971), IV, 89–136.

9 For a discussion of spiritual autobiography in England and its possible influence on Defoe, see George Starr, *Defoe and Spiritual Autobiography* (Princeton: Princeton University Press, 1965). A consideration of Defoe's work within the context of "Providence" literature is provided by J. Paul Hunter, *The Reluctant Pilgrim: Defoe's Emblematic Method and Quest for Form in "Robinson Crusoe"* (Baltimore: Johns Hopkins Press, 1966). Echoes of contemporary religious works are unquestionably present in Defoe's novels, but they function primarily as aesthetic devices to heighten verisimiltude and cohesiveness, a fact perceptively pointed out in Rader, "Defoe, Richardson, Joyce," p. 69, n. 11.

10 For a discussion of Defoe's possible indebtedness to a tradition of casuistical reasoning, see George Starr, *Defoe and Casuistry* (Princeton: Princeton University Press, 1971). For Moll's ambiguous attitude toward her children, see Michael Shinagel, "The Maternal Theme in *Moll Flanders:* Craft and Character," *The Cornell Library Journal*, No. 7 (1969), pp. 3–23.

11 That Defoe's "circumstantial factualism" was based upon rational-seeming logic in an emotional context is suggested in Benjamin Boyce, "The Question of Emotion in Defoe," *Studies in Philology*, 50 (1953), 45–58, but until recently many critics have failed to perceive that the "realism" of *Moll Flanders* exists as a function of the relationship not between words and things, but between words and the narrator's evaluative perception of things. For different perspectives upon this situation, see George Starr, "Defoe's Prose Style: 1. The Language of Interpretation," *Modern Philology*, 71 (1974), 277–294; and Jean Weisgerber, "Aspects de l'espace romanesque: *Moll Flanders*," *Revue des langues vivantes*, 15 (1974), 503–510.

12 In theory English Puritans found asceticism congenial to their religious views, and that was one of the reasons for the popularity of Mabbe's translation of Alemán's *Guzmán;* however, in practice dissenting tradesmen tended to model their life-style upon that of the English gentry. Whenever Defoe had the

opportunity to satisfy his own aspirations in this direction, he did not hesitate to do so, and his portrayal of Moll's "natural" impulse toward gentility quite possibly represents a projection and generalization of his own fears and desires. For a discussion of Defoe's attitudes in this matter, see Michael Shinagel, *Daniel Defoe and Middle-Class Gentility* (Cambridge: Harvard University Press, 1968).

13 Daniel Defoe, *Life, Adventures and Piracies of Captain Singleton*, in *Novels and Miscellaneous Works of Daniel Defoe* (London: G. Bell, 1901), I, 182.

14 An attempt to define the semantic content of the word "prudent" within Defoe's idiolect is contained in Dirk Barth, *Prudence im Werk Daniel Defoes* (Bern: Herbert Lang, 1973). Barth concludes that prudence for Defoe is a mode of action based upon knowledge of facts, rational consideration of alternatives, control of passions, and cautiousness in acting so that goals are attained without sacrificing one's honesty or bringing about evil consequences. For a discussion of the woman's role in such a society, see Backscheider, "Defoe's Women."

15 Defoe, *Serious Reflections*, p. 2.

16 Defoe, *Serious Reflections*, p. 8.

17 Starr (*Defoe and Spiritual Autobiography*) defines this pattern in terms of the three basic stages: (1) preparation for conversion, (2) conversion, and (3) the consequences of conversion. In *The Reluctant Pilgrim*, Hunter identifies it with what he calls the characteristic stages of "Providence" literature: (1) rebellion, (2) disobedience, (3) punishment, (4) repentance, (5) conversion and (6) deliverance. Zimmerman (*Defoe and the Novel*) contends that Moll generates a new identity at this point by adopting the structure characteristic of the repentant criminal's life.

18 John R. Moore, *Daniel Defoe: Citizen of the Modern World* (Chicago: University of Chicago Press, 1958), pp. 150–162.

19 Watt, *Rise of the Novel*, pp. 36–61.

Chapter 10. The Picaresque Hero Arrives: Sentiment and Success in Lesage's "Gil Blas"

1 The enormous and enduring popularity of *Gil Blas* is demonstrated by the fact that it has appeared in over 200 French editions and in nearly as many translations. See Roger Laufer, *Lesage ou le métier de romancier* (Paris: Gallimard, 1969), pp. 18 and 28; Charles Dédéyan, *Lesage et Gil Blas* (Paris: Société d'Enseignement Supérieur, 1965), I, 27–28.

2 Laufer, *Lesage*, pp. 14–22.

3 Gabriel Laplane, "Les anciennes traductions françaises de *Lazarillo de Tormes*," in *Hommage à Ernst Martinèche: Études hispaniques et américaines* (Paris: Editions d'Artrey, 1937), pp. 153–154; Rolf Greifelt, "Die Übersetzungen des spanischen Schelmenromans in Frankreich im 17. Jahrhundert," *Romanische Forschungen*, 50 (1936), 57, 62–64.

4 *Le diable boiteux* had nine editions within its first seven months of publication and forty-two more by the end of the century. Between 1732 and 1883, Le-

sage's *Guzman* went through thirty editions. See Laufer, *Lesage*, pp. 28, 196; and Edmond Cros, *Protée et le Gueux: Recherches sur les origines et la nature du récit picaresque dans "Guzmán de Alfarache"* (Paris: Didier, 1967), p. 47.

5 Marie-Louise Dufrenoy, *L'Orient romanesque en France (1704–1789): Étude d'histoire et de critique littéraires* (Montreal: Beauchemin, 1946), I, 25. See also Laufer, *Lesage*, pp. 199–282.

6 Alain-René Lesage, "Préface du traducteur," *Roland l'amoureux*, in *Oeuvres de A.-René Lesage* (Paris: E. Ledoux, 1828), VIII, 3.

7 For examples of Lesage's use of documentation, see Jean Sarrailh, "A propos de A. R. Lesage américaniste," in *Cahiers de L'Institut de l'Amérique Latine*, 5 (1965), 36–54, 61–65; and Dédéyan, *Lesage et Gil Blas*, I, 95–99.

8 Alain-René Lesage, *Le diable boiteux*, ed. Roger Laufer (Paris: Mouton, 1970), p. 92.

9 Lesage, *Histoire de Gil Blas de Santillane*, ed. Maurice Bardon (Paris: Garnier, 1962), 2 vols. All subsequent references to *Gil Blas* appear between parentheses in the text and refer to volume and page numbers in this edition.

10 For a discussion of Gil Blas's need to have a master, see R. Joly, "La fiction autobiographique," in *The Triumph of Culture: 18th Century Perspectives*, ed. Paul Fritz and David Williams (Toronto: A. M. Hakkert, 1972), pp. 169–189.

11 The parallel servant-master relationships above and below Gil Blas in the social hierarchy are treated in Laufer, *Lesage*, pp. 11–12 and *passim*.

12 Alain-René Lesage, "Avant-propos," *Estévanille Gonzalez*, in *Oeuvres de A.-René Lesage*, VII, 2.

13 In "La composition et les sources du *Diable boiteux* de Lesage," *Revue d'histoire littéraire de la France*, 27 (1920), 483–488, Jean Vic shows how characters in *Le diable boiteux* were interpreted as caricatures of actual persons, and he conjectures that contemporary readers regarded *Gil Blas* as a similar sort of work. Detailed discussions of these identifications are furnished in Anthony F. Taras, "The Portrayal of French Manners in *Le diable boiteux* and *Gil Blas* of Alain-René Lesage," Diss. Fordham, 1961; and in Katherine W. Carson, *Aspects of Contemporary Society in Gil Blas* (Banbury: The Voltaire Foundation, 1973), Studies on Voltaire and the Eighteenth Century, Vol. 10. See also Dédéyan, *Lesage et Gil Blas*, I, 129–146, 168–169.

Chapter 11. The Picaresque Hero as Young Nobleman: Victimization and Vindication in Smollett's "Roderick Random"

1 Paul Gabriel Boucé, *Les romans de Smollett: Étude critique* (Paris: Didier, 1971), pp. 124–126.

2 A more or less complete bibliography of Smollett criticism is contained in Francisco Cordasco, *Smollett Criticism, 1770–1924, a Bibliography, Enumerative and Annotative* (Brooklyn: Long Island University Press, 1948); Cordasco, *Smollett Criticism, 1925–1945: A Compilation* (Brooklyn: Long Island University Press, 1949); and Donald M. Korte, *An Annotated Bibliography of Smollett Scholarship 1946–1968* (Toronto: University of Toronto Press, 1969). These

bibliographical listings are supplemented by Paul Gabriel Boucé, "Smollett Criticism, 1770–1924: Corrections and Additions," *Notes and Queries*, 14 (1967), 184–187; and Boucé, *Les romans*, pp. 454–456. Attention should also be drawn to an important collection of essays which appeared subsequent to the publication of Boucé's masterful study: *Tobias Smollett: Bicentennial Essays Presented to Lewis M. Knapp*, eds. George S. Rousseau and Boucé (New York: Oxford University Press, 1971). The plot, characterization, autobiographical details, picaresque elements, and satiric qualities of *Roderick Random* were summarily introduced in Robert D. Spector, *Tobias George Smollett* (New York: Twayne, 1968), pp. 39–60. Its form is viewed as a function of Smollett's moral intention and of his thematic concern with a young man's difficult maturation in Robert Giddings, *The Tradition of Smollett* (London: Methuen, 1967), pp. 92–97. The idea that it reflects Smollett's attempt to reconcile reason and emotion is proposed in Milton Goldberg, *Smollett and the Scottish School: Studies in Eighteenth-Century English Thought* (Albuquerque: University of New Mexico Press, 1959), pp. 22–49. Roderick is interpreted as an outsider buffeted by fortune and finally thrust into a sentimentalized world in Robert Alter, *Rogue's Progress: Studies in the Picaresque Novel* (Cambridge: Harvard University Press, 1964), pp. 58–79. One of the most perceptive discussions of the novel is contained in Boucé, *Les romans*, pp. 158–177. Boucé contends that Roderick's life is divided into three segments: the failure of a solitary combatant; the doubtful, confused struggle of a young man who learns the lessons of adversity; and the final happiness of a man who recognizes the world's perversity and withdraws from it. Boucé also contends that the novel follows a pattern of rising and falling fortune. A possible tension between the satiric and sentimental dimensions of *Roderick Random* is discussed in Ronald Paulson, "Satire in the Early Novels of Smollett," *Journal of English and Germanic Philology*, 59 (1960), 381–402; rpt. in *Satire and the Novel in Eighteenth-Century England* (New Haven: Yale University Press, 1967), pp. 165–218. A similar tension is identified and ascribed to contradictory impulses toward game-playing and moral constraint in Philip Stevick, "Smollett's Picaresque Games," in *Tobias Smollett: Bicentennial Essays*, pp. 9–23.

3 The influence of Lesage and Cervantes upon Smollett is discussed in Boucé, *Les romans*, pp. 125–154.

4 Tobias Smollett, *The Adventures of Roderick Random* (New York: Signet, 1964). All subsequent references to *Roderick Random* will appear between parentheses in the text and refer to pages in this edition.

5 The epigraph is a modified version of Juvenal's *Satura* 10. 51–52, and can be found in Tobias Smollett, *The Adventures of Ferdinand, Count Fathom*, in *The Works of Tobias Smollett, M.D.*, ed. James P. Brown (London: Bickets and Son, 1872), V, facing p. xx.

6 Not all caricature in the novel implies moral disapproval: Strap and Bowling are sometimes subjected to good-natured, humorous distortion; nevertheless, it is frequently employed to expose vice or folly. For discussions of the manner in which Smollett adopted techniques employed by caricaturists and comic dramatists, see Lee M. Ellison, "Elizabethan Drama and the Works of Smol-

lett," *PMLA*, 44 (1929), 842–862; George M. Kahrl, "The Influence of Shakespeare on Smollett," in *Essays in Dramatic Literature: The Parrott Presentation Volume*, ed. Hardin Craig (Princeton: Princeton University Press, 1935), pp. 399–420; and "Smollett as Caricaturist," in *Tobias Smollett: Bicentennial Essays*, pp. 169–200; Alan S. McKillop, *The Early Masters of English Fiction* (1956; rpt. Lawrence: University Press of Kansas, 1968), pp. 152–162; Thomas R. Preston, "The 'Stage Passions' and Smollett's Characterization," *Studies in Philology*, 71 (1974), 105–125; and Robert Moore, *Hogarth's Literary Relationships* (Minneapolis: University of Minnesota Press, 1948), pp. 162–195.

7 Letter to Alexander Carlyle (1747) in *The Letters of Tobias Smollett*, ed. Lewis M. Knapp (Oxford: Clarendon Press, 1970), p. 6.

8 The best treatment of Smollett's "cliché-ridden diction" and "ready-made formulas" remains Albrecht Strauss, "On Smollett's Language: A Paragraph in *Ferdinand, Count Fathom*," in *Style in Prose Fiction: English Institute Essays*, ed. Harold C. Martin (New York: Columbia University, 1959), pp. 25–54. The sentimental stereotypes in Smollett's portrayals of female characters are discussed in Edward Mack, "Pamela's Stepdaughters: The Heroines of Smollett and Fielding," *College English*, 8 (1947), 293–301. The possibility that Smollett modeled his marriage scenes upon a commonplace epithalamic *topos* is suggested in Herbert Foltinek, "Epithalamiums-Stellen in den Romanen Tobias Smolletts," in *Festschrift Prof. Dr. Herbert Koziol zum siebzigsten Geburtstag*, eds. Gero Bauer, Franz Stanzel, and Franz Zaic (Vienna: Wilhelm Braumüller, 1973), Wiener Beiträge zur englischen Philologie, 75 (1973), 63–73.

9 In *Smollett and the Scottish School*, Goldberg suggests that the conclusion of *Roderick Random* reflects Smollett's attempt to achieve a commonsense reconciliation between reason and emotion. Although exaggerated in some respects, this thesis seems relevant insofar as knowing and feeling represent equally important poles of the moral vision which permits Roderick to enjoy his peaceful country retirement at the end of the novel.

10 The motto is taken from Horace *Sermon* 2. 5.8. Attention is drawn to it in Lewis M. Knapp, *Tobias Smollett: Doctor and Man of Letters* (New York: Russell and Russell, 1963), p. 94, but his translation—"If it is of low birth and little virtue, it is of little value"—is somewhat misleading.

INDEX

*Abentheuerliche Simplicissimus Teutsch,
Der.* See *Simplicissimus Teutsch*
Acquisitiveness as theme. *See* Money
Adam, 100
Adaptability of picaresque hero. *See*
Role-playing
*Adventures of Ferdinand, Count Fathom,
The,* 228–29, 232, 235
Adventures of Peregrine Pickle, The, 243
Adventures of Roderick Random, The. See
Roderick Random
Adventure-story format: French comic
novel, 148–49, 152–53, 156, 157–58,
160, 161; novels by Lesage, 207,
208–9, 210, 212–13, 214, 226–27,
230, 244; novels by Salas and Cas-
tillo, 70–71, 93–96, 104; *Roderick
Random,* 228, 230, 235–36, 238–39,
240–41, 244–45
Aeneas, 135
"Agudezas," in *Buscón,* 268*n2. See also*
Wordplay
Agudeza y arte de ingenio, 260*n6*
Agüera, Victorio G., 260*n8,* 261*n13,*
261*n15,* 265*n23,* 269*n7,* 269*n11,*
270*n14,* 270*n16*
Albertinus, Aegidius, 143–45, 148,
166, 167, 272*n9*
Alcaláa Yáñez ỳ Ribera, Jerónimo de,
70, 71–72, 73, 75, 83, 87, 104, 105,
264*n12*
Alemán, Mateo, 3, 9, 12, 19, 43–65
passim, 66, 67, 71, 74, 87, 96, 99, 100,
103–4, 105, 106, 126, 144, 146, 147,
159, 167, 192, 196, 208, 209, 210,
212, 226, 258–62 *passim*
Alexander, Peter, 272*n7*
Allegory: Albertinus' translation of

Guzmán, 145–46, 167, 272*n11;
Alonso,* 72–73; 1555 sequel to
Lazarillo, 43; *Guzmán,* 45–46, 48–49,
59, 261*n14; Marcos,* 264*n12; Simplicissimus,* 167–70, 176–77, 179–80,
185–86; works by Defoe, 203
Allgemeiner Schauplatz. See *Piazza Universale*
Almanacs written by Grimmelshausen,
167, 175, 277*n11*
*Alonso: Mozo de muchos amos, El donado
hablador:* bourgeois preoccupations
of, 76–77, 82, 85–87, 105; character
as nature in, 71–73, 76–78, 82, 83,
84–85, 86–87, 104, 105; linked with
other picaresque novels, 70, 71–72,
74, 77, 86–87, 263–64*n11;* picaresque
narrative sequence in, 84–85, 104;
pseudoautobiographical perspective
of, 75–77, 83–84, 86–87, 104; social
commentary in, 82–85, 104; world
view in, 72–73, 75–76, 86–87
Alter, Robert, 250*n4,* 250*n5,* 283*n2*
Álvarez, Guzmán, 258*n1*
Amadís de Gaula, 252*n8*
"Amar sólo por vencer," 266*n30*
Ambiguity: *Lazarillo,* 36–37, 39, 40;
Moll Flanders, 188–91, 278–79*n1*
Ambush as image in *Guzmán,* 51–52,
58, 261*n12*
"Âme généreuse" (generous soul), 154,
156, 214, 235
Andersen, Hans H., 280*n8*
Anthony of Padua, Saint, 45
Anxiety (or fear) as theme: *Buscón,* 120;
Estebanillo, 128, 132–34, 136–37;
Guzmán, 55, 62, 77–78; *Hija de Celes-
tina,* 95; *Lazarillo,* 24, 28, 31, 36; Lu-

Index

291

Index

Laufer, Roger, 281*n1*, 281*n2*, 282*n4*,
  282*n8*, 282*n11*
Laurenti, Joseph, 249*n3*, 256*n1*, 262*n1*,
  266*n31*, 266*n34*
Lavernae, or the Spanish Gypsy, 161
"Lazarillo castigado" (Lazarillo
  punished or corrected), 43–44, 142,
  259*n3*
*Lazarillo de Tormes y de sus fortunas y
  adversidades, La vida de:* authorship of,
  19, 255–56*n29*, 256*n1*; compared
  with other picaresque novels, 44–45,
  54, 58, 62, 63, 64–65, 89, 91, 111,
  113, 114, 120, 126, 132, 135, 137–
  38, 142, 159, 188, 194, 195–96, 198–
  99, 205–7, 220, 228; critical views of,
  256–57*n1*; editions of, 22, 23, 43–44,
  67, 140–42, 147–48, 256*n1*; ending
  of, 13; 1555 sequel, 43, 101, 141–42,
  259*n2*, 266*n41*, 272*n5*; influence on
  later works, 44, 70–71, 87–88, 96,
  97–99, 101–5, 106, 127–28, 143, 151,
  166, 259*n5*, 263*n11*, 265*n22*, 269*n7*,
  270–71*n3*; linked with other picaresque novels, 3, 9, 10, 66, 67, 69–
  70; meaning of central character's
  name, 21–22; panorama of representative types in, 24–27, 33–34;
  picaresque narrative sequence in, 6–
  7, 11–12, 19, 27–30, 40–42, 78;
  placed on Index, 97; pseudoautobiographical perspective in, 7–8, 14, 21,
  24–27, 28–29, 34–42, 98, 103–4, 105,
  252*n10*, 257*n1*; realistic elements in,
  14; reception of, 43, 66–67, 70, 149;
  social criticism in, 24–28, 32–33, 36,
  39–41, 44, 66, 98, 188, 254*n20*;
  socializing process in, 11, 21, 24–33,
  34–36, 38–42, 66, 87, 98, 126, 157,
  188; sources of, 6, 21, 24, 251–52*n8*,
  256*n1*; translations of, 67, 97–98,
  139–42, 147–48, 166, 170, 207;
  upward social mobility in, 14; wordplay in, 37–39, 257*n2*, 258*n7*, 258*n9*;
  world view in, 41–42, 44

Lazarillo primitivo, 256*n1*
Lázaro Carreter, Fernando, 250*n5*,
  251*n8*, 252*n10*, 252*n13*, 256–57*n1*,
  258*n6*, 259*n5*, 265*n23*, 267*n1*, 267–
  68*n2*
Lazarowicz, Klaus, 277*n11*
Lazarus, 21, 256*n1*
Leander, 130
Leiner, Wolfgang, 274*n30*
Leloir, Maurice, 26, 29
Lerma, Duke of, 88, 214, 215, 216, 217,
  220, 221–22, 223, 240
Leroy, Jean-Pierre, 273*n25*
Lesage, Alain René, 3, 10, 12, 16, 165,
  207–27 *passim,* 228, 244–45, 283*n3*
Leube, Eberhard, 266*n34*
Lewis, C. S., 254*n19*
Lewis, R. W. B., 250*n5*, 251*n6*
"Libertinage," 154–56
Liber vagatorum, 42
"Libro de chanzas" (joke book) in *Este-
  banillo,* 133
Lida, Raimundo, 268*n2*, 270*n16*
Lida de Malkiel, María Rosa, 251*n8*,
  256*n1*
Life and Death of Young Lazarillo, The,
  148, 161, 273*n16*
L'Illusion comique, 149
"Limpieza de sangre" (purity of blood),
  17–19, 35, 45, 51, 54, 62, 64, 75, 84,
  100, 105, 109, 121, 264*n16*, 270*n14*,
  270*n16*
Lipsius, Justus, 107, 269*n3*
Long Meg of Westminster, 142
López de Cortegana, Diego, 252*n10*
López Velasco, Juan, 43–44
Love as theme: *Diablo cojuelo,* 128, 129,
  130, 131–32; French comic novel,
  153, 156, 158, 160, 274*n33*; Lesage's
  novels, 208–12, 214; *Marcos,* 81; *Moll
  Flanders,* 197–99; novels by Salas and
  Castillo, 91–93; *Roderick Random,* 235,
  236–37, 239; *Simplicissimus,* 175, 182
Lovejoy, Arthur O., 254*n19*
Luis de Granada, 46

DESIGNED BY EDGAR J. FRANK
COMPOSED BY THE COMPOSING ROOM, GRAND RAPIDS, MICHIGAN
MANUFACTURED BY THOMSON-SHORE, INC., DEXTER, MICHIGAN
TEXT IS SET IN JANSON, DISPLAY LINES IN CASLON AND JANSON

Library of Congress Cataloging in Publication Data
Bjornson, Richard.
The picaresque hero in European fiction.
Includes bibliographical references and index.
1. Picaresque literature—History and criticism.
I. Title.
PN3428.B5   809.3'3   76-11312
ISBN 0-299-07100-6